8/9

The Pro Football Hall of Fame

The Pro Football Hall of Fame

Players, Coaches, Team Owners and League Officials, 1963–1991

by

Denis J. Harrington

McFarland & Company, Inc., Publishers
Jefferson, North Carolina, and London

British Library Cataloguing-in-Publication data are available

Library of Congress Cataloguing-in-Publication Data

Harrington, Denis J., 1932–

    The Pro Football Hall of Fame : players, coaches, team owners and league officials, 1963–1991 / by Denis J. Harrington.
      p. cm
    Includes index.
    ISBN 0-89950-550-3 (lib. bind. : 50# alk. paper) ∞
    1. Pro Football Hall of Fame (U.S.) 2. Football players—United States—Biography. 3. Football—United States—Coaches—Biography.
4. Football—United States—Team owners—Biography. I. Title.
GV959.5.U6H37 1991
796.332'0973—dc20   91-52636
                                                CIP

Manufactured in the United States of America

McFarland & Company, Inc., Publishers
 Box 611, Jefferson, North Carolina 28640

*To all the players
whose names and deeds have faded
from both print and memory
but whose effort, commitment and devotion
will always enjoy an enduring monument
in the knowing hearts of those who have truly striven
and whose blood, sweat, and emotion
were no less expended than that
of their more honored brethren.*

*Without them
there could be no pro football,
hence no Hall of Fame.
To this willing legion of noble warriors
these pages are gratefully dedicated.*

Acknowledgments

I should like to express my appreciation to those organizations listed below which provided assistance most necessary to the production of this book. Special thanks is also due those members of the Pro Football Hall of Fame whose personal anecdotes and remembrances recorded herein lent so much to the recounting of their heroics and those of their fellow inductees:

> The National Football League
> Pro Football Hall of Fame
> NFL Alumni Association, Inc.
> The Touchdown Club of Washington, D. C.
> Chicago Bears Football Club
> Cincinnati Bengals Football Club
> Green Bay Packers Football Club
> New York Giants Football Club
> New York Jets Football Club
> Philadelphia Eagles Football Club
> Pittsburgh Steelers Football Club
> Washington Redskins Football Club

Denis J. Harrington

Table of Contents

ix

Pony Soldiers *(Ends and Wide Receivers)*

Armored Infantry *(Running Backs)*

Aerial Bombardment Group *(Quarterbacks and Placekickers)*

Trench Troops *(Defensive Linemen)*

Special Forces *(Linebackers)*

Rearguard Brigade *(Defensive Backs)*

Headquarters Company *(Coaches)*

General Staff *(Team Owners, League Officials)*

A Foreword

War is not among man's more laudable endeavors, yet it is an undertaking to which he has devoted much of his intellect and effort since the dawn of time. Even with the advance of civilization, the probability of open hostility became no less a threat. Today, though men everywhere profess an aversion to conflict, the masses continue to evince a curious fixation with that aspect of their history having to do with combat and its champions, clothing both in an ornate mantle of romanticism.

All through the centuries they have marched with heavy footsteps—Julius Caesar, Alexander the Great, Attila the Hun, Genghis Khan, Napoleon, Lord Nelson, Ulysses S. Grant, John Pershing, Douglas MacArthur, and Dwight D. Eisenhower—the lords of battle. Early in their academic experience Americans become intimately familiar with the men who derived fame by their facility at waging war, particularly if they have done so in the quest of righteousness and freedom. We are a people given to heroes and their deeds of derring-do. Small wonder, then, that we have taken so avidly to the game of pro football.

Warfare and the play-for-pay gridiron sport have much in common. Both institutions are confrontational in nature, with planning, strategy, leadership, tactics, logistics, execution, and discipline integral to success. Each employs infantry assaults, artillery barrages, aerial bombardment, counterattacks, rearguard actions, flanking maneuvers, defensive feints and forays, and prolonged sieges. And they share a common goal—total victory.

Pro football has produced its lords of battle—George Halas, Earl

"Curly" Lambeau, Jimmy Conzelman, Steve Owen, Paul Brown, Earle "Greasy" Neale, Vince Lombardi, Weeb Ewbank and Tom Landry—field generals whose footsteps echo just as resonantly through the years as those of their military counterparts. And their armies have performed with no less compelling brilliance.

This book profiles these lords of battle and those members of the rank and file whose attainments under fire have earned them a niche of immortality in pro football's war museum, the Hall of Fame at Canton, Ohio, where annually thousands of admirers convene to bestow upon their champions a personal mantle of romanticism.

THE GAME...

Football's origins appeared long before the Hall of Fame came into being. The game evolved from rugby (English football) as participated in by such eastern universities as Rutgers and Princeton back in the late 1860s. In 1876, the first American football rules were devised, but it wasn't until 1892 that any record of a man being paid to play the sport appeared. This honor fell to former Yale All-American guard William "Pudge" Heffelfinger, who signed on with the Allegheny Athletic Association (AAA) for $500 to perform against the rival Pittsburgh Athletic Club (PAC). On November 12 of that year the two teams met, and the AAA prevailed 4–0, the only score of the heated contest coming when Heffelfinger scooped up a PAC fumble and rambled 35 yards for a touchdown.

Early in 1893 the PAC club issued a contract to halfback Grant Dibert, or so the story goes, to play the entire season. Thus he became the recipient of the first known pro contract. It wasn't until 1896 that a team paid all of its players. The AAA gets the nod for a first in this category. However, in 1897, the Latrobe (Pa.) Athletic Association team became the first organization to use all professional players for an entire season. A year later, the value of a touchdown was changed from four points to five. The oldest continuous franchise still active in the National Football League had its beginning in 1899 when Chris O'Brien formed a neighborhood squad on the South Side of Chicago titled the Morgan Athletic Club. Shortly thereafter, the team came to be known as the Normals, then the Racine (a street in Chicago) Cardinals, the Chicago Cardinals, St. Louis Cardinals, and, presently, the Phoenix Cardinals.

1

In 1900, William C. Temple assumed liability for the Duquesne Country and Athletic Club, becoming the first individual club owner of record. Come 1902, the baseball Philadelphia Athletics, under the management of Connie Mack, and the crosstown Philadelphia Phillies established professional football teams. They joined the Pittsburgh Stars in establishing the National Football League, the first such organization formed in the play-for-pay gridiron game. After a season in which all three teams claimed to be champion, a World Series of pro football was conducted with five clubs competing. The players from the two Philadelphia teams composed one entrant, along with the New York Knickerbockers, the Syracuse Athletic Club, the Warlow Athletic Club, and the Orange (New Jersey) Athletic Club. Syracuse and the Philadelphia conglomerate met in the opening round at New York's Madison Square Garden on December 28 to play the first indoor game of record. A crowd of 3,000 spectators was on hand to see Syracuse, led by guard Glenn "Pop" Warner, triumph by a 6–0 margin. The upstate New York club also won the tournament.

Near the close of 1903, the Franklin (Pa.) Athletic Club captured the second and last World Series of pro football, defeating the Oreos (New Jersey) Athletic Club, the Watertown Red and Blacks, and the Orange Athletic Club. Not long afterward, the Massillon Tigers, an amateur team, signed up four Pittsburgh pros for an important season-ending contest with Akron. Gradually, the center of the pro game moved away from Pittsburgh to Ohio. As many as seven professional teams populated the Buckeye state in 1904, Massillon the best of the lot. Before the year was out, the scoring of a field goal dropped from five to four points, and halfback Charles Follis became the first black player to perform for money, signing with the Shelby Athletic Club.

The Canton Athletic Club, later to become the Bulldogs, fielded a pro team for the first time in 1905, but Massillon won the Ohio League title, the professional championship in those days, for the second successive year. In 1906, the forward pass was approved as a legitimate offensive ploy, and the inaugural completion occurred on October 27 when Massillon's George "Peggy" Parratt pitched a strike to Dan "Bullet" Riley. At that time Massillon and Canton dominated the money game, but their intense rivalry for players caused both clubs to spend themselves into financial difficulty. This development, along with a betting scandal, produced a loss of fan interest in pro football for a while. By 1909, the field goal was further devalued to three points. The worth of a touchdown rose to six points in 1912.

Jim Thorpe, a standout athlete for the Carlisle (Pa.) Indians, tried his hand at pro football a year after winning two gold medals in the 1912 Olympics. In 1915, he joined the Canton Bulldogs for $250 a game. From 1916 through 1919, the Thorpe-led Bulldogs won three consecutive Ohio League crowns. Earl "Curly" Lambeau organized the Green Bay Packers in 1919. The ensuing year, an attempt was made to formalize rules and standards for the conduct of all pro fooball. On September 17, 1920, teams from a four-state area met in Canton to initiate the American Professional Football Association (APFA), the immediate forerunner of the current National Football League. A prime mover in this new organization was George Halas, then of the Decatur (Ill.) Staleys.

With the onset of the 1921 campaign, the APFA comprised 22 teams, and the Staleys, who moved to Chicago under Halas's guidance, won the league championship. In 1922, the APFA officially became the National Football League, and the Staleys changed their name to the Chicago Bears. The New York Giants were one of five new franchises added to the NFL in 1925, but the big news that year was the signing of the University of Illinois' incomparable all-purpose halfback Red Grange to a Bears contract. On Thanksgiving Day, 36,000 fans, the largest crowd in the history of the pro game to that date turned out at Wrigley Field in Chicago to see him go against the Cardinals. Later, when the Bears went on a nationwide barnstorming tour, 73,000 people packed New York's Polo Grounds to watch him work his swivel-hip magic against the Giants. With the acquisition of the "Galloping Ghost," pro football went big-time.

Grange left the NFL in 1926 to start a new league when unable to reach a contract agreement with the Bears. In 1927, the NFL consolidated its ranks by eliminating the financially weaker teams and distributing the excess players among the more stable clubs. The Bears and Grange were reunited in 1929. Also that year the Providence Steam Roller team engaged the Cardinals in the league's first night game. By the onset of the 1932 campaign, the NFL complement of clubs had dropped to eight, an all-time low. The end of that season was marked by the first playoff game in league annals being contested indoors at Chicago Stadium due to extreme cold and heavy snows. It was played on an 80-yard field.

The pro football hierarchy changed a number of rules in 1933, making a final break with the collegiate version of the sport. Prominent among these alterations were the legalization of the forward pass from anywhere behind the scrimmage line and moving the goalposts up to the goal line. On August 31, 1934, the first college all-star game took place in Chicago before 79,432 spectators, with the Bears providing the pro opposition. Chicago halfback Beattie Feathers, a rookie, became the NFL's first 1,000-yard rusher that season. Famed announcer Graham McNamee broadcast the first pro game nationally over CBS radio, a Thanksgiving Day confrontation between the Bears and the Detroit Lions. That year the player waiver rule was adopted.

In 1936, the inaugural college draft took place, University of Chicago

Heisman Trophy–winning halfback Jay Berwanger the first player to be so selected. Also, the second American Football League (AFL) began operation. Meanwhile, in the NFL, 1937 marked the awarding of a franchise to Cleveland, and the Redskins moved from Boston to Washington, D.C. The Pro Bowl became a fixture in 1939, the initial contest conducted at Wrigley Field in Los Angeles. Later that year, the Philadelphia Eagles and Brooklyn Dodgers played the first NFL game to be televised, NBC beaming the contest to about 1,000 sets in the New York metropolitan area.

Still another American Football League was formed in 1940. That December, the Bears administered a 73–0 beating to the Redskins in the NFL championship game. Quarterback Sid Luckman, deftly utilizing the T-formation and the man-in-motion maneuver, engineered the stunning victory for Chicago. It was the first title contest to be broadcast on network radio. In 1941, Elmer Layden became the NFL's initial commissioner. Playoff games were introduced to decide ties in division races, and sudden death was the means for deciding the outcome of postseason games deadlocked after four quarters. The AFL folded.

When World War II ended in 1945, the hashmarks on the field were moved again, this time to a point 20 yards from either sideline. In 1946, Bert Bell became commissioner of the NFL. That year, free substitution was eliminated, and no more than three men could be inserted at one time. Forward passes that struck the goalpost were ruled incomplete. More significantly, the Rams moved from Cleveland to Los Angeles, and the All-America Football Conference (AAFC) set up business with an eight-team league.

A fifth official, a back judge, was added to game crews for the 1947 NFL season. In 1948, officials other than the referee were equipped with whistles instead of horns. Additional changes of note involved the outlawing of plastic helmets and the approved use of an artificial tee for kickoff placements. Halfback Fred Gehrke of the Los Angeles Rams painted horns on his helmet, the first such emblem in the modern era. On January 20, 1949, free substitution was adopted. Unlimited free substitution became the rule in 1950, giving rise to two-platoon football and position specialization. The Eastern and Western divisions of the NFL became the American and National conferences. Also, the Cleveland Browns, perennial champions of the defunct AAFC, joined the NFL and went on to win the league title in their first season.

In 1953, the American and National conferences were renamed the Eastern and Western conferences. Grabbing a player's face mask (other than that of the ball carrier) was adjudged illegal, and CBS began televising regular NFL games to selected markets nationwide in 1956. The Baltimore Colts defeated the New York Giants 23–17 for the 1958 league championship, the first such contest to be decided by a sudden-death overtime. On

August 22, 1959, the new American Football League came into existence, and that October 11, NFL Commissioner Bert Bell died of a heart attack while attending a Philadelphia–Pittsburgh game. Pete Rozelle was selected to be the next commissioner on January 26, 1960, while Lamar Hunt emerged as president of the AFL. The NFL and AFL agreed verbally to a "no tampering" rule regarding player contracts, and that March, the Cardinals moved from Chicago to St. Louis.

Canton, Ohio, the birthplace of the league that became the NFL in 1922, was named the site of the Pro Football Hall of Fame on April 27, 1961. The AFL Chargers moved their franchise from Los Angeles to San Diego. On May 21, 1962, Judge Roszel Thompson of the U.S. District Court in Baltimore disallowed monopoly and conspiracy charges brought by the AFL against the NFL. In other legal action, Judge Edward Weinfeld of the U.S. District Court in New York City ruled that the NFL could black out television coverage of home games within a 75-mile radius. On February 8, 1963, the AFL Dallas Texans transferred operations to Kansas City, Missouri, assuming the name Chiefs. That September 7, the Pro Football Hall of Fame was formally dedicated. And in November the U.S. Fourth Circuit Court of Appeals upheld the lower court decision which found for the NFL in a $10 million antitrust suit brought by the AFL.

Pete Gogolak of Cornell University became the first soccer-style kicker in pro football when he signed with the AFL Buffalo Bills in 1964. The NFL added a sixth official, a line judge, to its game crews for the 1965 schedule. Later that year, Atlanta was awarded an NFL franchise, and Miami got an AFL team. In 1966, the AFL–NFL war intensified, and that spring, secret merger talks commenced between the two leagues. The outcome of these talks was a June 8 agreement, which provided for a combined league of 24 teams with the number of clubs to become 26 in 1968 and 28 by 1970 or shortly thereafter. Separate schedules were to be maintained for the NFL and AFL franchises through the 1969 season, with an annual world championship game (Super Bowl) to decide the ultimate champion, beginning in 1967. Also that year, the AFL and NFL were to begin conducting a common draft. In 1970, the two leagues would become one and play a mutual slate of games, the teams divided into a pair of conferences. Rozelle became commissioner over the expanded NFL. Congress approved the merger on October 21, officially exempting the agreement from antitrust prosecution. New Orleans received an NFL franchise.

On January 15, 1967, the Green Bay Packers of the NFL defeated the AFL's Kansas City Chiefs 35–10 in Super Bowl I. The "slingshot" goalpost and a six-foot-wide border around the field were incorporated by the NFL. Bubba Smith, a defensive lineman from Michigan State Unversity, was the first player taken in the combined AFL–NFL draft. Cincinnati was awarded an AFL team, with former Cleveland coach Paul Brown assuming the multiple roles of field boss, general manager, and part owner. Green Bay made it two in a row on January 14, 1968, whipping the AFL Oakland Raiders 33–14 in Super Bowl II. Shortly thereafter, Vince Lombardi resigned as coach of the Packers but remained with the club as general manager. The Houston Oilers moved to the Astrodome to become the first pro team to play its home games indoors. Weeb Ewbank established an unprecedented double when his New York Jets won the AFL title; previously, he had directed the Baltimore Colts to NFL championships in 1958 and 1959.

The third time proved to be the charm for the AFL when the Jets defeated the favored NFL Colts 16–7 in Super Bowl III on January 12, 1969. On this occasion the term *Super Bowl* was officially recognized by the NFL. Baltimore, Cleveland, and Pittsburgh joined 10 AFL clubs to form the American Football Conference of the NFL. The other half of the teams composed the National Football Conference. On February 7, Lombardi was named part owner, executive vice president, and head coach of the Washington Redskins. That August, club founder George Preston Marshall died even as the NFL celebrated its 50th anniversary.

A measure of revenge was achieved by the Chiefs for the beating absorbed in the first big game when they overcome the NFL Minnesota Vikings 23–7 in Super Bowl IV on January 11, 1970. Lamar Hunt, owner of the Kansas City franchise, became president of the AFC, and Chicago Bears patriarch George Halas was selected as NFC president. Under the 26-team merger, all jerseys were to display the players' names, the conversion after a touchdown was set at one point, and the scoreboard clock became the official timing device for league games. The Pittsburgh Steelers moved to Three Rivers Stadium, and the Cincinnati Bengals took up residence at Riverfront Stadium. On September 3, Lombardi died of cancer at age 57. Tom Dempsey of New Orleans kicked an NFL-record 63-yard field goal on November 8.

Baltimore turned back the Dallas Cowboys 16–13 in Super Bowl V on January 17, 1971. The Boston Patriots changed their name to the New England Patriots and moved to Schaefer Stadium in Foxboro, Mass. Similarly, the Philadelphia Eagles switched from Franklin Field to Veterans Stadium, the Cowboys relocated from the Cotton Bowl to Texas Stadium, and the San Francisco 49ers left Kezar Stadium for Candlestick Park. Los Angeles Rams president Dan Reeves died at 58. The Cowboys bulldogged the Miami Dolphins 24–3 on January 16, 1972, to claim the Super Bowl VI crown. Once again the hashmarks were moved closer to the middle of the field, and tie games became worth a half game won and a half game lost. Robert Irsay bought the Rams franchise and then traded it to Carroll Rosenbloom for the Colts ownership. William V. Bidwell assumed sole control of the Cardinals.

Miami attained a perfect 17–0 mark and an NFL first by downing the

Redskins 14–7 in Super Bowl VII on January 14, 1973. That April 5, the league instituted a new jersey numbering system (1–19 for quarterbacks and specialists, 20–49 for running backs and secondary defenders, 50–59 for centers and linebackers, 60–79 for defensive linemen and interior offensive linemen, 80–89 for wide receivers and tight ends). Players active in 1972 were allowed to retain their old numerals. The Buffalo Bills quit War Memorial Stadium for Rich Stadium, and after September 23 the Giants played their remaining home games of the season at the Yale Bowl in New Haven, Conn. In October the World Football Leage (WFL) commenced operations. O.J. Simpson of Buffalo became the first running back in NFL history to rush for more than 2,000 yards in a season, carrying for 2,003 yards. The Dolphins successfully defended their world-champion laurels, winning Super Bowl VIII at the expense of the Minnesota Vikings 24–7 on January 13, 1974. Commissioner Rozelle was given a 10-year contract extension. Tampa Bay and Seattle received NFL franchises. Rules changes: One sudden-death overtime period was added for all preseason and regular-schedule games; the goalposts moved from the goal line to the back of the end zone; kickoffs were conducted from the 35-yard line instead of the 40; after missed field goals from beyond the 20, the ball went back to the scrimmage line; members of the punting unit had certain restrictions placed on them to enhance return possibilities; cutbacks and roll-blocking of wide receivers was prohibited; receivers were subjected to less obstruction downfield by defenders; the penalty for offensive holding, illegal use of the hands, and tripping infractions was reduced from 15 to 10 yards; and wide receivers blocking back toward the ball within three yards of the scrimmage line could not make contact below the waist.

On January 12, 1975, the Pittsburgh Steelers defeated the Vikings 16–6 in Super Bowl IX. Referees were equipped with wireless microphones for all games. The Detroit Lions played their home games in the Pontiac Silverdome, and the Giants used New York's Shea Stadium; the New Orleans Saints moved to the Louisiana Superdome. In October the WFL folded. Pittsburgh scored a double, edging Dallas 21–17 in Super Bowl X on January 18, 1976. A pair of 30-second clocks were mandated for all games. The Giants made their home at Giants Stadium in East Rutherford, N.J., and the Steelers beat the College All-Stars in the last game of this series. Also, the St. Louis Cardinals won 20–10 over the San Diego Chargers in a preseason game conducted in Tokyo, the first NFL game to be played outside North America.

Minnesota lost again in Super Bowl XI to the Oakland Raiders by a 32–14 margin on January 9, 1977. A 16-game regular season schedule and four exhibition contests were to be the NFL format beginning in 1978. Also in 1978, a second wild-card team would be added to the playoff menu of both conferences, with the two at-large qualifiers to play each other in the first round. Seattle was assigned to the AFC West Division, and Tampa Bay joined the NFC Central Division. Rules changes: Defenders could contact wide receivers only once; the headslap was banned; offensive linemen could no longer thrust their hands to an opponent's neck, face, or head; and wide receivers were prohibited from blocking back, even in the legal clipping zone. Chicago's Walter Payton set a single-game rushing record of 275 yards.

Dallas overcame the Denver Broncos 27–10 in Super Bowl XII on January 15, 1978, in the Superdome, the first time the title tilt was conducted indoors. A seventh official, a side judge, was added to NFL game crews. Rules changes: A defender could not contact a receiver deeper than five yards beyond the scrimmage line, and the extending of the arms and open hands was condoned in pass-blocking. New Orleans and Philadelphia played a preseason contest in Mexico City, another NFL first. On January 21, 1979, Pittsburgh slipped past Dallas 35–31 in Super Bowl XIII to become the first team to win the big game three times. Rules changes: During kickoffs, punts, and field goal attempts, members of the receiving team could not block below the waist; the wearing of torn, altered, or exposed equipment deemed to be a physical hazard was prohibited; the zone in which there could be no crackback blocking was extended; and officials were to exercise a "quick whistle" once a quarterback was clearly in the grasp of a tackler. Rams owner Carroll Rosenbloom died at 72. Pittsburgh became the first team to win four Super Bowls, defeating the Rams 31–19 on January 20, 1980. The Pro Bowl moved to Honolulu, Hawaii, the first time it was played in a non-NFL city. Rules changes: Players were barred from directly striking, swinging, or clubbing on the head, face, or neck of an opponent. Anaheim Stadium became the new home of the Rams.

Oakland won Super Bowl XV by a 27–10 count at the expense of Philadelphia on January 25, 1981, the first wild-card team ever to achieve this distinction. The NFL'a regular-season attendance set a record for the fourth successive year, the teams drawing better than 60,000 spectators per game. San Francisco defeated Cincinnati 26–21 in Super Bowl XVI on January 24, 1982, at the Pontiac Superdome, the first time the championship was played in the North. A jury ruled against the NFL in an antitrust suit brought by the Los Angeles Coliseum Commission and the Oakland Raiders, allowing the Raiders to switch their home operation to Los Angeles. A 57-day players' strike cut the NFL regular season from 16 to 9 games. To compensate for lost time, the playoff format was expanded to 16 teams competing in a Super Bowl tournament. On January 30, 1983, Washington came from behind to surpass Miami 27–17 in Super Bowl XVII. George Halas, owner of the Chicago Bears and a league cofounder, died at 88.

The Los Angeles Raiders crushed Washington 38–9 in Super Bowl XVIII on January 22, 1984. In March the Colts abandoned Baltimore for

Indianapolis and the Hoosier Dome. Later in the year, the New York Jets contracted to play their home games at Giants Stadium in East Rutherford, N.J. It was a season for records: Dan Marino, Miami quarterback, threw for 5,084 yards and 48 touchdowns; Eric Dickerson, Los Angeles Rams running back, rushed for 2,105 yards; Art Monk, Washington wide receiver, caught 106 passes; and Chicago running back Walter Payton set a new career rushing mark of 13,309 yards. San Francisco beat Miami 38–16 in Super Bowl XIX on January 20, 1985. President Ronald Reagan, via television, flipped the pregame coin for a contest that was witnessed on TV by 115,936,000 viewers, 6 million of whom watched in the United Kingdom and a like number in Italy. Chicago blew out the New England Patriots 46–10 in Super Bowl XX on January 26, 1986. The NFL team owners approved instant replay as an officiating aid on a limited basis. In the wake of an 11-week trial, the United States Football League (USFL) received a one-dollar award in its $1.7 billion antitrust suit against the NFL. The Bears faced down Dallas 17–6 at London's Wembley Stadium in the inaugural American Bowl, a preseason game destined to become an annual event for the English pro football market.

The New York Giants ran over Denver 39–20 in Super Bowl XXI on January 25, 1987. Fans in 55 foreign countries saw the game either live via television or on tape. The ESPN sports network signed a three-year pact to cover 13 NFL games each season, thereby putting the league on cable TV for the first time. More than 400 former pro football performers who had at least five years in the NFL and played all or part of their careers before 1959 when the current Bert Bell Pension Plan went into effect received the first payment of a special annuity program financed by the team owners. The regular season was reduced from 16 to 15 games due to a 24-day players' strike. Replacement teams were used during weeks four, five, and six of the walkout. Instant replay was retained for another year.

Washington blasted Denver 42–10 in Super Bowl XXII on January 31, 1988. The Second Circuit Court of Appeals in New York upheld a lower court decision to award the USFL only one dollar in its antitrust suit against the NFL. Instant replay survived for another year, given a 23–5 vote by team owners. The Cardinals moved operations from St. Louis to Phoenix, and the American Bowl preseason series expanded to a second game scheduled for Tokyo in August of 1989. Art Rooney, founder and owner of the Pittsburgh Steelers, died at 87. San Francisco squeezed past Cincinnati 20–16 in Super Bowl XXIII on January 22, 1989. Commissioner Rozelle announced his retirement in March, pending agreement by the team owners on a successor. Instant reply was extended for a fourth consecutive year. Tex Schramm, former president of the Dallas Cowboys, was selected to head the new World League of American Football (WLAF), a developmental league supported by the NFL with 10 teams to be located in the United States and Europe. The WLAF began play in March 1991 and the championship game was conducted in June of that year. On October 26, former Rozelle aide Paul Tagliabue became the new NFL commissioner.

San Francisco crushed Denver 55–10 in Super Bowl XXIV on January 28, 1990, to become only the second team in NFL annals to win four of the postseason classics; the Pittsburgh Steelers first accomplished the feat in 1980. Quarterback Joe Montana of the 49ers set a number of Super Bowl (SB) firsts while leading his team to a place in the record book. He established career SB marks for most career passes attempted (122), most career passes completed (83), best career completion percentage (68.0), most career passing yards (1,142), most career touchdown passes (11), most career passes without an interception (122), most touchdown passes in a game (5), and most consecutive passes completed in a game (13). Other SB records established were for most career pass receptions (20), most career touchdown passes caught (4), most touchdown passes caught in a game (3), most career punt return yards (94), highest career punt return yards average (15.7), most career kickoff returns (10), most career extra points (9), most extra points in a game (7), most career extra points attempted (10), most extra points attempted in a game (8), most points scored by a team in a game (55), largest margin of victory for a team in a game (45), most touchdowns by a team in a game (8), most passing touchdowns by a team in a game (5), most kickoff returns by both teams in a game (12), most extra points by a team in a game (7), and most extra points attempted by a team in a game (8).

In February, the NFL announced that it would play a regular schedule of 16 games over a 17-week period during the 1990 and 1991 seasons and a 16-game schedule over 18 weeks in 1992 and 1993. Under this new format, each team will have an open weekend during the 1990 and 1991 campaigns and two open weekends in 1992 and 1993. Another change involved the addition of two first-round games and two wild-card teams to the postseason format which began in 1990. This means that both the AFC and NFC playoff brackets will consist of three division winners and three wild-card teams, with both conferences having an extra elimination contest. Also, the American Bowl series was further enlarged to include preseason games in Canada, Germany, Japan, and England. A new NFL single season attendance record was set in 1990.

On January 27, 1991, the NY Giants edged the Buffalo Bills 20–19 in Super Bowl XXV.

...AND THE
HALL

On December 6, 1959, the Canton *Repository* stated in an eight-column headline that "Pro Football Needs a Hall of Fame—and Logical Site Is Here." Lest this be thought no more than hollow bravado, the newspaper's claim had a firm foundation in history. After all, Canton, Ohio, had served as the site of the Canton Bulldogs, who signed Jim Thorpe, the legendary Indian athlete and the money game's first big-name performer, in 1915 and then went on to win the Ohio League championship, at that time generally considered emblematic of pro football supremacy. It was also in Canton, on September 17, 1920, that the American Professional Football Association (APFA) came into being. Late in June of 1922 the APFA changed its official title to the National Football League. That fall, and again in 1923, the Bulldogs fashioned undefeated seasons and won back-to-back league titles, the first NFL team ever to do so.

Originally, NFL officials awarded the Hall of Fame site to Latrobe, Pennsylvania, in 1947, operating under the mistaken belief that the town had hosted the first pro football game back in 1895. However, construction never got underway, so the site designation remained a matter of spirited conjecture. Detroit made a bid for the Hall of Fame on January 23, 1960, but the Pittsburgh Steelers reminded the NFL hierarchy of the commitment previously made to Latrobe. Meanwhile, Cleveland Browns coach Paul Brown stated the case for Canton. On February 25 of that year, dignitaries representing Canton's Chamber of Commerce, the Jaycees, various service and civic clubs, and area industry strongly endorsed the *Repository*'s overture. Shortly thereafter, a steering committee was formed to pursue the issue.

Pro Football Hall of Fame

A formal proposal in support of Canton was posed to the NFL by William E. Umstattd of the Timken Roller Bearing Company on January 25, 1961. The ensuing spring, NFL emissaries Paul Brown, George Halas, and Edwin Anderson visited Canton to review the suggested site. On April 27, 1961, a roll-call vote of all the league clubs accorded Canton official recognition as the NFL's choice for the Hall of Fame.

By February 8, 1962, pledges in the amount of $378,026 had been received, the Timken Company donating $100,000 of this sum, to commence construction of the initially planned structures. Ground-breaking ceremonies were conducted on August 11, 1962, and on the same date, the inaugural Hall of Fame game involving the St. Louis Cardinals and New York Giants was played to a 21–21 deadlock.

Finally, on September 7, 1963, the Hall of Fame, consisting of two buildings, was formally dedicated, along with the induction of 17 charter-class members. On May 10, 1971, a third viewing area augmented the complex. A fourth addition admitted its first visitors on November 20, 1978, thereby increasing the total exhibit space to 51,000 square feet. On September 4, 1986, the Hall of Fame welcomed its four-millionth patron.

Upon entering the premises, visitors are confronted by an imposing 7-foot bronze likeness of Jim Thorpe situated directly beneath a 52-foot dome, which affords the site a unique appearance. Immediately beyond lies an upward-winding ramp that leads to the original Exhibition Rotunda where nearly century-old pro football is informally chronicled via a variety of memorabilia, commencing with the first play-for-pay game in 1892 and proceeding to the modern era. Among some of the more notable attractions in this area are a football used in the 1890s, a complete 1902 uniform, a great coat worn by a member of the old Duluth Eskimos, Jim Thorpe's sideline blanket while playing with the Canton Bulldogs, and the battered shoulder pads of quarterback Y.A. "Yat" Tittle. Continually updated team panels representing each of the 28 NFL clubs can also be seen here.

In the adjoining two buildings are twin enshrinement galleries where each of the inductees is afforded an individual niche containing a bronze bust, an action mural, and a biographical sketch. Occupying the center of the second building is the Pro Football Photo-Art Gallery, which presents the work of prize-winning professional photographers. The third building houses the Pro Football Adventure Room that treats a variety of subjects such as "The Story of Blacks in Pro Football," "The 1972 Miami Dolphins' Perfect Season" and "The Evolution of the Uniform from 1920 to the Present Day."

Featured in the fourth building are the enshrinees, shown with their respective teams. Also located here is the Mementoes Room, which includes items that had particular meaning for each of the honored players. The Vince Lombardi trophy dominates the special Super Bowl display, along with replicas of the rings that go to members of the clubs that have been victorious in the postseason classic. Picture panels depicting every Super Bowl to date provide eye-catching graphics, and visitors can veiw a special videotape of all the games.

Throughout the hall, videotape monitors, recordings of memorable moments in pro football, selective slide machines, and even quiz games await the visitor to enhance his or her enjoyment and quest for knowledge. An eight-foot illuminated pylon visually ranks the NFL's all-time leaders in rushing, receiving, passing, and scoring. It is kept current with changing events, as are some 40 to 50 other stations in the complex. Each hour, NFL action films can be viewed in a 350-seat movie theater, and for the especially dedicated student of the pro game there is a research library, the very heart of the archives section. Fans who want to take something home in remembrance of their tour can choose from a variety of items in a well-stocked museum store.

Easily the highlight of every year is the enshrinement process, which takes place on the front steps of the hall. Here, in late July or early August, more than 10,000 spectators sit and stand listening raptly to the reminiscences and expressions of emotion that color the acceptance speeches

EARL CAMPBELL
Running Back

JOHN HANNAH
Guard

STAN JONES
Guard

TEX SCHRAMM
Administrator

PRO FOOTBALL HALL OF FAME
Canton, Ohio
1991 CLASS OF ENSHRINEES

JAN STENERUD
Kicker

of one-time gridiron warriors, some only lately removed from the battle. That afternoon the AFC–NFC Hall of Fame Game, which annually kicks off the NFL preseason slate, takes place in nearby Fawcett Stadium for the benefit of those on scene and a nationwide ABC-TV audience. All the league clubs participate in this contest on a rotating basis, with the scheduling now complete into the next century.

On the Saturday morning of the induction proceedings, a parade is conducted, which suffices as a means of publicly introducing the players being honored. They ride in open-top automobiles to acknowledge the plaudits and cheers of some 200,000 admirers. It's this moment as much as any other during that once-in-a-lifetime weekend which lingers with the participant the rest of his days. Bobby Mitchell, a standout running back and receiver with both Cleveland and Washington, was admitted to the hall in 1983. So impressive was the experience that he returned the following year as an onlooker to savor the festivities one more time.

"The procession, those thousands of people, and what it means is simply unforgettable," he said. "I just wanted to go back and see it from another perspective. All very touching, very stirring."

Year after year, the curious, the thoughtful, and the imaginative travel the road to Canton, to 2121 George Halas Drive, N.W., from 50 states and many foreign countries to look, ponder, and wonder how it must be amid the din of the fray. They study the faces of those who have borne the fight, listen to their voices from the past, and watch enthralled as flitting celluloid or videotape resurrects their heroics. All that's missing are the stinging rivulets of perspiration seeping into the eye and the cloying taste of blood fresh on one's lips. But given the audio and visual stimulation, the mind works mightily to supply these effects as well.

The lords of battle, set apart from other men by their passage through the crucible of human conflict, will forever command our esteem. Such it has been time out of mind.

ASSAULT
TROOPS

Offensive Linemen

Morris "Red" Badgro

6'0", 190 pounds. End: New York Yankees (1927), New York Giants (1930–1935), Brooklyn Dodgers (1936). All-Pro: 1930 (unofficial), 1931, 1933, 1934. Inducted into the Pro Football Hall of Fame 1981.

All things come to he who waits. Those individuals who subscribe to this axiom have no better evidence to support their belief than the case of Morris "Red" Badgro, who at age 78, after 45 years of waiting, was finally admitted to the Hall of Fame. Whether his rather belated entry also makes a statement of sorts about the ultimate validity of the selection system or the acuity of 20-20 hindsight can be debated. But whatever, justice was finally served. And that's what counts.

Like a lot of talented athletes from the late 1920s and 1930s, he had difficulty deciding if baseball or football should warrant his serious attention. So he played with the New York Yankees of the NFL in 1927 and then retired to try his hand at the diamond sport. He remained a member of the St. Louis Browns baseball club for two seasons but failed to nail down a regular roster spot during that period, so he decided to give pro football another shot.

He signed on with the New York Giants in 1930 for $150 a game, determined this time to stay the course. At the close of his first season, he was named to the unofficial all-league team for his stellar performance as an end. In 1931, 1933, and 1934 he rated official All-Pro status. During his tenure with the Giants, they were a perennial contender, making it to the NFL championship contest on three successive occasions from 1933 to 1935 and winning the title once.

Versatility was his long suit. He prevailed as both a sure tackler and a good blocker. But he demonstrated a particular facility for catching passes. In 1934, he logged 16 receptions to share league honors in this category. While his production pales beside the number of receptions recorded today by wideouts in the modern NFL, he accomplished no small feat when the pro game was primarily run-oriented and the shape of the ball made it difficult to throw accurately. He was the first player to score a touchdown in an NFL championship contest, when the series had its inception in 1933. That afternoon the Chicago Bears owned a 6–0 advantage when he pulled down a 29-yard pitch to put the Giants ahead 7–6, if only briefly.

Given his ability to come up with the ball in traffic, he became a frequent target for passes under pressure conditions and seldom failed to deliver. His 17-yard reception against the Brooklyn Dodgers in 1930 iced a 13–0 decision for the Giants. The ensuing season he made a 14-yard clutch catch that turned the tide against the Portsmouth Spartans. And in the Giants' 1934 drive to the Eastern Division title and an NFL championship, he supplied a key 15-yard reception which enabled the New York club to register a 3–0 win.

When it's known that Badgro plied his trade in the company of such gridiron greats as Red Grange, Sammy Baugh, and the many stars that sparkled for the great Bears aggregations of that period, one quickly gains a better perspective of his several abilities.

He finished his career with the Dodgers in 1936 and then commenced the long wait for the recognition so much due him.

Roosevelt Brown

6'3", 255 pounds. Offensive Tackle: New York Giants (1953–1965). All-Pro: 1956–1963. Pro Bowl: Nine appearances. Inducted into the Pro Football Hall of Fame 1975.

Breaking into the National Football League was a difficult task for Roosevelt Brown, coming from a small all-black school with few of the advantages enjoyed by many of his contemporaries, who originated from big-time gridiron programs. However, precious few players ever adjusted so quickly and so completely to the pro grame or experienced so distinguished and rewarding a career.

He had been a star at little Morgan State College, but the magnitude of

Roosevelt Brown

making the grade in the pros seemed overwhelming to the somewhat intimidated 20-year-old who faced the task as a rookie back in 1953. To begin
with, the New York Giants training site was miles away from his home. And
then too, he had never played against a white man, let alone been coached

by one. Everything seemed new, even the lineman's stance they wanted him to use. Yet, deep down, he had the desire to be in the NFL and to be respected by his peers.

Giants head coach Steve Owen liked the young rookie's physical ability and size but wanted to test his heart. To do this, he sent him against All-Pro defensive tackle Arnie Weinmeister in a number of head-to-head drills. Battered from one end of the field to the other, Brown still managed to take a few laps on his own after the grueling session, a clear signal to Owen of his intention to stick it out.

With the advent of the regular season, he was firmly entrenched at an offensive tackle slot and stayed there throughout his 13-year tenure in the NFL. Early on, he established himself as a quick learner, mastering the techniques of pass protection and downfield blocking so well that his performance earned him All-Pro recognition eight successive seasons and nine invites to the Pro Bowl. When the occasion demanded, he possessed the speed and agility to pull out on sweeps or protect the quarterback in scrambling situations. And when the Giants were forced into goal-line-stand circumstances, he often came to the aid of the defensive unit by adding heft and savvy at both tackle and end.

It's not a matter of coincidence that he played with the teams that won six Eastern Conference titles and a league championship in 1956. That year the Giants annexed the NFL crown by a convincing 47–7 margin, and he was voted lineman of the game. Overall, he felt the men who labored in the pits to make the offense go went largely unnoticed, and this bothered him.

"There is an element of self-satisfaction to doing the job, and we have to make that do," he once said. "When the newspapers tell which back went fifty yards but don't tell who made the blocks, that hurts. After all, he had to have the blocks; he couldn't go far without them."

An attack of phlebitis dictated his retirement following the 1965 campaign. Once out of uniform, he signed with the Giants as an assistant coach. In 1969, he became head line coach and then, two yars later, switched to the club's scouting staff.

"No, there's no more talent out there than in my time," he said. "A lot of the young players now are bigger and faster, and that's due to training methods and nutrition. Both of these areas are better understood than was previously the case. Overall, though, the game hasn't changed much, except that practically everybody is a specialist anymore. Plus, I just don't think offensive linemen block as well as before down by the goal line. In those situations you have to get your shoulder into a man and move him out of there. This technique has been largely lost because of the rules changes that allow offensive linemen to use their hands. So not everything has progressed."

George Connor

6'3", 240 pounds. Tackle, Linebacker: Chicago Bears (1948–1955). All-Pro: 1950–1954. Pro Bowl: Four appearances. Inducted into the Pro Football Hall of Fame 1975.

By the time George Connor entered the National Football League, he was a made product. Perhaps no lineman in the annals of the pro game came so well prepared and so well equipped to do the work destined for him. Significantly, he performed up to his potential throughout a notable career.

As a collegian he thrice earned All-America honors, once while attending Holy Cross and twice at the Notre Dame. During his tenure with the Fighting Irish he played on national championship teams, which further added to his personal luster. He was selected in the first round of the 1948 NFL draft by the Boston Yanks, but the Chicago Bears acquired him before the onset of that year's regular season.

He held forth at tackle initially, on both offense and defense. Physically, he prevailed as an imposing specimen of gridiron might at 6'3" and 240 pounds, all of which constituted classically proportioned muscle. What's more, he commanded a keen football mind plus the speed and agility to execute the mission his perception had dictated for him only moments before. But he generated an even greater impact on the opposition when circumstances forced him to function behind the line of scrimmage.

In the course of his second campaign, the Bears were facing the Philadelphia Eagles, defending league champions enroute to another title. Coming into the game, the Eagles had been making particularly effective use of their Hall of Fame halfback Steve Van Buren behind a phalanx of blockers. The Bears considered several antidotes to this threat but finally opted for the most feasible of these alternatives, dropping Connor off to an outside linebacker spot. From this position and operating in conjunction with a defensive end, he succeeded in repeatedly muscling his way through Van Buren's wall of interference and bringing the big ball carrier to a screeching halt. As a result, Chicago dealt Philadelphia its lone defeat of the 1949 schedule, 38–21.

Connor rated All-Pro honors at three positions—offensive tackle, defensive tackle, and linebacker. From 1951 through 1953, he was accorded all-league status on both offense and defense. He also participated in four consecutive Pro Bowls.

Injuries compelled him to retire after the 1955 slate. When he doffed his uniform for the last time, Bears owner and head coach George Halas paid him public tribute: "He parlayed leadership and intelligence and fine ability into one of the great careers of our time."

George Connor

From 1956 through 1957, Connor served the Bears as an assistant coach and then moved up to the TV booth as a color commentator for their games.

Albert Glen "Turk" Edwards

6'2", 260 pounds. Tackle: Boston Braves (1932), Boston Redskins (1933–1936), Washington Redskins (1937–1940). All-Pro: 1932, 1933, 1936, 1937. Inducted into the Pro Football Hall of Fame 1969.

The term *ironman* fit Turk Edwards like a given name. Large for any era, 6'2" and 260 pounds, he played tackle on both sides of the ball for the Redskins franchise when it initially resided in Boston as the Braves and later in Washington, D.C. During one 15-game schedule he performed offensively and defensively in every game save for intermittent breathers totaling only 10 minutes.

Prior to joining the National Football League, he prevailed as an All-America tackle at Washington State University. In his junior year he blocked a punt and returned it for a touchdown, enabling the Cougars to remain undefeated and earn a trip to the Rose Bowl. When he left the college game, there were many offers to play professional football. He ultimately narrowed his options to the Boston Braves (Redskins), the New York Giants, and the Portsmouth Spartans. The Braves (Redskins) won out simply because they made him the best deal, $1,500 for the 1932 campaign, which amounted to good money in those days. It was a mating that would persist for no less than 17 years.

Though not overly agile, he could move his bulk about with enough facility to cause the opposition no few problems. He rated All-Pro honors in 1932, 1933, 1936, and 1937. When the Boston club changed its designation to the Redskins before the 1933 bloodletting, he was already a well-established star in the NFL. He spearheaded the Redskins to a Western Division crown in 1936 and again in 1937 after they had relocated to Washington. That year, they went on to beat the Chicago Bears for the league championship.

Early in 1940, his career ended abruptly and under rather unusual circumstances. On September 22, the Redskins were hosting the Giants, and Edwards participated in the pregame coin toss. Once the ritual had been concluded, he shook hands with New York center Mel Hein, a close friend, and headed for the Washington bench. He never made it under his own power. In turning, he snagged his cleats and momentarily lost his balance. This sudden shift of his considerable bulk proved too much for an already battered knee, and it went out. Thus one of pro football's finest tackles was ported to the sidelines, though not on his shield given the misfortunes of battle. However, this somewhat inglorious end to his illustrious career did have a bright side to it. Later that year, the Bears humiliated the Redskins 73–0 in the NFL title game, and he was at least spared the ordeal of being a thoroughly defeated combatant.

No sooner did he doff his uniform than the club signed him as an assistant coach. He remained in that capacity for five seasons, then assumed the head-coaching responsibilities from 1946 to 1948. Under his leadership, the Redskins enjoyed only one winning campaign. Edwards died at age 65 on January 12, 1973.

Dan Fortmann

6'0", 210 pounds. Guard: Chicago Bears (1936–1943). All-Pro: 1938–1943. Inducted into the Pro Football Hall of Fame 1965.

The law of ballistics concerns the rate at which a projectile, given its size and mass, moves through the atmosphere and impacts an objective. By this ratio, a small smooth stone mortally felled the biblical Goliath. And it was this same equation that enabled Dan Fortmann to bring low the Goliaths of his day.

In 1936, Fortmann became the Chicago Bears' ninth-round pick in the inaugural National Football League draft. Back then, preparation for the selection process was so elemental that team owner and coach George Halas knew little more about his acquisition than the young man's name. "Fortmann," Halas mused to himself. "I like that name. I'll take him."

Chances are if Papa Bear had been aware that the aspiring pro lineman was a 19-year-old Phi Beta Kappa graduate from Colgate University who stood just 6'0" and weighed only 210 pounds he never would have worn a Chicago uniform. Life in the NFL trenches just wasn't the place for callow intellectuals, especially undersized ones. But Halas hadn't taken into consideration the law of ballistics.

When Fortmann made his appearance at the Bears' preseason camp, it didn't take him long to allay the doubts of his coaches and teammates. Early on, he proved to be a savage blocker, a human projectile that fairly hurled himself at an opponent, and a tenacious tackler. By the onset of the regular season, he had turned 20, thus becoming the youngest starter on the roster of any team in the league.

Offensively, he called all the blocking assignments and on defense proved to be particularly astute at diagnosing the opposition's plays. He lined up at left guard beside the Bears' first draft pick, tackle "Jumbo Joe" Stydahar, and together they were a formidable pairing. When vital short yardage or a goal-line plunge was needed, invariably the designated ball carrier got in behind them. And more often than not they delivered the required protection.

From 1938 to 1943, Fortmann earned All-Pro recognition at his position, so it was no coincidence that during his tenure with the Bears they finished first in the Western Division on five occasions and won three NFL championships. In the course of his relationship with Halas, they became fast friends and formed a mutual admiration club of sorts. While Halas much appreciated the contribution Fortmann made to the Chicago franchise, the sentiment was more than reciprocated by the heady little guard who deeply respected his gruff leader as a coach and a man. "George made it possible for me to pursue my medical studies while playing football," Fortmann related. "He allowed me to miss two weeks of summer practice each year so I could finish up in school. Without his understanding and cooperation, I never could have prepared for my future."

After the 1943 season, Fortmann stripped off his pads for the last time

Dan Fortmann

and turned his attention to building a medical practice, but not before he had given the law of ballistics a bit of classic application.

Frank Gatski

6'3", 240 pounds. Center: Cleveland Browns (1946–1949, AAFC), Cleveland Browns (1950–1956, NFL), Detroit Lions (1957). All-Pro: 1951–1953, 1955. Pro Bowl: One appearance. Inducted into the Pro Football Hall of Fame 1985.

In the best tradition of the strong, silent types of Western lore, Frank Gatski literally put himself on the line every Sunday for more than a decade to prove repeatedly that football is a game in which the toughest guys have the winning edge.

A quiet man of big dimensions, 6'3" and 240 pounds, he relied almost exclusively on his own brand of body language to impart the message of his mission: "They shall not pass." He played center on eight championship teams, excelling as a blocker to such an extent that even such resolute foes as Philadelphia Eagles Hall of Fame linebacker Chuck Bednarik was led to testify, "Gatski was an immovable object. He was the best and toughest I ever played against."

Tough is a descriptive term that had particular application to Gatski. During a tenure in football that spanned 20 years—counting his high school, college, and pro experience—he never once missed a practice session, never once missed a game, and never once called a time-out on his behalf. It's a matter of record that few opponents were able to make a similar boast after facing him across a scrimmage line. By his own admission, "You got to be tough to play football." It might have been added, to play football as he played it.

From 1946 to 1956, he served as the trigger to one of the most explosive attacks in the history of the gridiron sport. He was the pivot man in the offensive line of the Cleveland Browns when they reflected the innovative genius of general manager and coach Paul Brown, when Hall of Fame quarterback Otto Graham directed the team to 10 consecutive appearances in a league title contest provided support from such Hall of Fame contemporaries as fullback Marion Motley, receiver Dante Lavelli, and tackle–placement specialist Lou "The Toe" Groza.

Given four championship seasons in the All-America Football Conference, the Browns were admitted to the National Football League in 1950, where they adhered closely to their winning ways. And through it all, Gatski was a fixture at the center of the action, snapping the ball with unerring efficiency and methodically cutting down defenders intent upon invading the Cleveland backfield. In recognition of his stellar performance, he was accorded All-Pro status on four occasions and participated in one Pro Bowl.

Upon departing the Browns following the 1956 campaign, he was the proud owner of no less than seven rings emblematic of pro football supremacy. He would obtain still another one upon joining the Detroit franchise. In 1957, the Lions claimed the NFL crown, manhandling the Browns in the deciding contest. That afternoon, when facing his former comrades in arms, he could have been forgiven a little knowing smile that silently bespoke the sentiment "I could have told you I wasn't done yet."

Life prevailed as something of a hard proposition for Gatski from the outset. He was born into the coal-mining community of Farmington, West

Virginia, and for all intents and purposes, ultimately faced the bleak prospect of extracting carbon deposits from the bowels of the earth so long as heart and lungs should endure. But a year after finishing high school he received a reprieve from this molelike existence to try out for the Marshall College football team. Those candidates who earned a uniform would be given campus jobs to sustain them in their studies. All the hapless souls who couldn't so qualify were sent back to the pits. He made it and never looked back.

In essence, football offered Gatski a passport to an eminently better potential than his heritage would have. If this freedom had to be bought at the price of a little sweat and pain, it was still well worth the cost. And for a truly tough guy like Gatski, it went down like a piece of cake, considering the alternative.

Forrest Gregg

6'4", 250 pounds. Offensive Tackle, Guard: Green Bay Packers (1956, 1958–1970), Dallas Cowboys (1971). All-Pro: 1960–1967. Pro Bowl: Nine appearances. Inducted into the Pro Football Hall of Fame 1977. Coach: Cleveland Browns (1975–1977), Cincinnati Bengals (1980–1983), Green Bay Packers (1984–1987). Won-lost record: Cleveland Browns (18–23–0), Cincinnati Bengals (34–27–0), Green Bay Packers (25–37–1). Championships: Central Division (AFC), 1981; AFC, 1981.

Few linemen in the history of the National Football League devoted more personal time and effort to developing their job skills than did Forrest Gregg. Small wonder he made it to the Hall of Fame.

It can be said he played out of position most of his 15-year career in the NFL. When he joined the Green Bay Packers in 1956 as their first draft pick, it was as a defensive lineman, a classification which best encompassed his speed and agility. But once preseason camp got underway, he found himself competing for an offensive tackle post, a role for which his 6'4", 250-pound frame seemed a mite spare.

Undaunted by this switch in plans, he set about working long hours over and above normal practice sessions, preparing himself both physically and mechanically for what lay ahead. If not laboring to enhance his overall body strength, he was locked away in the film room studying the techniques of the better offensive tackles around the league. Early on, he determined that a solid grasp of fundamentals and no little finesse were the ingredients needed to overcome larger defensive ends who would be his opposition in the upcoming season.

He learned his lessons well, earning All-Pro recognition every year from 1960 through 1967. But twice during this span, in 1961 and again in

Forrest Gregg

1965, team injuries dictated that he be moved to guard, thus necessitating more adjustment and preparation. And he did it all without complaint and with his usual attention to detail. He mastered the modes and methods required to combat opposing defensive tackles so thoroughly that in 1965 most selectors voted him to All-Pro status at both guard and tackle.

In the course of his lengthy pro football tenure, he played in 188 consecutive games, a period extending from 1956 to 1971, then a league record. He also acquired three Super Bowl rings and was a member of seven championship teams. After the close of the 1963 season, he had it in mind to retire and accept a coaching job at the University of Tennessee. But Packers head coach Vince Lombardi convinced him he should stay on for another year.

He commenced both the 1969 and 1970 campaigns as an assistant with the Green Bay staff. But on each occasion he ended up in uniform, forced back into the lineup, courtesy of the heavy toll injuries had imposed upon the club. Once again he sought to retire just prior to onset of the 1971 schedule only to be recruited by Dallas Cowboys mentor Tom Landry with pleas of dire need. Finally, in the wake of Super Bowl VI, at the age of 38, he shed his game armor for the last time.

Thereafer he turned to teaching the skills his efforts had so arduously perfected. In 1975, he was hired as head coach of the Cleveland Browns. He retained this position until late in the 1977 season, resigning with three games left on the slate and an 18–23–0 won-lost mark. When the Cincinnati Bengals handed him their coaching reins in 1980, it was to direct a talented veteran aggregation. He responded by taking them to Super Bowl XVI where they grudgingly submitted to the San Francisco 49ers by a 26–21 margin. When he left the club in 1983 with a 34–27–0 record, it was to coach the Packers. He remained in Green Bay through the 1987 schedule before calling it quits, the Packers having gone 25–37–1 under his tutelage. Later, he became head coach at Southern Methodist University, his alma mater.

Lou Groza

6'3", 250 pounds. Offensive Tackle, Placekicker: Cleveland Browns (1946–1949, AAFC), Cleveland Browns (1950–1959, 1961–1967, NFL). All-Pro: 1951–1955, 1957. Pro Bowl: Nine appearances. 1954 NFL Player of the Year. AAFC Kicking Leader: 1946. NFL Kicking Leader: 1950–1955. Inducted into the Pro Football Hall of Fame 1974. Career: Touchdowns, 1; PATs, 810; field goals, 264; total points, 1,608.

Every placekicking specialist today owes his lucrative livelihood to Lou "The Toe" Groza, the man who literally put the foot back in football. He elevated the field goal to a par almost equal with that of the touchdown.

Back in the early 1950s, it was Groza who prompted Cleveland Brown coach Paul Brown, even then an offensive strategist of paragon status, to start thinking, and thinking seriously, about the place of the field goal in the pro game. The more Brown thought, the more percentages ran through his computerlike mental processes. And with all this cerebrating about numbers and their relationship to probabilities evolved ponderings as to the psychology of oneupmanship—getting on the scoreboard first, the importance of going downfield and not coming up empty, forcing the opposition to play catchup, and all the rest of the emotional weights and measures so routinely considered by coaches in the modern National Football League.

Groza initiated all this by being one of the most accurate kickers from placement ever to grace pro football. In 1946, his rookie year with the Browns, he kicked almost exclusively but was carried on the roster as an offensive tackle. Not until late in the 1947 campaign did he finally become a regular with Cleveland's offensive "pit crew." From that juncture until a back injury sidelined him for the entire 1960 schedule, he was a lineman first and a kicker second. And that's the way he preferred it. He earned All-Pro recognition six times, given his ability as both a run and a pass blocker. On no less than nine occasions he participated in the Pro Bowl, with six of these invitations citing him as a starter at tackle. In 1954, he was accorded NFL most-valuable honors. Unlike the current crop of placement artists, he was a real football player.

His legendary consistency as a kicker had much to do with preparation. Not a person to leave anything to chance, he devised a six-foot tape marker which enabled him to check his alignment and pace prior to every field-goal attempt. He fixed one end of the tape where the ball was to be held and the other end at the point of his setup, thereby assuring himself that the proper number of approach steps would be taken each time.

No matter the prevailing weather conditions, he performed his placement duties with a machinelike consistency. He was particularly effective from long range. This fact alone laid a heavy burden on the opposition's defensive minions, as they knew a superior effort would be required to hold the Browns beyond Groza's conversion potential. If they failed in this endeavor, it very likely meant a three-point deficit on the scoreboard, which could grow very quickly. On the other hand, they didn't have the benefit of such a weapon, and touchdowns were dearly bought, so being on the short side of such odds made for a long afternoon indeed.

He sat out the 1960 season due to a back problem. Upon his return to the team the following fall, he was 37 and well past his prime as a lineman. Only then did he become a kicking specialist. In this capacity he continued to make his uniformly significant scoring contributions until retiring after the 1967 slate.

Curiously enough, the one field-goal conversion which stood out from all the many others in his career of more than two decades was a comparative "gimme" by his lofty standards. But the stakes, and therefore the pressure attending it, were considerable. The clock was running down in the final quarter of the 1950 NFL championship game, and the Browns trailed the Los Angeles Rams 28–27. With the outcome riding on a 16-yard field-goal try, Groza methodically conducted his preliminary ritual, seemingly unmindful of the biting cold that gripped Cleveland's cavernous Municipal Stadium and a treacherous gusting wind that raked the playing field. At the putdown of the ball, he stepped foward and toed it perfectly between the uprights. The 30–28 victory represented the successful culmination of the Browns' inaugural season in the league after coming over from the defunct All-America Football Conference just a few months earlier. It proved beyond all reasonable doubt that they belonged in pro football's mainstream. "My biggest thrill," Groza testified afterward.

Lou Groza (left)

Overall, he spanned the gap between two eras, ushering out the age of the ironman and introducing the new order of the specialist. Few individuals have been able to play so substantive a role in the pro game's development.

John Hannah

6'3", 265 pounds. Guard: New England Patriots (1973–1985). All-Pro: 1976–1985. Pro Bowl: Nine appearances. NFLPA Offensive Lineman of the Year: 1978–1981. Inducted into the Pro Football Hall of Fame 1991.

It came as no surprise to gridiron savants that John Hannah earned election to the Pro Football Hall of Fame on first becoming eligible. Rather, it would have been something of a shock if he hadn't been accorded this ultimate honor.

Long before shucking his battle armor for the last time he was roundly regarded by friend and foe as one of the greatest offensive linemen ever to ply his skills in the National Football League. At 6'3" and 265 pounds, he rated All-Pro selection at guard for 10 successive seasons (1976–1985) and nine invitations to the Pro Bowl. From 1978 through 1981, his peers voted him the National Football League Players Association Offensive Lineman of the Year. He was similarly honored by the respected Seagram's Seven Crowns of Sport poll in 1978 and 1980.

When the New England Patriots made him their first-round pick in the 1973 NFL draft, he had already gained notoriety at the University of Alabama as a two-time All-American. With the Crimson Tide he held forth as a devastating run blocker in a ground-oriented wishbone offense. But any misgivings that pro scouts may have harbored about his ability to master pass-protection techniques were quickly dispelled once he arrived in the Pats preseason training camp as a physically awesome rookie. Almost from day one, he favorably impressed the coaching staff with his overall athletic ability and dexterity afoot.

It wasn't long after Hannah's conversion to the pro game that then New England offensive coordinator Jim Ringo, himself a Hall of Fame center with Green Bay and Philadelphia, was extolling the virtues of his massive young charge by comparing him to the standout guards with the Vince Lombardi–era Packers. "John has better pulling speed than Jerry Kramer and Fuzzy Thurston," Ringo said, "although he's twenty pounds heavier than either of them."

During the 1978 campaign Hannah bulwarked an offensive line that led the Patriots to an NFL single-season rushing record of 3,165 yards. In 1985, he was a key factor in New England's drive to the American Football Conference championship and a berth in Super Bowl XX. He had 10 career fumble recoveries, one of which went for a touchdown against the Miami Dolphins in a 1974 game.

The ultimate force to which there was no immovable object, he particularly distinguished himself in short-yardage situations where a quick jump off the ball and sheer power are the factors which produce the keep-the-drive-alive first down or put six points on the scoreboard that spells the difference between victory and defeat.

It will be some time before the likes of John Hannah comes down the NFL pike again.

Ed Healey

6'3", 220 pounds. Tackle: Rock Island Independents (1920–1922), Chicago Bears (1922–1927). All-Pro: 1922–1927. Inducted into the Pro Football Hall of Fame 1964.

Ed Healey didn't coin the adage "If you can't beat 'em, join 'em," but he gave a classic example of how it applies.

The incident took place in 1922 when he was playing tackle for the Rock Island (Ill.) Independents. In a home game against the Chicago Bears, he hunkered down opposite the visitors' player-coach George Halas, who held forth at end. Previously, Healey had done a number on Halas, and the Bears' hard-shell mentor didn't intend to take another manhandling. So he employed a new style of blocking, the basic technique of which involved grabbing the front of Healey's jersey and holding on for dear life. Healey howled in indignation and launched a haymaker intended to dislodge Hallas's head. And from that juncture on, the proceedings took a definite downturn.

In the wake of this unpleasant confrontation, Halas determined it wouldn't do for him to face Healey across a scrimmage line again. With this in mind, he purchased the rights to Healey for $100, just the amount of an oustanding debt the Independents owed the Bears. This exchange amounted to the first sale of a player in National Football League history. Ultimately, it proved to be one of the best deals Halas ever made.

Curiously enough, Healey performed three years at end for Dartmouth College with only moderate distinction. His case was uniformly one of a late bloomer. Following graduation, he accepted a coaching position in Nebraska that also entailed loading railroad cars in the summer to make financial ends meet. One day he heard of a pro football league forming back in Illinois and promptly boarded a train for Rock Island. There he joined the Independents on a trial basis. In his first pro outing, he took a beating but was impressive enough to earn $100 and a permanent contract. The year was 1920. He remained with the club until 1922 when the Bears added him to their payroll.

During the next five seasons, he rated All-Pro recognition and became universally respected for his prowess at tackle. He was deceptively fast for his 6'3", 220-pound bulk. In a 1924 game he displayed his speed in preventing a teammate from carrying the ball across the wrong goal line. After intercepting a pass, a Bears defender became confused and inadvertently headed for the Chicago end zone. Healey promptly gave pursuit and after a 30-yard chase, brought the erring fellow safely to ground.

He proved to be exceptionally agile. Following the 1925 season, the Bears were playing an all-star team in Los Angeles as part of a barnstorming tour. In this contest a fleet-footed back named George Wilson turned the corner on the Chicago defensive front and appeared a cinch to put six points on the scoreboard, but Healey deftly vaulted over several of his fallen comrades to get the angle on Wilson and then ran him down. His acrobatics drew a roar of appreciation from the 60,000 spectators looking on.

In 1927, the Bears finished the campaign with the third best winning percentage in the league, and on that note Healey called it a career. His retirement incited Halas to laud him as "the most versatile tackle of all time." Just five years later he became the first president of the club's alumni association. Healey died on December 9, 1978, at the age of 83.

Mel Hein

6'2", 225 pounds. Center: New York Giants (1931–1945). All-Pro: 1933–1940. Inducted into the Pro Football Hall of Fame 1963 (charter member).

All things considered, Mel Hein is probably the most multitalented member of the Hall of Fame to be designated as a center. Needless to say, he excelled at the duties of his position, but his abilities would have allowed him to achieve the same distinction if assigned a variety of other gridiron responsibilities.

From 1931 to 1945, he played nearly every minute of every game both offensively and defensively. The term *ironman* could have been coined especially for him. As a snapper, he prevailed without peer, and this was when the single wing still sufficed as the preferred method of attack. He unerringly centered to the tailback, one time just inside the lead knee to facilitate the spinner pivot. Another time he placed the snap right at the waistline for a direct handoff to a crossing back. Still another time he would float it back for easy handling in passing and punting situations. This required precision under pressure and in all weather with a ball that resembled a melon more than the easy-to-handle configuration of today.

Defensively, he employed methods that are still fashionable in the modern era. From his linebacker spot he utilized what has come to be known as "dogging," controlling an offensive lineman and then slipping off to break into the backfield and sack the passer. On such occasions as he was assigned to coverage, his agility and speed enabled him considerable range of latitude, so much so that he was able to contain the great Green Bay receiver Don Hutson along the sidelines, preventing him from reaching the open field where his maneuverability could be used to best advantage. Hein was that kind of an athlete.

During his tenure at Washington State University, he starred as a tackle, guard, and center at one time or another. In 1930, he earned selection to a number of All-America teams at each of these designations and was named to the squad of famed sportswriter Grantland Rice as a utility lineman, a special category which singled him out as able to play anywhere with the best of his breed. Still, the pros didn't evidence that much interest in him at the outset.

He was reduced to writing three NFL clubs and asking them for a try-out. The Providence Steam Roller franchise answered first, offering him $135 a game if he made the team. He fired off an affirmative reply, only to hear from the New York Giants. They were willing to compensate him at a rate of $150 per contest given the same contingencies. Quickly, he withdrew the agreement made with Providence and headed for the big city. He arrived there flat broke and had to be advanced $200 by the Giants management to cover living expenses. In training camp he faced the task of beating out two veterans for a spot on the 25-man roster. This he did and then settled down to doing his job above reproach for a span of 15 years.

He was among the most determined competitors ever to grace the National Football League. Only once was a time-out called on his behalf and then just briefly to treat a broken nose. Season after season, he lined up on both sides of the ball despite injuries that would have benched less resolute individuals. Though aggressive to a considerable degree, he never resorted to underhanded or outright illegal tactics to gain an advantage as did many of his contemporaries.

In 1945, his last year with the Giants, he held forth as the best-remunerated lineman in the league with a contract worth $5,000. When he left the game, his famed No. 7 jersey was retired by the club. He rated All-Pro recognition eight successive seasons and was honored as the NFL's Most Valuable Player in 1938.

To say that they don't make them like Mel Hein anymore is not just to invoke a timeworn cliché.

Wilbur "Pete" Henry

6'0", 250 pounds. Tackle: Canton Bulldogs (1920, 1921, APFA), Canton Bulldogs (1922, 1923, 1925, 1926, NFL), New York Giants (1927), Pottsville Maroons (1927, 1928). Inducted into the Pro Football Hall of Fame 1963 (charter member).

In a time when might largely made right in pro football, Wilbur "Pete" Henry was particularly well qualified for his line of work. He made his living at tackle both offensively and defensively, a legitimate 60-minute man, and possessed the dimensions, 6'0" and 250 pounds, to make a go of it.

Nicknamed "Fats" for obvious reasons, he gave the appearance of being soft, even flabby, a popular misconception which prompted no few assaults on his person that uniformly ended in dread for the perpetrators. A classic example of this folly occurred when an opposing coach proposed to "show that fat guy who's boss out there." His plan was simple enough:

Send a phalanx of blockers right at Henry and bury him. Then the ball carrier could all but tippy-toe through his vacated tackle spot. Like a lot of theories, it proved a disaster in practice. On the snap of the ball, a knot of outsize humanity barreled at "Fats," a glint of malice in their eyes. His reaction was to plow headlong into the midst of the burly assemblage strewing bodies about like so many faded leaves blown by a strong autumn wind. Then he laid a crunching tackle on the runner, throwing him for a substantial loss. Well, back to the drawing board.

Henry had earned a considerable reputation for himself prior to turning pro as a three-time All-America pick at Washington and Jefferson College. So when he signed to play for the Canton Bulldogs of the American Professional Football Association (APFA), it sufficed as big news locally. His act of penmanship rated a "War Over" kind of headline on the front page of the Canton *Repository*. Ironically, he joined the Bulldogs on the very day, September 17, 1920, that the APFA was being formed. This happening got little more than agate type on an inside page. No one, let alone the newspaper editor, could possibly have foreseen the significance of the meeting that went on in a downtown auto dealer's showroom — that out of the APFA there would shortly bloom the National Football League, the most successful athletic endeavor ever undertaken. But back then, Henry generated the headlines in northern Ohio.

Lest it be thought his talents were limited to knocking people around in awesome fashion, nothing could be further from the truth. He prevailed as an offensive threat of no mean magnitude as well. By placekicking or dropkicking the ball, he could score three points from almost anywhere on the field. In 1922, he boomed a 50-yard dropkick flush between the uprights for a league record. Later that year he notched a 40-yard placement to preserve a 3–3 tie and an unbeaten season for Canton. He was also a pretty fair country punter, loosing a 94-yard boot against the Akron Indians in a 1923 contest. Needless to say, this prodigious effort established an NFL mark. What's more, he occasionally carried the ball with success. He had been a fullback in high school and despite his size exhibited a certain deceptive quickness. Given the old "tackle over tackle" maneuver, he usually managed to get the needed short yardage.

The Bulldogs won back-to-back championships in 1922 and 1923, with Henry bulwarking the line both offensively and defensively. He joined the New York Giants in 1927, and they too won an NFL title. In 1928, he closed out his career with the Pottsville Maroons. He died on February 7, 1952, at 54.

Robert "Cal" Hubbard

6'5", 250 pounds. Tackle, End, Linebacker: New York Giants (1927, 1928, 1936), Green Bay Packers (1929–1933, 1935), Pittsburgh Pirates (1936). All-Pro: 1928–1933. Inducted into the Pro Football Hall of Fame 1963 (charter member). Tackle: 50-Year, All-Time, All-NFL team.

By any measure,. Cal Hubbard was a giant. He towered over two professional sports, football and baseball, as few individuals have done in the long history of either game. He is the only person to ever be memorialized in two major halls of fame, those of football and baseball.

Hard and roughhewn as life on a Missouri farm at the turn of the century could make a boy, young Hubbard early developed a deep affinity for the game of football. He liked it enough to attend the high school in a neighboring town because the one nearest him didn't have a team. Following graduation, he enrolled at Centenary College in Louisiana and there exercised his considerable gridiron talents under the tutelage of famed coach Alvin "Bo" McMillin. He finished out his scholastic tenure at Geneva College in Pennsylvania, there earning All-America recognition.

In 1927, no less than three NFL clubs sought his services. Confused by such attention, he inquired of McMillin what the best course of action would be. McMillin advised Hubbard to accept the offer tendered by the New York Giants because "they were most likely to pay him." And that he did.

With the Giants, Hubbard held forth at both tackle and end on offense, usually the biggest man on the field at 6'5" and 250 pounds. Defensively, he played linebacker, excelling as a run stuffer and, given his height, a most effective antidote to the forward pass. Besides that, he presided as something of a cop, ensuring that the opposition cheap-shot artists wouldn't practice their dubious avocation for fear of being suddenly consigned to a hospital bed.

His initial agreement with the New York franchise afforded him the handsome salary of $150 a game. The Giants made a killing on the deal as he proved to be a dominant force and led them to the 1927 NFL title. He was particularly imposing on defense, spearheading a prevent corps that limited opponents to just 20 points in 13 games. In spite of his bulk, he commanded surprising speed, an attribute that allowed him considerable range along the line of scrimmage, and he used this advantage like a club to consistently beat the other linemen in the league.

When playing against the Green Bay Packers in 1928, Hubbard became smitten with the bucolic atmosphere of the Wisconsin countryside and decided that he preferred it to New York City. That offseason, he refused to sign with the Giants again, threatening to quit football if they didn't trade him to the Packers. Finally, when faced with an outright loss on their investment, they acceded to his demand, and he headed for more rustic surroundings.

He became a tackle full-time with the Packers and made All-Pro each of his five seasons in Green Bay. In 1936, he returned to the Giants but closed out the year with the Pittsburgh Pirates. At the end of the campaign, he retired and concentrated on a career in baseball as an umpire. He would prove outstanding in this capacity, prevailing as the game's "great arbitrator" for many years.

.But even in this less physically combative occupation, Hubbard never lost his natural aggressiveness. He always made it a point to let the players and managers know who was boss between the lime lines. On one occasion, the perennially pugnacious Leo "Lippy" Durocher charged Hubbard, then working home plate, and proceeded to shower him with invectives. Hubbard looked on stonily. Then Durocher accentuated his tirade with a spray of dirt kicked onto Hubbard's pants and shoes. A numbing punch to the jaw ensued, and "The Lip" was ported unconscious to his dugout. Hubbard died on October 17, 1977, at 76.

Stan Jones

6'1", 250 pounds. Offensive Tackle, Guard; Defensive Tackle: Chicago Bears (1954–1965), Washington Redskins (1966). All-Pro: 1955, 1956, 1959, 1960. Pro Bowl: Seven appearances. Inducted into the Pro Football Hall of Fame 1991.

A standout performer on both offense and defense, Stan Jones was among the last of his breed to demonstrate a laudable versatility that would soon thereafter be reduced to but a fond memory, given the inexorable onrush of the specialist's era in pro football.

He came to the Chicago Bears in 1954 following a spectacular senior year at the University of Maryland as college lineman of the year and an All-America selection. During his rookie season with Chicago, he was an offensive tackle but moved over to guard the ensuing campaign and remained there through 1961. A shortage of quality personnel forced him to play on both sides of the ball the entire 1962 schedule. In 1963, he switched exclusively to the prevent corps and was a pivotal performer for the Bears as they drove to the NFL title. He went to Washington in 1966 and finished out his career with the Redskins that year.

By virtue of an arduous weight-training program he packed 250 pounds on his 6'1" frame and became an All-Pro selection in 1955, 1956, 1959, and 1960. He also earned an invitation to seven consecutive Pro Bowls from 1955 to 1961. Good size coupled with admirable agility and determination marked him as a standout pass blocker offensively and a daunting, tenacious defender. Durability was also a distinguishing characteristic as he missed only two starts because of injuries during his first 11 years with Chicago.

Admission to the Hall of Fame has long been his due.

Walt Kiesling

6'2", 245 pounds. Guard: Duluth Eskimos (1926, 1927), Pottsville Maroons (1928), Chicago Cardinals (1929–1933), Chicago Bears (1934), Green Bay Packers (1935, 1936), Pittsburgh Pirates (1937, 1938). All-Pro: 1932. Coach: Pittsburgh Pirates (1939), Pittsburgh Steelers (1940–1942, 1954–1956). Inducted into the Pro Football Hall of Fame 1966. Career: Coach: Won-lost record: Pittsburgh Pirates (1–6–1), Pittsburgh Steelers (24–33–3).

Without a strong supporting cast, no production, regardless how finely crafted, can achieve sustained success; the star system alone can't carry the show. In the course of the National Football League's long-run popularity, it has been blessed with a fine underbill of talent, not the least of which was Walt "Big Kies" Kiesling.

He hove onto the scene in the formative years of the pro game when it was confined to unkempt brickyards within the shadow of foundry smokestacks. During that period of the 1920s and 1930s, he performed as a big (6'2", 245 pounds), roughhewn guard on a variety of clubs, most of which long ago became just so many lines of agate type in NFL annals.

The Duluth Eskimos took him on as a rookie out of St. Thomas (Minn.) College in 1926. He moved to the Pottsville Maroons in 1928 for a single season before stopping over with the Chicago Cardinals from 1929 to 1933. His tenure in a Cardinals uniform provided him with a forum in which he could show to best advantage. In 1932, he earned All-Pro recognition despite the fact the Chicago franchise finished down in the standings. He traveled crosstown in 1934 to star with the Bears, who went undefeated during the regular schedule. Thereafter he bumped heads for the Green Bay Packers (1935, 1936) and then the Pittsburgh Pirates. He was a player-coach with the Pirates in 1937 and 1938 before shedding his uniform for the last time.

In 1939, he officially commenced his coaching career as an assistant with Pittsburgh and later that season became the field boss. He retained his position when the club became the Steelers in 1940 but was replaced prior to the onset of the next campaign. Near the end of the 1941 schedule, he reclaimed the head job and held it through 1942, that year leading Pittsburgh to a 7–4 record and second place in the Eastern Division. In 1943, due to the shortage of players imposed by World War II, the Steelers merged with the Philadelphia Eagles, and he served as co-coach along with Earl "Greasy" Neal. The following year, Pittsburgh joined the Cardinals under the same shared-leadership arrangement.

· From 1945 to 1948, Kiesling worked as an assistant coach under close friend "Curly" Lambeau of the Packers. In 1949, he returned to Pittsburgh in the same capacity but took over the head coaching reins again with the start of the 1954 season. He relinquished his duties after the 1956 campaign because of failing health. Even then he remained on the Steelers staff as something of a "coach emeritus," offering assistance in any way possible.

Only briefly did Kiesling's name make it in lights, the year he was named to the all-league team. But his most valuable contributions to the NFL were the caring administrations applied as a coach. Without his wisdom and presence along the way, it is doubtful that pro football, particularly in Pittsburgh, would have survived so well. He died on March 2, 1962, at 58.

Frank "Bruiser" Kinard

6'1", 218 pounds. Tackle: Brooklyn Dodgers (1938–1944), New York Yankees (1946, 1947, AAFC). All-Pro: 1940, 1941, 1943, 1944; All-AAFC: 1946. Inducted into the Pro Football Hall of Fame 1971.

A bullet has speed, force of impact, and a capability for lethal effect far greater than its size would seem to warrant. Much the same can be said of Frank "Bruiser" Kinard, a standout two-way tackle of the late 1930s and mid–1940s.

During most of his nine-year tenure in pro football he didn't weigh more than 195 pounds soaking wet, yet the nickname Bruiser epitomized his style of play. He was, in the parlance of the game, a "native hitter." Quick off the mark, rock-hard of body and savage in intent, he regularly intimidated men much larger than himself and frequently compelled opponents to avoid his position. Defensively, he prevailed as a sure and punishing tackler who commanded the ability to make stops from sideline to sideline. On offense, he held forth as a devastating blocker, so much so that plays for needed yardage frequently were called for the hole where he did business. In all, he was a dominant 60-minute man.

He twice earned All-America recognition as a tackle while attending the University of Mississippi, so when he entered the NFL draft in 1938, the Brooklyn Dodgers wasted no time in making him their second-round pick despite his lack of size. And though he joined a club that didn't want for talent, his presence in the lineup was felt almost immediately. Before long, he established himself as a mainstay both offensively and defensively. From 1940 to 1944, he achieved All-Pro status four times, missing nomination only in 1942.

The U.S. Navy called him to duty in 1945, and when afforded an opportunity to play football, he made the most of it, being voted to the all-service team. Given his discharge a year later, he jumped to the newly formed All-America Football Conference as a member of the New York Yankees. In 1946, he led the Yankees to a divisional title and was All-AAFC, the first man to be selected as an All-Pro in both leagues. Following the 1947 campaign, he retired and ended a brilliant career, one built for the ages on a foundation of determination and commitment to purpose.

Once out of uniform, Kinard returned to his beloved Ole Miss to serve initially as an assistant coach, then interim head coach, and finally athletic director. He died on September 7, 1985, at 70.

Jim Langer

6'2", 255 pounds. Center: Miami Dolphins (1970–1979), Minnesota Vikings (1980, 1981). All-Pro: 1974–1977. Pro Bowl: Six appearances. Inducted into the Pro Football Hall of Fame 1987.

Nobody's perfect, the saying goes, and pro football headhunters can certainly cite this observation in their defense. While they hit on a very high percentage of their picks, some "blue chippers" escape their notice. Enter, stage left, Jim Langer, a premier center who very nearly slipped through the National Football League cracks.

Being from North Dakota State University didn't help him activate the NFL talent sensors to any great degree. And a guy who plays in the middle of the offensive line, a fairly anonymous group of individuals per se, isn't going to be all that visible as a matter of course. So Langer attempted to join the NFL as a free agent in the preseason of 1970 and got waived by the Cleveland Browns for his trouble. But the Miami Dolphins quickly fished him out of the discard tank and gave his ambitions new life.

Down in the sun capital of the nation he sat on the bench for much of two years, except for getting some reps on special teams or a backup stint at both guard and center. Finally, in 1972, Dolphins head coach Don Shula decided to give him a shot at the snapper spot. Langer was paired off against veteran pivot man Bob DeMarco, with the winner to be accorded starter status. When the smoke of their head-to-head battle had cleared, Langer emerged as the victor, and the center spoils were his.

Suffice it to say his coming of age took place at a most propitious time, the onset of the Dolphins' perfect 17–0 season of 1972. He didn't miss a down during that historic campaign and distinguished himself as one of the finest practitioners of his trade. From 1974 through 1977, he held forth as a perennial All-Pro and appeared in six Pro Bowls during his career.

He routinely prevailed as a fine blocker, both in passing and running situations. After the 1972 schedule, film studies revealed that of 500 blocking assignments, he required assistance on only three occasions. At 6'2" and 255 pounds, he had the size to dig out recalcitrant defenders and regularly did so with such vigor that members of the loyal opposition were regularly reduced to picking themselves up after mixing birdcages with him. Given good balance and quickness of foot, he could make the snap and then adroitly backpedal into position to seal the seam of the protective passing pocket. Seldom did he need help in maintaining his turf on a man-to-man basis.

Prior to Super Bowl VIII, Minnesota Vikings head coach Bud Grant remarked to reporters that Langer was one of the most error-free centers in his memory. Small wonder, then, after Langer had played out his string with Miami in the wake of the 1979 slate that he was appropriated by Grant's Vikings. Langer retired at the close of the 1981 schedule.

William Roy "Link" Lyman

6'2", 252 pounds. Tackle: Canton Bulldogs (1922, 1923, 1925), Cleveland Bulldogs (1924), Frankford Yellowjackets (1925), Chicago Bears (1926–1928, 1930, 1931, 1933, 1934). Inducted into the Pro Football Hall of Fame 1964.

By best record, William Roy "Link" Lyman was the father of the tactics now widely employed by defensive linemen and linebackers in the National Football League. His mobility at the line of scrimmage made him nigh impossible to block effectively, and defensive coordinators are still borrowing pages from his book of tricks.

At 6'2" and 252 pounds, he held forth as one of the biggest linemen of his day and wouldn't have been overmatched even now. He utilized shifting, sliding maneuvers that confused the opposition's blocking angles and assignments. With surprisingly quick footwork for a man of his dimensions, he stepped back and forth from one side to the other after members of the offensive line had set themselves and couldn't move. Then, at the snap, he would "shoot the gap" between them and often arrived in the backfield right along with the ball. On other occasions, he engaged in a series of feints, some of them directed backward as if he intended to drop off the line and loop around for an outside rush, others' forward thrusts giving the impression he was bent upon beating the snap count. More often than not, the offense got whistled for a motion penalty, frustration having overcome the better judgment of a befuddled guard or tackle.

Lyman explained the genesis of his moves as more reflexive than conceptual. He instinctively felt the need to be in motion, the better to get an explosive start and make the most of his considerable bulk. As time went on, he consciously developed a routine to take advantage of his success at confounding would-be blockers. This repertoire, coupled with his native ability to diagnose enemy formations and perceive their intended outcome before they could actually reach fruition, presented no small problem to the other teams in the league. In direct response to the threat he posed, offensive linemen had to employ new stratagems of their own such as cross-blocking, trapping, and assignment-switching signals.

Not until entering the University of Nebraska in 1917 did Lyman play organized football. But he proved to be an enthusiastic student once exposed to the game, so much so that by 1921, his senior season, he had reached superstar status and served as the spearhead of a fine Cornhusker team. After graduating, he signed on with the Canton Bulldogs and played an integral part in their NFL champion squads of 1922 and 1923. When the franchise moved to Cleveland the following year, he stayed with them, and the outcome was another league crown. In 1925, he split his time between the Bulldogs and the Frankford Yellowjackets. The next season he joined the Chicago Bears and was a pivotal performer for them through 1934. However, he took two leaves of absence, one in 1929 to play semipro football and again in 1932 to deal with pressing business problems.

According to Bears owner and head coach George Halas, Lyman got better with age. While he held forth at tackle in 1933 and 1934, his last two years in pro football, Chicago topped the Western Division twice and won an NFL title.

Said New York Giants head coach Steve Owen: "Link was the first defensive lineman to ever move from his position before the ball was centered. His movements kept you guessing all the time, and most of the time you guessed wrong." Lyman died on December 16, 1972, at 74.

Mike McCormack

6'4", 250 pounds. Tackle: New York Yanks (1951), Cleveland Browns (1954–1962). Pro Bowl: Six appearances. Inducted into the Pro Football Hall of Fame 1984. Career: Coach: Seattle Seahawks (1982). Won-lost record: 4–3–0 (season shortened due to players' strike).

Contrary to popular belief, football is not a game of passing, running, and kicking. Rather, it's a matter of confrontation, pure and simple. No *X*s

Mike McCormack

and *O*s, however brilliantly configured, will result in even the slightest advance without the trench war being fought to advantage. And it was up front in close combat that Mike McCormack held forth as a literal mover and shaker who served as the key to a National Football League dynasty.

Hall of Fame field boss Paul Brown, founder and mentor of the

Cleveland Browns, once said of McCormack, "He was the finest offensive lineman I ever coached."

It was for this reason that Brown went to no little trouble to acquire the 6'4", 250-pound tackle after his fine rookie season with the New York Yanks in 1951. Even while McCormack was away from the NFL in 1952 and 1953 doing a hitch with the army, he was much a part of Brown's plans. Cleveland needed a premier pass blocker to initiate a balanced attack, one with an explosive quick-strike facet. So it was that Brown inaugurated a 15-player swap with the Baltimore Colts (formerly the New York Yanks and Dallas Texans) which brought McCormack to the Browns even before he had been discharged from the service.

"Paul (Brown) said he traded for me because I could pass-block," McCormack related. "I was lucky because my line coach at the University of Kansas, a former pro player and coach with the old Brooklyn Dodgers named Pop Warner, taught me all the techniques. You couldn't use your hands in those days. You had to keep them up against your chest. So it was all body position. You had to keep your man between you and the quarterback, and you had to do it with your feet and your head. It was like trying to stop somebody from getting through your doorway."

When McCormack reported to the Browns' preseason training camp in 1954, he learned his ample presence would also be required on defense due to the fact that a sufficient replacement for recently retired middle guard Bill Willis had not been found. But this was no big deal as he went both ways for the Yanks in his freshman campaign and was used to the regimen. He performed on both sides of the ball in laudable fashion, and Cleveland prevailed to claim the NFL title that year.

From 1955 through 1962, he played solely at right offensive tackle and during this period earned five invitations to the Pro Bowl. In 1957 and 1958, Hall-of-Famers Jim Brown and Bobby Mitchell joined the Browns, and McCormack immediately began utilizing his unusual mobility to pull out and lead sweeps featuring both members of the dynamic ball-carrying duo.

"Not many tackles would be asked to do that back then," McCormack said. "But not many teams had a Brown or a Mitchell, either." Nor a McCormack, for that matter.

In addition to his regular duties, big No. 74 also served as team captain for a span of seven years. His enthusiasm, dedication, and confidence proved to be highly contagious, readily infecting his teammates, but as the situation required, he could lend a little muscle to his leadership responsibilities and get equally good results.

When questioned about McCormack's influence on his comrades, Brown said, "I've never had, or known of, a finer captain or leader. He was a football player who never gave less than his best."

During his tenure in the NFL, McCormack had to contend with some of the best defensive practitioners ever to ply their skills in the pro game. "I always felt like Gino Marchetti was the best I ever played against," he said. "But there were so many good ones. Gene Brito, Andy Robustelli, Jim Katcavage, Darris McCord. I played against Bob Lilly and Deacon Jones when they were breaking into the NFL. They were all good."

McCormack retired following the 1962 season and thereafter remained in the league as both an assistant and a head coach. He also served as president and general manager of the Seattle Seahawks for several years.

At the time of his induction into the Hall of Fame, he remarked, "You know, you hear a lot of old-timers say they wish they could have played in the modern era. Well, I don't wish that. I don't think I could have played in a better era. Television was just coming in, and the game was just starting to get popular. I wouldn't trade my era for anyone's. I had a great time. And yeah, I think the Cleveland Browns teams I played on could hold their own today."

Mike McCormack thinks he could hold his own today too.

Mike Michalske

6'0", 209 pounds. Guard: New York Yankees (1926, AFL), New York Yankees (1927, 1928, NFL), Green Bay Packers (1929–1935, 1937). All-Pro: 1929–1931, 1935. Inducted into Pro Football Hall of Fame 1964 (first guard to be so honored).

For all the opposition knew, "Iron Mike" Michalske was indeed sculpted out of an ingot. During a pro career that spanned 12 years, he never seemed susceptible to injury, while those who came in contact with him fared much less fortunately.

Though but 6'0" and 209 pounds, he left many a larger opponent lying worse for wear on the greensward while affecting something akin to an immunity against the disabling mishaps so inherent to the position of guard. "I just didn't get hurt," he once commented, looking back on his playing days. "Don't ask me why. It got so the guys on the team began kidding me about getting paid by the minute."

When one knows the many and varied duties of a 60-minute lineman of the 1920s and 1930s, it becomes all the more amazing that Michalske managed to avoid being incapacitated. Offensively, a guard was expected to engage the strength of the enemy's trench troops on inside running routes. If sweeps were called, his prime responsibility amounted to getting ahead of the back and taking on ends and other outsize types converging to cover the play. When the ball changed hands, he was supposed to close off the middle against power thrusts and put pressure on the passer. In this latter capacity he excelled, utilizing a tactic known even then as "blitzing."

Once he had the passer in hand, there weren't so many strictures guiding his behavior as are now on the books. "We used to work the guy over pretty good," he admitted, "even after the ball was thrown. It may not have been ethical, but it didn't count as illegal either."

He played guard and fullback as well as end and tackle at Penn State University and earned All-America recognition in 1925. The following year he joined the pro ranks with the New York Yankees of the American Football League. When the AFL folded after one season, the Yankees were absorbed by the NFL, and so was he. In the wake of the 1928 campaign, the franchise went under, and he jumped to the Green Bay Packers. There he anchored lines that forged NFL titles from 1929 through 1931. During his eight years in the Wisconsin hamlet, he was named All-Pro four times.

He is credited with instituting the practice of converting fullbacks into guards, thereby making maximal use of their speed and hitting ability. Packers head coach "Curly" Lambeau, given the example set by Michalske, made use of this transformation process for many years thereafter, proving its worth over and over again. In the 1960s another Green Bay mentor of note, Vince Lombardi, evidenced much the same mentality in formulating his devastating ground attack.

On October 26, 1930, Michalske died at 80.

Ron Mix

6'4", 255 pounds. Offensive Tackle, Guard: Los Angeles Chargers (1960, AFL), San Diego Chargers (1961–1969), Oakland Raiders (1971, NFL). All-AFL: 1960–1964, 1966–1968. AFL All-Star Game: Seven appearances. All-Time AFL team: 1960–1969. Inducted into the Pro Football Hall of Fame 1979.

Ron Mix's professional career was marked by two noteworthy distinctions. He never cared much for football, and he was whistled only twice for holding infractions in 11 years. Not bad for an offensive tackle with all-league credentials.

In high school he harbored aspirations of earning his livelihood as a baseball player. He was also pretty fair at track. Football? Uh-uh, no love lost there. Nonetheless, he played the game well enough to rate a scholarship at the University of Southern California. While there, he frequented the team training table often enough to put on no less than 100 pounds. This substantial addition of adipose and a good work ethic produced on-field results sufficient unto attracting the attention of scouts from both the National Football League and the American Football League (AFL).

When the Los Angeles Chargers of the AFL waved the most money under his nose, he promptly signed on the dotted line. His original intent

Ron Mix

was to play just long enough, a couple of years at most, to get a stake in life and then do something more to his liking. But early success turned his head, and he decided knocking folks down on Sunday afternoons wasn't all that bad, after all.

By the time the Chargers were settled in San Diego a few seasons, Mix had become an established star. At 6'4" and 255 pounds, he held forth as one of the biggest men in the league at his position. What's more, he possessed unusual speed and agility for his size, which gave him another up on the opposition. In the early going his technique was relatively simple. He would make first contact at the snap of the ball, then keep applying pressure until the pass was thrown, the ball carrier got by safely, or the opposing linemen crumpled into a heap. Not too tough a way to earn a nice buck.

Gradually, as the AFL matured, Mix found the opposition linemen more skilled and larger of stature. As a result, his somewhat simplistic methods for dealing with them necessarily underwent change. He had to develop more moves to get the advantage that brute force previously accorded him. But he proved equal to the task, becoming more "coachable" in the process. Given his speed and impeccable balance, he could make an initial hit at the line of scrimmage, shed his man, then race downfield to get in on the action there.

In 1969, his last year with the Chargers, he was named to the All-Time AFL team. By then, he had been an All-AFL selection eight times as a tackle and once as a guard. He also played in five of the first six AFL championship games as a Charger. All that remained was an invitation to the Pro Football Hall of Fame, and that came in 1979.

George Musso

6'2", 270 pounds. Tackle, Guard: Chicago Bears (1933–1944). All-Pro: 1935, 1937, 1938. Inducted into the Pro Football Hall of Fame 1982.

It can be said that George Musso is the only Hall of Fame member to be acquired at a discount price. Depending upon whom one is inclined to believe, here is how the story goes.

After watching Musso perform in a 1933 East-West All-Star game for college seniors in Chicago, Bears owner and coach George Halas offered the young giant $90 a game if he made the team and an extra $5 to pay his way to training camp. Musso jumped at the opportunity. Now the plot thickens.

Halas claimed to have been unimpressed with the mammoth rookie (6'2", 270 pounds) in early scrimmages and wanted to cut him from the squad. But the young man, desperate to play pro football, refused to leave and was finally allowed to stay when he agreed to have his salary discounted to $45 a game until able to prove himself. The rest is history.

Musso told the tale a mite differently. When Halas wanted to farm him out to a development team in Cincinnati, he declined, asking instead for an outright release. He told Halas that the Green Bay Packers had promised him a roster spot and his plans were to sign on with them. Only then, Musso contended, did Halas make him the half-pay proposal. Take your pick of these renditions.

Whatever, it had to be one of the best deals the cagey Halas ever made. Musso not only proved himself; he went on to become one of the Bears' great linemen both offensively and defensively. During his 12-year tenure with the team, he provided protection for the likes of Harold "Red" Grange, Sid Luckman, and George McAfee, and played alongside Bill Hewett, Clyde "Bulldog" Turner, and Joe Stydahar, Hall-of-Famers all.

George Musso

Musso earned All-Pro honors as a tackle in 1935 and then repeated in 1937 and 1938, only as a guard, the first player in NFL history to be so recognized. His contribution as the middleman in the Bears' defensive front was considered to be of greater moment than the blocking he performed on the offensive side of the ball. However, he stood out in either capacity.

Years after their first meeting, Halas said of Musso, "George was one of the finest guards ever in professional football. He was tough, mobile, agile, and intimidating, with an indomitable competitive spirit."

Upon first seeing a photo of Musso, Grange snorted and observed, "This guy will never make it. He looks like a walrus." But later the two men became fast friends, and Musso credited Grange with encouraging him in those early, precarious days as a rookie.

Affectionately referred to as "Big Bear" by his teammates, Musso held forth as captain of the talent-laden Chicago aggregation for nine consecutive seasons. From time to time, Halas even allowed him to deliver the pregame oration.

"He was a great team leader, and from his third year on he was our team captain," Halas said. "He could get along with anybody."

Grange added, "George was the team captain. The players wouldn't have anyone else. He had great spirit, and his pep talks really got the players fired up."

In the course of his college days at Millikin, Musso accumulated 12 varsity letters. But he almost didn't get to attend school at all. His father, a coal miner, wanted him to work in the mines. It took the persistence of friends to persuade his father to permit him to enroll in high school and later to accept an athletic scholarship to college.

When Musso had Halas make the presentation speech during his induction into the Pro Football Hall of Fame, he was asked whether the Bears owner had been given travel expenses to Canton for the ceremony. "Yep," Musso replied, "I just sent him the same $5 he gave me back in 1933."

Jim Otto

6'2", 255 pounds. Center: Oakland Raiders (1960–1969, AFL), Oakland Raiders (1970–1974, NFL). All-AFL: 1960–1969. All-Pro: 1970–1972. AFL All-Star Game: Nine appearances. Pro Bowl: Three appearances. AFL All-Time team: 1960–1969. Inducted into the Pro Football Hall of Fame 1980.

To begin with, Jim Otto wore the number 00, a significant departure from the norm in itself. And then he started every regular and postseason game in a 15-year span. He did so despite serious infirmity, especially toward

Jim Otto

the end of his career when both knees were so badly battered they would have disqualified a lesser human being. Color him a maverick. And it just makes sense that he played his entire career for a classic organization of mavericks—the Oakland Raiders.

When he made himself available to the National Football League fresh out of the University of Miami (Fla.), his desirability rating was adjudged next to nil. He couldn't get an expression of interest from even one NFL club. Not that he wasn't a good center and all. Simply put, he just didn't possess the physical equipment thought to be necessary for survival in the pros. At 6'2" and only 205 pounds, he wasn't as big as some of the backs in the league. Sorry, kid, maybe some other time.

Undaunted, he packed his gear and headed for the American Football League (AFL), then in its first year (1960) of operation. The Raiders had given him a nod to try out, and that's all he required, at least to his way of thinking. He intended to make the team one way or another. And so he did. Meanwhile, he worked slavishly to build up his body to take the pounding that was indigenous to playing center for money. Given his addiction to work, he soon tipped the scale at 255 pounds and would ultimately become the bulwark of the Oakland offensive line.

He was a starter from the outset and after his rookie campaign earned All-AFL recognition. Now his telephone rang with offers from the NFL to join their ranks. Suddenly he had real football appeal. But he politely declined all such overtures, loyal to the AFL which had given him the chance to make good. He more than proved his worth to the Raiders, rating All-AFL selection 10 times and nine invitations to the AFL All-Star game. In 1967, his pivot play constituted an important element in Oakland's acquisition of the AFL title. He was also selected as the snapper on the AFL All-Time team in 1969.

When the Raiders joined the NFL prior to the 1970 campaign, he promptly established himself as the cream of the centers in that league too, gaining All-Pro honors three consecutive seasons and making the same number of appearances in the Pro Bowl. Besides being sure-handed in his duties and an excellent blocker in both passing and running situations, he held forth as the team leader, given his persistence in playing through pain and injury without so much as a glance toward the bench as if to say some relief would be appreciated. His attitude was I'm the center, and that's it.

His retirement following the close of the 1974 schedule left a large hole in the Raiders' offensive front. At that time he had been there for the club in no less than 308 games.

Jim Parker

6'3", 273 pounds. Tackle, Guard: Baltimore Colts (1957–1967). All-Pro: 1958–1965. Pro Bowl: Eight appearances. Inducted into the Pro Football Hall of Fame 1973.

Before food additives, weight-training programs, and chemical enhancements, there was Jim Parker, the ultimate prototype for offensive linemen of the modern era.

Jim Parker

He was 6'3" and 273 pounds au naturel. Before arriving in the National Football League, he had his football skills honed to an All-America edge at Ohio State University as an offensive and defensive tackle. In his senior year he earned the coveted Outland Award, emblematic of the finest lineman in the college game.

Woody Hayes, the brilliant but frequently choleric OSU head coach, felt the best chance for Parker to make the pros would be as a defensive tackle, despite the fact he had been an exceptional run-blocker, given the Buckeyes' traditional "five yards and a cloud of dust" offensive strategy.

But Baltimore Colts field boss Weeb Ewbank had an entirely different role in mind for his number-one draft pick of 1957. Right from the outset, Ewbank envisioned Parker as an offensive lineman, more particularly a personal pass-blocker for star quarterback Johnny Unitas. Ewbank entertained the conviction that Unitas, with his cool generalship and strong throwing arm, was the fuse to the Colts' explosive attack. Therefore, it stood to reason he had to be kept out of harm's way at all costs. And Parker became a most unwitting heir to this rather demanding assignment.

"You can be the most unpopular man on the team," Ewbank told him, "if anything should happen to John. Your job is to protect the quarterback. Nothing else matters. Should anything happen to John, I don't know if I could forget that."

The fact was, Parker hadn't done all that much pass-blocking in college. But there were two big things going for him, size and ability. In his quiet, unassuming manner, he went about mastering the mechanics and techniques of his position with an unremitting sense of purpose. And he succeeded so well as to be accorded All-Pro status on eight consecutive occasions, four times as a tackle and four as a guard, between 1958 and 1965. He also earned as many invitations to the Pro Bowl. During this period, the Colts won back-to-back NFL championships in 1958 and 1959, and three Western Conference titles, tying for another.

In 1967, Baltimore finished in a deadlock for the lead of the Western Conference Coastal Division, but Parker performed below par for the first time in his 11-year tenure due to a series of hobbling injuries. He could see that the Colts were building for another run to the top of the league and didn't feel his familiar presence in the left side of the offensive line would be up to providing the impetus needed to help sustain such a drive. So rather than hamper the efforts of his teammates to attain a Super Bowl ring, he opted to retire and let his attainments speak for themselves. He was, in the finest sense, an organization man.

When Parker entered the Pro Football Hall of Fame in 1973, he did so as the first lineman ever to play exclusively on offense. Indeed he was the ultimate prototype for those of his breed in the modern era. And it couldn't have happened to a nicer guy.

Jim Ringo

6'2", 230 pounds. Center: Green Bay Packers (1953–1963), Philadelphia Eagles (1964–1967). All-Pro: 1957–1962. Pro Bowl: 10 appearances. Inducted into the Pro Football Hall of Fame 1981.

The old axiom "It's not the size of the dog in the fight that counts but the size of the fight in the dog" most aptly applies to Jim Ringo, who was virtually in the center of conflict throughout a 15-year NFL tenure.

At 6'2" and 230 pounds, he was among the frailer snappers in the pro

Jim Ringo

game during his career. In fact, he weighed just 211 pounds when he
reported to the Green Bay Packers in 1953 as a rookie out of Syracuse
University. The first thing that caught his eye in preseason camp was the
size of the other players. Cowed by their bulk, he did an about-face and
headed back home to Easton, Pennsylvania. But his wife and father prevailed upon him to give the pro game a try. He agreed and returned to
Green Bay for an 11-year stay.

It wasn't long before he established himself as a starter. And in the process he also managed to put on 20 pounds. This added weight better enabled
him to take on the middle of the defensive line, whose members regularly
resorted to double-team tactics, their combined avoirdupois often totaling
more than half a ton. A natural consequence of his occupation was all manner of injuries, ranging from sundry lumps, bumps, and abrasions to fractures, a staph infection, and bronchial pneumonia. But no matter the extent of his affliction, he always made the lineup on game day.

He didn't miss a starting assignment for a string of 182 games, an NFL
record at the time, 126 of these being logged with the Packers. During a
bout with mononucleosis, he would lie abed in the hospital from Monday
through Friday night, then rouse himself each weekend for a trip to the
ballpark and Sunday's game. A real profile in dedication and courage? Not
necessarily, testified Ringo.

"I was more afraid of losing my job than anything," he confessed. "Back then, there were only thirty-three guys on a team, so that left a lot of good players waiting around to take your job. No way I was going to help them out."

From 1957 to 1963, he was an almost perennial All-Pro and Pro-Bowl selection. Despite his lack of size, he held forth as a standout blocker both downfield and in pass-protection situations with good speed, mastery of mechanics, and bulldog tenacity. When the offense needed short yardage for a first down or six points, more often than not the play called went through his hole. He had a way of getting in and under defending linemen and moving them away from the running lanes.

Although quiet and unassuming by nature, Ringo nevertheless proved an exceptional team leader. He could crack the verbal whip over lagging teammates when necessity demanded. So it was rather surprising when the Packers traded him to the Philadelphia Eagles in 1964. But Green Bay coach and general manager Vince Lombardi had his rules concerning loyalty, and they suffered no abridgment.

Thus, Ringo's departure from the Packers came rather abruptly when his agent visited Lombardi's office one day to negotiate a new contract, or so the story goes. Lombardi, not one to abide intermediaries intruding in intimate money matters, let the agent cool his heels while he made a telephone call. Finally, upon admitting the man to his inner sanctum, he greeted him with the news that "You've come to the wrong place. Mr. Ringo is no longer employed by the Packers. He now works for the Philadelphia Eagles." Lombardi had made a quick trade over the phone with the Philadelphia front office. In his mind, an unwritten rule of loyalty had been violated, and no compromise could be considered.

In the City of Brotherly Love, Ringo continued to perform in Pro-Bowl fashion year after year until 1967. Overall, he made 10 appearances in the postseason classic and was one of a few players to start for both the East and West teams.

Bob St. Clair

6'9", 265 pounds. Offensive Tackle: San Francisco 49ers (1953–1964). All-Pro: 1955. Pro Bowl: Five appearances. Inducted into the Pro Football Hall of Fame 1990.

Wherever Bob St. Clair went, he attracted attention. And this wasn't due solely to his 6'9", 265-pound dimensions. Off the field he proved to be a character, given to flamboyant behavior and high-profile shenanigans. Between the lime lines, his physical play and almost fanatical hustle made him a crowd favorite, qualities that ultimately earned him a niche in the Hall of Fame.

Hitting people held a special attraction for him from his youth. As a teenager he became involved with the street gangs which inhabited his neighborhood in a tough section of San Francisco. Fighting prevailed as a way of life, and he reveled in it. But he managed to escape the dire fate of imprisonment and death that befell many of his boyhood friends, thanks to the intervention of football. While a sophomore in high school he became enamored of the game, fascinated by the vigor and violence of the action, and sought to join the team. His initial attempt to do so met with disappointment. The coach turned him away because he was only 5'9" and 150 pounds. After a year devoted to rigorous bodybuilding, he reported for the squad again, this time weighing 210 pounds and standing 6'4". Needless to say, he got a uniform.

His play on the secondary level earned him a football scholarship at the University of San Francisco. While there, he played alongside such future National Football League stars as Ollie Matson and Gino Marchetti, both destined to become Hall of Fame inductees. Following the 1951 season, San Francisco dropped the gridiron sport, and St. Clair transferred to the University of Tulsa where he gained All-Missouri Valley Conference honors as a defensive end.

When he joined the San Francisco 49ers in 1953 as a third-round draft pick, it was to become an offensive tackle. He and 12 other rookies were faced with the task of trying to win a spot on a largely veteran team. Right from the outset, the coaching staff put him up against All-Pro tackle Leo "The Lion" Nomellini to see if he had "the stuff to stick." These were necessarily brutal encounters in which, overall, St. Clair gave as good as he got.

"Knocking a man down, really hitting him, is a thrill," he confessed. "It kind of gets you, gives you a jolt of the old adrenaline. That's what football is all about, and I love it."

Due to his strength and fondness for contact, St. Clair quickly impressed upon members of the opposition that he was a man to be feared and respected. He went up against all the best defenders in the league and left each of them with a very definite impression of his prowess, even old teammate Marchetti. "Gino brings out the best in me," he once said, "and I do the same for him."

To abet his reputation as being something other than human, he ingested steak, fish, chicken, and even raw liver along with such earthy supplements as wheat-germ oil and honey. Often he would sit down with a number of the team's younger players and begin feasting on an uncooked repast, rivulets of blood trickling down his chin. Before very long, he was all alone at the table, chuckling to himself. While still plying his skills for the 49ers, he served both as a councilman and then mayor of Daly City, California.

Bob St. Clair

St. Clair captained the 49ers for several years, the force of his play and personality establishing him as a natural leader. A classic example of the inspiration he generated for his teammates came in a 1959 game against San Francisco's arch rival, the Los Angeles Rams. On a 105-yard kickoff return, he ran interference all the way for ball carrier Abe Woodson, laying six blocks that ensured the effort would result in a touchdown. He provided similar protection for such Hall-of-Famers as quarterback Y.A. Tittle and running backs Joe Perry, John Henry Johnson, and Hugh "The King" McElhenny. He was accorded All-Pro status in 1955 and five invitations to the Pro Bowl.

It goes without saying that he routinely merited a lot of double- and triple-team attention from the defense. And despite his considerable bulk, he endured his share of injuries. He played with a fractured vertebra in his back for an entire season and remained in a game for several plays after incurring a painful and debilitating shoulder separation that ultimately benched him for seven weeks. Later he suffered a pair of Achilles tendon tears, the latter ending his career during the 49ers' 1964 preseason training camp.

Looking back on his tenure in the NFL, St. Clair expressed no regrets, save that his team never managed to win a league championship. But he can rest easy in the knowledge that it wasn't his fault it didn't happen.

Art Shell

6'5", 285 pounds. Offensive Tackle: Oakland Raiders (1968, 1969, AFL), Oakland Raiders (1970–1981, NFL), Los Angeles Raiders (1982). All-Pro: 1973, 1974, 1977. Pro Bowl: Eight appearances. Inducted into the Pro Football Hall of Fame 1989. Career: Coach: Los Angeles Raiders (1989–   ). Won-lost record: 20–10–0. Championships: Western Division (AFC), 1990.

Only the scale knew how much Art Shell actually weighed. But to opponents bent upon invading the Oakland–Los Angeles Raiders backfield he seemed like the Colossus of Rhodes, his sphere of influence extending far beyond the parameters of a tackle's usual purview.

According to the Raiders' press guide, his poundage varied anywhere from 265 to 285, but little did the media types know that these figures were purely guesswork on the part of the club's public relations staff.

"John Madden [then Raiders head coach] told me as long as I performed, it didn't matter how much I weighed," Shell related. "So when everybody else got on the scales, I would just walk on by."

However, even he wondered at times just how much muscle and suet adorned his 6'5" frame. Curiosity finally got the better of him the morning of Super Bowl XI only hours prior to the Raiders taking on the Minnesota Vikings for all the National Football League marbles. "I went into the locker room before the game and weighed myself," he recalled. "I weighed three hundred and ten pounds."

That afternoon, he really threw his ample adipose around, personally shutting down Minnesota's much-heralded defensive end Jim Marshall in unprecedented fashion. "When somebody told me I had a perfect game," Shell said, "I was shocked because I had no idea Marshall had not been in on even one play. I was too busy to keep track."

During the first half of the contest, the Raiders ran 27 of 33 plays through Shell's side of the line. It was simply a matter of putting strength on strength, and Oakland prevailed easily, 32–14.

Bulk notwithstanding, he was amazingly agile and possessed exceptional balance. In high school he played basketball as well as football with distinction. At Maryland State College, he also held forth as a two-sport standout, his accomplishments on the hardwood nearly rivaling those attained on the gridiron. It was this somewhat different mating of skills that caught and held the attention of the Raiders' scouts.

"The primary thing we saw in Art was his great size," Madden said. "But we were also excited about his skill as a basketball player. That ability to move so well combined with his size made us feel we had a quality prospect."

Although Shell commanded both talent and an imposing physical presence, making the transition to the NFL was still a difficult task for him.

"Coming to the pros amounted to an eye-opening experience," he said. "The toughest assignment was pass-blocking. In college, we ran more than we passed. And when we did pass-block, it was like taking the guy right there on the line in what you call a short set. In the pros you can't do that every time. Sometimes you have to change up ... deep drop, medium and short."

But he had fortified himself with good self-discipline and a deeply ingrained work ethic, attributes which served to give him the needed edge. He submitted wholly to the learning process, investing long hours in mastering all the intricacies of his trade. "I always did my best" sufficed as his creed, and his best effort proved to be more than enough.

Finally, in the 1970 preseason, he got his chance to become a regular. It was a status he wouldn't relinquish until the moment of his retirement. "Yeah, I really wanted to start," he said, contemplating that early juncture in his career. "I didn't know if I could hold the job once I had it, but I knew the best man would win it." And that he did.

He enjoyed a marked freedom from debilitating injuries, despite the rigors of his position. He played every game for 12 years before a ruptured knee ushered him to the sidelines on the eve of the 1979 campaign. It was generally conceded that he had been lost to the Raiders for the duration. Not so. He pushed himself through a most demanding regimen, sometimes working out several times a day to strengthen the weakened joint. To everyone's surprise, he was back on the field just seven weeks later, playing with his patented verve.

In all, he appeared in 156 successive games until put out of action. Then he ran another streak of 51 starts before injuries again consigned him to the bench. He played in 207 regular season contests, 24 playoff games, and 8 Pro Bowls, his tenure in the NFL touching on three decades. Though a fierce and dedicated performer, he never was one to lose his temper in the heat of battle or resort to reprehensible conduct. "My coaches always thought I would do a whole lot better if I was mean," he said. "But I'm just not a mean person. On the field before a game I would say to a guy I knew on the other team, 'Hey, how are you doing today? Let's have a good game.' That's just the way I am. I want to greet the guy and have a good, tough game. We can do that without being vicious or taking cheap shots."

Added Madden: "Art was one of the quiet leaders who commanded respect just by being a great player. He never, ever, acted like a tough guy. He was always nice and businesslike. But whether you were his teammate or an opponent, you knew this was a man who deserved your deepest respect."

Following the 1982 season, Shell retired and joined the team's coaching staff. In 1989, he became head coach of the Raiders, the first black man to be so elevated in modern times.

Joe Stydahar

6'4", 230 pounds. Tackle: Chicago Bears (1936–1942, 1945, 1946). All-Pro: 1937–1940. Inducted into the Pro Football Hall of Fame 1967. Career: Coach: Los Angeles Rams (1950–1952), Chicago Cardinals (1953, 1954). Won-lost record: Los Angeles Rams (19–9–0), Chicago Cardinals (3–20–1). Championships: National (Western) Conference, 1950, 1951; NFL, 1951.

Of the Chicago Bears' famed "Monsters of the Midway" in the early 1940s, no one better epitomized this awesome aggregation than "Jumbo Joe" Stydahar, a massive tackle who dominated his position throughout the colorful era.

Despite the fact that he spent his undergrad tenure at the University of West Virginia, then considered to be the outback of collegiate football, his considerable attainments did not completely escape public notice. In his senior year he rated All-Eastern, Little All-America, and All-America mention in various publications. But he still might have escaped discovery by the Bears had not owner-coach George Halas been tipped off to his availability.

When the first National Football League draft was conducted in the spring of 1936, the Bears took Stydahar as their first pick. Though 6'4" and 230 pounds, big for a lineman of that time, he commanded unusual quickness and agility. Upon joining the Chicago franchise, he declined to wear a helmet until the league made it a requirement. He quickly settled in at left tackle, both offensively and defensively, and became a regular 60-minute man. From 1936 to 1942, he earned All-Pro recognition four times and, not coincidentally, the Bears recorded four Western Division firsts and won two NFL titles.

In the wake of the 1942 season he entered the U.S. Navy and spent the duration of World War II in a legitimate active-duty status. Unlike many of his gridiron contemporaries, he didn't get the opportunity to play service football. He felt this fact would militate heavily against him upon his return to the pro game and openly expressed his concern about the matter to Halas upon rejoining the Bears in 1945. "I'm just about washed up as a player,"

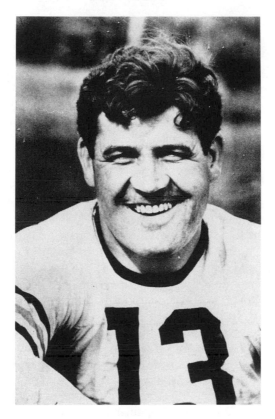

Joe Stydahar

he said. "Besides, I haven't played in three years. So put down anything on my contract you feel is fair."

Halas gave Stydahar $8,000 for the year, twice as much as he had ever made with the club. "That's the kind of guy Halas was," he observed later. "Whatever success I had, I owe it all to him."

For the next two seasons Stydahar made a supreme effort to prove himself worthy of his paycheck. It took him a while to shed the rust of inactivity during the 1945 campaign, and Chicago finished down in the standings. But he came roaring back the following year, and the Bears went all the way once more, whipping the New York Giants 24–14 for league laurels.

Following his retirement, Stydahar tried his hand at coaching. He directed the Los Angeles Rams to successive appearances in the NFL championship games of 1950 and 1951, the Rams prevailing the second time. He later served as the Chicago Cardinals field boss from 1953 through 1954. On March 23, 1977, he died at 65.

George Trafton

6'2", 235 pounds. Center: Decatur Staleys (1920, APFA), Chicago Staleys (1921, APFA), Chicago Bears (1922–1932, NFL). All-NFL: Eight times. Inducted into the Pro Football Hall of Fame 1964.

When in football togs, George Trafton adhered assiduously to his version of the Golden Rule: "Do unto others and then cut out." He held forth as the ultimate warrior, and taking prisoners definitely was not on his agenda. Just plain contentious was he? Well, not a few of his contemporaries thought so.

Perhaps the fabled Red Grange put it best when he said, "Big George was the toughest, meanest, most ornery critter alive."

Trafton held forth with the Chicago Bears (the early Decatur and Chicago Staleys) during the first 13 years of the National Football League's existence. He played center and snapped the ball unerringly with only one hand. In fact, there is no evidence that he ever made a miscue in his lengthy tenure as a pro. But there are plenty of indications he harbored a penchant for violence which freely expressed itself.

According to aged press clippings, the fans in every NFL town had a strong dislike for him, save for Green Bay and Rock Island where he was outright hated, with good reason. In the course of one afternoon, he reportedly caused four Rock Island stalwarts to be carted off the playing premises in sundry stages of disrepair. On another occasion, he broke the leg of a Rock Island running back against a fence far out of bounds in what can be euphemistically described as an outrageously late hit. At the sound of the game-ending gun, he rushed from the ballpark and hailed a cab as the stands angrily erupted behind him. Later, he thumbed his way back to Chicago.

Not to be overlooked in all this was his technical ability. He could block and tackle according to the book, and given his particular zest for these tasks, the outcome qualified as slightly spectacular. Though not exactly an innovator, he did prevail as one of the first up-front defenders to rove from his over-the-middle post. As some detractors have pointed out, this was probably more for predatory reasons than anything else. Nonetheless, his defensive abilities were exceptional, and although no official All-Pro ratings existed prior to 1931, Bears archives indicate that sportswriters of that era considered him the best center in the NFL for 8 of his 13 seasons.

Despite his indulgence in mayhem, he clearly distinguished himself as a 60-minutes player whose credentials compare favorably with any of the more lionized linemen of his day. Trafton died on September 5, 1971, at 74.

Clyde "Bulldog" Turner

6'2", 235 pounds. Center, Linebacker: Chicago Bears (1940–1952). All-Pro: 1941–1943, 1946–1948. Pro Bowl: Two appearances. Inducted into the Pro Football Hall of Fame 1966. Career: Interceptions, 16; return yardage, 289; yards per return, 18.1; touchdowns, 2.

If anyone ever belonged in the National Football League, it was Clyde "Bulldog" Turner. From day one of his professional experience, he held forth at center in the offensive line of the Chicago Bears when they were the "Monsters of the Midway," one of the most dominant teams in the history of the play-for-pay game.

During the pre–1940s, scouting in the NFL prevailed as something of a hit-or-miss proposition at best. Back then, league clubs didn't resort to scouting combines composed of talent hunters equipped with computer stat sheets on practically every college player in the United States. Far from it.

About all the teams subscribed to in the good old days were various sporting publications which primarily previewed the programs of the major football schools and their name players. Very infrequently did these magazines and tout sheets dip into the ranks of the smaller colleges to offer any kind of assay of the gridiron activities conducted there. Even so, Turner still couldn't escape notice in the big time.

He labored Saturday afternoons for little Hardin-Simmons University, hardly a stop on the main line for sportswriters who covered the many headline-making institutions of higher football learning in the great state of Texas. Still, as a junior, he came to the attention of both the Bears and the Detroit Lions via word of mouth. Telephoned tips and the mails brought word of a big hard-nosed kid with halfback speed who could play with anybody, bar none.

As a senior, Turner earned All-America recognition and received an invitation to display his wares in the East-West Shrine Game. Bears scout Frank Korch attended the postseason classic in San Francisco just to file a firsthand report on the young man. What he saw deeply impressed him. Upon his return to Chicago, he told Bears owner and head coach George Halas that the Hardin-Simmons product was for real. Halas listened and then put the burly Texan at the top of his draft list.

Unknown to Halas et al. was the fact that Detroit Lions owner Dick Richards already had made contact with Turner and felt quite confident he had done such a super sales job that the gifted center-linebacker wouldn't think of signing with any club but his. So convinced was Richards that the Lions didn't even bother to draft Turner. But when Chicago made Turner its first pick, the distraught Richards tried desperately to recoup his loss, only to merit a $5,000 fine for his trouble, the standard NFL penalty imposed when one team is caught tampering with a player previously committed to a rival's draft list.

In 1940, the Bears won the NFL championship, and Turner, though only a 20-year-old rookie, was a strong contributing factor to the success of his team offensively and defensively. The following season he rated All-Pro honors, the first of six times this distinction would be accorded him. For 13 seasons he proved to be an unerring snapper and a superior blocker, excelling both at pass protection and providing interference. When the opposition had the ball, his performance as a linebacker was no less impressive. He could maneuver his 6'2", 235-pound frame with the quickness and agility of a man half his size. And he was particularly astute at diagnosing plays even as they were forming, an ability which enabled him to blunt offensive ploys effectively with a monotony that had a thoroughly disheartening effect on Bears opponents.

Given his surprising lightness afoot, he regularly fooled quarterbacks and receivers into thinking passes could be completed over his head in the short drop zone. When this stratagem was tried, he would backpedal with the ease of a defensive back and more often than not deflect the ball away or pick it off. In 1942, he led the NFL with 8 interceptions and had 16 thefts overall during his career.

Unusual versatility also placed him a notch above his contemporaries. Besides playing center and linebacker, he could fill in at guard or tackle with equal facility. And he even served as a ball carrier on occasion. Once, in 1944, he romped 48 yards for a touchdown, outrunning some of the enemy's fastest defenders en route. In 1947, he wove his way through the entire Washington Redskins team to score on a 96-yard interception return. This bit of heroics sufficed as the biggest thrill of his NFL tenure.

Turner could do it all and did, longer and better than all but a very few of his breed.

Gene Upshaw

6'5", 260 pounds. Guard: Oakland Raiders (1967–1969, AFL), Oakland Raiders (1970–1981, NFL). All-AFL: 1967–1969; All-Pro: 1970, 1972, 1974. AFL All-Star Game: 1968. Pro Bowl: Six appearances. Inducted into the Pro Football Hall of Fame 1987.

The advent of the big guard as a singular offensive weapon which ultimately would presage a new philosophy of attack commenced not incoincidentally with the arrival of Gene Upshaw into the National Football League. When he joined the Oakland (later Los Angeles) Raiders in 1967,

Gene Upshaw

his massive presence lent considerable credence to a long-standing team credo: "We don't take what they give us. We take what we want."

As was the wont of Raiders managing general partner Al Davis, he went looking for a big interior lineman who could wipe out ponderous defensive tackles on a one-to-one basis while leading a sweep, spearheading a short-yardage thrust, or protecting a passer. He wanted a man up front next to the snapper who embodied the physical ability and mentality to do a number on the folks in wrong-color jerseys from the first whistle to the final gun. And he found him in Upshaw.

A 6'5", 260-pound guard, Upshaw gave nothing away to enemy tackles in size or mobility. He could contend with them favorably not only on a brawn basis but in foot and hand speed as well. Equally important, he enjoyed hitting and quickly adapted to the Radiers' confrontational style of play.

"When a defensive lineman gets ready to play us, he doesn't have to wonder what we're going to do," Upshaw once said. "He knows we're coming after him. We just pound it to him play after play—power stuff in the first quarter and power stuff in the fourth quarter. We just figure if we keep coming after him, by that last quarter he's gonna be ours."

Though skilled at both head-up and pass-blocking, he really excelled when leading the interference on wide plays that required him to turn the corner ahead of the ball carrier and clear out the secondary defenders. And as the sweep was a staple of the Raiders' power-oriented ground game, he had any number of opportunities to display his wares in this respect. "My play is the sweep," he said. "I get my kicks pulling in front of the back and cleaning house. Hey, if it was up to me, we'd call the sweep every down. The thing I concentrate on most is getting out of my stance right at the snap and going top speed. I run a four six or four seven in the forty-yard dash, but most backs do better than that, so I have to get the jump on them. You don't want to be holding up the ball carrier getting to the corner. When I turn upfield, I'm already drawing a bead on the defensive back working that side. He's two ten at most and one eighty-five some of the time. To my way of thinking, he hasn't got a chance. If he goes to the outside, I'm going to put him out of bounds. If he goes inside, I'll knock him in. And if he stays there, comes at me—man, I'm going right over the top of him."

Even when the play didn't result in six points or a long gainer, Upshaw knew his effort hadn't been wasted, that such tactics would ultimately produce a desirable accumulative effect as the game wore on. "I wind up on those dudes (defensive backs) every trip," he said. "That's because I'm thinking beyond the sweep we're running at the time. I'm also thinking about the whole game. If I get out there and put it to that guy a few times, I'm going to wear him down. Because most of those guys aren't built to absorb a lot of punishment, I know I can take something out of him. So when it comes time for him to cover our wide receiver, he's going to miss a step. And that may be just the edge we need to score. Running over those defensive backs is my biggest thrill in football, and that's why I just love the sweep."

Unlike most of his contemporaries, Upshaw didn't play organized football until his senior year in high school. After graduating, he enrolled at Texas A & I College, but without benefit of a scholarship. That didn't come until he had proven himself as a walk-on. When the Raiders made him their number-one draft choice, it was like starting over again. "I was all right as far as physical technique was concerned," he recalled, "but when I look back, I still don't know how I got by in my rookie year. I didn't have any idea what was going on. I was just reacting as fast as I could. Everything seemed like a totally new experience."

No matter what the task, he always has been a quick learner, and catching on in the NFL was no different. By career's end, he had earned All-Pro status six times in two leagues and as many Pro-Bowl invitations. Then came the ultimate recognition for a job well done, induction into the Pro Football Hall of Fame.

Currently, Upshaw serves as the executive director of the NFL Players Association.

Bill Willis

6'2", 215 pounds. Guard: Cleveland Browns (1946–1949, AAFC), Cleveland Browns (1950–1953, NFL). All-AAFC: 1946–1949. All-Pro: 1950, 1952, 1953. Pro Bowl: Three appearances. Inducted into the Pro Football Hall of Fame 1977.

Being the first black man in a new league promised to be something of a precarious situation, but Bill Willis didn't mind the pressure or the portent. He knew his abilities, and they were considerable. The idea was to make sure the other people involved understood that you belonged. And this he did admirably.

When the Cleveland Browns were forming up during the summer of 1946 to begin play in the inaugural season of the All-America Football Conference (AAFC) head coach Paul Brown received a letter of inquiry from Willis. He had been a member of Brown's national championship team at Ohio State University in 1942. He wanted to know if there was any prohibition against a black man playing in the AAFC. Brown replied that he knew of none but suggested that the young man report a few weeks late for the preseason camp, just to make sure there wouldn't be any problem.

Once assured of his squad's composition, Brown told Willis to report, and he did, causing no little stir among his teammates-to-be as well as the media types. At 6'2" and 215 pounds, he held forth as the smallest lineman in the Cleveland fold but also the quickest. In his first full-dress scrimmage, he lined up at middle guard and repeatedly beat veteran center Moe Scarry with his sprinterlike start. After that workout, Brown signed him to a contract. Thus began a precedent-shattering career that would culminate in the Hall of Fame.

Initially, Willis played on both offense and defense with distinction. But his reputation really began to grow when he concentrated solely on bulwacking the middle of the Browns' five-man prevent front. In this role he terrorized opposing quarterbacks, blowing past their interior blockers to make one sack after another. But fleetness afoot wasn't his lone glowing attribute. He proved to be an intimidating tackler and could fend with shoulder and forearm as well as men inches taller and many pounds heavier.

Still, his speed is what made such a difference to the Browns defensively. He could move off the line and chase down backs, turning either end, or even catch a runaway ball carrier. This is just what he managed to do when Cleveland and the New York Giants were involved in a 1950 playoff contest for the American (Eastern) Conference title. With the outcome of the game in the balance, he took off after Giants running back Gene "Choo-Choo" Roberts, who had broken through the secondary and seemed headed for a certain touchdown. It took Willis 44 yards, but he got his man just shy of the goal line, and Cleveland hung on to win 8–3.

He earned all-league honors seven of his eight seasons in the pro game and received an invitation to three Pro Bowls. Following the 1953 campaign, he retired.

Alex Wojciechowicz

6'0", 235 pounds. Center, Linebacker: Detroit Lions (1938–1946), Philadelphia Eagles (1946–1950). Inducted into the Pro Football Hall of Fame 1968. Career: Interceptions, 16; return yardage, 142; yards per return, 8.9; touchdowns, 0 (no statistics were kept 1938–1940).

Although something of a self-appointed comedian, Alex Wojciechowicz ("Wodgihoewutz") was definitely no joke on the field. He was a legitimate ironman, playing both center and linebacker, and held forth as a superb pass defender throughout his lengthy career.

Ruggedly handsome with the physique of a bodybuilder, he excelled at three sports in high school and went on to star for Fordham University as a two-time All-America selection. He was the pivot man in the Rams' famed "Seven Blocks of Granite" line, playing alongside another young man who would distinguish himself in the National Football League—Vince Lombardi.

In 1938, Wojciechowicz joined the Detroit Lions as their first pick that year. He played both ways in the Motor City, snapping on offense and backing the line defensively. At 6'0" and 235 pounds, he proved to be a solid, sure tackler capable of handling big offensive linemen on rushing downs. But he also possessed the speed and range to cover well in the shallow secondary, picking off seven passes during the 1944 campaign to set a team record that stood for several years.

Midway through the 1946 schedule, the Lions unexpectedly waived him, but he was quickly claimed by the Philadelphia Eagles. Head coach Earl "Greasy" Neale had a definite role in mind for his windfall acquisition. The Eagles' field boss had developed a defensive ploy he called the "chug" (now referred to as chucking) which involved the use of the hands and forearms as well as good footwork to prevent potential pass receivers from getting downfield under a full head of steam. Right at the outset, Wojciechowicz demonstrated a special aptitude for chugging. As a result, he always drew the opposition's best pass catcher with orders to shut him down.

He did an especially impressive job on Washington Redskins end

Bill Willis

Hugh "Bones" Taylor, who uniformly performed well at the expense of the Eagles. "In our 1948 opening game, Taylor caught five touchdown passes against us," Neale recounted. "So the next time we played Washington, I put Wojie on Bones. The guy never caught a pass all afternoon. And he didn't catch one against us the next three years either. Wojie made sure of that."

As a center, Wojciechowicz had few peers. He lined up with his feet spread to a width of five feet and four inches, but this extra broad base in no way impaired his blocking ability. Strong and durable, he bulwarked the offensive line of Eagles teams that won three division crowns and two NFL championships from 1947 to 1949. Curiously enough, he was never an All-Pro selection, this honor repeatedly eluding him for Hall of Fame contemporaries Mel Hein (New York Giants) and Clyde "Bulldog" Turner (Chicago Bears).

When Wojciechowicz retired after the 1950 season, his 13 years of service to pro football represented the second-longest tenure in NFL annals.

PONY SOLDIERS

Ends, Wide Receivers

Lance Alworth

6'0", 184 pounds. Wide Receiver: San Diego Chargers (1962–1969, AFL), San Diego Chargers (1970, NFL), Dallas Cowboys (1971, 1972). All-AFL: 1963–1969. AFL All-Star Game: Seven appearances. AFL Leading Receiver: 1964–1966. Wide Receiver: All-Time, All-AFL team (1960–1969). Inducted into the Pro Football Hall of Fame 1978. Career: Receptions, 542. Receiving yardage, 10,266. Yards per reception, 18.9. Touchdowns, 85. Rushing attempts, 24. Rushing yardage, 129. Yards per carry, 5.4. Touchdowns (rushing), 2. Punt returns, 29. Return yardage, 309. Yards per return, 10.7. Touchdowns, 0. Kickoff returns, 10. Return yardage, 216. Yards per return, 21.6. Touchdowns, 0.

When they made all those football epics in the late 1950s and the 1960s, the producers missed out big by not casting Lance Alworth in the lead role, for a couple of very cogent reasons. One, he had a matinee idol's good looks. Two, he wouldn't have needed a stuntman or any special effects. He could have performed the on-field derring-do required of the hero without a hassle. And that's because he did it every Sunday afternoon in-season for 11 years.

In his era he prevailed as the pro game's premier pass receiver. He combined 9.6 speed with a pair of seeing-eye hands and the ability to levitate far above and beyond the rest of his breed. Although an All-America halfback at the University of Arkansas, he didn't physically fit the mold of a pro-type ball carrier at 6'0" and 184 pounds. But given his fleetness afoot and aerialist attributes, he more than qualified for the flanker (wide receiver) spot. Scouts from both the National Football League and the rival American Football League (AFL) fully appreciated his kind of talent.

73

Lance Alworth

But the AFL got there first, in the person of Al Davis, then an assistant coach with the San Diego Chargers. He obtained Alworth's signature on a contract just before the start of the 1962 Sugar Bowl game in New Orleans. Looking back, it can be said this was probably the best possible move for the young Razorback product. At that time, the Chargers, under head coach Sid Gillman, boasted the most innovative passing attack of any team in either league. It was the system which could make optimal use of the things Alworth did best.

Despite all these pluses, he didn't enjoy a very rewarding rookie campaign. An injury kept him out of 10 games, but he still managed to catch 10 balls for 226 yards, an average of 22.6 yards per reception, and three touchdowns. But his sophomore season was a complete turnaround. He was on the receiving end of 61 aerials, 9 of them coming in a single outing, which netted 1,205 yards and 11 TDs as well as a league-high average of 19.8 yards. The next three years—1964, 1965, and 1966—he held forth as the top catcher in the AFL. In 1965, he picked up 1,602 yards, an average of 23.2 yards every time his fingers closed around the ball, and the following year he logged 73 receptions, all career highs.

From 1962 through 1969, he was voted all-league status seven times and played in as many All-Star games. He caught at least one pass in each of 96 successive starts and thus earned a spot on the All-Time, All-AFL team. By the time the Chargers joined the NFL in 1970, he had peaked and at the close of that schedule went to Dallas in a trade. With the Cowboys he was relegated to largely spot duty but did have one last hurrah. That came in Super Bowl VI against the Miami Dolphins. His seven-yard catch in the second quarter gave the Cowboys a 10–3 lead, and they went on to win handily, 24–3. After the 1972 slate, he retired and gained admission to the Hall of Fame in 1978, the first AFL player to be so honored.

Raymond Berry

6'2", 187 pounds. End: Baltimore Colts (1955–1967). All-Pro: 1958–1960. Pro Bowl: Five appearances. Inducted into the Pro Football Hall of Fame 1973. Career: Receptions, 631. Receiving yardage, 9,275. Yards per reception, 14.7. Touchdowns, 68. Coach: New England Patriots (1984–1989). Won-lost record: New England Patriots (50–42–0). Championships: AFC, 1985; Eastern Division, AFC, 1986.

The trademark on Ray Berry's football career could well read Self-Help Industry. If ever there was a do-it-yourself success story, it has to be the chronicle of his life and times in the National Football League.

Physically, by any measure of an NFL scout's appraisal, he simply didn't command the tools to be a potential Hall of Fame candidate. He was lean of build, so nearsighted that contact lenses were required for him to play, and had a lower-back condition that frequently left him with one leg shorter than the other. What's more, he couldn't qualify as either fleet of foot or a power runner.

On the plus side, he possessed good hands and a prodigious capacity for work. And intellectually he graded out perceptive, inventive, and highly motivated. In the final analysis, these qualities outweighed his deficiencies to the extent that he became one of the finest pass receivers ever to play in the pro game.

He didn't play regularly in high school until his senior season, despite the fact his father coached the team. Unable to attract an offer from a college with a major football program, he opted to attend a two-year school in the hope of enhancing his gridiron credentials. During his only campaign at Schreiner Institute in Kerrville, Texas, he caught 32 passes and tallied eight touchdowns. As a result, he was granted an athletic scholarship to attend Southern Methodist University.

As a sophomore at SMU, he saw only spot duty on offense, handling just five passes. The following year he played more frequently and logged 16 receptions. His productivity slipped to 12 catches as a senior. In all, he pulled down just 33 aerials in his three-season college stint and scored only one TD. Not impressive numbers by NFL expectations, but he still managed to get drafted, the Baltimore Colts taking him in the 20th round.

In the summer of 1955, he reported to the Colts' preseason camp as a borderline prospect to make the team but somehow managed to win a spot on the depth chart and lasted out the schedule. The next year he paired up with a hard-faced young quarterback from Pittsburgh named John Unitas and started to attract the attention of the coaching staff. And his work habits didn't escape notice either.

When practice sessions were finished and the last player had trekked wearily off to the showers, Berry remained behind to complete his personal regimen. He would run patterns and practice moves (there were 88 of them in his repertoire) aimed at eluding secondary defenders. Then he caught passes from anybody available to throw them. His partners in this regard ranged from groundskeepers and equipment managers all the way to his wife. Time after time, he had the ball thrown at his feet, behind him, overhead, at any number of difficult angles, and then tried to make the catch. All the while he imagined himself in a game situation, ever anticipating the hit that often followed close after hand and hide had made contact. Still another drill was devoted to safely securing the ball, putting it away, once caught. Finally, he worked on recovering fumbles. Interestingly enough, he was charged with only one turnover in his 13-year NFL tenure.

Such hard work and attention to detail paid big dividends. From

Ray Berry

1958 to 1960, he led the league in receptions. In 1959 and 1960, he was the best of his breed in the total-yardage and touchdown categories as well. He earned All-Pro recognition three times and participated in five Pro Bowls.

Perhaps his finest hour came in the famous 1958 NFL championship game between Baltimore and the New York Giants at Yankee Stadium. It was the first title contest to be nationally televised and the first such encounter requiring a sudden-death overtime period to determine the winner. Given these historic conditions, he caught 12 passes for 178 yards, both records, and scored a touchdown. His sure-handed receptions enabled the Colts to get the position necessary for a last-minute field goal that forged a tie at the end of regulation play. Then, in the extra period, he performed similar heroics to ensure the winning touchdown.

He retired at age 34 with a then all-time NFL-high 631 receptions, which resulted in 9,275 yards gained and 68 TDs. Thereafter, he served as an assistant with the Dallas Cowboys, Detroit Lions, Cleveland Browns, New England Patriots, and the University of Arkansas before taking over as head coach of the Patriots in 1984. Under his tutelage they made it to Super Bowl XX and won the 1985 AFC crown en route.

In all, Berry's attainments are a monument to the virtues of hard work and dedication.

Fred Biletnikoff

6'1", 190 pounds. Wide Receiver: Oakland Raiders (1965–1969, AFL), Oakland Raiders (1970–1978, NFL). All-AFL: 1969. All-Pro: 1970, 1972. Pro Bowl: Four appearances. NFL Reception Leader: 1971. Most Valuable Player: Super Bowl XI. Inducted into the Pro Football Hall of Fame 1988. Career: Receptions, 589. Receiving yardage, 8,974. Yards per reception, 15.2. Touchdowns, 76.

Attention to detail, mastery of fundamentals, determination, and perseverance equals success, a formula which can produce results that often exceed those derived solely from native talent and ability. It's the formula that Fred Biletnikoff utilized to gain admission to the Hall of Fame.

Even while he was enjoying no small distinction at Florida State University as a premier collegiate receiver, pro scouts were compiling a profile on him. Oh yes, they took note of the fact he was the object of four touchdown passes in the 1964 Gator Bowl. These heroics were duly recorded along with his other accomplishments and synthesized into final report form. And the bottom line read like this: "Great hands, hard worker but does not possess breakaway speed." For a 6'1", 190-pound wide receiver, one such negative reference can have an adverse affect on his ultimate standing in the drafting process.

So when Biletnikoff learned that the Oakland Raiders of the upstart American Football League were willing to make him their second-round pick, he went for it. Right from the outset he experienced difficulty adjusting to the way the pros did things. He sat on the bench until the seventh game of his rookie season before finally getting the coach's nod. That afternoon he made an auspicious debut, logging seven catches for 118 yards. But even then, inconsistency continued to plague him. On occasion he had difficulty even handling the ball, and this was due largely to a lack of sync in timing his moves to those of the quarterback.

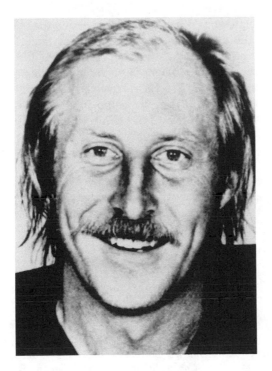

Fred Biletnikoff

Not until 1967, his third year in the AFL, did he finally hit his stride, posting 40 receptions for 876 yards and five TDs. From that juncture on, he improved dramatically, becoming the receiver the Raiders routinely went to in clutch situations. Still, he drove himself in the quest for perfection, staying after practice to run his patterns over and over again. He also spent much extra time in the film room studying himself and opposition defensive backs, ever in search of ways to match his strengths against their weaknesses. Little things that would give him an edge, enable him to come up with the ball in must-yardage situations, were what he strove to find and exploit. Through it all, he constantly berated himself for even the slightest error. And always he worried, worried, until beset by a stomach ulcer. Before a game he alternately ingested ample doses of antacid and chewed his finger nails. Once on the field, however, he became a nerveless scoring machine.

Perhaps Oakland head coach John Madden put it best when he said, "Fred is not a gifted receiver. Not one of those guys who just goes out and does it on ability alone. He's had to work very hard for everything he has achieved. He is one of the most dedicated athletes I have ever known."

Biletnikoff earned All-AFL honors in 1969 with 54 catches for 837 yards and 12 touchdowns. When the Raiders joined the National Football League in 1970, he continued to be a dominant factor, rating All-Pro recognition that season and again in 1972. He led the NFL in receptions with 61 during the 1971 campaign, 9 of them resulting in touchdowns. He also participated in four Pro Bowls from 1970 through 1974. But the high point of his 14-year pro tenure came in Super Bowl XI when he snagged 4 aerials worth 79 yards, 3 of them leading directly to TDs which contributed substantially to the Raiders' 32–14 margin of victory. Given his part in this winning scheme, he was voted the game's Most Valuable Player.

At the close of the 1978 schedule, he retired, having compiled a record of 589 catches for 8,974 yards and 76 touchdowns.

Guy Chamberlin

6'2", 210 pounds. End: Canton Bulldogs (1919, pre-NFL), Decatur Staleys (1920, APFA), Chicago Staleys (1921, APFA), Canton Bulldogs (1922, 1923, NFL), Cleveland Bulldogs (1924), Frankford Yellowjackets (1925, 1926), Chicago Cardinals (1927). Coach: Canton Bulldogs (1922, 1923), Cleveland Bulldogs (1924), Frankford Yellowjackets (1925, 1926), Chicago Cardinals (1927, 1928). Inducted into the Pro Football Hall of Fame 1965. Coach: Won-lost record: Canton Bulldogs (21–0–3), Cleveland Bulldogs (7–1–1), Frankford Yellowjackets (27–8–1), Chicago Cardinals (1–5–0). Championships: NFL, 1922, 1923, 1924, 1926.

Some people have a way with winning, and Guy Chamberlin was of this breed. In the very early days of the National Football League he excelled in the dual role of player and coach, a feat all the more remarkable given the vagaries of the pro game at that time.

He came to the play-for-pay version of the gridiron sport from the University of Nebraska where his credentials as a 60-minute end included recognition as a two-time All-America selection. Initially, he signed on with the pre-NFL Canton Bulldogs in 1919, given his admiration for the legendary Jim Thorpe, who represented the team off the field as well as on it.

The following season, George Halas recruited him for the Decatur-Chicago Staleys franchise. He proved to be a big-play maker on offense with surprising speed to abet his 6'2", 210-pound dimensions. In a must-win game for the Staleys in 1920, he participated in a 70-yard bit of pitch-and-catch that provided the needed margin of victory.

Defensively, he demonstrated the same capacity for breaking open a game with a single sterling effort. In 1921, the Staleys outlasted the Buffalo All-Americans 10–7 when he picked off an errant enemy pass and returned it 75 yards for the lone TD of the afternoon. Overall, he was in on every down of every game and a prime reason why the Staleys finished second in the league standings in 1920 and topped them the ensuing season.

Next, Chamberlin returned to Canton as player-coach of the Bulldogs. Despite the loss of Thorpe, he assembled a powerhouse squad that annexed the NFL championship in 1922 and 1923, the first such double to be accomplished in the league's young history. When the team moved to Cleveland in 1924 under new ownership, he went about the rebuilding process once more and produced the same result, another NFL crown.

With the advent of the 1925 campaign, he became player-coach of the Frankford Yellowjackets and promptly guided them to a 13–7–0 mark. The next year, he took them to the forefront of the league, winning his fourth NFL title in five attempts. In 1927, he hired out to the Chicago Cardinals as just a player and thereafter hung up his cleats for the last time. He agreed to coach the team during the 1928 campaign and suffered his only losing season.

Upon his retirement from the game, he could boast a 56–14–5 coaching record and a .780 winning percentage. He was, in the words of New York Giants field boss Steve Owen, "the Winningest."

Chamberlin died on April 4, 1967, at 73.

Mike Ditka

6'3", 225 pounds. Tight End: Chicago Bears (1961–1966), Philadelphia Eagles (1967, 1968), Dallas Cowboys (1969–1972). All-Pro: 1961–1964. Pro Bowl: Five appearances. NFL Rookie of the Year: 1961. Inducted into the Pro Football Hall of Fame 1988. Career: Receptions, 427. Receiving yardage, 5,812. Yards per reception, 13.6. Touchdowns (receiving), 43. Fumble return, 2. Rushing attempts, 2. Rushing yardage, 2. Yards per carry, 1. Touchdowns, 0. Kickoff returns, 3. Return yardage, 30. Yards per return, 10. Touchdowns, 0. Coach: Chicago Bears (1982–). Won-lost record: Chicago Bears (96–51–0). Championships: Central Division, NFC; 1984, 1985, 1986, 1987, 1988, 1990; NFC, 1985; Super Bowl XX.

The light that possesses the eyes of Mike Ditka is reflective of an inner forge, capable of volcanic heat on occasion, in which his emotions have been plunged and seared to such a temper that even life's passing years are not likely to dull their fervent incandescence. Then, as now, he prevailed as a man of smoke and fire.

He came well recommended to the Chicago Bears in 1961 following an All-America collegiate tenure at the University of Pittsburgh. For the Panthers he labored offensively as an end and defensively as a linebacker. And when not so occupied, he punted with distinction. But the Bears liked even more his attitude on the field, that of a mugger in cleats. He fit their style of play as though tailored to it.

In his freshman season he won NFL Rookie-of-the-Year honors, given 56 catches for 1,076 yards, a per-reception average of 19.2 yards, and 12 touchdowns. He imparted new meaning to the term *tight end*, playing the position with a physical presence that could best be described as awesome. His 6'3", 225-pound dimensions seemed more the measure of concrete than human flesh. The harder hit, the harder he retaliated.

"Naw, I don't mind getting hit," he once said. "And I like hitting other people too."

He rated All-Pro recognition from 1961 through 1964 and was a Pro Bowl invitee five successive years, 1962 to 1966. In 1964, he set an NFL high-water mark for tight ends with 75 receptions. But it was his intensity that often had a more galvanizing effect on his teammates than what he accomplished during a game.

Recalling his first exposure to Ditka always elicits a disbelieving shake of the head by Dick Butkus, the Bears' All-Time Hall of Fame linebacker. "When I was a rookie," Butkus said, "Mike had been with the Bears for a few years. I recall on this particular occasion we were in the locker room, and the coaches had just finished talking to us. When we filed out to the field, Ditka was standing by the door yelling at everybody, screaming at everybody, exhorting them to play their best. And it was just an exhibition game. That incident will always stand out in my mind. It best exemplifies how Mike approached the game of football."

The Bears returned to glory in 1963 after a 17-year hiatus by edging the Lombardi-coached Green Bay Packers in the Western Conference standings. And they owed much of their rejuvenation to the inspired play of Ditka, who repeatedly made clutch catches, key blocks, and not-to-be-denied runs that enabled them to record victories where defeats might otherwise have been warranted. In the NFL title game, he continued to give Chicago an advantage, finally sealing the 14–10 win for the Bears over the New York Giants with a 12-yard reception that set up the deciding TD.

While with the Bears, he overcame all manner of injuries to start 84 games in succession during a six-season period. Finally, in 1967, he went to the Philadelphia Eagles, generally feeling unappreciated by his former employers. He played intermittently in the City of Brotherly Love until 1969 when the Dallas Cowboys acquired his services via a trade. Down in Texas he seemed to find himself, and the competitive juices began to flow once more.

Dan Reeves, then a running back with Dallas, didn't know quite what to make of Ditka. "I remember once when we were playing cards," Reeves said, "Mike got real upset because he was losing. He picked up his chair and smashed it against a wall. The legs of the chair stuck in the wall. And then he grabbed the deck of cards and tore them all up. I'm sitting there saying to myself, 'What kind of a guy is this?' Mike was pretty emotional in those days."

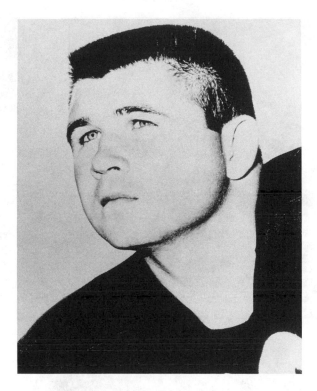

Mike Ditka

The Cowboys' championship season of 1971 was an equally important one for Ditka. He handled 30 balls during the regular campaign, and in Super Bowl VI his seven-yard catch for a touchdown helped give Dallas a 24–3 victory over the Miami Dolphins. After the completion of the 1972 schedule, he hung up his uniform for the last time.

He then served as an assistant coach with the Cowboys from 1973 to 1981, tutoring receivers and special teams. In 1982, he became head coach of the Bears, and his team won Super Bowl XX by mauling the New England Patriots 46–10.

In 1988, he was inducted into the Pro Football Hall of Fame as the first tight end to be so recognized. When advised of his acceptance, he said, "It's not an individual honor. I had coaches, teammates, and a quarterback who threw me the ball. I had a coach who designed an offense that threw the ball to a tight end and changed the look of pro football in the early nineteen sixties. I just played the position as good as I could the way Mr. [George] Halas designed it."

The Hall of Fame without a niche for "Iron Mike" would be unconscionable.

Tom Fears

Tom Fears

6'2", 215 pounds. End: Los Angeles Rams (1948–1956). All-Pro: 1949, 1950. Pro Bowl: One appearance. NFL Leading Pass Receiver: 1948–1950. Inducted into the Pro Football Hall of Fame 1970. Career: Receptions, 400. Receiving yardage, 5,397. Yards per reception, 13.5. Touchdowns, 38. Interceptions, 2. Return yardage, 37. Yards per return, 18.5. Touchdowns (interception returns), 1. Coach: New Orleans Saints (1967–1970). Won-lost record: New Orleans Saints (13–34–2).

If anyone can be said to have been on the cutting edge of the modern era in the National Football League, it was Tom Fears. He played a prominent role in implementing the high-scoring, multiple-receiver offense of today, his every attainment lending further credence to its validity as the new aerial age.

His first three campaigns in the pro game, he logged an NFL-record 212 receptions, more passes than many of his fellow Hall of Fame inductees had handled in their careers. In 1948, he caught 51 balls, 77 in 1949, and 84 in 1950, each a league-leading total for the season. With him as the prime target, the Los Angeles Rams introduced a throw-oriented attack that crisscrossed the opposition defense with more flight patterns than an air traffic controller saw in a week.

Despite his startling stats, Fears didn't measure up as the ultimate receiver when his qualifications were matched against the textbook checklist. He had acceptable size (6'2", 215 pounds), yet he failed to satisfy the requirements for speed and elusiveness. But he more than compensated for these shortcomings with a highly developed sense of perception, the intuitive ability to exploit defenses at their weakest point, just plain native intelligence, and a fierce desire to excel. What's more, he executed his routes with the precision of a diamond cutter.

Curiously enough, the Rams had him pegged as a defensive specialist when he signed on as a rookie. In his first game for the club, he had two interceptions and returned one for a touchdown. However, Los Angeles head coach Clark Shaughnessy wisely opted to make use of his sure hands and orientation for the end zone as integral elements in a wide-open, pass-dominated scoring scheme.

Although designated on the roster as an end, Fears actually functioned much like the wide receivers of today. He usually lined up 10 yards outside the right tackle while a tight end and a flanker assumed the same position on the opposite side of the field. With the snap of the ball, he often ran underneath the defensive secondary to make a clutch catch in heavy traffic. Other times he hooked out toward the sidelines for the percentage reception so frequently utilized when first-down yardage was needed. Then, just as the enemy coverage came in to play him tight, he would slip deep over the middle for a touchdown. In essence, he could do it all.

He had any number of big games. But among his more memorable outings was an 18-catch performance against the Green Bay Packers in 1950. That afternoon's accomplishment constituted a league record that still stands. Later that year, he gathered in three TD pitches to enable the Rams to overcome the Chicago Bears 24–14 for the Western Division title. In the 1951 NFL championship game against the Cleveland Browns, he worked himself clear for a 74-yard scoring reception that gave Los Angeles the decision by a 24–17 margin. Overall, he caught 400 passes for 5,397 yards and 38 touchdowns.

Prior to turning pro, Fears was a two-time All-America end at UCLA. In 1949 and 1950, he earned All-Pro honors and played in one Pro Bowl.

Bill Hewitt

5'11", 191 pounds. End: Chicago Bears (1932–1936), Philadelphia Eagles (1937–1939), Phil-Pitt (1943). All-Pro: 1933, 1934, 1936, 1937. Inducted into the Pro Football Hall of Fame 1971. Career: Receptions, 101. Receiving yardage, 1,606. Yards per reception, 15.9. Touchdowns (receiving), 24; (defensive), 1.

If Bill Hewitt could play today, he might not choose to do so. He might just turn up his nose and walk away after considering all the equipment the modern performers wear and the rules designed to protect certain skill players. Perhaps it just wouldn't seem like the game of pro football he had known.

Back in the 1930s, his heyday with the Chicago Bears and Philadelphia Eagles, he stood just a shade under six feet and tipped the beam at 191 pounds. Not imposing proportions for an end by modern standards, but the position he played with distinction both offensively and defensively.

Hewitt put in better than 50 minutes a game during a National Football League career that spanned nearly a decade. What's more, he didn't care to have a lot of equipment hindering his movements. Just the patented moleskins and a minimum of padding composed his game-day uniform. And as an indication of how little the specter of injury haunted him, he didn't even bother to wear a helmet his first eight seasons in the league. He donned headgear in 1939 only because that year it became mandatory. If not for this legislation, he very likely would have remained bareheaded throughout his playing tenure.

Despite his lack of intimidating size, he prevailed as a force to be reckoned with down after down. He had a pug's profile, arms that would have done a smithy proud, a barrel chest, and powerful underpinnings. On defense, he fairly rocketed from his stance and all but beat the snap into the opposition backfield. Because of his quick start, he frequently was whistled for being offside while not actually having committed an infraction. He enjoyed contact and had a well-deserved reputation for being a fearsome tackler. And when his combative nature was abetted by an uncanny ability to discern the opponent's offensive intent, he held forth as an awe-inspiring defender indeed.

Offensively, he was no less effective. His forte consisted of making the big play just when circumstances demanded. Also, he proved to be innovative, devising various trick plays to take advantage of the enemy's defensive weaknesses. One such bit of gimmickry enabled the Bears to win the first NFL championship game in 1933. This particular innovation had him catching a jump-pass just over the line of scrimmage and then lateraling to a teammate who was already en route to the end zone.

He gave the Bears a winning edge from 1932 to 1936. In the course of his tenure with the Chicago franchise, he earned All-Pro honors three times. Following a 1937 trade to Philadelphia, he again rated all-league recognition and thus became the first player in NFL annals to be so designated with two clubs. From 1940 through 1942, during the early years of World War II, he was out of football. He returned to the pro game in 1943 and played with a team composed of personnel from both the Eagles and Pittsburgh Steelers. At season's end, he retired.

Always personifying a granitelike quality, he undoubtedly would have excelled in any era, though not necessarily as an end. Given his speed, intelligence, perceptiveness, and hitting ability, he could have carried the ball or played in the secondary with any of today's NFL aggregations. He was that kind of a talent.

On January 14, 1947, at 37, Hewitt died in an automobile accident.

Elroy "Crazylegs" Hirsch

6'2", 190 pounds. Running Back, End: Chicago Rockets (1946–1948, AAFC), Los Angeles Rams (1949–1957, NFL). All-Pro: 1951, 1953. Pro Bowl: Three appearances. Inducted into the Pro Football Hall of Fame 1968. Flanker: 50-Year, All-Time, All-NFL team. Career: Receptions, 387. Receiving yardage, 7,029. Yards per reception, 18.2. Touchdowns, 60. Rushing attempts, 207. Rushing yardage, 687. Yards per carry, 3.3. Touchdowns (rushing), 3. Punt returns, 21. Return yardage, 286. Yards per return, 13.6. Touchdowns (punt returns), 1. Kickoff returns, 21. Return yardage, 566. Yards per return, 27.0. Touchdowns, 0. Passes attempted, 22. Passes completed, 12. Completion percentage, 54.0. Passing yardage, 156. Touchdowns (passing), 1. Interceptions, 1. Extra points, 9. Points scored, 9. Interceptions, 15. Return yardage, 251. Yards per return, 16.7. Touchdowns, 0.

The ball cut a high, arching trajectory through the thick veil of rain. Below, defender and receiver matched steps across the sodden field, their cleated feet kicking up sprays of fractured turf.

As the ball commenced its wobbly descent, the defender cast an apprehensive glance over his shoulder. The receiver, seemingly indifferent to its flight, churned on to an indeterminate destination. Suddenly he performed an intricate little shuffle step, leaned in on his running mate, and made the catch overhead without breaking stride. Touchdown!

Elroy "Crazylegs" Hirsch had done the acrobatic and improbable once again.

Crazylegs, a tag coined by a sportscaster along the way, aptly described the way Hirsch ran in pursuit of a pass. When he set out downfield, his powerful legs appeared to gyrate in all directions. This idiosyncrasy posed no small problem for the unfortunate defenders assigned to cover him.

But perhaps the most distinctive facet of Hirsch's receiving style was his uncanny ability to gather in the ball on the dead run when it plummeted down on him from directly above. He just seemed to sense where it would be at precisely the right time. This he did repeatedly throughout his illustrious career.

His unique method of running was not a natural affectation, but a schooled technique resulting from a youthful game. "Growing up in Wausau [Wis.]," he related, "I used to practice dodging around the trees near my home. I ran as close as I could without actually hitting them. I kind of weaved in and out of the tree line. I did this by the hour. That's how I came by my peculiar way of running."

As a schoolboy, Hirsch spent more time carrying the ball under arm than chasing after it. Early on at the University of Wisconsin he established himself as an outstanding running back. Later, at Michigan, while attending the university under the auspices of a V12 program during World War II, he gained further national recognition for his ball-carrying feats.

When it came time to consider a professional football career, he entertained offers from both the National Football League and the newly organized All-America Football Conference (AAFC). He elected to sign with the Chicago Rockets of the AAFC, largely because NFL contacts indicated his playing duties would not be all that concerned with running the ball.

In the course of three seasons (1946–1948) with the hapless Rockets, Hirsch endured constant coaching changes, consistent losing, and a succession of injuries, the most severe a fractured skull which not only threatened his career but his life. For a time, he lost control of his reflexes. Undaunted, he worked doggedly to rehabilitate himself until finally regaining his health.

The Los Angeles Rams of the NFL approached him in early 1949, and he quickly accepted their offer. His initial campaign with the Rams was largely spent sitting on the bench. But in 1950 he accepted a position switch to offensive end, and thereafter his pro career took off. For a while he wore

Elroy "Crazylegs" Hirsch

a specially constructed helmet to protect that area of his head (immediately above the right ear) which had been seriously fractured. Eventually, he discarded the helmet as too cumbersome. "I hated that helmet," he said, "and so I eventually got rid of it. I felt it hindered my play, and I wasn't really worried about reinjuring my head."

Combining with Hall of Fame quarterbacks Bob Waterfield and Norm Van Brocklin, Hirsch became a long-ball scoring threat any time he left the line of scrimmage under full throttle. In 1951, he led the NFL in receptions (66), receiving yardage (1,495), average yards per reception (22.7), and touchdown receptions (17). His 1,495 reception yards that year prevailed as a league record for more than two decades.

Although designated as an end, he actually functioned as a wide receiver. Looking back, it can be said that he was the bridge between a relatively ball-control-oriented era and modern times, with the forward pass serving as the principal means of attack. Yet he remains one of a kind.

"Back when I played, there weren't a lot of big linemen in the game as is the case today," he said. "Why, if a guy weighed 240 pounds, we would just stand around and stare at him. But big doesn't mean better. In the skill positions we were as good as anybody playing now. Let me pick the offensive people from my time, and I guarantee we'd score on anybody, absolutely anybody."

Blessed with the photogenic good looks of a matinee idol, Hirsch did appear on the silver screen in a film portraying himself. After quitting pro football in 1957, he remained on the West Coast to work briefly in the oil business and then served a stint as general manager of the Rams. Recently, he retired from the University of Wisconsin following a lengthy tenure as director of athletics.

Don Hutson

6'1", 180 pounds. End: Green Bay Packers (1935–1945). All-Pro: 1936, 1938–1945. NFL Most Valuable Player: 1941, 1942. NFL Receiving Leader: 1936, 1937, 1939, 1941–1945. NFL Scoring Leader: Five times. Inducted into the Pro Football Hall of Fame 1963 (charter member). End: 50-Year All-Time, All-NFL team. Career: Receptions, 488. Reception yardage, 7,991. Yards per reception, 16.4. Touchdowns, 99. Rushing attempts, 42. Rushing yardage, 236. Yards per carry, 5.6. Touchdowns (rushing), 1. Interceptions, 24. Return yardage, 365. Yards per return, 15.2. Touchdowns (returning), 1.

Pass defense entered an entirely new era when Don Hutson joined the National Football League as a sticky-fingered deep threat the likes of which the league had never before seen.

Right from the outset of his professional experience, he was double-teamed. Both the Green Bay Packers and the Brooklyn Dodgers claimed him as their property. NFL president Joe Carr, in an effort to be even-handed about the matter, ruled that the club which mailed its contract the earliest had first rights to the former University of Alabama All-America end. The Packers won out, having posted their offer 17 minutes earlier than the Dodgers.

Unknown to Hutson, this was a stroke of good fortune for him, as

Green Bay was a pass-oriented team while Brooklyn favored a ball-control offense. Had he gone with the Dodgers, his career might have proven to be much less illustrious than was the case.

It didn't take him long to make a lasting impression on the pros once in a Packers uniform. On his very first play from scrimmage, he fielded a pass and turned it into a dazzling bit of pitch-and-catch that went 83 yards for a touchdown. From that point on, it was "Katy bar the door" as it soon became apparent that he had more moves and speed than any defensive back in the money game.

Still, there remained some concern that given his slight frame, he might be injury-prone and more susceptible to a career-ending "accident." But he played 11 years in All-Star fashion without any serious mishap, thus giving credence to the old adage that appearances can be deceiving. As one member of the sportswriting fraternity put it, "You can't hurt what you can't hit."

Despite Hutson's almost electric impression on the NFL, there were still skeptics in the league who felt that he still could be contained using conventional defensive methods. One such unbeliever was Dodgers head coach Jock Sutherland. It didn't take him long to become disabused of this view after Hutson all but shredded the Brooklyn secondary with six receptions, two of which went for TDs.

In an effort to neutralize the Packers' fleet-footed receiving ace, opponents resorted to double coverage, bump-and-run tactics downfield, and jamming at the scrimmage line, all ploys very much in favor even now. But he had more going for him than just his speed, elusiveness, and impeccable timing. During his tenure with Green Bay, he enjoyed the additional advantage of catching passes from a strong-arm quarterback who could put the ball on the money time and again. First there was Arnie Herber and then Cecil Isbell, both of whom ably abetted his phenomenal capabilities.

No less than nine times the sandy-haired 'Bama export earned All-Pro recognition and twice rated NFL Player of the Year honors. He topped the league in receiving eight seasons and was the pro game's leading scorer on five occasions. From 1937 to 1945, he caught passes in 95 successive contests. Overall, he was on the business end of 99 scoring pitches, a record that stood for more than four decades, and handled 488 balls, which resulted in 7,991 yards worth of gains.

In addition to his catching ability, he held forth as an accomplished placekicker, his toe generating nearly 200 points for the Green Bay cause. He also did his share of the ball-carrying chores, rushing 42 times for 236 yards, an impressive per-attempt average of 5.6 yards, and a touchdown. Among his fondest memories are an end-around play that scored and an option pass he threw which also added six points to the Packers' total.

He wasn't half bad on defense either. In his last five campaigns, he picked off 24 aerials playing a safety position and returned them for 365 yards and a TD. And he did a bit of tackling too, taking on the large and the small without fear or favor.

It can be said that Don Hutson was years ahead of his time. Few of his many admirers doubt that he wouldn't have done just as spectacularly in the NFL today.

Dante Lavelli

6'0", 199 pounds. End: Cleveland Browns (1946–1949, AAFC), Cleveland Browns (1950–1956, NFL). All-AAFC: 1946, 1947. All-Pro: 1951, 1953. Pro Bowl: Three appearances. Inducted into the Pro Football Hall of Fame 1975. Career: Receptions, 386. Receiving yardage, 6,488. Yards per reception, 16.8. Touchdowns, 62.

Like a lot of Italian performers, Dante Lavelli had a flair for the dramatic. He liked being the center of attraction on the football field even though the crowd attracted was largely hostile. Whenever the going got tough, his basso-profundo voice could be heard above the din of battle calling for the ball. With it in his possession, the outcome would surely be a heroic one and just before the final curtain too. And more often than not, that's the way it worked out.

When he showed up for the Cleveland Browns' preseason camp in 1946, he had not much more than considerable self-confidence to recommend him. He could point to a total of only three college games as prior experience. Yet he managed to beat out five better-qualified contestants to become the starting right end. He then grandly proved his right to the job as a rookie by commandeering All-America Football Conference (AAFC) honors at his position and leading the league in receptions. What's more, he caught the deciding touchdown pass in that year's AAFC championship game.

He earned All-AAFC recognition again in 1947 and gained the reputation of a superior clutch player. When the Browns joined the National Football League in 1950, he continued to be impressive, gaining All-Pro status in 1951 and 1953 as well as participating in three Pro Bowls. He and quarterback Otto Graham formed one of the most productive pitch-and-catch combinations in the history of pro football.

Generally, he was a perfectionist in the execution of his pass routes. But if the game was hotly contested and the Browns needed a score, he would sprint down the field in search of an opening and yell for the ball to be thrown to him. And not infrequently that's how the scenario went because he had that special knack for making the catch in a crowd. This

Dante Lavelli

happened so often that he became known to friend and foe as "Glue Fingers."

Nobody appreciated more what Lavelli meant to the Browns in a tight situation than Graham. "Yeah, he had quite an ego," Graham said. "It didn't matter if there was a mob covering him, he still wanted the ball. But you can bet I went to him whenever I could. He really did have glue fingers. Of all the great receivers we had on the Browns, he was as competitive as anybody."

One of Lavelli's most memorable outings took place against the Los Angeles Rams in the 1950 NFL title contest. It marked the culmination of the Browns' first year in the senior league, and the prospect of a win over their "betters" provided every team member with an extra stimulus. But no one was more pumped for the test than he. That afternoon, he caught 11 aerials and scored a pair of touchdowns in Cleveland's stirring 30–28 come-from-behind victory.

He retired after the 1956 season.

Don Maynard

6'1", 185 pounds. Wide Receiver: New York Giants (1958), Hamilton TigerCats (1959, Canadian Football League), New York Titans (1960–1962, AFL), New York Jets (1963–1969, AFL), New York Jets (1970–1972, NFL), St. Louis Cardinals (1973). AFL All-Star Game: Four appearances. Wide Receiver: All-Time AFL team 1960–1969. Inducted into the Pro Football Hall of Fame 1987. Career: Receptions, 633 (CFL, 1). Receiving yardage, 11,834 (CFL, 10). Yards per reception, 18.7 (CFL, 10.0). Touchdowns, 88 (CFL, 0). Rushing attempts, 24. Rushing yardage, 70. Yards per carry, 2.9. Touchdowns, 0. Punt returns, 25. Return yardage, 126. Yards per return, 5.0. Touchdowns, 0. Kickoff returns, 15. Return yardage, 349. Yards per return, 23.3. Touchdowns, 0.

With his chiseled features, weathered face, long sideburns, and cowboy boots, Don Maynard looked as if he had stepped right out of a Marlboro advertisement. But despite his wide-open-spaces orientation, he didn't smoke or drink or even ride a horse all that much. His thing was catching passes, which he did in record numbers for 15 years.

As incongruous as it may seem, he was much a part of the New York City sporting scene, toiling first for the Giants and later the Titans and Jets. He came to the Big Apple from Texas Western University at the invitation of the Giants in 1958. That was during the heyday of "Chuckin' Charley" Conerly, Frank Gifford, et al., so he naturally spent a lot of time warming the bench. He did manage to play briefly in the "greatest game ever" between New York and the Baltimore Colts for the NFL title that year, which went into sudden-death overtime and was nationally televised. Shortly thereafter, the Giants cut him loose, and he drifted to the Canadian Football League for a one-season stand with the Hamilton TigerCats.

In 1960, he returned to New York and joined the Titans of the newly formed American Football League (AFL). That season, he caught 72 passes for 1,265 yards, a per-catch average of 17.6 yards, and 6 touchdowns. He had finally found a football home. His performance fell off a bit the ensuing year, but he enjoyed another stellar campaign in 1962, fielding 56 balls for 1,041 yards, a per-reception average of 18.6 yards, and 8 scores.

When Weeb Ewbank moved over from the National Football League Colts to the AFL in 1963 and became head coach of the newly named New York Jets, he was immediately impressed with Maynard's reception statistics but not his method of running patterns. Unlike the top catch personnel in the NFL, he tended to freelance his routes with scant attention given to what had been diagramed on the chalkboard. Some of this undisciplined behavior had to do with the scrambling tactics employed by Jets quarterbacks, who usually were forced to run for their lives. Under these conditions, he found it necessary to keep adjusting, to keep trying to get open.

In 1965, Joe "Willie" Namath signed on as the Jets' field general, and almost immediately Maynard began to execute more-precise patterns. With a better quarterback throwing the ball more accurately, he was able to improve his performance too. "Joe helped me learn to run patterns effectively," he said. "Right from the start, when we would miss on a pass, we'd get back and discuss it right away. What happened? Was I too early, or were you late, or what? And we got it right. We told each other, 'Let's get together. I'll help make you famous, and you help make me famous.' Mutual respect, that's what our relationship was all about."

Practice, practice, and more practice made Maynard not only more consistent but more confident in what he could do under game pressure. "You have to be real alert on every play," he said. "Say I'm going to run twenty yards and then break to the inside. As I run down the field, I've got to feel where the linebacker is in there behind me while I'm driving the cornerback deep in front of me. When I break in, I can't let the linebacker wind up standing between me and the quarterback. I have to know whether to break in hard, or just turn and stop. I have to read the defense even as the quarterback is doing the same thing. And we both have to do it right. Needless to say, it takes some practice to get the timing between us just right."

Maynard's biggest game was the 1968 AFL Championship matchup between the Jets and the Oakland Raiders. That afternoon, he caught six passes for 118 yards and two touchdowns, the latter giving New York a 27–23 win. On January 12, 1969, the Jets upset the Colts 16–7 in Super Bowl III. Maynard didn't have a reception in that contest, but he repeatedly decoyed the Baltimore secondary into covering him deep while other New York receivers ran underneath for the catches which ultimately forged the victory.

In considering his illustrious career, he said, "I've always thought that success in football is about ten percent physical and ninety percent mental attitude. I had it in my mind that I was going to catch the ball. I concentrated on it, got both hands on it, and when I did get ahold of it, I kept both hands on it. As a result, I only fumbled once in my fifteen years of playing professionally. The right attitude is the key to everything in the world. If you want to be a winner, then you get the attitude that you want to be a winner. And then you train for it. The rest just comes."

Currently, Maynard still owns the NFL record for most 100-yard reception games with 50 and is third on the all-time career-yards-catch list with 11,834.

Wayne Millner

6'0", 191 pounds. End: Boston Redskins (1936), Washington Redskins (1937–1941, 1945). Inducted into the Pro Football Hall of Fame 1968. Career: Receptions, 124. Receiving yardage, 1,578. Yards per reception, 12.7. Touchdowns, 12. Coach: Philadelphia Eagles (1951) (assumed the head coaching position after two games of the season). Won-lost record: Philadelphia Eagles (2–8–0).

Rare is the talent that can accomplish the spectacular without making the process seem spectacular. Wayne Millner was thus endowed. But because he made it seem so easy, his true ability went largely uncelebrated, and even greater things came to be expected of him as a matter of course.

He was an end by job description, the last of a dying breed who could dispatch both offensive and defensive responsibilities with equal aplomb. While at the University of Notre Dame, he twice earned All-America recognition with a penchant for making clutch catches when they were most needed. A classic example of his flair for such histrionics occurred during the famous 18–13 comeback victory by the Fighting Irish over heavily favored Ohio State in 1935. Even as the final seconds ticked off the game clock with his team trailing by the narrowest of margins, he calmly slipped free in the end zone and made a leaping reception of a pass that capped this giddiest of triumphs.

So when he joined the Boston Redskins as a product of the 1936 college draft, it was with no little fanfare. His presence in camp prompted new head coach Ray Flaherty to exclaim, "If we don't take the championship now with that big Yankee out there on the wing, then I ought to resign." The Redskins did manage to annex the Eastern Division crown with a 7–5 record but lost a 21–6 decision to the Green Bay Packers in the NFL championship game at New York's Polo Grounds. Millner had much to do with his club's success, snaring 18 aerials on the season for 211 yards and a per-catch average of 11.7 yards. And he did this despite the fact the Boston franchise favored a mode of attack weighted toward running the ball.

In 1937, the Redskins moved to Washington, D.C., and acquired a sensational rookie quarterback named Sammy Baugh. Right from the outset, the lanky Texas pitching whiz and Millner established themselves as perhaps the most explosive big-play combo in the NFL. That year, the Redskins registered another Western Division first on the strength of a fine 8–3–0 record and played in their second successive league title game. Providing the competition on that occasion were the Chicago Bears, and they went to the locker room at the halftime intermission with a 14–7 lead. But the second 30-minute period was no sooner under way than Baugh hit Millner on the fly for a 55-yard scoring strike. Shortly thereafter, the Bears forged back ahead, only to have Baugh and Millner bring the score level again. This time they combined for a 78-yard bomb that had Millner going in for the tally without breaking stride. Finally, Baugh threw for the deciding TD when Millner, this time acting as a decoy, suckered a couple of Chicago defenders out of position to allow unheralded halfback Ed Justice to make the reception without impediment.

With the Redskins prevailing 28–21 for the championship, Millner finished the day with eight catches for 181 yards and two touchdowns. His feline grace, acrobatic agility, and fierce determination were never more in evidence than during this sterling performance.

He also acquitted himself well as a blocker, particularly on behalf of standout running back Cliff Battles. Not infrequently, a breakaway burst by Battles was directly attributable to Millner's having paved the way for him. Not one to covet the spotlight, Battles said, "I always knew if I could get in the open, Wayne would be there to block for me. His involvement in the play determined whether or not I would get away for a long gain."

Defensively, Millner could hold his own with the best of his breed. He turned plays inside, given good mechanics and speed. And his natural elusiveness enabled him routinely to beat larger blockers and get quickly into the opposition backfield.

Following the 1941 campaign, he entered the U.S. Navy and remained on active duty for the duration of World War II. He rejoined the Redskins for the 1945 season and thereafter retired. At that juncture he had 124 career catches to his credit, the best such mark in the club's history until then, for 1,578 yards, a per-reception average of 12.7 yards, and 12 TDs.

He died on November 19, 1976, at 63.

Pete Pihos

6'1", 210 pounds. End: Philadelphia Eagles (1947–1955). All-Pro: 1948, 1949, 1952–1955. Pro Bowl: Six appearances. NFL Receiving Leader: 1953–1955. Inducted into the Pro Football Hall of Fame 1970. Career: Receptions, 373. Receiving yardage, 5,619. Yards per reception, 15.1. Touchdowns, 61.

Pete Pihos

All references to the "Golden Greek" in the sporting press of the post–
World War II years were reserved exclusively for Pete Pihos, historically
one of the National Football League's most uniquely talented performers.
Back then, the pro game underwent a period of substantive change, but this
transition was never so rapid that the all-purpose pride of the Philadelphia
Eagles didn't continually remain one step ahead.

In 1947, he joined the Eagles after a two-year military stint and a collegiate career at Indiana University in which he earned All-America

recognition as a fullback and an end. He commenced his NFL tenure during the waning years of the 60-minute player. But he fit right into this mode, being as gifted at tackling and rushing the quarterback as blocking and catching the ball. He served with distinction on both offense and defense for the better part of his nine years in the league, rarely repairing to the sidelines for so much as a breather.

From 1947 through 1949, the Eagles enjoyed three championship seasons, winning a trio of Eastern Division titles and two NFL championships. Pihos had a major role in this Philadelphia success story, rating All-Pro honors twice for his accomplishments as a two-way stalwart. But he particularly shone as a clutch receiver, handling 103 passes which resulted in gains of 1,632 yards and 22 touchdowns. He compensated for a lack of breakaway speed with impeccable timing, good hands, exceptional balance, and superior physical effort. Defensive backs found him not only punishing to cover but worth their life to bring down after making a catch, a tribute to his upbringing as a fullback.

With the advent of the two-platoon system, he was moved to defensive end full-time in 1952 when injuries to key players on the prevent side plagued the Eagles. Sportswriters named him All-Pro for a third time. The next year, he moved back to the offensive unit and proceeded to lead the NFL in receptions with 63 catches for 1,049 yards and 10 TDs. He repeated this process the following two years, making All-Pro again on both occasions. In 1954, he was on the receiving end of 60 aerials for 872 yards and 10 scores. He caught 62 balls for 864 yards in 1955 and crossed the opposition goal line 7 times. Overall, he participated in six consecutive Pro Bowls.

He retired in the wake of the 1955 campaign while still at the height of his powers.

Charley Taylor

6'3", 210 pounds. Running Back, Flanker (Wide Receiver): Washington Redskins (1964–1975, 1977). All-Pro: 1966, 1967, 1969. Pro Bowl: Eight appearances. Inducted into the Pro Football Hall of Fame 1984. Career: Receptions, 649. Receiving yardage, 9,140. Yards per reception, 14.1. Touchdowns, 79. Rushing attempts, 442. Rushing yardage, 1,488. Yards per carry, 3.4. Touchdowns (rushing), 11. Passes attempted, 16. Passes completed, 3. Completion percentage, 18.9. Passing yardage, 99. Touchdowns (passing), 1. Interceptions, 1. Kickoff returns, 5. Return yardage, 133. Yards per return, 26.6. Touchdowns, 0. Punt returns, 5. Return yardage, 63. Yards per return, 12.6. Touchdowns, 0.

There wasn't any way that Charley Taylor wouldn't make the Hall of Fame, either as a running back or a split end (flanker). He had the requisite size, speed, moves, and good hands as well as the quiet determination of a consummate achiever.

Despite these sterling attributes, he didn't enjoy the notoriety bestowed upon less-gifted contemporaries. Perhaps it was his unassuming demeanor that tended not to attract attention to himself. He was always one to let his actions on the field do the talking. But the people who appreciated him most were those who knew how much he did for them.

One such admirer was Sonny Jurgensen, a Hall of Fame quarterback with the Washington Redskins when Taylor prevailed as a most inviting target for his aerial salvos. "I wanted to get the ball in Charley's hands at every opportunity," Jurgensen said. "And that's because I knew he was going to make a big play for us. Unlike a lot of receivers, he knew what to do with the ball once it was in his possession. He just made things happen."

When Taylor came out of Arizona State in 1964, he was the Redskins' first pick in the college draft. In the minds of the coaches there was no doubt that he would make the team. However, they disagreed concerning the best means of utilizing his considerable abilities. One faction lobbied to keep him at running back, while another wanted to try him out at cornerback, a position then badly in need of shoring up. Ultimately, Washington field boss Bill McPeak decided that Taylor would best benefit the franchise with a football under his arm, so he remained in the offensive backfield.

As it turned out, he made McPeak look like a genius, winning NFL Rookie-of-the-Year honors with his ball-carrying heroics. He also caught 53 passes for 814 yards, a per-reception average of 15.4 yards, and 5 touchdowns. He was just as devastating a runner in 1965. And that year he also pulled down 40 pitches for 577 yards, a 14.4 yards-per-catch average, and 3 TDs. Then the unexpected happened.

In 1966, Otto Graham, a Hall of Fame quarterback with the great Cleveland Browns teams of a decade earlier, took over as head coach of the Redskins and immediately opted to open up the passing game. In studying his personnel, it occurred to him that Taylor would be an even more effective receiver if given that duty full-time. He had the size to catch the ball over the middle in traffic and was an excellent blocker. So his job description abruptly changed.

Though not one to say much, Taylor let it be known that he wasn't happy with the switch. Still, he didn't let his disappointment come into play on the field. In his first start as a split end (flanker), the equivalent of a modern wideout, he handled 8 aerials totaling 111 yards. The following weekend, he was on the receiving end of 11 passes. By season's end, he sat atop the NFL standings in his specialty with 72 receptions for 1,119 yards, a per-catch average of 15.5 yards, and 12 scores. It was more of the same in 1967 when he snared 70 balls worth 990 yards, a per-reception average of 14.1 yards, and 9 touchdowns. He would average 60 catches a year until injuries largely sidelined him in 1971.

Charley Taylor

Taylor regained his form in 1972 and continued to be a potent performer until he spent all of the 1976 campaign on injured reserve. He retired following the 1977 season and became a scout for the Redskins. In 1981, he was named receivers coach and retains that responsibility with the team to this day. He rated All-America recognition as a running back at Arizona State University. During his 13 years in the NFL, he earned All-Pro status three times and participated in eight Pro Bowl games. He finished his career with 649 receptions, the best mark in NFL history at that time.

Paul Warfield

6'0", 188 pounds. Wide Receiver: Cleveland Browns (1964–1969, 1976, 1977), Miami Dolphins (1970–1974), Memphis Southmen (1975, WFL). All-Pro: 1964, 1968, 1969, 1971, 1972, 1973. Pro Bowl: Seven appearances. NFL Reception Leader: 1968, 1971. Inducted into the Pro Football Hall of Fame 1983. Career: Receptions, 427 (25, WFL). Receiving yardage, 8,565 (422, WFL). Yards per reception, 20.1 (16.9, WFL). Touchdowns, 85 (3, WFL). Rushing attempts, 22. Rushing yardage, 204. Yards per carry, 9.3. Touchdowns, 0.

It was something like being a thoroughbred consigned to running in sulky events. This is the kind of frustration that beset Paul Warfield for the greater part of his 13-year tenure in the National Football League. A man endowed with speed and grace granted few of his breed, he can but wonder what might have been if only his talents were given their full rein.

He was a premier wideout by every measure except the one that matters the most—career statistics. In his time he pulled down 427 aerials for 8,565 yards, an all-time high per-average gain of 20.1 yards, and 85 touchdowns. But he had 100 less catches than at least a dozen other receivers and trailed the overall leader in this category by more than 300 receptions. Given their opportunities, he very well could have been the best ever by a long shot.

When he exited Ohio State University in 1964, it seemed only natural for the Cleveland Browns to make him their number-one draft pick. A Buckeye born and bred, he had no complaints about the mating either. But the Browns weren't going to build their offense around him. In fact, they were pledged to a ball-control offense with such as Jimmy Brown and Leroy Kelly to do the toting and a fine run-blocking line.

As a rookie, Warfield did handle 52 balls for 920 yards and 9 touchdowns. But his catch production fell off markedly thereafter. Only his 1968 season total of 50 receptions for an NFL-leading 12 TDs even approached his first season's output. Still, all things considered, he wasn't that unhappy in Cleveland. The fans that filled cavernous Municipal Stadium liked him, and his duties weren't limited to running down the occasional long ball. He could and would go underneath for the clutch catch when needed. What's more, he consistently earned high marks as a blocker. The Browns finished first in their division five times and won an NFL championship between 1964 and 1969.

Given the caliber of his performance, it came as something of a shock when the Browns traded him to the Miami Dolphins prior to the 1970 campaign. Again, he was going to be working for a club with a ground-based attack. Back then, the Dolphins relied heavily upon the likes of Larry Csonka, Jim Kiick, and Mercury Morris to advance the ball, the pass being

Paul Warfield

used only as needed. Miami head coach Don Shula favored the grunt approach but did not wholly disdain the options that Warfield provided his offense as a quick-strike threat.

From 1970 through 1974, his reception stats were down except for 1971. That year he logged 43 catches for 996 yards and a league-high 11 touchdowns. When the Dolphins drove to a perfect 17–0 record in 1972 and annexed Super Bowl VII to close out their historic achievement, they were considered to have the perfect blend of pass and run. And not a few expert observers said that Warfield's ability to go all the way on any snap kept Miami opponents loose and unable to concentrate on shutting down the rushing game. Yet, despite two Super Bowl rings (SBs VII and VIII), he held forth as an unhappy employee due to his lack of involvement in the Dolphins' attack.

He jumped to the maverick World Football League and the Memphis Southmen in 1975 for money and other considerations. This venture lasted one year, during which he registered 25 receptions for 422 yards and 3 touchdowns. In 1976 he returned to the NFL with Cleveland and there closed out his playing days at the end of the 1977 schedule.

ARMORED INFANTRY

Running Backs

Cliff Battles

6'1", 201 pounds. Running Back: Boston Braves (1932), Boston Redskins (1933–1936), Washington Redskins (1937). All-Pro: 1932, 1933, 1937. NFL Leading Rusher: 1932, 1937. Inducted into the Pro Football Hall of Fame 1968. Career: Rushing attempts, 873. Rushing yardage, 3,622. Yards per carry, 4.1. Touchdowns, 23.

Perhaps the most appropriate caption for the abbreviated career of Washington Redskins running back Cliff Battles is "what might have been." Were it not for a contract dispute with then team owner George Preston Marshall, he doubtless would have continued to terrorize opposition defenders with his electrifying breakaway jaunts and made an even more lasting mark in the annals of professional football.

Battles first caught Marshall's eye when playing with little West Virginia Wesleyan College in a losing cause against Georgetown University. Despite the lopsidedness of the game, Battles displayed a combination of raw power and attention-getting speed that convinced Marshall he had found a potent offensive weapon for his newly acquired National Football League team, the Boston Braves.

In 1932, his rookie season with the Braves, Battles led the NFL in rushing with 576 yards and was accorded All-Pro honors. However, he was the only bright spot in a largely lackluster campaign for the Boston franchise. The public stayed away in force, and the club lost money, so much so that Marshall's partners pulled out, leaving him the sole owner.

The following year, Marshall retitled his property the Boston Redskins, and Battles again distinguished himself as the premier ball carrier in the pro game. His 5.0 yards-per-try average was the best in the league, and he earned All-Pro recognition once more. On any play, he could go all the way and not infrequently did just that. In one game during the 1933 season he rushed for more than 200 yards, a startling attainment by any measure. But despite his headline-making play, attendance did not increase appreciably, and Marshall began considering ways to enhance his investment.

Finally, in 1937, the Redskins moved to Washington, D.C., and commenced to build one of the most illustrious and profitable entries in the league. That first year in the nation's capital brought Battles into partnership with a newly recruited passing sensation named Sammy Baugh. Right from the outset, they proved to be a sensational combination. As the weeks rolled by, it became increasingly apparent that the Redskins and the New York Giants were going to battle it out for Eastern Division supremacy. On the final Sunday of the regular schedule, Washington and New York squared away in the Polo Grounds to settle the matter.

Several thousand Redskins fans had trained to New York for the encounter, complete with the team's marching band outfitted in buckskins and Indian headdress. The entire entourage marched up Broadway to the stadium, and their display of support would not prove to be for naught. With Baugh throwing bullets and Battles notching scoring runs of 4, 73, and 76 yards, Washington overwhelmed the Giants by a 49–14 margin and claimed the division crown.

The next weekend, the Redskins were on the road again, this time to Chicago. In a hard-fought contest, Washington bested the Western Division champion Bears 28–21 and annexed the NFL title, an historic first for the club. Battles finished the campaign as the league's leading rusher for the second time with 874 yards to his credit. Little did anyone suspect that he had played his last game of professional football.

Later that year, Marshall became so embroiled in trying to sign Baugh to a new contract that he virtually ignored Battles, who also wanted more money. After some weeks of being unable to meet with Marshall, Battle let his frustration get the better of him and announced his retirement. He then accepted an assistant coaching position at Columbia University for $1,000 more than he had been making with the Redskins. So ended one of the NFL's most brilliant careers on the most curious of notes.

He died on April 28, 1981, at 70.

Jim Brown

6'2", 228 pounds. Running Back: Cleveland Browns (1957–1965). All-Pro: 1957–1961, 1963–1965. Pro Bowl: Nine appearances. NFL Rookie of the Year: 1957. NFL Most

Valuable Player: 1958, 1965. Running Back: 50-Year, All-Time, All-NFL team. Inducted into the Pro Football Hall of Fame 1971. Career: Rushing attempts, 2,359. Rushing yardage, 12,312. Yards per carry, 5.2. Touchdowns, 106. Passes attempted, 12. Passes completed, 4. Completion percentage, 33.3. Passing yardage, 117. Touchdowns (passing), 3. Interceptions, 0. Kickoff returns, 29. Return yardage, 648. Yards per return, 22.3. Touchdowns (kickoff returns), 0. Receptions, 262. Receiving yardage, 2,499. Yards per reception, 9.5. Touchdowns (receiving), 20.

Inside, outside, up-the-gut, underneath, or downtown, Jim Brown was a man for all occasions on a football field. He could score carrying the ball and catch passes underneath or down deep to put six points on the board. Perhaps no big man in the history of pro football embodied so many offensive weapons as the Cleveland Browns' mercurial No. 32.

The word *gifted* truly applied to Brown. Athletically there was little he couldn't do. Just name a sport. In addition to his undeniable abilities with a football under arm, he also excelled in basketball, track, and lacrosse in high school and at Syracuse University. As a sophomore for the Orangemen, he finished fifth in the national decathlon championships, a series of 10 events testing the participant's skill at running, jumping, and throwing activities. The record notes that he actually bettered the efforts of the immortal Jim Thorpe in six of these competitions.

He was the Browns' number-one pick in the 1957 draft and became a starter in the Cleveland backfield from day one of training camp. Although head coach Paul Brown traditionally relegated rookies to backup status no matter their college credentials until they had mastered his system, he didn't hesitate to make an exception in the case of the big Syracuse graduate. He liked to win football games and league championships as well as the next coach and realized that No. 32 was integral to this process.

With Jim Brown coming out of the Cleveland backfield from 1957 to 1965, the Browns were a perennial title contender. During this nine-year stint, Cleveland logged three first-place finishes in the NFL's Eastern Division, was second four times and third only twice. In their three league-championship appearances, the Browns beat Baltimore 27–0 (1964) and lost to Detroit 59–14 (1957) and Green Bay 23–12 (1965). Not coincidentally, Brown supplied the offensive impetus for Cleveland's surge to the top in 1957. In that season he led the league with 942 yards on 202 rushes for a per-carry average of 4.7 yards and 9 touchdowns. This performance earned him not only Rookie-of-the-Year recognition but Player-of-the-Year honors, a classic double which remains unequaled to this day.

From 1958 through 1961, he led the NFL each year in rushing with totals of 1,527, 1,329, 1,257 and 1,408 yards. These eye-opening statistics were established in 12-game schedules, with the exception of 1961 when the league went to a 14-game slate. In 1962, he fell off to 996 yards but from

Jim Brown

1963 through 1965, produced consecutive efforts of 1,863, 1,446, and 1,544 yards. Thus, for eight out of nine years in the NFL, he topped all league rushers in the gross output category and five times exceeded a 5 yards-per-carry average on the year. His heroics entitled him to All-Pro selection eight times and nine invites to the Pro Bowl. In 1958 and 1965 he was voted the NFL's Most Valuable Player.

At 6'2" and 228 pounds, he combined bulk and speed with devastating effect. He could sprint for big yardage, outrunning the opposition secondary in the process, or crunch through a wall of writhing bodies from two yards out with equal facility, alternating speed and power gears as the occasion demanded. And this was all done with the hashmarks much nearer the sidelines than today.

"Back then, it wasn't difficult to figure out who was going to get the ball most of the time in the Cleveland offense," said Sam Huff, a former standout linebacker with the New York Giants. "In fact, I keyed on Brown every play. And when the ball was spotted at the hashmark, we would flop all of our best lineman to the wide side of the field, knowing just where Brown would have to run. And he'd still get five yards or more. There was just no stopping him."

Probably the most fearsome sight for a secondary defender of that era was to see Brown bearing down on him and know that if he didn't make the tackle, a touchdown would surely result. Jim Patton, an All-Pro defensive back with the New York Giants, was in this unenviable position many times in his career. "If you tried to tackle Brown up high, he would simply run over you," Patton said. "So your best bet was to hit him low, just under the knees. Personally, I developed a method that was kind of like lassoing him around the ankles. I'd throw a rolling block at him and then snare his legs when he tried to hurdle me. Sometimes it worked, and sometimes it didn't. But the important thing is I'm here to tell about it."

During the off-season following his banner year of 1965, Brown caught all of pro football flat-footed when he announced his retirement from the game. He was making a movie overseas at the time and felt his future lay in the entertainment business. At age 30, he still had several peak seasons left in his magnificent body, so his abrupt departure from the NFL left many an admirer wondering what further heights he might have scaled before the years finally caught up with him. That bit of conjecture must remain forever unanswered.

In retirement, Brown watched with considerable chagrin as his all-time NFL rushing record of 12,312 yards was surpassed. He felt that because the nature of the pro game had changed so much, the seasons were longer, and the modern rules so much favored scoring, it made for an unfair comparison. It galled him to be removed from the record book by players who had not really surpassed his performance.

"When you change the rules, it becomes a different game," he said, "and the resulting performances are suspect. You have a lot of guys making one thousand yards rushing in a season now. But it doesn't mean anything. The regular schedule today is sixteen games. I set my record in nine years playing twelve- and fourteen-game schedules. So one thousand yards doesn't mean much anymore. But they [NFL hierarchy] are still talking about a record based upon this criterion. It's just ludicrous."

No matter what standard of measure is used, there will always be only one Jim Brown. His kind come along but once in a lifetime.

Earl Campbell

5'11", 233 pounds. Running Back: Houston Oilers (1978–1984), New Orleans Saints (1984, 1985). NFL Most Valuable Player: 1978, 1979, 1980. All-Pro: 1978, 1979, 1980. Pro Bowl: Five appearances. Inducted into the Pro Football Hall of Fame 1991. Career: Rushing attempts, 2,187. Rushing yardage, 9,407. Yards per carry, 4.3. Touchdowns, 74. Receptions, 121. Receiving yardage, 806. Yards per reception, 6.7. Touchdowns, 0.

The term *power back* has no more apt application than to Earl Campbell, a 5'11", 233-pound brute of a ball carrier who sufficed as the prime mover of a fine Houston Oilers attack during the late 1970s. Dubbed "Thunder Thighs" for his exceptionally strong underpinnings, he topped all NFL rushers from 1978 to 1980 while leading his team to the American Football Conference championship game each of those years.

A consensus All-America choice at the University of Texas and 1977 Heisman Trophy designate, he was the first player taken in the 1978 NFL draft, scouts having already tagged him as a future superstar. He didn't disappoint the prognosticators. Making the transition from college to pro football in spectacular fashion, he was the league's most productive ground gainer and earned All-Pro, Rookie-of-the-Year, and Most Valuable Player honors for his efforts.

In 1980, he bulled his way through, over, and around the opposition for 1,934 yards, the third highest output ever by an NFL running back. During the course of that campaign, he enjoyed four 200-yard rushing performances. The previous year he ran for 100 yards or more in 11 contests. On a Monday night in 1978 he awed an ABC national television audience by shredding the Miami Dolphins defense for 199 yards and four touchdowns. He eclipsed the 1,000-yard mark in five of his first six seasons as a pro. When not packing the ball under arm, he frequently came out of the backfield to catch a clutch pass that kept the Oilers moving.

Shortly after the advent of the 1984 schedule, Campbell was traded to New Orleans where he finished out his career the following year. He could look back at his attainments with no little pride. In just eight campaigns (1978–1985) he rushed for 9,407 yards, ninth best total all time, while averaging 4.3 yards per carry and tallying 74 TDs. He also caught 121 passes for 806 yards. No less than three times he was named the league's MVP, played in five Pro Bowls, and thrice rated All-Pro recognition.

It was these sparkling stats that assured him of admission to the Hall of Fame as a first-time applicant.

Tony Canadeo

5'11", 195 pounds. Halfback: Green Bay Packers (1941–1944, 1946–1952). All-Pro: 1943, 1949. Inducted into the Pro Football Hall of Fame 1974. Career: Rushing attempts, 1,025. Rushing yardage, 4,197. Yards per carry, 4.1. Touchdowns, 26. Receptions, 69. Receiving yardage, 579. Yards per reception, 8.4. Touchdowns (receiving), 5. Passes attempted, 268. Passes completed, 105. Completion percentage, 35.4. Passing yardage, 1,642. Touchdowns (passing), 16. Interceptions, 20. Punt returns, 45. Return yardage, 509. Yards per return, 11.3. Touchdowns, 0. Kickoff returns, 71. Return yardage, 1,626. Yards per return, 22.9. Touchdowns, 0. Interceptions, 9. Return yardage, 129. Yards per return, 14.3. Touchdowns, 0. Punts, 45. Yards per punt, 37.0.

Being a jack of all trades and pretty good at most will take you far in the National Football League, even to the Hall of Fame. Tony Canadeo is a classic case in point.

He wasn't all that big (5'11", 195 pounds) for a halfback, given the pro football standard of weights and measures. And he didn't command the type of speed NFL ball-carrying types were supposed to possess. But he ran effectively with or without blocking. And he could throw the ball pretty fair to middlin' too. What's more, he did a little better than all right returning kicks and punts, coming out of the backfield to catch passes and playing defense. If a job needed doing, he was ready and willing to do it. This kind of attitude and adaptability bodes to be ever in demand, no matter the age and era.

After a little All-America background at Gonzaga University, a less than prestigious gridiron academy, Canadeo entered the NFL in 1941 as a seventh-round draft pick of the Green Bay Packers. Back then, the Packers, under the direction of head coach "Curly" Lambeau, were a pass-oriented powerhouse and perennial title contender. Early on, he served as an understudy to Cecil Isbell, Green Bay's veteran aerial artist. By 1943, he had taken over the throwing chores and deported himself well enough to rate All-Pro recognition. After the 1944 campaign he entered the service for a year of military duty.

When he rejoined the Packers in 1946, new names graced the team roster, and his strong right arm was no longer in demand. The club had ceased to be a serious participant in the annual quest for championship status. Given a perceptive assessment of the situation, he determined that his best chance of making and staying with the team lay in becoming a dependable every-down running back. And this he did, delivering repeatedly when the must yardage was needed. In 1949, he evidenced the tenacity, courage, and commitment to duty that enabled him to rush for 1,000 yards, only the third player to do so at that time, and earn All-Pro distinction once more. He retired at the close of the 1952 campaign. During his 11 seasons with Green Bay, he averaged 75 yards an outing by virtue of his jack-of-all-trades offensive abilities.

When out of uniform he continued to support the team. First he functioned as a color commentator for television broadcasts of the Packers' games. Later, when a drive got under way to build a new stadium, he was a leader in the effort to raise the necessary funding. Currently, he is a member of the club's board of directors and its executive committee.

Larry Csonka

6'3', 235 pounds. Fullback: Miami Dolphins (1968, 1969, AFL) Miami Dolphins (1970–1974, NFL), Memphis Southmen (1975, WFL), New York Giants (1976–1978,

Larry Csonka

NFL), Miami Dolphins (1979). All-Pro: 1971, 1972, 1973. Pro Bowl: Five appearances. Most Valuable Player: Super Bowl VIII. Inducted into the Pro Football Hall of Fame 1987. Career: Rushing attempts, 1,891 (WFL, 99). Rushing yardage, 8,081 (WFL, 421). Yards per carry, 4.3 (WFL, 4.3). Touchdowns, 64 (WFL, 1). Receptions, 106. Receiving yardage, 820. Yards per reception, 7.7. Touchdowns (receiving), 4.

Forging a hole where there was none, getting the short yardage in first-down and scoring situations, and just plain running out the game clock were the primary duties defined in the job description of Larry Csonka, who powered the ground attack of the Miami Dolphins in their glory years of the 1970s.

He was the treads upon which the Dolphins juggernaut ground to victory in three American Football Conference (AFC) championship contests from 1971 through 1973 and Super Bowls VII and VIII. In each of the AFC title tilts and both Super Bowl encounters he held forth as the leading rusher, and this was done primarily between the tackles. He slogged out 112 yards in SB VII and followed this performance with a Most Valuable Player effort of 145 yards, a record on that occasion, in SB VIII.

At 6'3" and 235 pounds, he was perfectly formed for the ball-control dictum tht Miami head coach Don Shula imposed upon his charges. Bull-shouldered and oaken of limb, he literally barged through the opposition, but at a terrible price. In the course of his career he suffered multiple fractures to his nose, a number of concussions, a badly battered elbow and knee, and a cracked eardrum, not to mention a daunting compendium of bruises and abrasions.

However, none of these maladies did he consider a particular burden to his work. They were expected if not all that welcome. "Fullbacks take a beating," he once observed. "It's no big deal. Naw, I don't like to use anything for pain. If I can't control it with my mind, then I don't belong out there. Playing hurt is all part of this business. You owe it to your teammates to do that. Actually doing it has to come from inside you. Call it pride, determination, or whatever."

In the wake of the 1974 campaign, Csonka jumped to the ill-fated World Football League and labored a season with the Memphis Southmen. When the WFL folded, he went to work for the New York Giants from 1976 to 1978. Then he returned to the Dolphins for the 1979 schedule before retiring. If there was an endearing legacy he left to the pro game, it was his aversion to fumbling, an error which afflicted him just 21 times in 1,997 carries.

Bill Dudley

5'10", 176 pounds. Halfback: Pittsburgh Steelers (1942, 1945, 1946), Detroit Lions (1947–1949), Washington Redskins (1950, 1951, 1953). All-Pro: 1942, 1946. NFL Most Valuable Player: 1946. NFL Triple Crown: 1946. Inducted into the Pro Football Hall of Fame 1966. Career: Rushing attempts, 765. Rushing yardage, 3,057. Yards per carry, 4.0. Touchdowns, 20. Receptions, 123. Receiving yardage, 1,383. Yards per reception, 11.2. Touchdowns (receiving), 18. Passes attempted, 222. Passes completed, 81. Completion percentage, 36.5. Passing yardage, 985. Touchdowns (passing), 6. Interceptions, 17. Punt returns, 124. Return yardage, 1,515. Yards per return, 12.2. Touchdowns (punt returns), 3. Kickoff returns, 78. Return yardage, 1,743. Yards per return, 22.3. Touchdowns (kickoff returns), 1. Interceptions, 23. Return yardage, 459. Yards per return, 20.0. Touchdowns (interceptions), 2. Punts, 191. Yards per punt, 38.2.

Though small and slow afoot, Bill Dudley nevertheless made it into the Hall of Fame with an intense competitive spirit and the ability to

Bill Dudley

dispatch a variety of gridiron responsibilities with largely unorthodox but thoroughly effective methods.

In addition to being a veritable football tortoise, he threw with a somewhat spastic motion and took no steps when placekicking, simply using a pendulumlike motion of his leg. But he got results, good results. What's more, he held forth as a most elusive runner, a reliable punter, and a fierce tackler. In essence, whatever needed doing, he could do it in winning fashion.

He graduated from the University of Virginia as the school's first All-America selection. This distinction afforded him the honor of being the Pittsburgh Steelers' top draft pick in 1942. His play, even as a rookie, made the team's officials look like so many geniuses. In his initial appearance with the Steelers, he tucked the ball under arm and ran 55 yards for a touchdown. The following weekend, he fielded a kickoff and went all the way with it. By season's end, he had rushed 162 times for 696 yards, both NFL bests, and was conferred All-Pro status.

The next two years, 1943 and 1944, he spent piloting B-29 bombers for the Army Air Corps in the South Pacific. When the war ended in 1945, he returned to the Steelers but played only briefly. He hit his stride again a year later, leading the league in rushing, punt returns, and interceptions. This feat, known as the Triple Crown, earned him further recognition as the NFL's Most Valuable Player. He was also named All-Pro for the second time.

Despite his attainments, the Steelers traded him to the Detroit Lions before the onset of the 1947 campaign. Reports had it that he and Pittsburgh head coach Jock Sutherland didn't get along all that well. In any event, the Lions welcomed him to the pride with a contract worth $25,000 annually, big money in those days. He finished his career with the Washington Redskins. During his first season in the nation's capital, he executed perhaps his most spectacular bit of broken-field running, returning a punt 96 yards for a touchdown. Ironically, it came at the expense of the Steelers.

In 1950 and 1951, Dudley received invitations to display his multiple skills in the newly instituted Pro Bowl on behalf of the American Conference team, a fitting finish to a most distinguished career.

Frank Gifford

6'1", 195 pounds. Halfback, Flanker: New York Giants (1952–1960, 1962–1964). All-Pro: 1955–1957, 1959. Pro Bowl: Seven appearances. NFL Player of the Year: 1956. NFL Comeback Player of the Year: 1962. Inducted into the Pro Football Hall of Fame 1977. Career: Rushing attempts, 840. Rushing yardage, 3,609. Yards per carry, 4.3. Touchdowns, 34. Receptions, 367. Receiving yardage, 5,434. Yards per reception, 14.8. Touchdowns (receiving), 43. Passes attempted, 63; passes completed, 29. Completion percentage, 46.0. Passing yardage, 823. Touchdowns (passing), 14. Interceptions, 6. Punt returns, 24. Return yardage, 118. Yards per return, 4.9. Touchdowns, 0. Kickoff returns, 18. Return yardage, 480. Yards per return, 26.7. Touchdowns, 0. Interceptions, 2. Return yardage, 112. Yards per return, 56.0. Touchdowns (interceptions), 1.

Frank Gifford

From the very outset of his tenure in the National Football League, Frank Gifford was a class act in an occupational endeavor not known for its refinement and urbanity. His performance was always impeccable, both on and off the field. Perhaps New York Giants executive Jack Mara put it best when he said, "Frank lent a certain dignity and tone to an entire organization."

In 1952, the Giants made Gifford their first pick in the college draft. He was fresh from the University of Southern California with All-America good looks and a gridiron reputation to match. He could do it all offensively and defensively, a truly versatile performer. During his first two years in the NFL, he did just that—everything. The coaching staff very nearly burned him out in his sophomore campaign, using him regularly on both sides of the ball and as a kick returner.

Ultimately, sanity prevailed when Vince Lombardi joined the New York franchise as an assistant coach in 1954 and promptly assigned Gifford exclusively to the offensive unit. A strong bond developed between the two men, and Gifford's career took off, as did the football fortunes of the Giants. He earned All-Pro honors four times thereafter and NFL Player of the Year in 1956. That same season, the Giants won the league championship and for nearly a decade held forth as the team to beat in the Eastern Division.

Recalling his sudden surge to prominence in the mid–1950s, Gifford said, "Everything I accomplished in this game I owe to Vince [Lombardi]. I considered him a very special man. The people who've written about him don't have a clue as to what he was really like. I tried to tell them about him, but I've given up on that. He made the difference between my being a good pro player and just another halfback."

Gifford was at the height of his powers in 1960 when a head injury nearly ended his playing days and his life. The near-fatal accident happened as the result of a crushing tackle by Philadelphia Eagles linebacker Chuck Bednarik. After the collision, Gifford lay still on the ground and had to be removed by stretcher. Giants linebacker Sam Huff remembers that awful moment vividly. "They took him off the field with a towel over his face," Huff said. "We all thought he was dead."

Bednarik also recalled the circumstances of that fateful day. "For years afterward a lot of people called it a cheap shot," he said. "It was just a good clean hit. When the hole opened, I was on the left side and stepped up to meet him coming through. His head was down, and we actually made contact straight on. I was 230 pounds, and he only weighed 190 or so. That made the difference. All the papers carried a picture the next day of me standing over Frank like I was celebrating. I didn't know he was hurt. He had fumbled, and we recovered to preserve a 17–10 lead. I still get asked about that hit to this day."

X-rays and neurological examinations revealed there had been some subcranial bleeding. Prior to the 1961 season, doctors gave Gifford clearance to play again, but he decided to retire. During that off year, he worked as a sportscaster with an eye to preparing for the future. But he missed football and returned to the Giants in the summer of 1962. Given the nature of his injury, it was decided he could be used most effectively as a flanker out where contact would likely take place on a more equitable basis.

Initially, he had difficulty adjusting to his new assignment. But hard work and determination paid off, and he finished the schedule as NFL Comeback Player of the Year. He went on to establish himself as a standout flanker. After the 1964 slate, he retired again, this time for good. He did so with the distinction of having been the only player to participate in seven Pro Bowls at three positions—defensive back, halfback, and flanker (wide receiver).

Today, he is a nationally known network sports personality.

Harold "Red" Grange

6'0", 185 pounds. Halfback: Chicago Bears (1925), New York Yankees (1926, AFL), New York Yankees (1927, NFL), Chicago Bears (1929–1934). Inducted into the Pro Football Hall of Fame 1963 (charter member). All-America: University of Illinois (1923–1925).

Although Red Grange's glory days in the National Football League were minimal, his impact on the pro game was maximal. He served as the NFL's first major gate attraction, the man who initially got the turnstiles clicking persistently and set the precedent for the success the league enjoys today.

During his college days at the University of Illinois, he was the most storied running back in the land, his wraithlike feints and dodges leaving opponents grappling with air and their fondest fantasies. Thus he became known as the Galloping Ghost, and his number 77 constituted the most familiar double digit in America's mathematics primer.

Grange's name was box-office big time, and this fact of football life didn't escape George Halas, proprietor of the Chicago Bears. In those days, college stars did not readily gravitate to the pros as in the modern era. And the reason couldn't have been more basic: no lucrative contracts as commonplace today, and the money game prevailed as something of a pimply faced pretender to legitimacy in many people's minds. Halas also knew this, and it was just another goad to get Grange into a Bears uniform.

Much as it went against his grain, Halas dug deep to sign Grange in 1925, just 10 days after he had doffed Illinois colors for the last time, but it was an investment that paid handsome dividends almost immediately. When Grange first trotted onto the turf of Wrigley Field to work his running magic against the Chicago Cardinals, there were 36,000 worshipers on hand to accord him a throaty welcome to the NFL. It was Thanksgiving Day. Later that season, the Bears took on the New York Giants at the Polo Grounds to the roar of 70,000 fans. Pro football was officially on its way.

C.C. "Cash and Carry" Pyle, Grange's agent, possessed about as acute a homing sense for folding legal tender as anyone. He had only to glimpse the crowds turning out to see Grange wearing Chicago moleskins, and his mind, operating in cash-register fashion, promptly conceived of a barnstorming tour at season's end which would not only sell the league to the paying populace, a trump card to deal Halas, but amply line his pockets and those of his client.

The tour consisted of 18 contests, 9 in the first 17 days, and snaked its way across the country to the West Coast. In Los Angeles, the Bears played before 75,000 onlookers in the cavernous confines of the Coliseum.

Harold "Red" Grange

Overall, the Chicago troupe with Grange starring put more than 400,000 fans in the seats. When the brutal sojourn finally finished, it was January 31, 1926.

Negotiations between Halas and Pyle concerning Grange's second-year contract reached a stalemate, so the opportunistic front man started the rival American Football League (AFL). Its principal franchise was dubbed the New York Yankees and featured Grange. Hastily contrived, the league just as hastily destructed, with only the Yankees, given Grange's considerable presence, making anything resembling a profit. In 1927, the Yankees were absorbed into the NFL, but, ironically, Grange severely damaged a knee against the Bears and never regained his unparalleled running ability.

"I was just an ordinary ball carrier after that," he admitted later. "I missed the entire 1928 season. And when I came back, I couldn't begin to do the things that before came so easily."

At the onset of the 1929 campaign, Grange joined the Bears once more. He remained with them through 1934, developing into a fine defensive back. His tackle in the waning moments of the 1933 NFL championship game prevented a Giants touchdown and preserved a 23–21 Chicago win.

Few personalities in the annals of sport have so captivated the public's imagination. It was fortunate indeed for the NFL that he came along at just the right time.

Joe Guyon

6'1", 180 pounds. Halfback: Canton Bulldogs (1919, 1920), Cleveland Indians (1921), Oorang Indians (1922, 1923, NFL), Rock Island Independents (1924), Kansas City Cowboys (1924, 1925), New York Giants (1927). Inducted into the Pro Football Hall of Fame 1966.

In death as in life, Joe Guyon has been overshadowed by the only other full-blooded American Indian to become enshrined in the Hall of Fame—Jim Thorpe.

He and Thorpe were teammates on four National Football League teams, and the story was always the same. Thorpe got the notoriety even though Guyon was equally talented and, all things considered, perhaps an even more versatile athlete. Not until his very last year in the NFL did he manage to claim the spotlight for himself.

Born of the Chippewa tribe on the White Earth Indian Reservation in Minnesota, he was able to advance only to the sixth grade under the auspices of the U.S. government. From there he went to the Carlisle (Pa.) Indian School and as a 20-year-old upperclassman played on the institution's 1912 national championship team. He later enrolled at Georgia Tech and was a member of the 1917 Ramblin' Wrecks squad which won the national collegiate title.

In 1919, he joined the Canton Bulldogs and held forth with them as a triple-threat back and a defensive standout for two seasons. Thereafter he went to the Cleveland Indians for the 1921 campaign. Once again, in 1922 and 1923, he and Thorpe shared a backfield, this time with the Oorang Indians. He was the prime offensive threat and the club's most prolific scorer, but as usual, Thorpe, as player-coach, garnered the headlines.

Late in 1924 they parted company for good when Guyon left the Rock Island Independents for the Kansas City Cowboys. He remained with the Cowboys until the close of the 1925 slate and then went his separate way. Finally, in 1927, he got his long-awaited chance to play in a major metro center. He signed on with the New York Giants, who were well stocked with veteran performers and priming for a rush to the top of the league standings. Defense was the name of the game for the Giants as they shut out 10 of 13 opponents. Offensively, Guyon showed to best advantage — passing, running, and punting — and was the prime mover behind what points the New Yorkers did put on the scoreboard.

A classic example of his importance to the team was amply demonstrated in a pivotal game against the Chicago Bears late in the season. He was engineering a sustained drive when George Halas, the Bears' player-coach, broke through the offensive line from his end position and bore down on him. Just as it appeared Halas would administer a crippling tackle, Guyon whirled around and extended a knee in protective fashion. It caught the charging Halas full in the chest, cracking four of his ribs. Then, adding insult to injury, Guyon fell to the turf and writhed in pain, pretending that he had suffered a particularly vicious hit. His emoting elicited the hoped-for response. The Bears were whistled for a 15-yard unnecessary-roughness penalty, and Halas went to the hospital for repairs. Moments later, Guyon threw a touchdown pass that gave the Giants a 13–7 victory and their first league crown. It was his finest hour.

Guyon's belated rise to pominence, despite disadvantaged circumstances and the strictures traditionally imposed upon minorities, constitutes a study in courage and determination that is a lesson worthy of study for the ages.

He died on November 27, 1971, at 79.

Franco Harris

6'2", 225 pounds. Running Back: Pittsburgh Steelers (1972–1983), Seattle Seahawks (1984). All-Pro: 1977. Pro Bowl: Nine appearances. Inducted into the Pro Football Hall of Fame 1990. Career: Rushing attempts, 2,949. Rushing yardage, 12,120. Yards per carry, 4.1. Touchdowns, 91. Receptions, 307. Receiving yardage, 2,287. Yards per reception, 7.5. Touchdowns (receiving), 9.

It's rare that an athlete, especially one of noteworthy attainment, suffers a loss of identity due to his affiliation with a particularly stirring play which occurred under uniquely memorable circumstances, but this is exactly what happened to Franco Harris.

The year was 1972, and the Pittsburgh Steelers trailed the Oakland Raiders 7–6 at Three Rivers Stadium with time running out in a first-round American Football Conference (AFC) playoff game. Pittsburgh quarterback Terry Bradshaw put aloft a desperation pass intended for running back John "Frenchy" Fuqua, who was racing downfield. But Oakland safety Jack Tatum leaped to intervene, and the ball struck him on the shoulder pad, rebounding backward. There waiting to receive it was Harris. Cradling the ball against his chest, he scurried into the end zone to give the Steelers a come-from-behind 13–7 victory. Since then, his unscheduled catch has gone down in the annals of pro football as the Immaculate Reception and bodes to outlive him as a subject of discussion.

Equally unique is the fact that no one actually saw the ball strike Tatum on the shoulder pad, thereby legalizing Harris's catch, save for umpire Pat Harder. "When we [game officials] huddled after the play," Harder recounted, "our crew chief (referee) asked if any of us actually saw what had happened. I was the only one who saw it. When the ball went up, I turned and followed it with my eye all the way. A kind of tunnel opened up among the players, and I distinctly saw the ball hit Tatum on the shoulder and rebound into Harris's hands. I made the call on that one before thousands in the stands and millions more on television. That was the biggest call of my seventeen years as an NFL official."

As for Harris, then a rookie, it sufficed as a happy happenstance which rewarded him for his dedication and hustle. "I just ran down there hoping I could help out in some way," he confessed, "to make something happen. Suddenly the ball popped up, and I simply caught it and ran in for the touchdown."

Unlike other players touched by the divine, Harris prevailed as a bona fide standout just embarking upon the road to superstardom. He finished the 1972 campaign with 1,055 yards rushing, only the fifth first-year performer to do so in NFL history. Earlier, during the fifth game of the season, he came off the bench and ran for 115 yards on 19 carries, leading the Steelers to a 24–7 win over the Houston Oilers. Thereafter he gained more than 100 yards in six successive outings while Pittsburgh went on a 5–1 winning streak. Sighs of relief could be heard from the coaching staff.

He had been drafted out of Penn State University with a reputation for

Franco Harris

being a big-play performer. But his behavior in training camp did little to assure the front office that he was going to develop in this mode. Steelers offensive backfield coach Dick Hoak put into words what all his associates were thinking. "We thought maybe we had a dud," he said. "Franco would burn up the first thirty yards in the forty-yard dash, and then coast in. Everything he did, walk, talk, practice, seemed to be in slow motion."

As the preseason developed, Harris gradually accelerated his pace until he broke a 70-yard jaunt in an exhibition game and served notice he was approaching the proper mental state. On that occasion, he bowled over an opposing linebacker, faked out two more defenders, then tromped on the gas. By the time the regular schedule arrived, he had more than allayed the fears of the Pittsburgh hierarchy.

"I don't ever recall seeing him get caught from behind," Hoak said. "He was a 225-pounder who ran like he weighed 195 pounds."

For most of the 1973 slate, injuries slowed him to a trot, and he closed out the season with just 698 yards on the ground. But he came roaring back the following year, carrying for 1,006 yards and proving highly instrumental in the Steelers' drive to the AFC title and victory in Super Bowl IX. He scored twice in the conference championship game and won Most Valuable Player honors for his then Super Bowl rushing record of 158 yards.

When Pittsburgh annexed Super Bowls X, XIII, and XIV, he also played a major role in this all-conquering scenario. "Franco was the guy who really lifted the Steelers to a new plateau, a level of confidence that made us believe we could win," said "Mean Joe" Greene, an All-Pro defensive tackle for the Steelers during that era. "Franco did things for our offense that nobody else had done in the four or five years I had been there."

Added Pittsburgh Hall of Fame linebacker Jack Ham: "The constant factor became our running game—in bad weather, in good weather, in wind, whatever, you could always count on Harris and our running game."

In the course of his 13 years in the pro game, Harris carried 2,949 times for 12,120 yards and 91 touchdowns. He also caught 307 passes for 2,287 yards and 9 TDs, and owned or shared 24 NFL records. To date, he remains No. 4 in rushing output and combined running and receiving yardage (14,622). In addition, he prevails as one of only six players to score 100 touchdowns. He has eight 1,000-yard seasons to his credit and forty-seven 100-yard games. He was the leading ground gainer in 13 of 19 playoff contests, carrying 400 times for 1,556 yards and 16 TDs. He logged 101 running attempts in four Super Bowls for 354 yards and 4 six-pointers. Even more important, the Steelers never suffered a losing campaign while he worked for them.

With the advent of the 1980s, Harris drew ever closer to the all-time NFL rushing mark of 12,312 yards established by legendary Cleveland running back Jim Brown. Doubtless he would have caught the "Browns' bomber" had not the 1982 campaign been cut short by a players' strike, costing him any number of ball-carrying opportunities. He did pick up 1,007 yards in 1983 yet still lacked 363 yards. In 1984, he became involved in a contract dispute with the Pittsburgh front office and was released. He then signed with Seattle but played in only eight games for the Seahawks, adding just 170 yards to his total. At the close of that schedule, he retired.

Clarke Hinkle

5'11", 201 pounds. Fullback: Green Bay Packers (1932–1941). All-Pro: 1936–1938, 1941. NFL Scoring Leader: 1938. Inducted into the Pro Football Hall of Fame 1964. Career: Rushing attempts, 1,171. Rushing yardage, 3,860. Yards per carry, 3.3. Touchdowns, 33. Passes attempted, 54. Passes completed, 24. Completion percentage, 44.4. Passing yardage, 316. Touchdowns (passing), 2. Punts, 87. Yards per punt, 43.4. Placekicking, 31 PATs, 28 field goals. Total points, 115.

Pound for pound, Clarke Hinkle was one of the hardest-hitting backs in the history of pro football. He never went around people when going over them was just as easy, being forever on the lookout for a challenge, real or imagined.

As a fullback with the Green Bay Packers from 1932 to 1941, he frequently had occasion to encounter archrival Bronko Nagurski of the Chicago Bears. Though a good 30 pounds lighter than the storied Bronk, he never hesitated to take on his granitelike adversary when circumstances dictated that they should meet head-on.

In one game involving the Bears and the Packers, he found himself trapped along the sideline by the powerful Nagurski. Undaunted, he simply lowered his head and went at his big opponent in battering-ram fashion. Nagurski had to be helped from the field in a semiconscious state, having suffered a broken nose and a fractured rib. Hinkle reasoned, "I have to get the Bronk before he gets me."

But he prevailed as more than just a hard-nosed thumping ball carrier. He also commanded the speed to get outside and turn the corner upfield for a long gainer at any time. He could throw and catch with equal facility and excelled as a punter and placekicker. When called upon to block, he numbered among the best practitioners of this chore, particularly in pass-protection situations. Defensively, he held forth at linebacker, presenting a terror to both running backs and receivers. He once boasted that only a single pass was caught behind him in 10 years.

In spite of his many gridiron skills, the former Bucknell University All-American managed largely to escape the attention of the pro scouting gentry during the course of his collegiate career. However, he blew his cover, so to speak, by being the leading ground gainer in the East-West Shrine Game of 1932. Packers head coach "Curly" Lambeau was on hand for the postseason classic in San Francisco and promptly made Hinkle a $125-per-game offer to play for Green Bay. The deal was closed right there.

By the end of his decade-long stint with the Packers in 1941, Hinkle had his name inscribed in the National Football League record book any number of times. But each entry was methodically expunged years after his retirement as rules changes and new techniques inexorably altered the very fabric of the game. Still, he earned All-Pro recognition four times and did more things well on a football field than all but a very few of his fellow Hall of Fame inductees.

Paul Hornung

6'2", 220 pounds. Halfback: Green Bay Packers (1957–1962, 1964–1966). All-Pro: 1960, 1961. Pro Bowl: Two appearances. NFL Most Valuable Player: 1960, 1961. NFL Leading

Scorer: 1959–1961. NFL All-Time Single-Season Leading Scorer: 1960 (176 points). Inducted into the Pro Football Hall of Fame 1986. Career: Scoring: 62 TDs, 190 PATs, 66 FGs. Total points 760. Rushing attempts, 893. Rushing yardage, 3,711. Yards per carry, 4.2. Touchdowns, 50. Receptions, 130. Receiving yardage, 1,480. Yards per reception, 11.4. Touchdowns (receiving), 12. Passes attempted, 55. Passes completed, 24. Completions percentage, 43.6. Passing yardage, 383. Touchdowns (passing), 5. Interceptions, 4. Kickoff returns, 10. Return yardage, 248. Yards per return, 24.8. Touchdowns, 0.

The media referred to Paul Hornung as Golden Boy, and he was that, one of the most complete offensive players ever to gain admission to the Hall of Fame. He could score in many ways—running, passing, receiving, and kicking—and did, to set a National Football League record for the most points tallied in a season. Yet he had to overcome a tarnished image acquired off the field before full credit could be given him for his many contributions on the gridiron.

Hornung's blond good looks graced the covers of magazines the land over as a consensus All-America selection and Heisman Trophy winner while plying his considerable skills at Notre Dame. He was the versatile all-conquering quarterback of the immensely popular Fighting Irish and therefore commanded adulation from their considerable public akin to that normally accorded Celtic patron saints.

Thus it was something of a comedown to be a 1957 bonus pick of the lowly Green Bay Packers, then the resident walkovers of the NFL. His first two years in the outback of Wisconsin were anything but memorable. During his rookie and sophomore seasons, he spent the balance of his time shuffling back and forth between quarterback and halfback, taking a pounding in the process. Needless to say, he was no longer a news item, far from it. In fact, he became so despondent over his lot that serious contemplation was given to quitting pro football for the real world.

But in 1959, Vincent Lombardi took over as head coach of the Packers, and suddenly things began to turn around. One of his first official acts was to situate Hornung at left halfback permanently, a key role in the new offensive scheme of things. Almost immediately the former Notre Dame standout began to regain some of his luster, as did the Green Bay franchise overall, developing into a legitimate divisional power as in days of yore.

In 1960, the Packers reached the NFL championship game against the Philadelphia Eagles before succumbing 17–13. Hornung was a major factor in this success, setting an all-time scoring mark for the campaign with 176 points, and earned league Most Valuable Player honors. The following year he reclaimed the Most Valuable accolade and again topped all scorers for the third successive season, a playoff-high 19 points coming in the title contest as Green Bay began its nearly decade-long reign over the pro football roost. It was more of the status quo in 1962, the Packers retaining NFL supremacy and Hornung supplying much of the punch to their vaunted attack on the ground and through the air.

But just as the Golden Boy came back to the covers of the nation's sporting periodicals, he took an unexpected and nearly career-ending tumble from his lofty pedestal. An established lover of night life, with all of its glitzy trappings and shady denizens, he thoughtlessly became involved with gambling, some of it to do with NFL games, and merited suspension from the league for a year. So he spent 1963 out of uniform, dourly considering his folly and watching younger men steal his headlines. It sufficed as a sobering experience.

He was reinstated in 1964 and promptly rejoined the Packers in quest of his bygone excellence. On the year he scored 107 points, but Green Bay could do no better than a tie for runner-up status in the Western Conference. In 1965, the Packers rebounded back to the league pinnacle, and Hornung amply abetted their arrival there by scoring five touchdowns in a crucial regular-season encounter and then accounted for the winning TD in the championship game. He closed out his NFL tenure with sharply curtailed duties in 1966, having been significantly slowed by the effects of injuries sustained before and shortly after returning from his year's enforced sabbatical. But he remained long enough to be a part of Green Bay's triumph in Super Bowl I and to acquire a coveted championship ring, the first of a kind for a very special one of a kind.

John Henry Johnson

6'2", 225 pounds. Fullback: Calgary (1953, CFL), San Francisco 49ers (1954–1956, NFL), Detroit Lions (1957–1959), Pittsburgh Steelers (1960–1965), Houston Oilers (1966, AFL). All-Pro: 1962. Pro Bowl: Three appearances. Inducted into the Pro Football Hall of Fame 1987. Career: Rushing attempts, 1,571. Rushing yardage, 6,803. Yards per carry, 4.3. Touchdowns, 48. Receptions, 186. Receiving yardage, 1,478. Yards per reception, 7.9. Touchdowns (receiving), 7.

"John Henry was a steel drivin' man.
John Henry was gonna beat that hammer down, down,
Gonna beat that hammer down...."

The fabled John Henry of folklore and ballad is not the John Henry Johnson considered here, but there are definite similarities between the two. John Henry Johnson also did some driving and hammering, for the Steelers and several other clubs in three leagues. And when he hit people, with or without a ball under arm, the feeling he left them with was definitely one of having been hammered.

A couple of things set him apart from other fullbacks of his time. One, he had unusual speed for a 6'2", 225-pound power runner and used it like a breakaway back once in the open. Two, he held forth as an exceptional blocker, a task which elicited almost as much pride on his behalf as grinding out a short-yardage touchdown plunge.

While Johnson was enjoying his premier years with Pittsburgh, no one appreciated his contribution as a blocker any more than Bobby Layne, then the Steelers' signal caller of note. "John Henry is my bodyguard," Layne once stated. "Half the good runners will get a passer killed if you keep them around long enough. But a quarterback hits the jackpot when he gets a combination runner-blocker like Johnson."

When Johnson emerged from the college ranks in 1953, the Steelers had it in mind to make him their number-two draft pick of that year. But he disdained their overtures and headed north to the Canadian Football League (CFL) and signed with Calgary for more money. As a rookie, he became the CFL's Most Valuable Player, and this singular feat did not escape the notice of the San Francisco 49ers. They promptly obtained his rights from Pittsburgh and in short order convinced him that he should pack his gear and head for the City by the Bay.

He occupied the inside running spot the 49ers so much needed in a backfield that already included such gridiron luminaries as quarterback Y.A. Tittle and big-yardage threats Hugh "The King" McElhenny and Joe "The Jet" Perry. By the end of the 1954 campaign, Johnson had accumulated 681 yards rushing, second-best mark on the club, despite the fact he was often held in to block for Tittle and didn't get the ball-handling opportunities available to Perry and McElhenny.

Thereafter, Johnson's situation deteriorated somewhat due to injuries and a change in coaches. In 1957, he went to the Detroit Lions where conditions proved to be no better for him. Finally, in 1960, he found his way to the Steelers. With Pittsburgh he had his number called more often and responded by crunching out 1,000-yard seasons in 1962 and 1964, an accomplishment that didn't happen that much back then.

Following the 1965 schedule, he displayed his wares in still another league, the American Football League (AFL), as the property of the Houston Oilers. At the conclusion of that slate, he retired, then pro football's number-four rusher all-time.

Alphonse "Tuffy" Leemans

6'0", 200 pounds. Halfback, Fullback: New York Giants (1936–1943). All-Pro: 1936, 1939. NFL Rushing Leader: 1936. Inducted into the Pro Football Hall of Fame 1978. Career: Rushing attempts, 919. Rushing yardage, 3,142. Yards per carry, 3.4. Touchdowns, 17. Passes attempted, 383. Passes completed, 167. Completion percentage,

43.6. Passing yardage, 2,234. Touchdowns (passing), 25. Interceptions, 32. Receptions, 28. Receiving yardage, 422. Yards per reception, 15.1. Touchdowns (receiving), 3. Punt returns, 19. Return yardage, 262. Yards per return, 13.8. Touchdowns, 0. Interceptions, 3. Return yardage, 35. Yards per return, 11.7. Touchdowns, 0.

The nickname Tuffy fit Alphonse Emil Leemans like the proverbial glove. He preferred it to the rather baroque handle his parents afforded him. He was indeed a tough multipurpose running back who gave the New York Giants not only their primary offensive impetus but much of their identity during the team's championship years of the late 1930s and early 1940s.

Like a lot of college standouts in that era who plied their football skills at schools with less than national reputations, he didn't rate the attention from the pro scouts his abilities deserved while at George Washington University. Because of the rather catch-as-catch-can methods employed by NFL talent hunters in those days, he might have been passed over altogether had it not been for the fact that the son of Giants owner Tim Mara saw him play. The occasion was a game in which Leemans showed to advantage against the University of Alabama. What young Wellington Mara saw that day prompted him to tell his father about the triple-threat back. As a result, the New York club took him in the second round of the 1936 draft.

In his first play-for-pay outing, the College All-Star game, Leemans earned Most Valuable Player honors. Thereafter, he joined the Giants and promptly became a star, leading the league in rushing as a rookie. He carried the ball 206 times for 830 yards and two touchdowns that year. He also threw for three scores in addition to serving as a receiver and a punt returner. When the ball changed hands, he stayed on the field to perform as a secondary defender. These heroics got him elected to All-Pro status, the only newcomer to rate this distinction.

During his tenure with the Giants, he doubled as a halfback and a fullback, mixing his running routes inside and outside. The club also made use of two platoons back then, each unit playing an equal time on offense and defense, and he was no exception to this rule. While he held forth in his varied capacities, the New York franchise won three Eastern Division titles and the 1938 NFL championship. In 1943, he functioned as a player-coach and earned the top salary of his eight-year career—$12,000.

The fact that he didn't have the good fortune to play in the modern NFL when his versatility would have been worth six or seven figures was not a source of regret to him. "I just loved the game," he once confessed. "I knew a lot of players back then, myself included, who would have played for nothing."

He retired following the 1943 campaign. On January 19, 1979, he died at 66.

George McAfee

6'0", 177 pounds. Halfback: Chicago Bears (1940, 1941, 1945–1950). All-Pro: 1941. Induced into the Pro Football Hall of Fame 1966. Career: Rushing attempts, 341. Rushing yardage, 1,685. Yards per carry, 4.9. Touchdowns, 22. Receptions, 85. Receiving yardage, 1,357. Yards per reception, 16.0. Touchdowns (receiving), 10. Passes attempted, 22. Passes completed, 6. Completion percentage, 27.2. Passing yardage, 94. Touchdowns (passing), 1. Interceptions, 1. Punt returns, 112. Return yardage, 1,431. Yards per return, 12.78. Touchdowns (punt returns), 2. Kickoff returns, 11. Return yardage, 265. Yards per return, 24.1. Touchdowns, 0. Punts, 39. Yards per punt, 36.9. Interceptions, 21. Return yardage, 294. Yards per return, 14.0. Touchdowns (interceptions), 1.

Just like Gale Sayers two decades later, George McAfee shone briefly though brilliantly before fading from the National Football League firmament. But just like Sayers, also a Chicago Bears running back, he glittered so brightly in the short period allotted him that it proved sufficient to earn his induction into the Hall of Fame.

An All-America selection at Duke University, he was the Bears' number-one draft pick in 1940. However, even as team owner and coach George Halas made his choice, he harbored doubts about McAfee's being able to make it in the NFL. These misgivings had nothing to do with the young recruit's capacity to perform. He carried the ball with a fleet-footed surety, could come out of the backfield and make the clutch catch, and possessed the elusive moves and courage to be a quick-strike threat as a kick returner. Ability he had in spades.

No, it was his physical endurance which concerned Halas. Papa Bear wondered if the slim speedster could hold up under the pounding routinely administered to running backs in the NFL. McAfee stood 6'0" tall and weighed 177 pounds, acceptable dimensions for the man on the street but not for heavy-duty service in pro football. But Halas's fears were quickly dispersed once the Chicago training camp opened and he saw the former Duke star perform. McAfee easily outmanuevered heavier, more imposing defenders and darted to daylight with the innate sense for preservation of a hunted rabbit. Watching him run, Halas not only ceased to worry but congratulated himself for being such a perceptive judge of talent.

From day one, McAfee didn't need to be told what his role with the Bears involved. He was expected to make the big plays, whether taking a handoff, catching a pass, or fielding a kick. Once his teammates got him into the clear, he would be expected to make things happen and if at all possible, put points on the scoreboard.

Despite his triple-threat potential, he didn't break into the starting lineup immediately. In fact, much of his rookie season was spent sitting on the bench watching and waiting. He received the same treatment as a second-year man in 1941. This state of affairs prevailed because the Bears had experienced personnel at every position. Still, he made good use of the limited opportunities afforded him during his sophomore season and managed to gain All-Pro recognition.

In 1942, with the United States fully immersed in World War II, he joined the navy and spent the duration of the conflict serving his country. These were prime football years lost to him, years never to be recaptured, so what he might have accomplished in a Chicago uniform instead of navy blue can only be the subject of conjecture. He rejoined the Bears late into the 1945 NFL campaign. The next season he saw only limited action due to a variety of injuries. But from 1947 to 1950, he played without serious interruption and was universally referred to as One-Play McAfee, given his penchant for scoring from anywhere on the field.

Again like Sayers, he displayed an amazing versatility. Besides his ordinary chores of running the ball, catching passes, and returning kicks, he threw successfully on the halfback-option series, punted creditably, and conducted himself with distinction in the defensive secondary.

Until just a few years ago, McAfee boasted the best punt-return average in NFL annals—12.78 yards. In 1940, he ran back a punt 75 yards for a touchdown; later that year, he broke a 93-yard kickoff return. Still later, he scampered 34 yards with a stolen pass to register another six points. The designation One-Play McAfee was well deserved.

Hugh McElhenny

6'1", 198 pounds. Running Back: San Francisco 49ers (1952–1960), Minnesota Vikings (1961, 1962), New York Giants (1963), Detroit Lions (1964). All-Pro: 1952, 1954. Pro Bowl: Six appearances. NFL Rookie of the Year: 1952. Inducted into the Pro Football Hall of Fame 1970. Career: Rushing attempts, 1,124. Rushing yardage, 5,281. Yards per carry, 4.7. Touchdowns, 38. Receptions, 264. Receiving yardage, 3,247. Yards per reception, 12.3. Touchdowns (receiving), 20. Punt returns, 126. Return yardage, 920. Yards per return, 7.3. Touchdowns (returns), 2. Kickoff returns, 83. Return yardage, 1,921. Yards per return, 23.1. Touchdowns, 0.

Like a rabbit on a hot road, Hugh McElhenny scurried hither and yon with such unpredictable precision that would-be tacklers were routinely left grappling with an armful of air and evidencing somewhat sheepish expressions. Nicknamed The King, he held forth as perhaps the greatest broken-field runner ever to play football for money.

When he came out of the University of Washington with All-America credentials in 1952, the San Francisco 49ers promptly designated him as their number-one pick in the college draft. Inside of a year he did much more than simply justify their confidence in him. He made them look like nothing short of prophets.

On his initial play from scrimmage as a pro, he ran 42 yards for a touchdown. And then things got even better. Later that season, in the course of returning a punt, he managed to scamper 94 yards for another TD. Shortly thereafter, he swivel-hipped his way 89 yards through the opposition in spectacular fashion to record six more points. For the year, he logged 1,731 yards with the ball under arm and crossed the opponents' goal line 10 times. He notched 684 of these yards by rushing, his per-carry average of 7.0 yards representing the best such effort in the National Football League. The balance of his output came from 26 pass receptions netting 367 yards and kick returns totaling 680 yards.

Given this phenomenal performance, he was NFL Rookie of the Year and garnered support in some quarters as the league's Player of the Year. He also was a consensus All-Pro selection and scored two touchdowns in his first Pro Bowl appearance. There just wasn't much more he could have done other than outrace a speeding bullet or leap over buildings in a single bound. His exciting heroics sent the turnstiles to clicking, putting people in the seats where they had stayed away in droves before. This sudden influx of revenues served to shore up a tottering franchise, and thus the 49ers' front office personnel looked upon him as nothing less than money in the bank.

Following the 1960 campaign, he was traded to the newly formed Minnesota Vikings, and with the fledgling "purple gang" he enjoyed one of his more productive seasons, accumulating 1,067 yards of the all-purpose variety and rating a sixth trip to the Pro Bowl. But a decade of dipping, dodging, twisting, and turning had taken its toll. The constant grinding together of the thigh- and shinbones at their point of juncture had actually worn away the cartilages in both knees. What enemy defenses were unable to accomplish McElhenny did to himself with his unusual running style.

In 1963, he moved on to the New York Giants and finally realized his dream of playing with a championship club. That year the Giants finished atop the Eastern Conference standings with an 11–3 record before losing a 14–10 decision to the Chicago Bears for the NFL title. Due to his physical problems, he saw only spot duty but still filled in admirably when called upon as a ball carrier, receiver, and kick returner.

Said Giants coach Allie Sherman: "Because Hugh's knees were shot, we could only use him sparingly. As always, though, he gave us his very best in whatever we asked him to do."

McElhenny closed out his sparkling career with the Detroit Lions in 1964 as only a shadow of his former self. His knees simply were no longer able to support one of the greatest running talents ever to grace the pro game. In 13 seasons, he gained 11,375 yards in a variety of roles, just one of three players in NFL annals to carry a football that far, and scored 60 touchdowns.

Hugh McElhenny—The King indeed.

John "Blood" McNally

6'0", 185 pounds. Halfback: Milwaukee Badgers (1925, 1926), Duluth Eskimos (1926, 1927), Pottsville Maroons (1928), Green Bay Packers (1929–1933, 1935, 1936), Pittsburgh Pirates (1934, 1937–1939). Inducted into the Pro Football Hall of Fame 1963 (charter member).

There was a time when America wore its shirt open at the collar, callused hands were considered a social attribute, and lunch did come free for the price of a cool brew. Such was the time when John "Blood" McNally plied his considerable skills in the National Football League with all the color and diversity so characteristic of the Roarin' Twenties.

His life and experiences were the stuff of which period novels are made. As a boy, he evidenced an intellect beyond the ordinary, completing high school while still a callow youth of 14. Though small and somewhat immature for his years, he grew quickly in both stature and savvy as a student at St. John's College of Minnesota. While an upperclassman, he captained the basketball team and lettered in football, baseball, and track.

During his senior year, a curious interlude served as an entree to his long association with the NFL. He and a friend were out walking one day when they chanced to pass a movie theater. Inadvertently, his eyes were drawn to the marquee and the title of the featured film, *Blood and Sand*. Like an electric shock, the answer to how he could preserve his college eligibility and still make money playing football came to him. He would use an assumed name. "That's it," he exclaimed to his friend. "I'll be Blood and you be Sand." And so the curtain rose on the brilliant but ofttimes zany career as Johnny Blood.

McNally (Blood) was a running back with sprinter's speed, good moves, and respectable power. He also doubled as an outstanding receiver and an accomplished passer and punter. Defensively, he had a nose for the ball and tackled with authority. In a nutshell, he could do it all. However, he didn't always do it all to the best of his ability. Should his team be the proprietor of a comfortable lead, he was given to loafing and even clowning a bit for the benefit of the fans.

Off the field he displayed a total disregard for training rules. He summarily ignored curfew, as it seriously impinged upon his nightly drinking excursions. Long after lights-out for the rest of the team, he could be found with a bottle of distilled spirits in hand and a collection of empties close around. Once, when he was the sparkplug of a fine Green Bay aggregation, Packers head coach "Curly" Lambeau offered him $10 more a game just to lay off the "happy juice." McNally politely declined the offer but did agree to go on the wagon after Wednesday of each week during the season.

When not occupied with professional football, he played a number of other roles in life, ranging from able-bodied seaman and bartender to poet, hotel desk clerk, and even a cryptographer in China. But his most memorable performances came on the gridiron. He wore the uniform of five clubs in the span of 15 years, but his best efforts were devoted to the Packers. Given his multitalented contribution, Green Bay methodically ground to league titles in 1929, 1930, 1931, and 1936. More than five decades later, he is still listed among the club's leading scorers with 224 points.

He closed out his remarkable NFL tenure in 1939 as player-coach of the Pittsburgh Pirates. In spite of his excesses, he lived to be 82, quitting this mortal coil on November 28, 1985.

Ollie Matson

6'2", 220 pounds. Halfback: Chicago Cardinals (1952, 1954–1958), Los Angeles Rams (1959–1962), Detroit Lions (1963), Philadelphia Eagles (1964–1966). All-Pro: 1954–1957. Pro Bowl: Five appearances. Inducted into the Pro Football Hall of Fame 1972. Career: Rushing attempts, 1,170. Rushing yardage, 5,173. Yards per carry, 4.4. Touchdowns, 40. Receptions, 222. Receiving yardage, 3,285. Yards per reception, 14.8. Touchdowns (receiving), 23. Kickoff returns, 143. Return yardage, 3,746. Yards per return, 26.2. Touchdowns (kickoff returns), 6. Punt returns, 65. Return yardage, 595. Yards per return, 9.2. Touchdowns (punt returns), 3. Passes attempted, 15. Passes completed, 5. Completion percentage, 33.3. Passing yardage, 119. touchdowns, 0. Interceptions, 1. Interceptions, 3. Return yardage, 51. Yards per return, 17.0. Touchdowns, 0.

One man does not a team make, but Ollie Matson did his best to disprove this aged axiom. Not unlike others of his fellow Hall of Fame colleagues, he labored throughout a lengthy career with teams that rightfully could have been sued for nonsupport and so never achieved the heady experience of playing with a championship aggregation. But this fact in no way diminished his marvelous achievements.

When he came into the National Football League in 1952, it was as an All-America standout from the University of San Francisco. He had speed to burn, having won bronze and goal medals the previous summer as a sprinter with the U.S. team in the Helsinki Olympics. Given these credentials, the Chicago Cardinals, his new employer, fully expected him to rescue the club from its lowly status. After all, what's a number-one draft pick for if not to perform a miracle or two. During his first season, he did produce, sharing NFL Rookie-of-the-Year recognition. He carried the ball 96 times for 344 yards and three touchdowns.

In 1953, he served a commitment to the army before resuming his football pursuits. For all intents and purposes, he sufficed as the Cardinals' offense not only as a running back but as a kick returner and receiver. He warranted All-Pro selection from 1954 through 1957 and an annual invitation to the Pro Bowl. By the end of the 1958 campaign, his last in the Windy City, he had rushed 761 times for 3,331 yards and 24 TDs, caught 130 balls for 2,150 yards and 16 scores, and topped once each the league's punt-and kickoff-return rankings.

The Los Angeles Rams picked him up in 1952 for the price of nine players. Out on the sun coast he continued to contribute as a triple threat on offense. Despite his yeoman contribution, the club remained mired deep in the second-division standings, so he moved on to the Detroit Lions for a season's span and then to the Philadelphia Eagles in 1964. While in the City of Brotherly Love, he served largely as a spot performer following his initial campaign with the club. Slowed by years of pounding as the principal weapon in the arsenal of four teams, he nevertheless had spurts of greatness left in him. Halfway into his last year with the Eagles he was beckoned from the bench in a game against San Francisco with the 49ers up 20–7. Time and again he wacked out needed yardage with a bygone gusto and capped off the afternoon with a leaping TD reception that gave Philadelphia a come-from-behind 35–34 win. It was a fitting exit for one of the pro game's most gifted practitioners.

Bobby Mitchell

6'0", 195 pounds. Running Back, Wide Receiver: Cleveland Browns (1958–1961), Washington Redskins (1962–1968). All-Pro: 1962, 1964. Pro Bowl: Four appearances. Inducted into the Pro Football Hall of Fame 1983. Career: Receptions, 521. Reception yardage, 7,954. Yards per reception, 15.3. Touchdowns, 65. Rushing attempts, 513. Rushing yardage, 2,735. Yards per carry, 5.3. Touchdowns (rushing), 18. Kickoff returns, 102. Return yardage, 2,690. Yards per return, 26.4. Touchdowns (kickoff returns), 5. Punt returns, 69. Return yardage, 699. Yards per return, 10.1. Touchdowns (punt returns), 3. Passes attempted, 3. Passes completed, 3. Completion percentage, 100. Passing yardage, 61. Touchdowns (passing), 1. Interceptions, 0.

In truth, Bobby Mitchell led two football lives during his 11-year career in the National Football League, first as a running back and later as a flanker, excelling in both capacities, given his diversity of talent and physical ability.

He prevailed as a big-play threat anytime his hands touched the ball.

Not only did he possess sprinter's speed, but he commanded a variety of moves that more often than not left defenders off balance and out of position. While attending the University of Illinois, he had nurtured dreams of trying out for the 1960 U.S. Olympic team but abandoned them when the Cleveland Browns nodded in his direction.

If he harbored any doubt about being able to make the grade in the pro game, it concerned his size. At 6'0" and 195 pounds, he felt his most effective role would be as a wide receiver, but the Browns needed a halfback, and that was that. He paired up with the incomparable Jim Brown to give the Cleveland franchise the most potent ground attack in the league. During his rookie campaign, he rushed for 232 yards in one contest, going inside and outside with quick, darting facility.

The Browns also utilized him as a kick returner, and here again he dazzled them with his footwork. In the course of his freshman season, he ran back a kickoff 95 yards to paydirt and shortly thereafter scampered 78 yards with a punt. Another big plus for Cleveland was his knack for coming out of the backfield and making the money catch. He could read defenses like a book and would sucker the opposition into a mismatch. This accomplished, he simply beat his cover man to a weak point in the defense, gathered in the pass, and then lit up all the burners en route to the distant goal line.

Following the 1961 schedule, he moved to Washington in a trade, and so began his second football life. With the Redskins he got his wish to be a wide receiver and made the most of the opportunity. His initial season in the nation's capital, he caught 72 aerials for 1,384 yards, both league bests in 1962, and scored 11 touchdowns courtesy of a per-reception average of 19.2 yards. In addition, he saw spot duty as a running back with patented effectiveness.

Upon coming to Washington, he earned another distinction of sorts. He was the first black player to remain with the Redskins for any length of time. The experience was anything but gratifying. Somehow he managed to shrug off the ever-present burden of discrimination that blighted his off-field life and could still play all-out on Sunday afternoons. But the lessons of that era were not forgotten and still profoundly affect his social consciousness.

He earned All-Pro honors in 1962 and 1964 and received four Pro Bowl invitations. Before the onset of the 1969 season, he retired and joined the Redskins' front office. Currently he is assistant general manager of the club, one of the few black executives in the NFL.

Leonard "Lenny" Moore

6'1", 198 pounds. Flanker, Running Back: Baltimore Colts (1956–1967). All-Pro: 1958–1961, 1964. Pro Bowl: Six appearances. NFL Comeback Player of the Year: 1964.

Inducted into the Pro Football Hall of Fame 1975. Career: Rushing attempts, 1,069. Rushing yardage, 5,174. Yards per carry, 4.8. Touchdowns, 63. Receptions, 363. Receiving yardage, 6,039. Yards per reception, 16.6. Touchdowns (receiving), 42. Passes attempted, 12. Passes completed, 3. Completion percentage, 25.0. Passing yardage, 33. Touchdowns (passing), 2. Punt returns, 14. Return yardage, 56. Yards per return, 4.0. Touchdowns, 0. Kickoff returns, 49. Return yardage, 1,180. Yards per return, 24.1. Touchdowns (kickoff returns), 1.

In the parlance of the prize ring, Lenny Moore was a combination artist, a guy who could hurt you in a number of ways. During his tenure in the National Football League, the opponents of the Baltimore Colts felt the same way whenever "Sputnik" was on the field as a running back, receiver, or a kick returner. No matter the role, he always found a way to make the big play.

At the outset, the Colts weren't all that sure they wanted the Penn State product. It was nearing the time they would be making their picks in the 1956 NFL draft, and some of them felt he might not prove durable enough for the pro game. They reasoned that his 198 pounds fit kind of sparingly on a 6'1" frame, hardly the build that traditionally absorbed the Sunday poundings so well. Maybe he'd prove to be overly brittle and injury-prone.

Once again, the Baltimore front office put in a call to Penn State seeking assurance that Moore had the physique to make the grade in the bigs. The response came from then assistant coach Joe Paterno, who said, "Tell [Colts head coach] Weeb Ewbank not to miss this guy, because if he does, it will be the greatest mistake he could ever make."

The club elevated Moore to its first pick, and he never gave anyone cause to second-guess his lofty selection. During the 12 seasons he wore Baltimore's blue-and-white battle ensemble, his performance earned him All-Pro recognition five times and six invitations to the Pro Bowl. He tallied 113 touchdowns by a variety of means, evidencing a nose for the end zone that is rarely seen among the finest of offensive practitioners. In 1964 alone he crossed the opposition goal line in 11 successive games and scored 20 TDs overall. He could go all the way on any down and not infrequently did, as perhaps one of the most complete performers ever to line up on the attack side of the ball.

Initially, he saw action as both a flanker and a ball carrier, but his primary responsibility was as a receiver coming out of the backfield. He excelled in this capacity, especially when Johnny Unitas took over as quarterback for the Colts. The two of them led Baltimore to bookend NFL titles in 1958 and 1959, dazzling the enemy with their pitch-and-catch derring-do.

Moore was particularly effective in 1958, rushing for 598 yards and a league-leading attempt average of 7.3 yards. He also caught 50 aerials worth 938 yards and had a per-reception average of 18.8 yards. In all, he gained 1,633 yards and notched 14 touchdowns. Against the New York Giants for the NFL championship, generally referred to "as the greatest game ever played," he hauled in six passes for 101 yards, one of them being a 60-yard scoring shot that got the hostilities under way. He also ran "sweeps" to either side that kept the New York defense spread out and the middle open for Unitas's underneath offerings.

In 1959, he prevailed in only slightly less spectacular fashion by accounting for 1,268 yards total offense and 8 TDs. He continued to do yeoman duty in 1960 and 1961, exceeding the 1,000-yard mark for total offense both seasons. But he underwent a position change in 1962 with the arrival on scene of young receiver Johnny Orr. He moved into the backfield, and Orr was given his flanker post. In this restricted capacity he carried the ball more frequently and only rarely figured in the passing game. He promptly began to absorb more punishment, his native speed and agility negated by the inside routes routinely assigned to him. This pounding took its toll in 1963, relegating him to the sidelines for all but seven of the scheduled games.

But Moore had never been a quitter or a complainer. In 1964, he experienced perhaps his finest year by accentuating the positive. He rushed 157 times for 584 yards and 16 touchdowns. And even though no more passes came his way than usual, he managed to work them into long gainers. He caught just 21 balls, the same number as the previous campaign, but picked up 472 yards given an average reception of 22.5 yards. This effort and determination earned him NFL Comeback of the Year honors and All-Pro status for the fifth time.

He retired after the 1967 season.

Marion Motley

6'2", 238 pounds. Fullback: Cleveland Browns (1946–1949, AAFC), Cleveland Browns (1950–1953, NFL), Pittsburgh Steelers (1955). All-Pro: 1950. Pro Bowl: One appearance. Inducted into the Pro Football Hall of Fame 1968. Career: Rushing attempts, 828. Rushing yardage, 4,720. Yards per carry, 5.7. Touchdowns, 31. Receptions, 85. Receiving yardage, 1,107. Yards per reception, 13.0. Touchdowns (receiving), 7. Kickoff returns, 48. Return yardage, 1,122. Yards per return, 23.4. Touchdowns, 0.

The slap of hide against hand ignited an explosion of mayhem. Rising from his backfield position, Marion Motley readied himself to block in an apparent pass-play scheme. Just as the protective pocket was shunting the defensive rush to the outside, he took a handoff and cradling the ball to his chest, bolted through the tangle of blockers. Once clear of the melee, he turned upfield, shedding an overmatched linebacker with the thrust of a brawny arm. Some yards further on, he thundered into a contingent of fast-closing defenders and finally went to ground, but not before notching yet another first down. Once more, Trap 34 had caught the opposition napping.

Coach Paul Brown of the Cleveland Browns had devised the play especially for his big fleet-footed power back, Motley. The two men went back a long way together. When Motley played football for McKinley High School in Canton, Ohio, the team lost only three games in as many years. But all these defeats were imposed by state rival Massillon High School, coached by Brown. Their paths crossed again during World War II at the navy's Great Lakes Training Center. During this encounter, Brown coached the facility's star-studded team, and Motley held forth as one of its brightest luminaries.

After receiving his discharge, Motley headed back to the University of Nevada intent upon completing his education and playing a little more football. But again Brown intervened in his life. "On my way out to Nevada, I got a call from Coach Brown," Motley related. "He told me about his forming a professional football team. And he asked me to play for him. So I turned around and went instead to Cleveland."

During the tenure of the All-America Football Conference (AAFC) from 1946 to 1949, the Cleveland Browns perennially topped the standings, with Motley supplying the bulk of the franchise's running attack while also performing at linebacker on defense. In 1948, he concentrated solely on his offensive duties and was the league rushing leader with 964 yards, 157 carries, and a per-attempt average of 6.1 yards. Once in possession of the ball, he ran out of a crouch, his shoulders bobbing rhythmically until contacting a would-be tackler. At that point he would raise up, lifting the hapless player off his feet, and then casually shed him like a dog ridding itself of a pesky flea.

When the AAFC dissolved after the 1949 season, the Browns were absorbed into the older and more prestigious National Football League. Prior to that, certain team owners in the NFL had publicly made disparaging remarks about the Cleveland aggregation, intimating that its gridiron attainments were tainted by "playing in a bush league." It was also openly speculated that the poorest NFL team would have no trouble handling the Browns. So in 1950, when Cleveland joined "their betters," it became put-up-or-shut-up time.

The Browns' opening game that year pitted them against the defending NFL champion Philadelphia Eagles. The contest took place in Philadelphia's cavernous Memorial (now JFK) Stadium before a crowd in excess of 70,000, many of whom expected to see an Eagles rout. By the final gun, the Cleveland upstarts had gained a generous measure of revenge with a

Marion Motley

convincing 35–10 victory, and no one enjoyed the sweetness of it all more than Motley.

He fairly feasted on NFL defenses that year with a statistical relish. By the end of the regular schedule, he led all rushers with 810 yards on 140 carries for a per-try average of 5.8 yards. In the playoffs he again paced the Browns' ground game as they went on to win the league championship and further embarrass their establishment critics. He was 30 at the time, some of his most productive years having been spent in military service and the AAFC.

Recalling his heyday, Motley said, "On occasion I would intentionally run into a defensive back instead of trying to avoid him. I just wanted to sting him, work on his mind a little bit. You run over a guy, and the next time through, he isn't going to be there. That's when you break a big one."

After his retirement from the NFL, he continued to stay close to the pro game and still participates in NFL alumni golf tournaments, which fund a variety of charities. He frequently attends Browns' home games at Cleveland Stadium but isn't completely happy with the way the proceedings are being conducted of late. "I just don't care for all that hand-fighting the offensive linemen do now," he said. "I think they've forgotten how to put a shoulder into a guy and really move him out of there. And that's why they don't get the ball into the end zone on short yardage plays so well anymore."

For a fact, nobody ever put a shoulder into a man quite like Marion Motley. Comparisons with perfection are necessarily less than satisfying.

Bronko Nagurski

6'2", 225 pounds. Fullback, Tackle, Linebacker: Chicago Bears (1930–1937, 1943). All-Pro: 1932, 1933, 1934. Inducted into the Pro Football Hall of Fame 1963 (charter member). Career: Rushing attempts (no records for 1930–1931), 610. Rushing yardage, 2,708. Yards per carry, 4.4. Touchdowns, 18.

It was said of Bronko Nagurski that he ran his own interference. And to those unfortunate members of the opposition assigned the task of halting his progress with a ball under arm, he did seem like a crowd.

Consider the testimony of Ernie Nevers, a Hall of Fame fullback and a pretty fair thumper in his own right. "Tackling Bronko," Nevers said, "is like tackling a freight train going downhill. I had seen him play in college, and it looked to me as if he ran a little too high, so I thought I probably could tackle him pretty easily if I hit him high. The first time I had a chance to tackle him, I hit him high. But he caught me right in the chest, bowled me over, and darn near killed me. After that, I always made sure to tackle him low."

Added Red Grange: "When you tackle the Bronk, it's like an electric shock. If you hit him above the ankles, you could get killed."

Yet another Hall of Famer, quarterback Earl "Dutch" Clark, figured out a safer means of tripping up the Chicago Bears juggernaut. "Bronko ran in a sort of bent-over slant position," Clark related. "He would kill you if you tried to tackle him around the knees or the body. The only way I could stop him was to just hit the ground right at his ankles."

Bronko Nagurski

New York Giants coach Steve Owen devised all manner of defensive alignments in an attempt to prevent Nagurski's inevitable march down the field. None of them got the job done. One of his innovative schemes involved assigning a linebacker to plug the hole into which the Bears' big banger seemed to be headed. This happened on the very first rushing play of a game at the old Polo Grounds, and the result was not unpredictable. "A couple of things happened that we hadn't counted on," Owen said. "One, Nagurski gained eight yards. And two, the linebacker had to be carted off on a stretcher."

Finally, Owen hit upon the perfect solution to his problem. With a perceptible note of pride in his voice, he announced, "Shoot Nagurski before he leaves the dressing room."

No doubt the ploy would have worked. However, the rules frowned on such behavior, even in the 1930s when padding was negligible, helmets were frequently disdained, and everybody qualified as a 60-minute player. So Nagurski remained virtually unstoppable.

The closest anything came to holding its own against Chicago's one-man wrecking crew was a concrete wall at Wrigley Field. Story has it that Nagurski, running full tilt, slammed through a phalanx of enemy defenders and careening off the field, proceeded into a dugout where he encountered a wall head-on. Eyes glazing over, he staggered backward and wheezed, "Gee, that last guy really hit me."

Of Polish-Ukrainian descent, he was born in Rainy River, Ontario, Canada, but moved to International Falls, Minnesota, as a young boy. He played for a high school team that went winless during his tenure there. The way he was recruited to play for the University of Minnesota has become one of the most colorful tales in football annals.

It goes something like this. On a hot summer day, a Minnesota scout pulled off a country road seeking directions. Getting out of his car, he noticed a young man in a nearby field plowing without the benefit of a horse. In response to a plea for assistance, the young man gestured off into the distance—with the plow. The scout recruited him on the spot.

With the Golden Gophers, Nagurski shone at both fullback and tackle with his bone-rattling style of play. He earned All-America recognition in his junior and senior years. And in 1929, the New York *Sun* named him to its All-America team as a fullback and a tackle. The following year he signed on with the Bears and promptly began terrorizing the NFL with his punishing rushes. He also proved to be a savage blocker and tackler. What's more, he could pass a little better than all right. His aerials, usually of the jump-and-lob variety to a back cutting over the middle, provided the margin of victory for Chicago in the 1932 and 1933 league-championship games.

After failing to wrangle a salary hike out of Bears owner and coach George Halas following the 1937 season, Nagurski retired and turned to wrestling full-time. In 1943, a full six years after hanging up his cleats, he pulled on a football uniform once more at the behest of Halas and again supplied the Chicago franchise with the needed impetus for yet another NFL title. He continued to wrestle for another decade before calling it quits in 1953 and returning to his home in International Falls. There he hunted, fished, and operated a gas station. At age 70, he resigned himself to a rocker on the front porch, complaining, "My legs were bothering me."

A quiet, private man by nature, Nagurski remained in seclusion until 1984 when he was enticed into appearing at the coin-toss ceremony preceding that year's Super Bowl game in Tampa, Florida. On the evening of January 7, 1990, at 81, he died of cardiopulmonary arrest in his hometown.

Ernie Nevers

6'1", 205 pounds. Fullback: 1926, 1927 (Duluth Eskimos), 1929–1931 (Chicago Cardinals). All-Pro: 1926, 1927, 1929–1931. Inducted into the Pro Football Hall of Fame 1963 (charter member).

Perhaps *indestructible* is the word that best describes Ernie Nevers, a charter member of the Hall of Fame who could do everything that needed to be done on a football field.

While at Stanford University, he accumulated 11 letters in athletics, excelling in baseball, basketball, and football, but he gained the most notoriety porting a pigskin under arm in heroic fashion. Accounts of his Herculean performance against Notre Dame in the 1926 Rose Bowl still circulate to this day. On that occasion he rushed for 114 yards, despite a pair of fractured ankles, and was Most Valuable Player.

Heralded as the "paleface Jim Thorpe," he emerged from college at a most propitious time for him, as pro football was badly in need of a superstar. He filled the bill in every respect. Besides signing with the Duluth Eskimos of the National Football League for $15,000, top money in those days, he also penned contracts in professional baseball and basketball. However, the gridiron sport is where his light truly shone.

Duluth officials determined that if they were going to make money with Nevers wearing an Eskimos uniform, it would be necessary to show-case him, to enable the greatest number of people to see him in action. To accomplish this objective, the team played only one of its 29 games in Duluth during the 1926 season, the rest conducted on the road at sites where maximum crowds could be attracted. (Yes, that's right—29 games.) By schedule's end—with Nevers calling signals, running, passing, blocking, tackling, and placekicking—the Eskimos compiled a respectable 19–7–3 record while traveling some 17,000 miles.

Easily the most eye-opening statistic resulting from this odyssey of football was the fact that The Blond Bull missed less than a half hour of playing time out of 1,740 minutes. He completed another wearying season with the Eskimos and then sat out 1928 with an injury to his spinal column, a broken transverse process of a vertebra. In 1929, he became player-coach of the Chicago Cardinals and promptly resumed his amazing NFL career. In one game that year he personally outscored the crosstown rival Bears by a 40–6 margin; the ensuing week, he again did all the tallying for the Cardinals, leading them to a 19–0 victory over Dayton—a total of 59 points in two outings, an attainment that no one is ever likely to equal, let alone surpass.

Though still in his prime, Nevers quit after the 1931 campaign. He had accomplished everything it was possible for him to achieve. Of all the Hall of Fame inductees, he had the shortest tenure in pro football, just five years. But he was a unanimous all-league selection every season and dominated the NFL of his era as no one else has ever done. And when all the games he participated in are summed up along with his playing time, an average of nearly 60 minutes per contest, it computes to approximately a 10-year span, given modern schedules and today's degree of specialization.

Nevers died at 72 on May 3, 1976.

Joe Perry

6'0", 200 pounds. Fullback: San Francisco 49ers (1948, 1949, AAFC), San Francisco 49ers (1950–1960, 1963, NFL), Baltimore Colts (1961, 1962). All-Pro: 1953, 1954. Pro Bowl: Three appearances. AAFC Rushing Leader: 1949. NFL Rushing Leader: 1953, 1954. Inducted into the Pro Football Hall of Fame 1969. Career: Rushing attempts, 1,929. Rushing yardage, 9,723. Yards per carry, 5.0. Touchdowns, 71. Receptions, 260. Receiving yardage, 2,021. Yards per reception, 7.8. Touchdowns (receiving), 12. Kickoff returns, 31. Return yardage, 737. Yards per return, 23.8. Touchdowns (kickoff returns), 1.

Joe "The Jet" Perry is one of only a few Hall of Fame inductees who did not play the gridiron game in college before achieving stardom in the National Football League. But then if circumstances hadn't deemed otherwise, he would never have chosen to play the sport professionally anyway.

In the beginning, music was his first love, a passion of no small moment. And as a means of indulging this desire, he intended to pursue a career in engineering, a game plan that would assure him the best of both his worlds. Sports was just something he did, given a natural talent for them and a body capable of doing what his abilities commanded. He excelled at track and field early in his high school tenure. Later he added basketball, baseball, and football to his athletic repertoire.

His mother didn't want him going out for the football team, fearing that he might suffer an incapacitating injury. With or without her approval, he was determined to play and sought to do so secretly. This attempt at subterfuge was promptly exposed, however. On the oaccasion of the squad's first scrimmage, he suffered a broken ankle. Fortunately for him she ultimately withdrew her objections and became his staunchest backer.

Following graduation, he enrolled at Compton (Calif.) Junior College to prepare himself to achieve his academic goals. While there, he starred for the school football team, scoring 22 touchdowns as a freshman. Before he could embark upon his sophomore year, World War II intervened and duty to country called. He entered the service and subsequently played with the Alameda Naval Station squad. While there, he caught the eye of San Francisco 49ers tackle John Woudenberg, who reported his sensational find to team owner Tony Morabito. Though somewhat disbelieving, Morabito did invite Perry for a tryout following his discharge from the navy.

Suddenly he was faced with a difficult decision, one that bode to change his chartered course in life. More than 14 colleges had offered him aid to play football, but he also needed a source of income, expecially to assist his mother. And he felt drawn to test his ability against the best. In the end, he opted to turn pro. Neither he nor the 49ers would live to regret his choice.

As a rookie, he had to learn a degree of finesse to go along with his native power and speed, but he quickly learned to feint and change pace effectively and soon became one of the most elusive ball carriers in the All-America Football Conference (AAFC). In his second year, he acquired the nickname The Jet when San Francisco quarterback Frankie Albert said, "I'm telling you, when that guy gets a handoff, his slipstream darn near knocks you over. I've never seen anybody get such a fast start. He's strictly jet-propelled."

His first two seasons he led the AAFC in touchdowns with a total of 18 and topped all rushers in 1949 with 783 yards on 115 attempts for a per-gain average of 6.8 yards. When the 49ers joined the NFL in 1950, he was more than ready for the challenge. In 1953, he led all running backs with 192 carries for 1,018 yards, an average of 5.3 yards, and a league best 10 TDs. He duplicated this feat in 1954, picking up 1,049 yards via 173 rushes for a per-carry average of 6.1 yards and 8 scores. Both seasons he rated All-Pro honors.

For more than a decade, Perry paced the San Francisco ground attack and supplied another pair of sure hands when a clutch catch was needed. In the wake of the 1960 campaign, he was traded to the Baltimore Colts, with whom he labored largely as a spot back. Finally, in 1963, he rejoined San Francisco to finish out his career. When he stripped off his pads for the last time, his rushing total amounted to 9,723 yards, second only to the incomparable Jim Brown at that time.

Gale Sayers

6'0", 200 pounds. Running Back: Chicago Bears (1965–1971). All-Pro: 1965–1969. Pro Bowl: Five elections, four appearances. NFL Rookie of the Year: 1965. Inducted into the Pro Football Hall of Fame 1977. Running Back: 50-Year, All-Time, All-NFL team. Career: Rushing attempts, 991. Rushing yardage, 4,956. Yards per carry, 5.0. Touchdowns, 39. Passes attempted, 18. Passes completed, 4. Completion percentage, 22.2. Passing yardage, 111. Touchdowns (passing), 1. Interceptions, 0. Receptions, 112. Receiving yardage, 1,307. Yards per reception, 11.7. Touchdowns (receiving), 9. Kickoff returns, 91. Return yardage, 2,781. Yards per return, 30.6. Touchdowns (kickoff returns), 6. Punt returns, 28. Return yardage, 391. Yards per return, 14.0. Touchdowns (punt returns), 2.

A shooting star streaking across the darkened firmament—so went the pro football career of Gale Sayers.

Following an All-America tenure at the University of Kansas, he burst onto the National Football League scene in 1965 with meteoric brilliance.

As a Chicago Bears rookie, he scored a record 22 touchdowns, 14 of them running from scrimmage, 6 as a pass receiver, 1 returning punts, and 1 more fielding kickoffs. He was elusive as vapor, swift as quicksilver, and amazingly versatile. In all, he tallied 132 points, 36 in one game against the San Francisco 49ers with a record-equaling 6 touchdowns while averaging 5.2 yards per carry. He could turn on a dime, making would-be tacklers miss him in even the most confining circumstances.

"When I was active," he said, "I think you had better all-around players in the league. I'm not saying this was true in all cases, but as a rule. I ran back kickoffs. I ran back punts. I caught passes out of the backfield, and I ran from the line of scrimmage. Back then, I felt that doing all these things gave me just one more offensive play, another opportunity to get my hands on the ball, and another chance to score."

In 1966, Sayers laughed at the sophomore jinx by leading all rushers with 1,231 yards and a 5.4-yards-per-attempt average. He continued to perplex defenses around the league with his darting ways until a fateful afternoon in 1968 when his right knee was badly damaged. The injury occurred in a game with the 49ers, a team he had badly embarrassed as a rookie. But even though he went out with five games left on the schedule, his attainments for the year were still impressive—856 yards rushing and an NFL best per-carry average of 6.2 yards.

At the earliest possible moment after surgery, he began rehabilitating his knee, exercising it two and three times a day despite intimidating pain. "No knee injury was going to keep me out of my game," he said. "I knew I'd be back. And I wanted to do it right away. Most runners are afraid of a knee injury. They've been brainwashed. They think it's supposed to take a long time to recover. I wanted to prove you could be ready by the next season."

When it came time for the Bears to open their 1969 slate, Sayers was on hand and raring to go. To the surprise of almost everyone, he led the league in rushing attempts with 236 and rushing yardage with 1,032. And what's more, he continued to be an effective receiver as well as a kick returner. However, the ligaments in his left knee would be badly torn in 1970, an injury from which he would not be able to come back effectively. He played on briefly in 1971 and then retired.

Reflecting on his truncated career, he said, "During my first four years in pro football, the coaches still weren't big on the use of weight training, especially for running backs. But it's been proven that the proper use of weights can build both quickness and speed. If I had worked with weights, I believe I would have strengthened my legs, and perhaps my knee injuries wouldn't have been so severe. The way I ran, the way I cut, my knees were so loose that I was just waiting for an injury. Because of the way I ran, the way I cut, I put so much pressure on my joints, on my ligaments, that I

Gale Sayers

needed strong legs. Not working with weights, I am now convinced, was my downfall."

Shortly after his retirement, Sayers served as director of athletics at Southern Illinois University. Then he entered private business in the Chicago suburb of Northfield and worked as a commentator for radio broadcasts of the Bears' games.

"I still like the pro game, even with all the specialization there is nowadays," he said. "I think the public is missing something in not seeing the great athletes perform like they should in a variety of capacities. They don't allow them to run back punts and kickoffs or catch passes. Instead, they put in specialists to do the job. But I think it's a game just made for Gale Sayers. And I say this because of the artificial turf, the I-formation, the one-back offense, the hashmarks being in close to the middle of the field, all of it. I think it would be ideal for me to play today."

When asked to capsulize the abilities that made him such a devastating runner, Sayers replied, "The big key to my success was an innate quickness. And then I had a certain sixth sense that told me when and where to cut. I could actually feel pressure building around me. Plus, I had great peripheral vision. I could see all around, and this helped me a great deal."

He gained entry into the Pro Football Hall of Fame at age 34, the youngest player ever to be so honored. "Yes, I was kind of surprised to have it happen that soon," he said. "The average time for most players to be inducted into the Hall of Fame is ten years. I played only sixty-eight games for the Chicago Bears. You can break that down into just four and a half years of actual playing time. A very, very short period to impress the so-called experts. But then again, I did so many things. So I guess you could say I impressed people in many, many ways in a very, very short time."

And that he did.

O. J. Simpson

6'1", 212 pounds. Running Back: Buffalo Bills (1969, AFL), (1970–1977, NFL), San Francisco 49ers (1978, 1979). All-Pro: 1972–1976. AFL All-Star Game: One appearance. Pro Bowl: Five appearances, MVP 1973. NFL Rushing Leader: 1972, 1973, 1975, 1976. NFL Player of the Year: 1972, 1973, 1975. Inducted into the Pro Football Hall of Fame 1985. Career: Rushing attempts, 2,404. Rushing yardage, 11,236. Yards per carry, 4.7. Touchdowns, 61. Receptions, 203. Receiving yardage, 2,142. Yards per reception, 10.6. Touchdowns (receiving), 14. Passes attempted, 16. Passes completed, 6. Completion percentage, 37.5. Passing yardage, 110. Touchdowns (passing), 1. Interceptions, 0. Kickoff returns, 33. Return yardage, 990. Yards per return, 30.0. Touchdowns (kickoff returns), 1.

One of the few Heisman Trophy winners to live up to his potential in professional football was O. J. "The Juice" Simpson. In a gridiron career that spanned more than a decade, he blossomed into one of the finest running backs ever to grace the money game and thereafter the Hall of Fame.

When he entered the American Football League (AFL) as a two-time All-American from the University of Southern California in 1969, the "can't miss" label was firmly affixed to his future prospects. But not long after he joined the Buffalo Bills, a team then in the throes of transition, thoughts of early retirement became commonplace in his thinking.

His rookie year was substantive but hardly sensational—697 yards rushing on 181 attempts for a per-carry average of 3.9 yards and two touchdowns. No bell ringer, but he did receive an invitation to participate in the 1969 AFL All-Star game.

In 1970, the Bills, along with the rest of the teams in the AFL, were absorbed into the National Football League, and life on Sundays began anew. But things didn't change much for Simpson. He was still an all-purpose performer, which included returning kicks as a member of special teams. While serving in this capacity, he tore up a knee late that season and repaired to the sidelines, seriously considering the possibility of calling it quits.

The following season, Lou Saban returned to Buffalo as the Bills' head coach and immediately contemplated how Simpson might be used to better advantage. With this in mind, he went out and acquired one of the best run-blocking offensive lines in the NFL. So as the centerpiece of the Bills' attack, "The Juice" suddenly commenced to attain the promise which had been roundly predicted for him. From 1972 through 1976, he held forth as the most dominant running back in the league. In 1973, he carried the ball 332 times for a single-season record of 2,003 yards, a per-attempt average of 6.0 yards, and 12 touchdowns. During this six-season stretch, he annexed four NFL rushing titles and was voted the league's Player of the Year in 1972, 1973, and 1975.

His ability to make would-be tacklers miss him in the most confining of circumstances gave rise to the theory that perhaps he had a special sixth sense not to be found in other mere mortals. "Yeah, I've had people suggest that," he said. "But that's not it. Preparation is the key. Knowing what you're doing. It's study and preparation. If you study the plays and then run them enough in practice, you just get a feel for where everybody is supposed to be at any one time. Once you can do this, then the secret lies in faking properly. You have to fake a guy tight. By that I mean you have to make a guy miss without leaving him. You just get him a little off balance and then blow right upfield. He can maybe touch you but not make the stop. The idea is to get to the end zone in the most direct manner possible without encountering a whole lot of people."

O. J. Simpson

Simpson hastened to add that practice and study were not to be engaged in on game days. "When I'm running well, my mind just goes blank," he related. "I'm not thinking about anything at all. Thinking is what gets you caught from behind. But even though I'm not thinking, I am still aware of everything going on around me. When I get to the end zone, I can tell you where everybody was, who blocked who. And I mean not just the guys near me, but all over the field."

Ultimately, the hits he did take slowed him down, and with passing time, the bruises and bumps required longer and longer to heal. In 1978, he went to San Francisco, his hometown, to finish out the string with the 49ers. By his standards, the two-year stint was anticlimactic, and he retired after the 1979 campaign.

Now Simpson can be seen doing television commercials and color commentary for network TV coverage of NFL games.

Ken Strong

5'11", 210 pounds. Halfback: Staten Island Stapletons (1929–1932), New York Giants (1933–1935), New York Yanks (1936, 1937, AFL), New York Giants (1939, 1944–1947, NFL). NFL Leading Scorer: 1933. All-Pro: 1934. Inducted into the Pro Football Hall of Fame 1967. Career: TDs, 35. PATs, 169. FGs, 39. Total points, 496. (No further statistics in other categories are available for his NFL years or those in the AFL.)

Despite the fact that Ken Strong was among the most versatile players ever to ply his skills in the National Football League, his career had less glory and gold to it than that of many lesser practitioners.

He came out of New York University as an All-America selection in 1928, a multitalented athlete seemingly destined to join the hometown Giants and bring them to league supremacy. And this surely would have been the scenario were it not for a bit of bad faith on behalf of the club.

When he met with members of the Giants' front office, the offer was $3,000 a year. No paltry sum in those days, but not the $4,000 team owner Tim Mara had authorized as the contract price. Rather than be shortchanged, he turned his back and walked away, deciding to play instead with the Staten Island Stapletons for much less money. He had his principles.

Shortly thereafter, he also agreed to play baseball with the New York Yankees organization. He was a gifted outfielder who could hit for distance. Back then, many gifted performers played both sports without difficulty, and he didn't anticipate any problems doing so either.

In 1931, he had an excellent season with a Yankees minor-league team but later injured his wrist. Corrective surgery proved unsuccessful, and he was no longer able to throw with power. This left him with only football as a viable means of livelihood. But after the 1932 campaign, the Stapletons folded, and he found himself out of work. He asked the Giants if they could find a spot for him on their roster, but Mara refused at first, still angry at having his offer turned down three years earlier. Still, he didn't want the former NYU star playing for someone else. Sensitive negotiations followed, and Strong finally wound up signing for the $3,000 he had refused earlier.

The Giants got their money's worth, and then some. In 1933, they reached the NFL championship game as Strong topped the league in scoring with 64 points. He took them right back to the title tilt the next year and all but won the contest single-handedly. Playing on a frozen field at the Polo Grounds, he donned basketball shoes prior to the second half for better traction and scored 17 points, 4 more than the entire Chicago Bears squad could muster, as the Giants won easily, 30–13. His record total, comprising a field goal, two touchdowns, and four extra points, prevailed for nearly 30 years. This effort earned him All-Pro honors.

When the inaugural college draft was conducted early in 1936, the team owners, already struggling financially, suddenly realized they were no longer so heavily dependent upon veteran players with a guaranteed supply of fresh talent available to them each year. So they summarily cut the salaries of their experienced personnel. Irate at having his pay reduced to $150 a game, considerably below his 1935 wage, Strong bolted to the rival American Football League (AFL) and the New York Yanks. As a result, the NFL hit him with a five-year suspension.

The AFL went out of business after the 1937 schedule, and Strong's exile was terminated a year later. He returned to the Giants for the 1939 season and then announced his retirement. The club lured him back in 1944 when World War II produced a drastic player drain in the NFL. At 38, he limited his on-field appearances to kicking situations, often disdaining to wear shoulder pads while dispatching his duties. He persisted in this limited role through the 1947 slate before calling it quits a second time.

During his heyday, he could do it all—run, pass, catch, punt, place-kick, block, and play defense—with distinction. Yet he was treated with something less than respect a good part of his 14 years in pro football. One must conclude there's just no accounting for the vagaries of human nature.

Strong died on October 5, 1979, at 73.

Jim Taylor

6'0", 216 pounds. Fullback: Green Bay Packers (1958–1966), New Orleans Saints (1967). All-Pro: 1961, 1962. Pro Bowl: Five appearances. NFL Leading Rusher-Scorer: 1962. Fullback: NFL Team of the 1960s. Inducted into the Pro Football Hall of Fame 1976. Career: Rushing attempts, 1,941. Rushing yardage, 8,597. Yards per carry, 4.4. Touchdowns, 83. Receptions, 225. Receiving yardage, 1,756. Yards per reception, 7.8. Touchdowns (receiving), 10. Kickoff returns, 7. Return yardage, 185. Yards per return, 26.4. Touchdowns, 0.

Football was Jim Taylor's game, as though the match were so ordained by no less than God. It afforded him a gladiatorial role which he played to perfection, given a mind, body, and spirit seemingly honed for confrontation from the moment of conception, the consummate warrior just made for a Sunday afternoon's bloodletting.

When he carried the ball, arms, legs, elbows, every part of his anatomy became a lethal weapon, a calculated means of grinding down the enemy in quest of that precious extra yard. He made no pretense of avoiding contact. Often he contrived the circumstances, intent upon intimidating the opposition with the full range of psychological and physical implications that attend such a hapless mating.

"I try to sting 'em," he once said of his intent toward would-be tacklers. "I like to make 'em pay a price, to make them think about next time. The idea is to get a little respect."

He came out of Louisiana State University in 1957 with an All-America tag firmly fixed to his gridiron pedigree and a reputation for being premier up-the-middle goods. The Green Bay Packers, then something of the National Football League doormat, made him their second pick in the college draft of 1958. Needless to say, his rookie campaign was not a particularly pleasant or memorable experience.

The next year, however, his entire outlook took a 180-degree turn for the better. And that was due to the arrival in Green Bay of new head coach Vincent Lombardi. Muck like the marines, the "Italian master" was in search of a few good men to promote a bare-knuckle style of play. He wanted men who could, who would, take it to the other team down after down until victory had been ensured. He promptly singled out Taylor as his kind of guy.

In the beginning, this relationship didn't appear to be one made in heaven. Both principals were tough and devoid of pretense—hard taskmasters. Yet each wanted the approval, the admiration, of the other and thus covertly harbored sensitivities easily bruised if the anticipated reaction wasn't readily forthcoming.

Looking back on that time, Taylor said, "Yeah, he [Lombardi] would

Jim Taylor (ball carrier)

get on you, ride you hard. It kind of bothered me at first, kind of got me down. Then I came to understand what he was trying to do for me, for all of us."

Ball control prevailed as the dominant theme of the Green Bay attack under Lombardi, and Taylor had a lot to do with its implementation on the field. He ran sweeps to the right and left, plied the guts of the defense in short-yardage thrusts, and caught the little pitchouts in the flat designed to set up the deeper slants and post patterns over the middle. He thumped the ball upfield so that his quicker, swifter confederates could use their mercurial talents to better advantage against a wearied and battered opponent.

The Packers had a galaxy of stars in that era, but Taylor personified what the team was really all about. In 1960, they took on the Philadelphia Eagles for the NFL title. With less than a minute left in the contest and Green Bay marching on the Eagles' goal line, Taylor got the call to make up a 17–13 deficit. Arms thick as wagon tongues flailed away at a web of grasping hands while oaken underpinnings churned relentlessly toward the nearby end zone. Then he collided with Philadelphia Hall of Fame linebacker "Concrete Charley" Bednarik and was wrestled to the turf just shy of the promised land. But enough time remained for another play. He struggled to rise, but Bednarik wouldn't let him up until the waning seconds were no more.

"Yeah, he [Bednarik] sat on me," Taylor testified. "He surely did. He wouldn't let me get up." Bednarik, recalling the incident, chuckled. "Jim said some very ungentlemanly things to me. But I didn't let him up until the clock ran down. I didn't want him getting his hands on the ball again."

In 1962 it was a different story. Taylor led all NFL rushers and scorers that year with 1,474 yards gained and 19 touchdowns. He then capped this epic season by accounting for the deciding TD in the Packers' 16–7 win over the New York Giants for the league championship. The game took place in the frigid wind-swept confines of Yankee Stadium. All afternoon he waged a brutal battle with the New York defense, particularly Giants linebacker Sam Huff. Near exhaustion and rubbed raw from repeated impactions upon the frozen ground, he banged over for the clinching six points and then, rising, shook the ball in Huff's face.

"Oh, I don't remember exactly what I said," Taylor explained. "It was something like, 'Well, Mr. Huff, that looks like it, and here's the ball as a memento of the occasion.' That's not it exactly, but you get the idea." When informed about Taylor's version of the exchange, Huff smirked. "That's nothing like I heard."

Following the 1966 slate, he went to New Orleans in a trade. He saw spot duty with the Saints during the 1967 schedule and then retired. Overall, he earned All-Pro recognition twice and played in five Pro Bowls. From 1960 through 1964, he rushed for more than 1,000 yards each year. Later, he was voted to the All-NFL team of the 1960s.

Jim Thorpe

6'1", 190 pounds. Halfback: Canton Bulldogs (1915–1917, 1919, 1920), Cleveland Indians (1921), Oorang Indians (1922, 1923 NFL), Rock Island Independents (1924), New York Giants (1925), Canton Bulldogs (1926), Chicago Cardinals (1928). President/American Professional Football Association: 1920. Inducted into the Pro Football Hall of Fame 1963 (charter member). Halfback: 50-Year, All-Time, All-NFL team.

Perhaps no athlete ever enjoyed so storied a career as Jim Thrope, a sports hero for the ages of whom much has been written, both fact and fable. His life reads like pages from a novel, full of glittering triumphs and saddening accounts of human frailty. But none of his accomplishments more starkly define his physical prowess than those he attained on the gridiron.

While the big Indian actively lent his considerable fame and presence to the pro game in excess of a decade, he had actually passed his prime as a player before the NFL officially became an entity.

He established his reputation in football by leading the Carlisle (Pa.) Indian School to a national collegiate championship in 1912. During that season, he scored 25 touchdowns and 198 points while earning All-America honors. When he signed a contract with the Canton Bulldogs in 1915 for $250 a contest, it was as a major gate attraction, something the play-for-pay endeavor desperately needed at that time.

A somewhat aging rookie at 27, he did everything that could be done with a football. As a running back, standing 6'1" and weighing 190 pounds, he possessed both speed and intimidating power. He could pass and catch with consummate skill and punt and kick in eye-opening fashion. When executing field goals, he did so flawlessly either from placement or by dropkicking. Blocking and tackling, more mundane chores of the game, he performed with a relish, liberally strewing members of the opposition in his wake.

Provided his talents in their backfield, the Bulldogs won the 1916, 1917, and 1919 Ohio League titles, the unofficial world championship of the pro game in those days. In 1920, the American Professional Football Association (APFA) was formed to provide more stability for the teams then in existence, and Thorpe became its first president by popular acclamation. He switched his allegiance to the Cleveland Indians in 1921 but played very little due to injuries. Thereafter he plied his waning skills with the Oorang Indians (1922, 1923), Rock Island Independents (1924), New York Giants (1925), Canton Bulldogs (1926), and finally, after a year's hiatus, the Chicago Cardinals (1928).

Given his awesome natural abilities, Thorpe didn't put much stock in practicing. Why go over and over what one could already do to perfection? he reasoned. As the seasons melded one into another, he adhered less and less to anything resembling a training regimen, and his magnificent body began to betray him. Still, when angered, he would perform prodigiously, aging sinews and failing reflexes notwithstanding.

Undoubtedly his greatest fame came from stirring victories in the decathlon and pentathlon events of the 1912 Olympics. He also played major-league baseball from 1913 to 1919. But football was his first love, the jarring give and take of combat most suiting his competitive personality.

In 1950, the nation's sportswriting community voted him the most outstanding American athlete of the twentieth century's first 50 years. Later, he was selected to the All-Time, All-NFL team.

He died on March 28, 1953, at 64.

Charley Trippi

6'0", 185 pounds. Halfback, Quarterback: Chicago Cardinals (1947–1955). All-Pro: 1948. Inducted into the Pro Football Hall of Fame 1968. Career: Rushing attempts, 687. Rushing yardage 3,506. Yards per carry, 5.1. Touchdowns, 23. Receptions, 130. Receiving yardage, 1,321. Yards per reception, 10.2. Touchdowns (receiving), 11. Passes attempted, 434. Passes completed, 205. Completion percentage, 47.2. Passing yardage, 2,547. Touchdowns (passing), 16. Interceptions, 31. Punt returns, 63. Return yardage, 864. Yards per return, 13.7. Touchdowns (punt returns), 2. Kickoff returns, 66. Return yardage, 1,457. Yards per return, 22.1. Touchdowns, 0. Punts, 196. Yards per punt, 40.4. Interceptions, 4. Return yardage, 93. Yards per return, 23.3. Touchdowns (interception returns), 1.

Back in the dark days of the late 1940s, Charley Trippi proved to be the linchpin upon which the survival of the National Football League hung, and the six-figure amount expended for his services was one of the best life insurance buys in the history of pro sports.

When the superstar running back from the University of Georgia closed out his collegiate career in 1946, the NFL was locked in a bitter war for playing talent with the upstart All-American Football Conference (AAFC). The Chicago Cardinals made him their top draft pick, as did the New York Yanks of the AAFC. Both leagues knew instinctively that the one to acquire his signature on a contract first would have irrevocably turned the tide of battle in its favor.

The Yanks felt so sure Trippi would sign with them that they called a news conference in New York to proclaim the occasion. But even as they did, the two-time All-America selection was affixing his signature to a Cardinals agreement in consideration of the then astronomical figure of $100,000, thus sealing his allegiance to the NFL for the ensuing four years. This coup tipped the scales in favor of the senior league, and thereafter the AAFC slipped inexorably down the hill to receivership.

Upon his arrival in Chicago, he joined the likes of quarterback Paul Christman, fullback Pat Harder, and halfback Marshall Goldberg to form what the press-box brigade would dub the Dream Backfield. His impact upon the Cardinals' gridiron fortunes was immediate. That first season he ran 83 times for 401 yards, a per-carry average of 4.8 yards, and two touchdowns. But his most endearing contributions were the big plays he made as a ball carrier and kick returner.

Given Trippi's presence, the Cardinals had just the edge they needed to beat out the Bears, their crosstown rival and longtime nemesis, for the Western Division crown. That set the stage for him to display his offensive wares to the fullest against the Philadelphia Eagles in the 1947 NFL championship game. Wearing basketball shoes to improve his traction on the frozen turf of Comiskey Park, he carried 14 times from scrimmage for 206 yards, one of these sorties a 44-yard touchdown jaunt. He also returned a punt 75 yards for another score. These electrifying thrusts proved to be the difference in the tightly fought contest as Chicago prevailed 28–21 to claim the league title.

In 1948 he earned All-Pro recognition with another premier campaign.

This time around, he rushed 128 times for 690 yards, an eye-opening 5.4 yards a try and 6 TDs. And again the Cardinals finished ahead of the Bears for the division crown. Once more they faced the Eagles, the winner's spoil pro football supremacy. The rematch took place in a blinding blizzard that obliterated the field markings to such an extent that the officials had to guess on almost every down where the ball should be spotted. In the end Philadelphia gained the victory by a 7–0 margin when Steve Van Buren scored on a controversial two-yard plunge.

"Frankly, I don't think he (Van Buren) got in with the ball," Trippi said some years later. "But the point is, the game never should have been played under those conditions."

Always a team player, he willingly accepted position changes whenever circumstances dictated. Through the 1950 season, he operated as a running back and fielded kicks. From 1951 to 1952, he switched to quarterback and threw for more than 2,000 yards and 13 touchdowns. He resumed his halfback duties for the 1953 schedule, then closed out his versatile career as a defensive specialist in 1954 and 1955. Also, he took care of the team punting chores with an overall average of 40.4 yards and held forth as a clutch pass receiver.

Trippi currently lives in Athens, Georgia, where he is still revered as the triple-threat back who led the hometown Bulldogs to the 1942 Rose Bowl and victory in the 1946 Sugar Bowl following an undefeated season.

Steve Van Buren

6'1", 200 pounds. Halfback: Philadelphia Eagles (1944–1951). All-Pro: 1944, 1945, 1947–1949. NFL Rushing Leader: 1945, 1947–1949. Inducted into the Pro Football Hall of Fame 1965. Career: Rushing attempts, 1,320. Rushing yardage, 5,860. Yards per carry, 4.4. Touchdowns, 69. Receptions, 45. Receiving yardage, 503. Yards per reception, 11.2. Touchdowns (receiving), 3. Kickoff returns, 77. Return yardage, 2,030. Yards per return, 26.4. Touchdowns (kickoff returns), 3. Punt returns, 34. Return yardage, 473. Yards per return, 13.9. Touchdowns (punt returns), 2. Interceptions, 9. Return yardage, 81. Yards per return, 9.0. Touchdowns, 0.

Few running backs in the annals of pro football have been accorded the distinction of being the prime mover behind the good fortune their teams enjoyed. And even fewer running backs can be said to have defined the very era in which they presided. But both these honors rightly rest upon Steve Van Buren, the Philadelphia Eagles' storied "moving van" of the late 1940s and early 1950s.

Although categorized historically as a halfback, he actually held forth

Steve Van Buren

as a power ball carrier who could go the distance on any down, over people as opposed to around them. He didn't possess great bulk by modern standards, standing just 6'1" and weighing but 200 pounds. However, he commanded that explosive velocity upon impact that fairly blasted him through areas of congestion, a rare capability that marks the true short-yardage man who can deliver the first down and touchdown when the strength of the opposition is ready and awaiting his impending thrust. His kind are few and far between.

Ironically, he was a mere mite of a lad in high school, tipping the beam at barely 125 pounds. Due to his lack of size, he was denied an opportunity to turn out for the football team. Undaunted, he went to work in an iron foundry and later returned to make the squad and earn a scholarship to Louisiana State University. At LSU, he blocked more than carried the ball as an underclassman. But in his senior season he finally got a chance to display his wares and did so, rushing for 832 yards. Then he failed to gain All-America recognition, as many an observer of that time felt was due him, and so went largely unnoticed by most of the teams in the National Football League.

Were it not for a tip from LSU head coach Bernie Moore, the Eagles might well have let Van Buren slip past them too. However, they didn't make that mistake, taking him as their first selection in the 1944 NFL draft. He immediately paid big dividends for them, picking up 444 yards via 80 rushes for an average of 5.5 yards per carry and 5 touchdowns. This rookie effort earned him All-Pro recognition, a height he would scale four more times in a span of five seasons.

In those days, the NFL schedule consisted of 10 games. Then it went to 11 dates, and finally 12 when Van Buren ran for 1,008 yards in 1947 and 1,146 in 1949. Back then, 1,000-yard campaigns meant something, primarily a per-game rushing average of 100 yards or more. On no less than four occasions he topped the league's ball-carrying category. Two of these times (1948 and 1949) Philadelphia won back-to-back NFL titles.

Less publicized were his exploits as a 60-minute man. When not hammering the scrimmage line, he returned both kickoffs and punts, caught passes coming out of the backfield, and played in the defensive secondary. He wasn't just a one-dimensional performer. But he made headlines carrying the ball, and two of his biggest outings involved NFL championship games. In 1948, he ran for 98 yards, more than the total yardage generated by the opposition Chicago Cardinals, on a snow-covered field and scored the only touchdown of the contest to give the Eagles a 7–0 win. A year later, he churned through a sea of mud for a record 196 yards in 31 carries to lead Philadelphia to a 14–0 victory.

Francis J. "Bucko" Kilroy, a standout tackle with the Eagles of that time, said, "We were basically a ball-control team, and that was because of Van Buren. He was the core of our offense. So how he went is how we went."

The "moving van" rolled to a stop after the 1951 season, hobbled by injuries and slowed by the batterings which attended his many ball-carrying sorties.

Doak Walker

5'11", 173 pounds. Halfback: Detroit Lions (1950–1955). All-Pro: 1950, 1951, 1953, 1954. Pro Bowl: Five appearances. NFL Scoring Leader: 1950, 1955. Inducted into the Pro Football Hall of Fame 1986. Career: Scoring: 34 TDs. 183 PATs. 49 FGs. Total points, 534. Rushing attempts, 309. Rushing yardage, 1,520. Yards per carry, 4.9. Touchdowns, 12. Receptions, 152. Receiving yardage, 2,539. Yards per reception, 16.7. Touchdowns (receiving), 21. Passes attempted, 28. Passes completed, 7. Completion percentage, 25.0. Touchdowns (passing), 2. Interceptions, 2. Punt returns, 18. Return yardage, 284. Yards per return, 15.8. Touchdowns (punt returns), 1. Kickoff returns, 38. Return yardage, 968. Yards per return, 25.5. Touchdowns, 0. Interceptions, 2. Return yardage, 60. Yards per return, 30.0. Touchdowns, 0. Punts, 50. Yards per punt, 39.1.

Doak Walker was the little man who was always there. He ran, passed, kicked, caught, and defended for the Detroit Lions in a fashion which enabled them to win three divisional titles and two National Football League championships in a span of six years. And he did his best work when the money was on the line.

He came to the NFL after one of the most illustrious careers in collegiate annals. While laboring for the Southern Methodist University Mustangs, he achieved All-America recognition three times and appropriated the coveted Heisman Trophy as a junior in 1948. But despite these attainments, there were those members of the Lions administration who took a look at their 1950 rookie halfback and wondered whether he would prove durable enough to survive the pounding of the pro game.

It took him no longer than the opening kickoff of his freshman season to allay their fears and doubts. That campaign he scored 128 points to lead the NFL and earned All-Pro honors and his initial invite to the Pro Bowl. Still, he provided a marked contrast to his teammates. While the Lions at large projected a free-wheeling, tough-guy image complete with boisterous behavior and highly quotable quotes, the diminutive Texan (5'11", 173 pounds) said little and then only in the most polite manner. Oddly enough, his closest associate on the club was fellow Lone Star State expatriate Bobby Layne, standout quarterback and the undisputed leader of the raucous, beer-drinking Detroit contingent. Living proof that opposites do attract, or so it seemed.

Though relatively small of stature, Walker proved to be quite durable, save only for the 1952 campaign in which he was sidelined for several games. But even then, he evidenced a not readily perceptible toughness by

Doak Walker

rejoining the Lions lineup in time for the playoffs, throwing a touchdown pass against the Los Angeles Rams in the National Conference showdown game and then rambling for a 67-yard TD to give Detroit a 17–7 win over Cleveland and the league crown. In 1953, when the Lions again faced the Browns for all the NFL marbles, he tallied the first six points of the conflict and later iced the verdict 17–16 with a perfect PAT placement.

After the close of the 1955 slate, he announced his retirement, though still in the prime of his playing life. Club officials tried mightily to change his mind by offering him a substantial raise in salary, but he had business interests in Texas that demanded attention. And he wanted to walk away from the game without a telltale hitch in his step.

Upon departing, he left on the league record book the indelible print of his scoring prowess—534 points produced in about every conceivable fashion.

AERIAL BOMBARDMENT GROUP

Quarterbacks, Placekickers

Sammy Baugh

6'2", 180 pounds. Quarterback: Washington Redskins (1937–1952). All-Pro: 1937, 1940, 1943, 1945, 1947, 1949. Pro Bowl: One appearance. NFL's Leading Passer: 1937, 1940, 1943, 1945, 1947, 1949. Inducted into the Pro Football Hall of Fame 1963 (charter member). Career: Passes attempted, 2,995. Passes completed, 1,693. Completion percentage, 56.5. Passing yardage, 21,886. Touchdowns, 186. Interceptions, 203. Interceptions 28. Return yardage, 407. Yards per return, 14.5. Touchdowns, 0. Rushing attempts, 318. Rushing yardage, 324. Yards per carry, 1.0. Touchdowns (rushing), 6. Punt returns, 11. Return yardage, 99. Yards per return, 9. Touchdowns, 0. Punts, 338. Yards per punt, 44.9.

The game of football has never fostered a purer passer than Sammy Baugh, a lean slingshot of a man whose aerial artistry remains the standard by which the efforts of all others of the quarterbacking genre must be judged.

But overshadowed by his pitching prowess were other abilities which also defy comparison. He was an excellent punter, his accomplishments in this endeavor still much with us via the pages of the record book. And he could perform defensively with few peers, a sure tackler and annually among the league's interception leaders. He was more than just a thrower. In every respect he was an all-around performer of considerable talent.

A versatile athlete as a schoolboy, he starred in three sports at the secondary level and later attended Texas Christian University on a baseball scholarship. While there, he was an All-America football pick twice.

Following his tenure at TCU, he signed with the St. Louis Cardinals baseball organization and seemed bound for a diamond career when pro football intervened in the person of George Preston Marshall, owner of the Washington Redskins.

The year was 1937, and Marshall had just moved his franchise to the nation's capital. He badly needed a drawing card, a premier attraction that would put fans in the seats and money in the club coffers. It was important that his Redskins establish a financial base that through the years would make them a profitable going concern. And he saw in Baugh just the marquee personality his team required to start the turnstiles clicking. Marshall waved a goodly amount of money for those days under the multitalented youngster's nose, $5,000 for a year's labor, and quickly got his attention. The rest is glorious history.

Baugh commenced his 16-year career in Washington as a tailback and promptly led the Redskins to the NFL title. In the championship encounter with the Chicago Bears, he pitched three touchdown passes and Washington won going away, 28–21. That season he led the league in passing by completing 81 of 171 attempts for 1,127 yards. He would reign as pro football's leading aerialist no less than six times, half of these honors being attained out of the single wing and the other half resulting from his accomplishments as a T-formation quarterback.

In 1943 he not only won the passing crown again but topped all of his contemporaries defensively with 11 interceptions. That same campaign he also held forth as the best punter in the money game. Perennially he was pitted against standout Chicago quarterback Sid Luckman during the regular season and not infrequently in postseason play. Always these duels provided a lot of spectacular pitch-and-catch histrionics from both men. But Baugh, though usually directing a less talented aggregation than that put forth by the Bears, generally proved nearly impossible to stop.

Whenever questioned about his rivalry with Baugh, Luckman would say, "Sammy is the best in the game. Nobody can match him. Nobody." Praise from Caesar is praise indeed.

Given Baugh's presence as the premier passer in the NFL, the entire face of pro football underwent a marked change. The offensive aspect of the sport opened up, intricate pass routes and multiple receivers becoming the order of the day. And gone forever were the brutal muscle matchups, the gritty grinding out of yardage with painstaking savagery, that had so epitomized the NFL in its early years. Even the shape of the ball would become more streamlined to better accommodate throwing it. Few players ever had so profound an effect on the status of the league as did the "Texas Tornado."

He wore well right to the end of his playing days. In 1947, then a battle-scarred 32, he passed for 355 yards and six TDs as the Redskins

Sammy Baugh

soundly defeated the Chicago Cardinals, who were then en route to the NFL title.

At the time of his retirement in 1952, he could look back on a career that fairly glittered and know that his place in pro football was unique, not subject to the usual ravages of passing time.

George Blanda

6'2", 215 pounds. Quarterback, Placekicker: Chicago Bears (1949–1958), Baltimore Colts (1951, one game), Houston Oilers (1960–1966, AFL), Oakland Raiders (1967–1969, AFL), Oakland Raiders (1970–1975, NFL). AFL All-Star Game: Four appearances. AFC Player of the Year: 1970. AP Male Athlete of the Year: 1970. Inducted into the Pro Football Hall of Fame 1981. Career: Passed for 36 touchdowns in 1961 (then a pro football record). Passes attempted, 4,007. Passes completed, 1,911. Completion percentage, 47.7. Passing yardage, 26,920. Touchdowns (passing), 236. Interceptions, 277. Rushing attempts, 135. Rushing yardage, 344. Yards per carry, 2.5. Touchdowns (rushing), 9. Scoring: TDs, 9. PATs, 943. FGs, 335. Total points, 2,002 (NFL record).

"George Blanda didn't invent football. But he knew the guy who did." This bit of wry wit, attributable to a member of the sportswriting fraternity, speaks to the longevity Blanda enjoyed in professional football. For 26 years (1949–1958, 1960–1975) he plied his skills as a quarterback and placekicker in the National Football League and the American Football League (AFL).

He began his lengthy play-for-pay career with the Chicago Bears in 1949, then joined the Baltimore Colts for one game in 1951 before returning to the Windy City later that year and remaining for the next eight seasons. In 1960, following a 12-month layoff, he signed on with the Houston Oilers of the AFL and remained there until 1966. The next fall he switched his allegiance to the Oakland Raiders. When the Raiders along with the rest of the league were adopted by the NFL in 1970, he came home, so to speak. At the end of the 1975 campaign, he finally hung up his cleats for good. He was just a month shy of his 49th birthday.

In the course of his long sojourn through pro football, he established himself as the game's all-time leading scorer. His record total of 2,002 points is composed of 9 touchdowns, 943 extra points, and 335 field goals.

Unlike most signal callers of note, Blanda is better remembered for what he accomplished with his foot than his arm. He was graying and pushing 40 when the Raiders took him on as a sometime quarterback and full-time placekicker. In 1970, he more than earned his keep during a five-week stint in which he threw three TD passes to beat the Pittsburgh Steelers, booted a 48-yard placement with three seconds left on the clock to tie the Kansas City Chiefs, added a scoring pass and a 52-yard field goal in the last

96 seconds of play to beat the Cleveland Browns, tossed yet another game-winning aerial at the expense of the Denver Broncos, and squeezed out the San Diego Chargers with a clutch kick at the gun. These heroics earned him AFC Player of the Year. Later, the Associated Press named him its 1970 Male Athlete of the Year. How sweet it was.

He presently resides in the Chicago suburb of La Grange Park, Illinois, and when not playing golf, still enjoys pro football as a spectator with a pointed view of the proceedings. Curiously enough, he decries the emphasis placed on statistics in the modern NFL, despite the fact his memory is preserved in the record book by some eye-opening figures. "I know this sounds funny coming from me," he said, "and no doubt I'm going to be at odds with most people, but I don't like all the statistics in the game now. I just think they take away from a team sport. Especially when you get involved in individual statistics. I never really believed in statistics other than winning and losing. Quite frankly, I feel that they detract from the unity concept of the game by singling out individuals."

Not surprisingly, Blanda maintains a keen interest in the kicking aspect of the pro game. "Today, you've got guys making several hundred thousand dollars a year just to kick," he observed. "They should be better. That's all they do. When you're paying a guy $250,000 or more, he should be expected to kick a high percentage of field goals. Back in the 1950s, we didn't put a premium on kicking. Whoever could kick did the kicking. If he kicked good, fine. And if he didn't kick good, fine. Basically, he got nothing extra in his pay envelope for kicking. So he didn't practice kicking all that much. The guys kicking now have it easier in that some years ago they brought the hashmarks in closer to the center of the field, which markedly improves the angle on the goalpost. Plus, they have special people holding for them. Even a special guy that just snaps for kicks. There's a big difference between then and now."

But some things never change, in his opinion, and getting the ball into the opposition end zone is one of them. "You still run the ball to control the clock and pass to score," he said. "That hasn't changed. And another thing is it's no easier getting a touchdown from inside the twenty-yard line. I hear a lot of criticism that NFL teams today don't score from close in like they used to do. They're supposedly too ready now to bring in the field-goal kicker instead of going for the touchdown. Let me say, inside the twenty-yard line has always been the hardest place from which to score. Quarterbacks like Bobby Layne and Johnny Unitas all had the same problem they have today. Down inside the twenty-yard line, the field shrinks. The defense has less area to cover, so you've really got to needle the ball in there. And I'm going back to many, many years ago when the scores were not as high as today. No, they couldn't get the ball in the end zone easier than now."

George Blanda

Take it from a man who knows, George Blanda, the Methuselah of pro football.

Terry Bradshaw

6'3", 210 pounds. Quarterback: Pittsburgh Steelers (1970–1983). All-Pro: 1978, 1979. Pro Bowl: Three appearances. AFC Player of the Year: 1978. Most Valuable Player: Super Bowls XIII, XIV. Inducted into the Pro Football Hall of Fame 1989. Career: Passes attempted, 3,901. Passes completed, 2,025. Completion percentage, 51.9. Passing yardage, 27,989. Touchdowns, 212. Interceptions, 210. Rushing attempts, 444. Rushing yardage, 2,255. Yards per carry, 5.1. Touchdowns (rushing), 32.

Among the finest guns ever in the National Football League was the one Terry Bradshaw carried on his right shoulder. It was a heavy-duty, long-range recoilless model with magnum-force muzzle velocity. It took him nearly five years to get it on target, but when he did finally take his best shots, they bagged four Super Bowl titles, as many conference crowns, and a covey of aerial records.

Few college gridiron heroes have debuted in the NFL with more fanfare than he. Accompanying him into the play-for-pay game were tales of an awesome throwing arm that could put the ball downtown big-time or through a brick wall. Despite his undisputed ability, he wasn't able to achieve instant stardom or immediately extricate the proud and aging Pittsburgh Steelers franchise from its long-standing doldrums.

"I was totally unprepared for pro ball," Bradshaw admitted some years later. "I had no schooling on reading defenses. I never studied the game films the way a quarterback should. So my rookie year was a disaster."

By any measure, this critique of his initial NFL campaign in 1970 wasn't far off the mark. He started eight games as a freshman, completing a puny 38.1 percent of his passes, with 24 of them being stolen by the opposition. These statistics ranked him right at the bottom of the quarterback heap. Not what the Steelers, or anybody else in the league, had expected from their golden boy.

"I can laugh now, but back then I had no idea what it meant to be the number-one draft choice in the NFL," he related. "I was an outsider who didn't mingle well. The other players looked on me as a Bible-toting Li'l Abner."

Big, at 6'3" and 210 pounds, and rawboned, he had simply overpowered the competition as a standout quarterback at Louisiana Tech. During his tenure at the little-known college, he passed for 7,149 yards and 42 touchdowns. Thus it was he gained such high ratings from the NFL scouting breed. So when he didn't perform in similarly spectacular fashion as an entry-level pro, critics were quick to attribute his failings to a "lack of smarts," a cruel indictment that severely scarred his young psyche.

"Sure I made some mistakes, particularly when I was a rookie," he conceded. "Like scrambling all over the field and then throwing an interception. So some guy wrote about me being dumb. When things didn't go right for me, it was because I was 'dumb.' I had nobody to defend me, either. Anytime I'd come out and defend myself, I'd just dig my hole deeper, so I finally just said the heck with it."

In 1971 Bradshaw prevailed as the main man under center in every game but one. A year later, he pitched the Steelers to their first divisional championship in 40 years of trying. Against Oakland in the playoffs he carved a unique niche for himself in football annals with what has become popularly known as the Immaculate Reception. With the clock running

Terry Bradshaw

down and Pittsburgh teetering on the brink of elimination, he dropped back and loosed a desperation bomb aimed at the imploring hands of intended receiver Frenchy Fuqua. En route, the pass caromed off the shoulder pads of Raiders safety Jack Tatum and fell conveniently into the grasp of Steelers running back Franco Harris, who had gone downfield just hoping to be helpful in some way. He was. Clutching the deflected ball to his bosom, he trotted into the end zone to give Pittsburgh a dramatic 13–7 victory. No one could believe it, least of all Brandshaw.

He suffered a shoulder separation in 1973 which cut into his playing time. The next year, Steelers head coach Chuck Noll decided to start Joe Gilliam at quarterback, and he sat on the bench again, this time for six games. Finally, Noll beckoned to him and said, "Go make your mistakes. We're going to win with you."

Looking back on that time, Bradshaw said, "When he [Noll] told me that, that's when I became a quarterback. Before that I wasn't making any progress. I knew that when I made mistakes, I was going to be benched."

Freed from looking over his shoulder, from the self-induced pressure of playing errorless football, he promptly became the most-feared field general in the league. After taking over the quarterback reins in early 1974, he led Pittsburgh all the way to Super Bowl IX. In the big game he hit tight end Larry Brown with a four-yard TD strike to close out the scoring and lift the Steelers to a 16–6 triumph over the Minnesota Vikings.

The ensuing season it was much the same story. Again Pittsburgh reached the Super Bowl, this time against the Dallas Cowboys, and again Bradshaw made the difference. With the Steelers holding onto a precarious 15–10 advantage in the fourth quarter, he unleashed a 64-yard money shot to wide receiver Lynn Swann that resulted in a touchdown and a 21–17 victory. Back-to-back NFL titles—not bad for a dumb quarterback.

In 1978 and 1979, Bradshaw led Pittsburgh to another double in Super Bowls XIII and XIV. After the regular season in 1978, he was accorded AFC Player of the Year. Then he was named the Most Valuable Player in Super Bowl XIII, given four touchdown passes that enabled the Steelers to claim a 35–31 edge over the Dallas Cowboys. Once more, in Super Bowl XIV, he delivered with the game on the line, recording a pair of scoring pitches to bring Pittsburgh from behind and into the winner's circle with a 31–19 win at the expense of the Los Angeles Rams. And again he earned MVP recognition.

Even as he belatedly attained superstar stature, a bit of Huck Finn still lingered in his on-field personality. He not infrequently would ignore an open receiver to force the ball into tight coverage, intent upon making the big play as opposed to a less ambitious advance. "I always wanted to go downfield with the ball at every opportunity," he said. "And sometimes I tried to make things happen when it wasn't the percentage thing to do. I never really did develop that feather touch, that light touch, especially over the middle. My inclination was always to put something on it [the ball]."

Ultimately, Bradshaw's cannon lost its fire power. Prior to the onset of training camp in 1983, he submitted to elbow surgery. And although the operation was deemed to be successful, his arm never regained its strength. He didn't appear in the Pittsburgh lineup until the next-to-last contest of the regular season, directing the Steelers to a couple of early touchdowns before taking himself out of the game with a painful elbow. That was his last hurrah.

Following his retirement in 1984, he became a color commentator for CBS telecasts of NFL games.

Earl "Dutch" Clark

6'0", 185 pounds. Quarterback (Tailback): Portsmouth Spartans (1931, 1932), Detroit Lions (1934–1938). All-Pro: 1931, 1932, 1934–1937. Inducted into the Pro Football Hall of Fame 1963 (charter member). Career: Rushing attempts, 580 (no records available for 1931). Rushing yardage, 2,757. Yards per carry, 4.8. Touchdowns (rushing), 23. Coach: Cleveland Rams (1939–1942). Won-lost record: 16–26–2.

Whether formally designated so or not, Earl "Dutch" Clark was always a coach on the field. As a team leader, he had few peers, even among his colleagues in the Hall of Fame.

Despite his slowness afoot, he prevailed as a feared triple-threat back throughout his career in the National Football League. It can truly be said that he could hurt the opposition in so many ways. When carrying the ball, he used his blockers to perfection, weaving back and forth from one sideline to the other until the sought-after opening finally appeared. Time and again he seemed to be trapped, only to emerge from a cluster of would-be tacklers and go for the big gain. He was an excellent broken-field runner who as the prime mover of a famed backfield of the 1930s known as the "infantry attack," helped to set a Detroit Lions' rushing record that stood for 36 years.

Instinctive and *reflective* were terms that best defined his mode of operation in a game situation. He could think on his feet and respond reflexively with amazing consistency, nearly always making the right move at the most opportune juncture of the proceedings. Deep in the enemy secondary he evidenced a kind of uncanny sixth sense, evading defensive perils that couldn't have been seen but only sensed with a last-second sidestep or spinning motion. It was as though he were equipped with some invisible but highly sensitive antennae that enabled him to detect pressure even as it was building and thereby quickly avoid the consequences.

He held forth at tailback, the quarterback position in the single-wing attack, and as such commanded individual scoring honors in the NFL on three occasions. Besides his ball-carrying prowess, he could throw effectively and was an excellent dropkicker, the last of that breed in the pro game. During his playing tenure he toed 15 field goals and 71 extra points through the uprights with this largely extinct mode of conversion. A quiet, unassuming man, he often avoided calling his own number for fear his teammates might misconstrue his intentions as those of a headline seeker.

Upon graduating from Colorado College, he left the little institution of higher learning with the legacy of having produced the only All-America football player in its history. He rated this honor as a senior in 1929. Thereafter nearly two years elapsed before he plied his skills in the NFL. In 1931 and 1932, he performed for the Portsmouth Spartans (forerunners of the Detroit Lions), earning All-Pro recognition both seasons.

He dropped out of the pro game in 1933 to serve as head coach at another obscure college, the Colorado School of Mines. Then a year later, it was back to the NFL and the newly christened Detroit franchise. Given his running, passing, and kicking, the Lions clawed their way to the 1935 league title tilt where they thoroughly mauled the New York Giants, 26–7. In 1937 and 1938, his final two seasons with the club, he served in the dual role of player-coach. As alluded to earlier, this change of status merely formalized what already had been in effect for years.

No less than six times he was cited as the best quarterback in the NFL. One season he completed 53.5 percent of his aerial attempts, this before the ball had been provided with a narrower tapered configuration to enable it to be thrown more accurately. He gained admission to the Hall of Fame in 1963 as a charter member. Contrary to popular misconception, nice guys don't always finish last.

On August 5, 1978, he died at 71.

Len Dawson

6'0", 190 pounds. Quarterback: Pittsburgh Steelers (1957–1959), Cleveland Browns (1960, 1961), Dallas Texans (1962, AFL), Kansas City Chiefs (1963–1969, AFL), Kansas City Chiefs (1970–1975, NFL). All-AFL: 1962, 1966. Pro Bowl: One appearance. AFL Individual Passing Champion: 1962, 1963, 1965, 1966. AFL Player of the Year: 1962. Super Bowl IV: Most Valuable Player. Inducted into the Pro Football Hall of Fame 1987. Career: Passes attempted, 3,741. Passes completed, 2,136. Completion percentage, 57.1. Passing yardage, 28,711. Touchdowns, 252. Interceptions, 187. Rushing attempts, 294. Rushing yardage, 1,293. Yards per carry, 4.4. Touchdowns (rushing), 9.

All things come to he who waits, or so goes the aged aphorism. Len Dawson will attest to its validity, but there was a time when he had his doubts. Just when it seemed his dreams had gone aglimmering, he got a much needed chance to prove himself and made the most of it. Now he's a respected Hall of Fame member. From little acorns great oaks do grow.

While at Purdue University, he distinguished himself as a quarterback who had a good command of all facets pertinent to his position. For this reason, the Pittsburgh Steelers made him their first pick in the 1957 draft. But they saw him as an insurance policy rather than a potential starter, so with veteran signal callers ahead of him on the depth chart, he mostly sat and watched.

At the close of the 1959 campaign, he went to the Cleveland Browns in a trade and was promptly consigned to the bench once more. There he languished until after the 1961 schedule. At that juncture of his uneventful career in the National Football League, he was handed his outright release. In five years with the Steelers and the Browns he threw only 45 passes in regular-season play.

But the good Lord had better things in mind for him, though Dawson would have been hard-pressed to be convinced of it back then. Across the way in the American Football League (AFL) his fallout from the NFL did not escape the notice of Hank Stram, head coach of the Dallas Texans. He had been an assistant coach at Purdue when Dawson was setting the Big Ten on fire and so wasted no time in getting his ex-pupil's signature on the dotted line. From that moment forward, Dawson did nothing but make Stram look like a genius.

His first year in the AFL, 1962, Dawson took over as the Texans' field general and passed them to the league title with a 20–17 double-overtime victory in the championship game serving as the icing on his comeback cake. His heroics earned him AFL Player of the Year. In 1963, the Texans became the Kansas City Chiefs, and both he and the team became destined for great things.

During the ensuing years, he held forth as the AFL's individual passing champion no less than four times and in the process, led the Chiefs to a trio of AFL crowns. He established himself as one of the more accurate practitioners of his trade, topping the league in the completion-percentage category on seven occasions. He also displayed a laudable ability to put the ball downfield when a quick-strike attempt was mandated. But perhaps his strong suit involved play calling, fitting his repertoire of options to the talents and abilities of those who shared the backfield with him. He had a reputation for being a heady tactician.

In Super Bowl I, Dawson saw a monumental opportunity to show the moguls of the NFL that they had made a mistake in letting him go. And he wanted to acquire a measure of revenge. But it was not to be, the awesome Green Bay Packers of Vince Lombardi prevailing in convincing fashion over the Chiefs, 35–10.

"Nothing could be done but live with it," he said afterward, "and hope to get another chance to redeem yourself."

Again the adage about waiting came to pass for him. The Chiefs made it back to the Super Bowl in January 1970 with the Minnesota Vikings providing the opposition. This time he starred, connecting on 12 of 17 aerial attempts for 142 yards and a clinching 46-yard pitch to wide receiver Otis Taylor. Kansas City prevailed by a 23–7 margin, and Dawson was voted the game's Most Valuable Player. All the old wounds were healed—and just by waiting.

John "Paddy" Driscoll

5'11", 160 pounds. Quarterback, Coach: Hammond Pros (1919), Decatur Staleys (1920), Chicago Cardinals (1920–1925, NFL), Chicago Bears (1926–1929). Inducted

into the Pro Football Hall of Fame 1965. Career: Coach: Chicago Bears (1956, 1957).
Won-lost record: 14–10–1. Championships: Western Conference, 1956.

Like everything else today, somebody in the distant past already thought of it. Take the designation *franchise player*. No, no, it's not the invention of some clever word merchant of the modern era. John "Paddy" Driscoll gave birth to the phrase 70 years ago, although in a bit different context than it is used currently.

In his heyday, 1919 to 1929, he was a triple-threat quarterback of no mean ability. He called signals out of the single wing and passed, ran, and kicked with explosive results. But punting and dropkicking the then overinflated hoghide was his real long suit. In all, he was a good part of the offense for any team that had his name on the dotted line.

However, his scoring talents were never more sorely tested than in 1920. At the time, he played for the Chicago Cardinals, who contended for fan support in the Windy City with a nonleague club dubbed the Tigers. Rather than fight a debilitating battle for gate receipts, the team owners struck upon a somewhat unique bargain. They agreed to have their minions play one another, and whoever won had the territory to themselves, the losers going out of business and stealing silently away.

As might be expected, it was a hard-fought contest with no quarter given or accepted. In the end, the Cardinals avoided extinction by a perilously narrow 6–3 margin, Driscoll's lone touchdown spelling the difference between victory and defeat. The reward for his heroics was a new contract worth $300 a game, big money in that era, and the distinction of being the first franchise player.

The Rochester Jeffersons gave up no less than 27 points to Driscoll in a 1923 confrontation, this total consisting of four touchdowns and three extra points. In 1925, he put on an eye-opening exhibition of dropkicking, converting field goal attempts of 23, 18, 50, and 35 yards to ensure the Cardinals yet another triumph.

When the Bears moved to Chicago in 1921, they promptly formed a no-love-lost rivalry with the crosstown Cardinals that persisted for many years. On such occasions, Driscoll never failed to give a premier performance. A classic example of the edge he afforded the Cardinals in these outings occurred in 1922. That year, he booted a pair of field goals to down the Bears 6–0 in an early-season showdown. Some weeks later in a rematch, he tallied three more field goals, and the Cardinals prevailed again, 9–0.

Perhaps the most galling experience for the Bears during this period took place in 1925 when the incomparable Red Grange made his National Football League debut against the Cardinals. A large crowd had turned out to see the famed Galloping Ghost do what he did best, break the big play. It was not to be, however. That afternoon Driscoll punted 23 times but only three of them got anywhere near Grange, and he was able to return but one of them. As a result, the game ended in a scoreless tie. Boos cascaded down on the balding Cardinals technician, but he merely shrugged them off. "I decided if one of us was going to look bad," he said afterward, "it wasn't going to be me. Punting to Grange is like grooving a pitch to Babe Ruth."

Driscoll went to the Bears in a 1926 trade and continued his scoring histrionics there until retiring after the 1929 campaign. He served as the team's head coach for two seasons, logging 14 wins against 10 loses and a lone tie. Under his tutelage, the Bears captured the 1956 Western Conference title but slipped badly in the standings the following year, and he resigned.

On June 29, 1968, he died at 72.

Otto Graham

6'1", 195 pounds. Quarterback: Cleveland Browns (1946–1949, AAFC), Cleveland Browns (1950–1955, NFL). All-AAFC: 1946–1949. All-Pro: 1951–1955. Pro Bowl: Five appearances. NFL's Leading Passer: 1953, 1955. Inducted into the Pro Football Hall of Fame 1965. Career: Passes attempted, 2,626. Passes completed, 1,464. Completion percentage, 55.8. Passing yardage, 23,584. Touchdowns, 174. Interceptions, 135. Rushing attempts, 405. Rushing yardage, 882. Yards per carry, 2.2. Touchdowns (rushing), 44. Interceptions, 7. Return yardage, 102. Yards per return, 14.6. Touchdowns (interceptions), 1. Punt returns, 23. Return yardage, 262. Yards per return, 11.4. Touchdowns, 0. Coach: Washington Redskins (1966–1968). Won-lost record: 17–22–3.

Otto Graham suffered from the surfeit of talent that surrounded him. Because of the great Cleveland Browns teams he quarterbacked, the annals of pro football have not accorded him the respect he is due. A curious anomaly.

Graham's penchant for accuracy was reflected in the National Football League record book for many years after he had retired from the pro game. Nonetheless, his prowess as a player has been largely forgotten. And even while still active he failed to merit the attention his deeds deserved. This can be largely attributed to the bevy of fine receivers that graced the Browns roster in the late 1940s and early 1950s, as well as the powerful offensive lines behind which he operated. In essence, he was strictly for connoisseurs.

If winning is the measure of success for a quarterback, then Graham must be dubbed the best ever. During a period of 10 seasons, four in the All-America Football Conference (AAFC) and six in the NFL, he directed the Browns into as many championship games. Cleveland was the victor in seven of these outings.

According to Pete Pihos, a Hall of Fame end with the Philadelphia Eagles of the 1950s, "Graham was the heart and soul of that Cleveland machine. Some people say he was just a robot carrying out Paul Brown's orders, but that's nonsense. You could tell that because the year after Graham left, the Browns fell to fourth place with a 5–7 record. The difference between that season and the ten consecutive championship games was Graham."

Chuck Noll, head coach of the Pittsburgh Steelers, played guard for the Browns during Graham's heyday. "Otto could pass long, short, or in between with the best of them," Noll said. "He could evade a pass rush and run with the ball. He could do it all. And he did."

With Graham as their field boss, the Browns annexed four AAFC crowns and compiled an eye-opening 52–4–3 mark. In the NFL, he led them to three championships and a 62–16–1 record in six seasons. What's more, he was the league's leading passer in 1953 and 1955. He was an all-league selection nine times (AAFC four times, NFL five times).

During his college years, he held forth as a multisport standout. He went to Northwestern University with the intention of playing basketball and studying music. But while participating in an intramural football game, he was spotted by a member of the coaching staff and invited to join the varsity. He directed the Wildcats' offense for three years as a tailback who could pass and run with equal facility. Later, he performed in a similar capacity for the Naval Pre-Flight team at the University of North Carolina.

In early 1946, Paul Brown wasted no time in signing Graham to quarterback his new Cleveland pro aggregation. And this was done despite the fact Graham had never played in a T-formation offensive scheme. But Brown had no qualms about this shortcoming. "Otto commanded all the qualities a good T-quarterback needed," Brown said. "He had poise, excellent ball-handling skills, and a distinct sense of leadership on the field. I knew learning the mechanics of the position would pose no problem for him."

Brown knew whereof he spoke. Graham went on to be named the AAFC's most valuable player two of the four years the league was in existence. He threw for 10,085 yards and 86 touchdowns during that period and earned all-conference honors four times. Then, in 1950, the Browns jumped to the NFL, and he continued his winning ways over there. "Unlike some of the other leagues that came along later," he said, "the AAFC truly was on a competitive level with the NFL. The good teams in both leagues were really good, and the poor teams were really poor. I don't think the Browns left any doubt when we entered the NFL that we were the best team in football, no matter what anybody had been saying for four years."

Cleveland met the Philadelphia Eagles, defending NFL champions, in

Otto Graham

the season opener of the 1950 campaign for both clubs. It was no contest after the first quarter, the Browns prevailing by a 35–10 count. That December they outlasted the Los Angeles Rams 30–28 to take the NFL title in their first attempt. Throughout the year, Graham sufficed as the trigger for Cleveland's high-scoring offense.

Easily the high point of Graham's professional career was the Browns' 56–10 defeat of the Detroit Lions in the 1954 NFL championship game. On that occasion, he threw for three touchdowns and ran for three more. But he was only slightly less impressive in his swan-song appearance, the 1955 title contest won by Cleveland 38–14 at the expense of the Rams. In that one he rushed for a pair of scores and then added another couple via the air.

Not one to sit still long, even in retirement, Graham tried his hand at coaching, with mixed results. He opened up the Washington Redskins' passing game but largely in vain as the team could do no better than 17–22–3 from 1966 to 1968. Also, he served as the College All-Stars' mentor several times for their August confrontation with the NFL champions in a charity exhibition game at Chicago's Soldier Field. Later, he tutored the Merchant Marine Academy team and then was the school's athletic director for many years. Now he splits his time between his homes in Connecticut and Florida, depending upon the season, and freely indulges a long-standing passion for golf.

Looking back on his playing days, he said, "I don't know if I'd do all that again. Sometimes I think I should've had my head examined for doing it."

There are some old opponents who wish he'd felt that way back in his prime.

Bob Griese

6'1", 190 pounds. Quarterback: Miami Dolphins (1967–1969, AFL), Miami Dolphins (1970–1980, NFL). All-Pro: 1971, 1977. AFL All-Star Game: Two appearances. Pro Bowl: Six appearances. NFL Passing Leader: 1977. Inducted into the Pro Football Hall of Fame 1990. Career: Passes attempted, 3,429. Passes completed, 1,926. Completion percentage, 56.3. Passing yardage, 25,092. Touchdowns, 192. Interceptions, 172. Rushing attempts, 261. Rushing yardage, 994. Yards per carry, 3.8. Touchdowns (rushing), 7.

The term *field general* applies to Bob Griese in all its varied contexts. For a fact, few quarterbacks in the Hall of Fame marshaled their troops as effectively as he. Whatever the strong suits of his receivers and backs, he played to them with the touch of a virtuoso. Yes, he ran, kicked, and passed with the best of them. But few of this number qualified as his peers when it came to directing the offense as a whole.

Bob Griese

What he meant to the Miami Dolphins can best be illustrated by his presence late in the "perfect season" of 1972. After nine weeks on the sidelines due to a debilitating injury, he was called into that year's American Football Conference championship contest, the Dolphins trailing the Pittsburgh Steelers 10–7 in the third quarter. Performing as though never out of the lineup and seemingly unmindful of the crushing pressure, he coolly engineered touchdown drives of 80 and 49 yards to give the Miami forces a 21–17 victory. In the process he completed three of five passes for 70 yards and otherwise served as the jump start the Dolphins needed to get their powerful ground game into overdrive.

Just two weeks later, it was more of the same in Super Bowl VII, Griese pulling all the right levers and his awesome running attack responding with a sock-it-to-'em 14–7 win over the Washington Redskins. And just to be sure his team's motor didn't overheat en route, he pitched TD connections of 28 yards and 47 yards, the latter effort being nullified by a penalty. Afterward, Miami head coach Don Shula stated for all to hear, "Bob is the master of the position of quarterback. He knows our people and how to use them. And he knows the defenses inside and out. There isn't much more you can say about him."

Sans Griese, it is doubtful the Dolphins would have posted that historic 17–0 campaign. He was the firing mechanism that discharged all those scoring explosives.

A two-time All-America pick at Purdue University, he led the Boilermakers to a 14–13 triumph over Southern California in the 1967 Rose Bowl as a senior. Still, the pro scouts were a bit leery of him because of his size, only 6'1" and 190 pounds. But Miami personnel director Joe Thomas knew a good thing when he saw it and wasted no time in getting the heady Hoosier to sign on the dotted line. "You could see he was going to be a good one," Thomas said. "He had live feet, a quick arm, and that fluid way of moving like a thoroughbred. He was very wide-eyed and alert. And he listened to you with an intelligent attentiveness."

If some of the Dolphins' front-office personnel had any doubts about Griese's ability to hack it in the bigs, they were quickly disabused of those negative thoughts early in his rookie season. Midway through the opening game of the 1967 schedule, he took over at quarterback for the injured starter and immediately made things happen. Within minutes, he drove Miami 80 yards for a score with his 27-yard aerial proving the clincher. By the final gun, he was 12 for 19 in the passing department for 193 yards and a pair of touchdowns. Oh yes, the Dolphins won 35–21.

During the early 1970s when Griese quarterbacked a dominating ball-control club, the rumor made the rounds that he didn't have the arm for the deep ball. But again he embarrassed his critics. Any number of his TD tosses were in the "bomb" category, one of them resulting in an 87-yard hookup with wideout Paul Warfield, a favorite target on the fly patterns the Dolphins would intermittently call to keep the opposition defense from stacking against the run. In 1973, he hit Warfield four times with six-point tallies in the first half of one game, a couple of them airborne a long time. And four years later he tapped the St. Louis Cardinals secondary for six TD passes in another outing. Not bad for a guy supposedly afflicted with a weak wing.

If Griese is to be believed, there's "no great mystery to quarterbacking. You move people around in various formations, looking for the defense's particular patsy, and then you eat him alive."

Overall, he attempted 3,429 aerials and completed 1,926 of them for 25,092 yards and 192 touchdowns. He led the NFL with 22 scoring passes in 1977. Yet he is most revered for his singular ability to run the vaunted Miami "grunt" attack in the club's glory years. And the best example of his handiwork in this regard occurred when the Dolphins won Super Bowl VIII by whipping the Minnesota Vikings 24–7. In that encounter he put the ball up just seven times while handing off on 53 occasions.

"Bob gets as much of a thrill calling the right running play for a touchdown as he does connecting on a bomb," Shula said. "That's just his makeup."

Griese excelled in spite of 20-200 vision in his right eye, a deficiency which adversely affected his perspective. He tried contact lenses and then glasses before finally reaching an accommodation with his problem. And then there were injuries that benched him five weeks in 1969, nine weeks in 1972, four weeks in 1975, five weeks in 1978, and 11 weeks in 1980, his final season.

He was an All-Pro selection twice and appeared in two AFL All-Star games and six Pro Bowls during his 14-year career.

Arnie Herber

6'1", 200 pounds. Quarterback: Green Bay Packers (1930–1940), New York Giants (1944, 1945). All-Pro: 1932. NFL Individual Passing Champion: 1932, 1934, 1936. Inducted into the Pro Football Hall of Fame 1966. Career: Passes attempted, 1,174. Passes completed, 487. Completion percentage, 41.5. Passing yardage, 8,033. Touchdowns, 79. Interceptions, 98.

In something of a Horatio Alger saga, Arnie Herber went from a clubhouse attendant for the pro club he had loved since boyhood to the star quarterback of the team during one of its most illustrious eras—by any measure, a story that could have been written in Hollywood, but wouldn't have been set in such a rustic site as Green Bay, Wisconsin.

As a youth, he was a local high school football and basketball standout and sold game programs on Sundays to see the Packers perform. Following graduation, he enrolled at the University of Wisconsin and then transferred to little Regis College in Denver to play under head coach Red Strader, who harbored visions of building the school into a gridiron power. But all such dreams were snuffed out by the hard hand of the 1929 stock-market crash and what it portended.

Herber returned to Green Bay and found employment in the Packers organization as a handyman. Finally, head coach "Curly" Lambeau agreed to give the inexperienced 20-year-old a tryout. The young man demonstrated a strong throwing arm, good speed, and no little punting ability. So for $75 a game the franchise got itself a homegrown quarterback who would merit his team and himself national headlines.

In his first outing as a rookie, he pitched a touchdown pass to give the Packers a 7–0 victory. Buoyed by his heady debut, he went on to lead the club to the National Football League title. The year was 1930. And he duplicated this feat in 1931, his long, accurate aerials triggering one of the most potent passing attacks of that day. He now held forth as the talk of the pro game, a far cry from his menial anonymity only months earlier.

While his ability to throw scoring bombs rated most of the sportswriters' attention, he could put points on the board in other ways. During a 1932 contest against the Staten Island Stapletons, he ran for touchdowns of 85 and 45 yards and saw to all the punting chores. Oh yes, he also pitched three TD strikes. In 1932, 1934, and 1936, he prevailed as the NFL individual passing champion. His aerial attainments were all the more remarkable because he didn't possess the broad span of hand thought to be a requisite for effectively throwing the rounded ball of that time. To compensate for short fingers, he hooked his thumb around the laces, a technique contrary to the conventional method, which ensured a firm grip and the desired tight spiral.

No sooner did a lanky end named Don Hutson join the team in 1935 than he and Herber mounted an all-out assault on the NFL record book. Given the elusive University of Alabama import's ability to get downfield in a hurry and the stocky Green Bay quarterback's slingshot arm, the Packers were ever in the hunt for league supremacy. They made it to the championship game on three occasions within a five-year stretch and came away winners in 1936 and 1939.

Herber retired after the 1940 campaign. But due to a player shortage imposed on the NFL by World War II, he suited up once more, only this time in a New York Giants uniform. In 1944, he helped put the Giants atop the Eastern Division but was unable to get them past Green Bay in the title contest. Following the 1945 season, he retired again, this time permanently.

On October 14, 1969, he died at 59.

Sonny Jurgensen

6'0", 203 pounds. Quarterback: Philadelphia Eagles (1957–1963), Washington Redskins (1964–1974). NFL Individual Passing Leader: 1966, 1967, 1969. Pro Bowl: Five invitations, four appearances. Inducted into the Pro Football Hall of Fame 1983. Career: Passes attempted, 4,262. Passes completed, 2,433. Completion percentage, 57.1. Passing yardage, 32,224. Touchdowns, 255. Interceptions, 189. Rushing attempts, 181. Rushing yardage, 493. Yards per carry, 2.7. Touchdowns (rushing), 15.

Perhaps it's only fitting that a quarterback often touted to have displayed the best throwing arm in National Football League history is named Christian Adolph Jurgensen, III. That is individuality to the max.

He enjoyed the admiration of his peers throughout a career that spanned 18 seasons. Baltimore Colts Hall of Fame flinger Johnny Unitas once said, "If I threw as much as Jurgensen, my arm would fall off. And if I could throw as well, my head would swell up too big to get into a helmet."

Yet another glowing testimonial came from "Dandy Don" Meredith back when his Dallas Cowboys regularly opposed Jurgensen's Washington Redskins in conference play. Said Meredith: "Sonny's the one person who can pass a defense to death. He's an uncanny passer, simply the best the game has had."

Like Bobby Layne before him, Jurgensen loved a good time almost as much as he did winning football games. In his heyday, he could be seen zipping around the nation's capital night after night in a racy sports car bearing license plates inscribed SONNY. A good-natured smile frequented his freckled open features, and more often than not an outsize cigar jutted from his lips. Wherever tart libation bathed with cubed ice he could be found. But the late hours notwithstanding, he never failed to bring his best form to the ballpark on game day.

After a noteworthy stint at Duke University, he began his NFL tenure with the Philadelphia Eagles as a backup signal caller. When the Eagles won the 1960 league title, he saw the game from the bench, waiting in reserve on the likes of Hall of Fame quarterback Norm Van Brocklin. The following year, after the Dutchman had retired, he took over the field-general duties and promptly went to the top of the passing charts with 235 completions for 3,723 yards and 32 touchdowns. In 1962, he repeated as the leader of the yardage-gained-throwing category with 3,261. The next year, hampered by injuries, his production fell off, and he was traded to the Redskins. His acquisition had to be one of the best moves the Washington franchise ever made.

Under head coach Bill McPeak, Jurgensen mixed the run and the pass more equitably than had been the case in Philadelphia, but his completion statistics continued to exceed the 50 percent mark. Then, in 1966, when Hall of Fame quarterback Otto Graham took over the Redskins coaching reins, he again reveled in a situation where the forward pass was designated as the principal weapon of attack. That year and the next he held forth once more as the NFL's pitching pacesetter, throwing for 3,209 yards in 1966 and 3,747 in 1967.

A dropback passer, he never made any bones about his inability to scramble effectively. "Just four seconds is all I ask of my offensive line," he said. "I'm not going to beat anybody running. But I can passing, only I need to stay on my feet to do it."

In 1969, Jurgensen maintained his position at the fore of the league quarterbacks, completing 62 percent of his aerials for 3,102 yards. But while he reigned almost perennially as the "top gun" in the NFL, his ambition to play with a championship team seemed a remote possibility at best. Then George Allen came to Washington in 1971, and hope sprang eternal once more. And well it might have, for the very next year the Redskins went all the way to the Super Bowl. But the downside of it was that Jurgensen tore

Sonny Jurgensen

an Achilles tendon and was forced to the sidelines for both the NFC and Super Bowl title games. Equally discouraging, Washington lost in the league-championship tilt, and he could but watch in frustration.

Upon retiring after the 1974 campaign, Jurgensen was able to look back at his attainments with no little pride. He won three individual NFL passing crowns, had five 3,000-yard seasons, and threw in excess of 400 yards five times and 300 yards in no less than 25 games.

Summing up, he said, "I don't think the job has ever been created that is more difficult than being a quarterback in the NFL. . . . It takes a special kind of person to really make it as a successful NFL quarterback."

It goes without saying that Sonny Jurgensen was that special kind of person.

Bobby Layne

6'2", 190 pounds. Quarterback: Chicago Bears (1948), New York Bulldogs (1949), Detroit Lions (1950–1958), Pittsburgh Steelers (1958–1962). All-Pro: 1953, 1954. Pro Bowl: Three appearances. NFL Individual Passing Leader: 1951. Inducted into the Pro Football Hall of Fame 1967. Career: Passes attempted, 3,700. Passes completed, 1,814. Completion percentage, 49.0. Passing yardage, 26,768. Touchdowns (passing), 196. Interceptions, 243. Rushing attempts, 611. Rushing yardage, 2,451. Yards per carry, 4.0. Touchdowns (rushing), 25.

Whether the stadium lights were up or the club lights were down, Bobby Layne always gave it his best effort. He liked to think he was here for a good time, not necessarily a long time.

Many a football aficionado has speculated how Layne would have fared in the modern National Football League with the coaching staff calling the plays and computerized game plans all the rage. The answer is that something would've had to give. And most likely it wouldn't have been the forthright Texan.

Shortly before his death on December 1, 1986, Layne discussed the subject of play calling and who should do it. "Nobody ever called plays for me," he said in a belligerent tone. "That's why I spent all those extra hours with the coaches for five or six days each week before a game. After all that, if I didn't know what the head coach wanted me to do on Sunday, then I shouldn't be the quarterback out there. During the week, we went over it and over it and over it. It was just quarterbacks and coaches drilling for the upcoming team. Sure, some plays came in from the sidelines on occasion, but the quarterback had the option to use them or not. On the field, the quarterback ran the game."

When it was submitted that coaches in the press box commanded a better perspective of the defensive maneuvers, Layne had a ready response. "Yeah, I admit they can see more from upstairs than the quarterback in the game," he said, "only it's different being up there than in the heat of the action. When you're in the middle of the battle, it's quite different. I got most of my information from the players in the game. They knew who they could block and who they could beat. If the players have confidence in you as a quarterback, you can call the worst play in the world and they'll make it work."

Like a general at the head of an army, Layne pointed the way, and his teammates dutifully did as bid. And if they didn't, they heard about it in terms unfit for a schoolmarm's ears. Perhaps there is no better illustration of this phenomenon than what transpired in the waning minutes of the 1953 NFL championship game. At that juncture of the proceedings, the Detroit Lions, quarterbacked by Layne, trailed the Cleveland Browns

Bobby Layne

16–10 with the ball on their 20-yard line and the clock rapidly running down.

"Just give ol' Bobby a little time," he chirped in his familiar rasping tone, "and we'll be in their end zone directly. Understand?" His eyes, speaking volumes more, panned the encircling faces. The full context of the message was understood right enough. He connected on four of his first six passes to put the Lions in scoring position. Then he threw a final completion of 33 yards for the go-ahead touchdown. And this was all accomplished within the fleeting span of 69 seconds. Detroit prevailed 17–16 to win the league title.

In all, the Lions annexed three NFL championships—1952, 1953, and 1957—out of four appearances in the title game during Layne's tenure with the club. He was traded to the Pittsburgh Steelers in 1958, and Detroit's halcyon football fortunes went with him. He was, in every sense of the word, a winner. And he also presided as something of a dictator, on and off the field. When Joe Schmidt, a rookie linebacker with the Lions in 1953, became a starter as the result of a veteran being traded away, it was Layne who sidled up to him and said, "You better be good, kid."

As a matter of course, Layne appropriated rookies to do his chores, everything from running errands to chauffeuring him on nocturnal excursions to a favorite Pontiac watering hole. This latter task supplied Alex Karras, a many-time All-Pro defensive tackle, with some bittersweet memories. "I'd drive him up to this place in Pontiac and then sleep in the car until he was ready to go," Karras related. "One night I went inside for a few beers, and when I came out, he was already behind the wheel. He drove back singing at the top of his lungs with one foot propped up on the dashboard. We must have been doing one hundred miles per hour. Ever after that, I made sure I was in the driver's seat before he got there."

Doak Walker, a multipurpose running back with the Lions and a friend of Layne's, once said, "Even the assistant coaches were afraid of Bobby. They knew the kind of power he had with the club."

But Layne could be autocratic and get away with it because he had that ability to put numbers on the scoreboard once the whistle blew. He was a winner. That's what counted.

One of the more persisting myths about him is the macho image he supposedly promoted by disdaining to wear a face mask. "I didn't want to get my face busted up any more than the next guy," he explained. "But I just didn't feel comfortable wearing a face mask. I tried all kinds of them in practice. Everything from a single bar to the cage kind that linemen wear. Only they all impaired my vision of the field and the receivers. So I didn't wear one. Maybe if I had worn one when I started playing football, it would have been different. But I didn't wear one because I was trying to be a tough guy or whatever."

With the advent of extensive rules changes in the late 1970s, Layne became critical of the emphasis placed on passing in the pro game to the detriment of running the ball. He felt that some things shouldn't be subject to tampering. "Back when I was with the Lions," he said, "we tried to keep the pass-and-run ratio at 60 to 40 either way. Every time we exceeded that kind of balance, we got beat. It doesn't matter if you're fourteen points behind, you still have to stick to your game plan, you still have to run at them. You can't throw every down because they'll just lay back their ears and come after your quarterback. If the defense can just play pass, they'll force you to make turnovers. Running complements passing and vice versa. Do what they don't expect you to do, only stay in balance. Through the years, winning teams have always done that."

Cancer was the culprit that put the final sack on Layne at the age of 59. But it didn't happen until his defenses had been dangerously weakened by too many dusk-to-dawn encounters with countless glasses of tart bubbly. Still, he went the way he knew best—playing hard. God love ye, Bobby.

Sid Luckman

Sid Luckman

6'0", 190 pounds. Quarterback: Chicago Bears (1939–1950). All-Pro: 1941–1943, 1945–1947. NFL Most Valuable Player: 1943. NFL Passing Champion: 1945. Inducted into the Pro Football Hall of Fame 1965. Career: Passes attempted, 1,744. Passes completed, 904. Completion percentage, 51.8. Passing yardage, 14,683. Touchdowns, 137. Interceptions, 131. Rushing attempts, 204. Rushing yardage, 209. Yards per carry, 1.0. Touchdowns (rushing), 2. Punt returns, 11. Return yardage, 107. Yards per return, 9.7. Touchdowns (punt returns), 0. Interceptions, 14. Return yardage, 293. Yards per return, 20.9. Touchdowns (interception returns), 1. Punts, 230. Yards per punt, 38.4.

The T-formation was an idea whose time had come when Sid Luckman entered the National Football League. Previous to that, it just looked good, very good, on paper.

When the stocky single-wing standout from Columbia University signed on with the Chicago Bears in 1939, the modern version of pro football had its inception. Bears owner and coach George Halas formally introduced him to the innovative offense while he was preparing for the College All-Star Game in the late summer of that year. Just a glance at the playbook caused the young recruit to shake his head in dismay. It goes without saying that this mating didn't exactly amount to a classic case of love at first sight.

Luckman found the transition to the T format difficult in the early going. Adjusting to the direct snap from center produced any number of fumbles, and he also had problems handing off to the running backs, the timing and positioning required being totally unfamiliar to him. As a result, he was moved briefly to halfback where his considerable ball-carrying skills could be better utilized. But he got a second chance to operate under center, and on this occasion the system took.

Perhaps he and the T-formation officially came of age in the 1940 NFL championship game between the Bears and the Washington Redskins. Before that historic meeting, he had experienced some success in his new role, but there were still a few more wrinkles to be ironed out. Clark Shaughnessy, head coach at Stanford University and a consultant to the Bears since his days at the University of Chicago, all but fathered the new mode of attack. He took Luckman under his wing and developed a man-in-motion deception that was just what the young quarterback needed to deal effectively with the Redskins.

Washington had defeated the Bears 7-3 during the 1940 regular season, and this was done by shifting linebackers to the side of the field the motion man moved, thereby neutralizing his effectiveness. So Shaughnessy added a counterplay to the Bears' game plan wherein an end was split out and the motion went away from him. But when the defense adjusted in the direction of the motion, a halfback took a pitch and ran toward the split-end side with his blockers operating against only a one-deep front. It would work to perfection.

On the first play from scrimmage in the title tilt, Luckman set one back in motion, and the Redskins linebackers moved right with him as expected. Then he pivoted inside, flipped the ball out to a second back crossing, and the play went 68 yards for a touchdown. It served to trigger a deluge of scores, Chicago prevailing 73-0 for the largest margin of victory ever in NFL annals.

That afternoon, Luckman put aloft only six passes, four of them connecting for 102 yards and a TD. He didn't throw more often because it wasn't necessary. But he played a brilliant game, directing the Bears' awesome running attack with deft faking, handoffs, and pitchouts that kept the Washington defenders out of position for the most part. Given this display of T-formation perfection, pro football suddenly found itself standing on the threshold of a new and exciting era.

Such was also true of Luckman's career. He would lead Chicago to three more league crowns while earning All-Pro recognition no less than six times in a seven-season span. In 1943, he was voted the NFL's Most Valuable Player, passing for 2,194 yards and 28 touchdowns to lead his quarterbacking contemporaries in both categories. That year, he also enjoyed two of his finest outings in a 12-year pro tenure. Facing the New York Giants at the Polo Grounds on Sid Luckman Day, he pitched a record-equaling seven TDs in directing the Bears to a 56–7 triumph. Later, in the championship game against the Redskins, his aerials accounted for 276 yards and five touchdowns, Chicago winning easily, 41–21.

In 1946, the Chicago Rockets of the All-America Football Conference offered Luckman $25,000 a year to be a player-coach, but he turned them down solely out of a deep-seated loyalty to the Bears. "How could I possibly have taken it," he said. "How could I quit a club that has done so much for me."

Even after retiring as a player following the 1950 campaign, he continued to have a close relationship with his beloved Bears.

Joe Namath

6'2", 200 pounds. Quarterback: New York Jets (1965–1969, AFL), New York Jets (1970–1976, NFL), Los Angeles Rams (1977). AFL Player of the Year: 1968. All-Pro: 1972. AFL All-Star Game: Four appearances. Pro Bowl: One appearance. Inducted into the Pro Football Hall of Fame 1985. Career: Passes attempted, 3,762. Passes completed, 1,886. Completion percentage, 50.1. Passing yardage, 27,663. Touchdowns, 173. Interceptions, 220. Rushing attempts, 71. Rushing yardage, 140. Yards per carry, 2.0. Touchdowns (rushing), 7.

"I absolutely guarantee it."

These words still ring down the annals of pro football, words uttered by Joe Namath, then the highly visible quarterback of the upstart New York Jets from the equally upstart American Football League (AFL). His words made headlines across the land and became etched in sporting stone when he made good on them in Super Bowl III, leading the Jets to an historic 16–7 victory over the Baltimore Colts, champions of the establishment National Football League.

Perhaps only Babe Ruth's calling his home run matches in audacity what Namath proposed and then accomplished before an audience of millions. It was gamesmanship pure and simple. And it worked, as the Colts overreacted in their eagerness to put down the arrogant "Broadway Joe," emotion and anger repeatedly subverting better judgment and a carefully prepared game plan. The big-city slicker had conned them and thus ensured himself a unique bit of football immortality.

But Hall of Fame honors are conferred for attainments of broader scope than just an isolated bit of derring-do, no matter its once-in-a-lifetime proportions. Namath could play football. His statistics and frequently demonstrated on-field leadership qualities prove this point beyond all dispute. Unfortunately, his public profile tends to obscure these documentable factors even now.

When he came out of the University of Alabama in 1965 with a much-heralded throwing arm and two battered knees, it was assumed that some NFL team would avail itself of his services. But he emerged at a turbulent time, a bidding war for playing talent going full bore in the AFL. So it came as something of a shock to those in the pro football know when he joined the Jets for a reported $400,000. That it constituted a coup for the AFL could not be denied by the NFL. Not a few observers felt that this single event did much to turn the tide of thinking in the senior league from an attitude of confrontation to one of conciliation. Obviously, the AFL could compete monetarily, and signing Namath merely signified its willingness to do so.

Once in a Jets uniform, he became the eye of a publicity vortex which had its origin in the front office. The idea was to put people in the seats, fill Shea Stadium for home games, and it had the desired effect. But the "party guy" image didn't make it easy on the young quarterback as every defensive headhunter in the league was after him. True, he enjoyed a little after-hours fun as well as the next person, but it wasn't the focal point of his life, as the media have been led to believe. His big paycheck and all the attending ink may have made him the envy of every male in America, but it didn't make his football life any easier. Yet, he somehow managed to grow into the role cast for him and still succeed on Sundays.

"I'm a pretty confident guy," he said. "I know what my abilities are. I know that if you add up all the things a quarterback needs—the ability to throw, to read defenses, to call plays, to lead the team—that nobody has ever played the position of quarterback any better than I do."

As a sophomore in 1966, he led the AFL in passing by completing 232 aerials out of 471 attempts for 3,379 yards and 19 touchdowns. On the downside, he also gave up a league-high 27 interceptions. The following year, he again threw the ball better than the rest of his AFL signal-calling contemporaries, connecting on 258 of 491 pitches for 4,007 yards and 26 TDs. It is noteworthy that he thus became the first quarterback in all of pro football to exceed the 4,000-yard mark in a single season. What's more, he attained this feat in a 14-game schedule.

The 1968 AFL championship game provided him one of his finest hours. Facing the formidable Oakland Raiders that afternoon, he threw for 266 yards and three touchdowns, which put the Jets into Super Bowl III and set the stage for his unforgettable theatrics. As a result of this performance, he was named the league's Player of the Year.

Many times in his career he enjoyed 300-yard passing games despite the fact that his damaged knees didn't allow him to roll out of the pocket to escape a pressing rush. In light of this fact, his accomplishments acquire an even greater luster.

In 1972, he paced all quarterbacks in the NFL with 2,816 yards on a 162-for-324 completion ratio and 19 TDs. Just five seasons later, he finished up his tenure in the pro game with the Los Angeles Rams. Injuries prevented him from leaving the league on a high note. "Yeah, I could consider it the worst experience of my life," he said of his year with the Rams, "but I'm not going to let it be. I'm just going to accept it as a great experience. I went through things emotionally I never went through before. And I am a wiser man for it."

Namath played in four AFL All-Star games and one NFL Pro Bowl. In 1969, he was voted to the All-Time AFL team. He earned All-Pro recognition in 1972.

Class is a term that fit him like the proverbial glove, both on and off the field.

Clarence "Ace" Parker

5'11", 168 pounds. Quarterback: Brooklyn Dodgers (1937–1941), Boston Yanks (1945), New York Yankees (1946, AAFC). All-Pro: 1938, 1940. NFL Most Valuable Player: 1940. Inducted into the Pro Football Hall of Fame 1972. Career: Passes attempted, 718. Passes completed, 335. Completion percentage, 46.7. Passing yardage, 4,701. Touchdowns, 30. Interceptions, 50. Rushing attempts, 498. Rushing yardage, 1,282. Yards per carry, 2.6. Touchdowns (rushing), 14. Receptions, 8. Receiving yardage, 229. Yards per reception, 28.6. Touchdowns (receiving), 3. Punt returns (1941–1946), 24. Return yardage, 238. Yards per return, 9.9. Touchdowns, 0. Kickoff returns (1945, 1946), 2. Return yardage, 27. Yards per return, 13.5. Touchdowns, 0. Punts (1939–1946), 150. Yards per punt, 38.3. Interceptions (1940–1946), 7 (no other data available).

The team that had Clarence "Ace" Parker as a quarterback held the trump card in any game of showdown, so much so that the opposition could legitimately claim they were the victims of a raw deal.

At the height of his powers, he often proved to be the "ace in the hole" that made the difference between victory and defeat more sure than the turn of a card. In 1940, while employed by the Brooklyn Dodgers of the National Football League, he singly outscored the Chicago Cardinals 14–9. Just two weeks later, he repeated this feat, tallying two touchdowns and converting the attending extra points to overcome the crosstown New York Giants by a 14–6 margin. The next year, 1941, he undercut the Giants once more by making a TD-saving tackle, throwing a scoring pass, and legging the ball 61 yards to set up the deciding six points.

Curiously, Parker didn't really have a football career in mind when he left Duke University as an All-America tailback in 1936. Baseball was his main game back then, and he quickly signed on with the Philadelphia Athletics. Football, in his view, would suffice as an offseason endeavor aimed at keeping him in shape and his bank account appropriately padded.

After the 1937 baseball campaign, he joined the Dodgers, intending simply to play out the slate and then return to the diamond sport. However, he continued to perform for the Brooklyn franchise through the 1941 schedule. When World War II intervened, early in 1942 he entered the service of his country. In 1945, he returned to the NFL, this time to ply his abilities as a member of the Boston Yanks. Finally, he closed out his pro football tenure in 1946 with the New York Yankees of the All-America Football Conference (AAFC). He enjoyed one of his best years ever, leading his team to the AAFC Eastern Division title. He threw for eight touchdowns and added three more with the ball tucked under his arm to account for nearly 1,000 yards.

Were it not for injuries incurred in baseball, he might well have persisted a bit longer on the gridiron and perhaps even flared a mite more brilliantly in the process. Broken ankles sustained between the foul lines hindered him in the pursuit of football accolades. During the first three weeks of the 1940 NFL slate, he was hobbled by a cumbersome 10-pound brace that encompassed his lower left leg. Yet he still managed to win Most Valuable Player honors for the year.

Though slowed by his baseball impairments, it is true he was never particularly fleet of foot. But he commanded a certain resiliency that enabled him to run, pass, catch, and kick the ball, as well as play defense in near top form right to the end of his pro football days. And always he remained the master of the Hollywood finish, an act of derring-do perpetually at the ready to transform a loss into a win just before the last scene faded to black.

He rated All-Pro recognition in 1938 and 1940. Also, he participated in the first professional football game televised. The year was 1939, and he pitched a touchdown strike to give the Dodgers a 23–14 edge over the Philadelphia Eagles.

Currently, Parker serves as a scout for the Phoenix Cardinals, his area of responsibility being the far-eastern United States.

Bart Starr

6'1", 200 pounds. Quarterback: Green Bay Packers (1956–1971). All-Pro: 1966. Pro Bowl: Four appearances. NFL Player of the Year: 1966. Most Valuable Player: Super Bowls I and II. NFL Passing Leader: 1962, 1964, 1966. Inducted into the Pro Football Hall of Fame 1977. Career: Passes attempted, 3,149. Passes completed, 1,808. Completion percentage, 57.4. Passing yardage, 24,718. Touchdowns, 152. Interceptions, 138. Rushing attempts, 247. Rushing yardage, 1,308. Yards per carry, 5.3. Touchdowns (rushing), 15. Coach: Green Bay Packers (1975–1983). Won-lost record: 53–77–3. Championships: Central Division (NFC), 1978 (shared).

In the ground-consuming machine the Green Bay Packers comprised during the 1960 decade of the National Football League, the ignition was undeniably Bart Starr. His intelligence and on-field leadership supplied the impetus and direction the aggregation of stars which surrounded him required to attain the laurels they did as a unit.

When he came out of the University of Alabama, there was no hue and cry for his quarterbacking services among the teams in the NFL. He didn't get picked until the 17th round of the 1956 college draft, and then nobody wanted him except the lowly Green Bay Packers. Despite the club's lack of talent at most positions, he didn't get much playing time during his first three seasons as a pro practitioner. But his fortunes took a definite turn for the better with the arrival of Vince Lombardi as the club's head coach in 1959.

Even then, there were team officials who didn't think Starr was the man to lead the Packers. But Lombardi knew otherwise. He had watched the young signal caller perform in practice and on film, and liked his sure manner, his ball-handling ability, and his strong, reliable arm. The basic equipment for success was all there. But the young man's confidence had to be built and then bolstered. And this didn't prove an easy task.

Lombardi's manner was that of a taskmaster. He yelled, ranted, and verbally prodded his charges in long, tiring practice sessions. This proved to be a problem for Starr, so, steeling himself, he asked his coach for a personal conference and got it.

"He (Lombardi) would criticize me in front of the other players," Starr recalled, "and I felt if it persisted, they wouldn't respect me as their quarterback. So I asked him if we could discuss the matter privately. He listened and agreed that if there were any problems in the future, we would settle them in his office."

Given this assurance, Starr quickly blossomed into a standout field general. But even at the height of the Packers' powers, he failed to derive the recognition due him. With Paul Hornung and Jim Taylor carrying the ball and Max McGee catching passes, it didn't seem to the unschooled eye as though he was doing all that much. This myth was easily perpetuated because he commanded a largely ball-control offense and never threw as many as 300 passes in a season. But when he did put the ball up, it went special delivery. His aerial offerings were rarely susceptible to interception.

More important was his consummate skill in operating the Green Bay attack. He excelled at reading defenses and often changed his calls at the line of scrimmage, frequently catching the opposition out of position or nullifying a carefully disguised blitz. A classic example of his ability to outwit an opponent occurred during the famous 1967 "Ice Bowl" NFL title game between the Packers and Dallas in subzero weather. With the outcome

Bart Starr (kneeling)

on the line in the waning seconds of play, he crossed up the Cowboys' defense by running a quarterback keep for the winning one-yard plunge instead of handing the ball off to one of his celebrated backs. Green Bay prevailed 21–17.

He figured heavily in the Packers' back-to-back wins in Super Bowls I and II. On both occasions, attending sportswriters voted him Most Valuable Player. In 1966, he rated All-Pro recognition and was named the NFL's Player of the Year.

Following his retirement as a player at the close of the 1971 season, he briefly tutored the Green Bay quarterbacks and then, from 1975 to 1983, served as Packers head coach.

Roger Staubach

6'3", 202 pounds. Quarterback: Dallas Cowboys (1969–1979). Pro Bowl: Five appearances. NFL Individual Passing Champion: 1971, 1973, 1978, 1979. Inducted into the Pro Football Hall of Fame 1985. Heisman Trophy, Maxwell Award Winner: 1963. Career: Passes attempted, 2,958. Passes completed, 1,685. Completion percentage, 57.0. Passing yardage, 22,700. Touchdowns, 153. Interceptions, 109. Rushing attempts, 410. Rushing yardage, 2,264. Yards per carry, 5.5. Touchdowns (rushing), 20.

Like the hero in those Saturday-afternoon adventure flicks of years gone by, Roger Staubach always saved his most daring histrionics until the last reel.

In an 11-year tenure as a quarterback with the Dallas Cowboys, "Roger the Dodger" was the trigger for 23 come-from-behind victories in the final period, 14 consummated after the intercession of the two-minute warning or in overtime. Nobody ever performed better more often than he did with the seconds ticking off the scoreboard clock and the muzzle of the game-ending gun pointed skyward.

"Confidence," he frequently said, was the secret of his ability to pull out the cliffhangers. "It's a circle. Work builds confidence. And more work builds more confidence. Hard work. There isn't any substitute for it. Some guys may get by for a little while on sheer talent, but if you want to stay on top, you have to like work."

Liking work was a trait of Staubach's that four years at the U.S. Naval Academy merely served to enhance. And it's what enabled him to keep his competitive edge while on active duty for another four years, years away from organized football. "I had it in mind to play pro ball," he said. "I knew how easy it is to lose your touch, your drive, when away from the game. But I wasn't going to let it happen. I had a regular exercise schedule— running, lifting weights, and so on. It just felt so good. You're out there, breaking a sweat, and the confidence comes right up. You know you can do it, and the work makes it all possible."

He reported to the Cowboys in 1969, four years after his glory days as a Heisman Trophy college star, and immediately set about learning how to be a signal caller in the National Football League. It took him better than two seasons to get a starting opportunity, but he made the most of it. That year, 1971, he won the NFL's individual passing title and his touchdown production totaled 15.

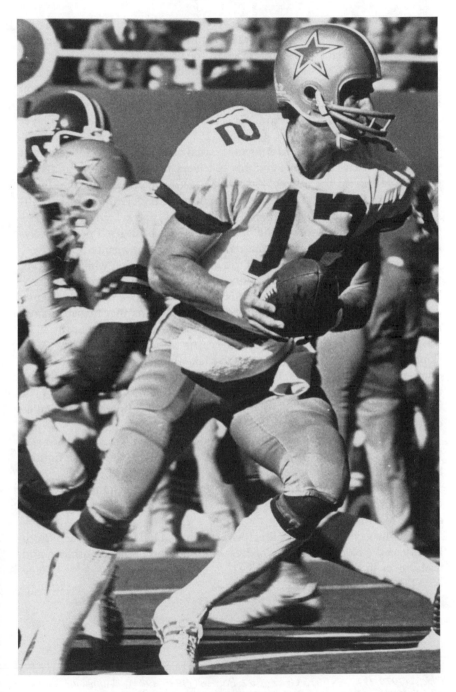

Roger Staubach

Once in the driver's seat, he never looked back. He repeated as individual passing champion in 1973, 1978, and 1979. And in 1977, he headed all of his quarterback contemporaries in four categories—attempts (361), completions (210), yardage (2,620), and touchdowns (18). With him directing the offense, Dallas amassed an 85–30 record during an eight-season span which included as many playoff appearances, four NFC crowns, and victories in Super Bowls VI and XII. He was voted Most Valuable Player for Super Bowl VI.

Much of the success he enjoyed related to his ability to move out of the pocket when pressured, give his receivers time to get free, and then deliver the ball on the money. And when his receivers couldn't get open, he could run for daylight with the best of his breed. Overall, he rushed 410 times for 2,264 yards, better than 5 yards a carry, and tallied 20 TDs. His scrambling invariably forced the opposition to commit itself prematurely, and he rarely failed to exploit the defensive gaps that resulted.

But it was his almost magical touch in the late going which will long twit the memory of fan and player alike when all his other attainments have been forgotten. One such miracle finish proved so disheartening for standout Washington Redskins running back John Riggins that he sat out the next year before returning to the game. It was the closing date of the 1979 schedule and Staubach's final regular-season appearance. Both the Redskins and the Cowboys needed a win to make the playoffs. With the fourth quarter on the wane, Washington owned a comfortable lead. But once again Staubach directed a down-to-the-wire rush and pulled out a 35–34 triumph for the Cowboys. So Riggins went home to recuperate, and Dallas captured division laurels for the 14th time.

"I thought we had a good chance to go all the way to the Super Bowl," Riggins said later. "But after the Cowboys won like they did, I just figured there wouldn't be another chance for me to play in the big one."

Riggo did come back to star in a Super Bowl, but Staubach retired, ending a brilliant sojourn in pro football that saw him become the league's all-time leading passer.

On the occasion of Staubach's departure, Dallas head coach Tom Landry said, "Roger might be the best combination of passer, athlete, and leader ever to perform in the NFL."

That says it all.

Jan Stenerud

6'2", 190 pounds. Placekicker: Kansas City Chiefs (1967–1969, AFL), Kansas City Chiefs (1970–1979, NFL), Green Bay Packers (1980–1983), Minnesota Vikings (1984, 1985). AFL All-Star Game: Two appearances. Pro Bowl: Four appearances.

MVP Pro Bowl: 1972. Inducted into the Pro Football Hall of Fame 1991. Career: Scoring: PATs, 580. FGs, 373 (NFL record). Total points, 1,699 (second highest in NFL history).

The Hall of Fame induction of Jan Stenerud constituted a noteworthy inaugural not only for the man but the shrine. His admission marked the first time a pure specialist had gained entrance to the hallowed Canton institution.

For nearly two decades he held forth in the National Football League as a noncombatant. His job description required him neither to block, tackle, nor otherwise make physical contact with the opposition. Yet he managed to prevail as the second most prolific scorer in NFL history.

Stenerud made his living kicking from placement, an occupation specifically insulated from violence by statute. Thus it is that the Hall of Fame, a structure dedicated to the perpetuation of the memory and deeds of men lionized for their aggressive behavior, now houses the bust of an individual who displayed no such penchant.

But just as the technical and operational aspects of pro football change with time, so do the kinds of players that apply them. In the modern era, the kicking phase of the game has become an element of paramount importance offensively and defensively. Enter Stenerud, his strong right leg as potent a weapon of aerial bombardment as the throwing arm of any quarterback to be granted a niche in the Hall of Fame.

A transplant from Norway, he harbored no aspirations for football fame and fortune until attending Montana State. And even then, it was not a purposeful thing. He originally enrolled at the university on a skiing scholarship but was spotted doing some kicking by the football coach, so his future took a new and unexpected direction.

Following graduation, he was selected by the Kansas City Chiefs in the 1966 American Football League draft and remained with the club for 13 campaigns (1967–1979). His rookie year, 1967, he topped the AFL in field-goal production with 36. In Super Bowl IV, he kicked three field goals, one a 48-yard effort which tied a record for the postseason classic, as the Chiefs upset the heavily favored Minnesota Vikings of the NFL.

When the AFL and the NFL merged in 1970, he again led all kickers in field goals with 42. He repeated this feat in 1975 with a total of 32 FGs. In 1980, he joined Green Bay as a free agent. While with the Packers in 1982, he set an NFL single-season record for field-goal accuracy with a success percentage of 91.6, converting 22 of 24 attempts (it stood for one year). During the summer of 1984, he was traded to the Vikings and finished out his career with the Minnesota franchise in 1985.

Among his most sparkling attainments are an NFL record-tying seven seasons in which he scored more than 100 points, an NFL mark of 17 field goals over 50 yards, two AFL All-Star games, four Pro Bowls, and an all-time league high of 373 field goals.

Fran Tarkenton

6'0", 185 pounds. Quarterback: Minnesota Vikings (1961–1966), New York Giants (1967–1971), Minnesota Vikings (1972–1978). All-Pro: 1973, 1975. Pro Bowl: Nine appearances. NFL Most Valuable Player: 1975. Inducted into the Pro Football Hall of Fame 1986. Career: Passes attempted, 6,467. Passes completed, 3,686. Completion percentage, 57.0. Passing yardage, 47,003. Touchdowns, 342. Interceptions, 266. Rushing attempts, 675. Rushing yardage, 3,674. Yards per carry, 5.4. Touchdowns (rushing), 32.

Without a doubt, Fran Tarkenton gave more people the runaround than anyone else in the history of professional football. Intentionally or otherwise, he changed the mode of quarterbacking from one of hanging tough to hit the moving target and in the process did a major overhaul on the record book.

From the outset of his tenure in the National Football League, the University of Georgia product proved he could put points on the scoreboard, and in bunches. His first time off the bench as a rookie with the Minnesota Vikings, he threw four touchdown passes in triggering a 37–13 upset of the Chicago Bears.

If something didn't develop off the designated play, then, unlike others of his breed, he would break out of the pocket, or what remained of it, and head for the high ground, giving his receivers time to readjust their routes and find an open spot. Give Plan A a shot, but should it not work, then improvise, go with Plan B, and try to make something happen. More often than not, he did. But when he didn't, the ball often ended up in enemy hands, and not infrequently the outcome of this impromptu liaison abetted the opposition cause by six points. And herein lay the crux of the criticism directed his way.

From 1961, his freshman year in the NFL, to 1966, he labored under the tutelage of Vikings first-time head coach Norm Van Brocklin, a Hall of Fame quarterback in his own right who harbored strong views on the conduct of the game and espoused them forthrightly. He definitely didn't like his young field general scrambling all over the greensward and putting the ball up for grabs when pressured. And he said so for all to hear. "He will win some games you might not have won," Van Brocklin observed, "and he'll also lose some games you should have won. But he'll never win you a championship."

Much of Tarkenton's early scrambling tactics were due to playing with

an expansion team. It was simply a matter of survival. The losses far outnumbered the wins in those early days, and players of varying talent and skill
came and went in steady profusion, reducing continuity to nil, particularly in
the offensive line. Without effective blocking, a quarterback's choices are
essentially two—stand and die, or run for it. He made the latter choice.

The fact that his elusive maneuvering forced opponents to adjust their
pursuit strategy didn't sit all that well with some of the game's more titled
prevent personnel of that time. Sam Huff, a standout middle linebacker for
the New York Giants, was in this group. "You really wanted to clobber the
guy when you finally caught up to him," Huff testified. "Let him know you
didn't appreciate all that running around he made you do. Especially if it
was a hot day."

Willie Davis, a premier defensive end for the Green Bay Packers, took
another tack in combating the Tarkenton syndrome. On one occasion,
after missing a sack attempt, he merely trotted after the Minnesota quarterback, then streaking for the opposite sideline in search of an open receiver.
When a teammate urged Davis to join the hunt more vigorously, he just
grinned and tapped a finger to his helmet. "No hurry," Davis assured his
buddy. "He'll be back directly, and we'll get another shot at him."

Moments later, Tarkenton returned, eyes still frantically tracing the
flow of jerseys downfield, and Davis nailed him. There's more than one
means of skinning a cat, surely.

In 1967 Tarkenton went to the New York Giants for four high draft
choices. After five uneventful campaigns in the Big Apple, he was traded
back to the Vikings, who were then legitimate contenders for championship
honors. Under his direction, the Minnesota franchise amassed a 62–22–2
record from 1973 to 1978. During this period, the Vikings made three
Super Bowl appearances, but all were losing excursions. In the end, Van
Brocklin's prediction assumed reality.

Although modern philosophy has it that scrambling tends to expose
the quarterback to a greater risk of injury, Tarkenton performed without
serious mishap for 16 years until bruised ribs set him down briefly in 1976.
Then, in 1977, he missed five starts with a broken leg. Following the 1978
schedule, he retired with NFL records for passes attempted (6,467), passes
completed (3,686), passing yardage (47,003), and touchdowns by passing
(342). He earned Most Valuable Player recognition in 1975, was twice an
All-Pro selection, and participated in nine Pro Bowls.

Y. A. Tittle

*6'0", 200 pounds. Quarterback: Baltimore Colts (1948, 1949, AAFC), Baltimore Colts
(1950, NFL), San Francisco 49ers (1951–1960), New York Giants (1961–1964). All-Pro:*

1957, 1961–1963. Pro Bowl: Six appearances. NFL Player of the Year: 1961, 1963. NFL Individual Passing Leader: 1963. Inducted into the Pro Football Hall of Fame 1971. Career: Passes attempted, 4,395. Passes completed, 2,427. Completion percentage, 55.2. Passing yardage, 33,070. Touchdowns, 242. Interceptions, 248. Rushing attempts, 372. Rushing yardage, 1,245. Yards per carry, 3.3. Touchdowns (rushing), 39.

With a name like Yelverton Abraham Tittle, a kid had to be a great fighter or a recluse. Not much is known about Tittle's childhood, but it's a matter of public record that he was some kind of a fighter during his 17-year tenure in the National Football League.

The "Bald Eagle" had a full head of rust-colored locks when he exited Louisiana State University in 1948 and went to work for the Baltimore Colts. Right from the outset, he proved his mettle in the pro game, completing 161 passes for 2,522 yards and 16 touchdowns. This performance earned him All-America Football Conference (AAFC) Rookie of the Year. He continued to conduct himself with distinction in 1949 as the AAFC's premier passer: 2,209 yards gained through the air and 14 TD tosses. After that campaign, the league folded.

In 1950, the Colts joined the NFL. The next year, he switched to the San Francisco 49ers, and this association persisted for 10 illustrious seasons. While quarterbacking the franchise by the bay, he connected on 1,387 of his aerial attempts for 17,900 yards and 116 touchdowns. His 17 TDs led the league in scoring during the 1955 schedule, and two years later he topped the standings again, hitting on 176 of 279 passes for an eye-opening completion percentage of 63.1. Also in 1957, he directed the 49ers to an 8–4 record and a share of the Western Conference title. In a playoff contest against Detroit, he put 18 points on the scoreboard all by himself, but the Lions mounted a late rally to edge San Francisco, 31–27.

After the 1960 season, the 49ers figured Tittle had seen better days and traded him to the New York Giants. This proved to be a serious miscalculation by San Francisco and a major boon to New York. But it definitely wasn't a case of love at first sight when he joined the Giants in August 1961. They were a close-knit veteran group with a quarterback in "Chuckin' Charlie" Conerly who was a proven quantity and an old buddy. It was common knowledge that Tittle had been brought in to take Conerly's job, and that didn't sit well with his friends. For the duration of the training camp, it was an awkward situation all around.

When the regular season commenced, Tittle and Conerly split time at the signal-calling chores. But as the weeks melded one into another and the Giants prevailed as serious Eastern Conference contenders, it became increasingly apparent that a transition had taken place at quarterback, like it or not. Given this impetus, the Giants dutifully fell in behind their new field general, between the lime lines and outside of them. Tittle's strong arm was pitching them into the playoff picture and bonus money, and after all, that's the name of the game.

New York edged Philadelphia for the conference crown but lost to Vince Lombardi's Green Bay Packers in the NFL championship encounter. Still, it had been a heady experience for the victory-starved Giants, and Tittle did nothing but cover himself with glory. He was named 1961 NFL Player of the Year. The ensuing campaign, he guided New York to the top of the conference heap once more and in the process, managed to better his stats across the board. He hooked up with his receivers on 200 aerial attempts for 3,224 yards and a league best 33 touchdowns. Once again, the Giants fell prey to the Packers in the league-title tilt.

"Y. A. just loves to play this game," said Frank Gifford, the Giants' star flanker. "He really gets fired up. And this is great for our young people because they get fired up, too."

Tittle was pushing 37 when he embarked upon the 1963 season, but on him age never looked better. In fact, for all intents and purposes, he reached his peak. Again, he drove New York to Eastern Conference supremacy and once more was NFL Player of the Year. This time he threw for 36 touchdowns and a completion percentage of 60.2, both league leading marks. But he wasn't to know how it felt to be king of the pro football hill, as the Chicago Bears narrowly defeated the Giants 14–10 for all the league marbles.

In 1964, he took a beating and thereafter called it a career. He was an All-Pro selection four times and participated in six Pro Bowls.

Recently he observed, "Today, twenty-nine out of thirty-six pass completions is nothing to get excited over. Back when I played, that was something to write home to grandmother about. Just about anybody can throw now. They pass fifty times a game and complete thirty. Don't get me wrong. I'm still a big supporter of pro football. Basically, I feel the game has improved markedly. It's better coached, and the players are bigger, stronger, and faster. Still, I like to feel I could have played with them."

Few are the souls who believe he couldn't.

Johnny Unitas

6'1", 196 pounds. Quarterback: Baltimore Colts (1956–1972), San Diego Chargers (1973). All-Pro: 1958, 1959, 1965, 1967. Pro Bowl: 10 appearances. NFL Most Valuable Player: Three times. Inducted into the Pro Football Hall of Fame 1979. Career: NFL records (at time of retirement): Most passes attempted, 5,186. Most passes completed, 2,830. Most yards gained passing, 40,239. Most seasons passing for 3,000 yards or more, 3. Most games passing for 300 yards or more, 26. Most touchdown passes, 290.

Postseason: Highest pass-completion percentage, 62.9. Most yards gained passing during championship play, 1,177. Passes attempted, 5,186. Passes completed, 2,830. Completion percentage, 54.6. Passing yardage, 40,239. Touchdowns, 290. Interceptions, 253. Rushing attempts, 450. Rushing yardage, 1,777. Yards per carry, 3.9. Touchdowns (rushing), 13.

The subway train emerged from its concrete burrow and ascended the elevated tracks with a metallic clatter. Leveling off, it rolled past the soot-stained spires of the upper Bronx. Its passengers, normally given to reading newspapers or just staring blandly at the graffiti-scarred walls, now crowded against the car windows, all eyes fixed on the brightly illuminated hulk of Yankee Stadium which slipped by below. In the distance, reflecting the glare of arc lights, the scoreboard told the story: New York 17, Baltimore 14. Left to play: 1:56.

Down on the stadium's worn turf, the Colts broke out of their huddle and trotted to the line of scrimmage. Johnny Unitas, lean and stoop-shouldered, the block number 19 on his jersey nearly obscured by grit, crouched under center and squinted at the Giants' end zone 86 yards away. At the slap of the ball against his hands, he drop-stepped quickly and lofted a pass that just skidded off the fingertips of his intended receiver. Then another pass missed the mark. It was third and 10. Once again, the opposing lines collided with a muffled thud, but this time Unitas didn't throw. Instead, he handed off to running back Lenny Moore, who scrambled for 11 yards and the desperately needed first down. Clutch call.

After a long look at the New York defense, Unitas leaned into the tight semicircle formed by his teammates and called a play. He passed once more. Incomplete. Undaunted, he went to the air again. The ball found the waiting arms of end Ray Berry. Even as the game clock winked off the precious seconds, Unitas threw to Berry twice in succession, and the Colts had another first down on the midfield stripe. Baltimore time-out. Left to play: 1:04.

His face an emotionless mask, Unitas stood poised in the pocket, seemingly unmindful of the conflict erupting all around him. At the last moment, he arched another aerial to Berry who gathered in the ball at the opposition 25. On the ensuing down still another Unitas-to-Berry pass connected, this time for 13 yards. Just nine seconds remained in the hard-fought contest. Out came Baltimore placekicker Steve Myhra and booted a 20-yard field goal to send the game into overtime, 17–17.

In the extra session, Unitas directed the Colts to their 40 on the first series of downs, artfully mixing his plays. But then the New York defenders stiffened, and he was sacked for an eight-yard loss. Rising, he casually dusted himself off and opted for a play the Giants had never seen before. The call was a spread formation featuring both ends split out and a third receiver lined up in the slot to the right side of the field. At the snap, Unitas

Johnny Unitas

retreated rapidly and once again looked for Berry. When the New York cornerback momentarily lost his footing, he coolly waved Berry farther downfield and then hit him with a perfect completion on the Giants' 42.

Minutes later, confronted with a short-yardage situation, the Giants' prevent corps tightened its ranks, fully expecting a frontal assault for the first down. But Unitas, ever a gambler, dumped a short pass just over the heads of the New York secondary, and Baltimore had the ball on the one-yard line. From there, the Colts went on to win their first NFL championship 23–17 in what has since been widely eulogized as "the greatest football game ever played."

Looking back on that memorable moment in his playing career, Unitas, now a successful Baltimore-area businessman, said, "I firmly believe the 1958 championship game between New York and Baltimore put professional football on the map. That was the first playoff game ever to go into overtime and the first game ever to be nationally televised. It got into more households than any other sporting event up to that time. Everything involved with the game, I think, served to catch the fancy of the viewing public. The strategies employed by both teams, the timing and coordination of the event itself and the trading back and forth in the scoring all worked perfectly to make it a great sales promotion for the National Football League."

Needless to say, the game also nationally advertised the quarterbacking skills and singular self-confidence of the young Unitas, all of which made it that much more difficult to believe he had been summarily discarded by the NFL just three years earlier as not a bona fide pro prospect. Back then, he was a rookie fresh out of the University of Louisville lacking a big-time college pedigree and impressive attainments. Though disappointed, he hung on. After a year of semipro football with the Bloomfield (Pa.) Rams, he got another tryout. This time he signed with Baltimore. It was the best deal the Colts ever made.

Unitas led Baltimore to a second NFL title in 1959, a 31–16 win over the Giants in the championship contest, making it a rare double, back-to-back crowns. Remarkably, he was still wearing a Colts uniform 12 seasons later when the Colts edged the Dallas Cowboys 16–13 in Super Bowl V. He started that game for Baltimore, but a painful rib bruise sustained in the second quarter put him out of action. During the regular campaign, he completed 166 of 221 pass attempts for 2,213 yards and 14 touchdowns. He also had thrown 18 interceptions on the year. At 37, his once incomparable abilities were sorely eroded.

On the eve of the Colts' 1971 Super Bowl matchup with the Cowboys, he conceded, "Sure, I know I don't throw the ball as far and run as fast as I used to do. And I've had my share of injuries. But a quarterback can't permit himself to think about such things, or he'll leave his best game in the locker room."

He spent the better part of the 1973 season sitting on the San Diego Chargers bench as a backup quarterback. When that year became history, he stripped off his high-top cleats for the last time and turned his thoughts to other endeavors. But never did he regret the toll 18 years of pro football had exacted both mentally and physically.

"Yeah, sure, it was worth it," he said, looking back on his career. "It's what I wanted to do. Football is a game of hit and be hit. And that's what I wanted. But it wasn't hard for me to retire, and I don't miss playing now. All those years. They were enough."

Unlike most Hall of Fame inductees, Unitas is almost as well known in the present generation as he was in his own. Through the years, his reputation as a quarterback has not diminished one whit. He remains the prototype, the standard by which all other professional signal callers are judged.

Weeb Ewbank, who coached the Colts when they won back-to-back NFL championships in 1958 and 1959, had this to say about Unitas: "John was the best quarterback I ever saw at throwing crossing patterns and the little sideline outs," Ewbank said. "And he could put the ball on the money no matter the defensive pressure. He could throw very accurately on the long routes, too. I'd have to say he was probably the best all-around quarterback I've ever seen or been associated with. And that covers some pretty good people."

Sid Luckman, the Chicago Bears' great quarterback of the 1940s, expressed his sentiments about Unitas even more succinctly. "In my opinion," Luckman said, "Johnny Unitas was the greatest pro football player of all time."

Norm Van Brocklin

6'1", 190 pounds. Quarterback: Los Angeles Rams (1949–1957), Philadelphia Eagles (1958–1960). All-Pro: 1960. Pro Bowl: Eight appearances. NFL Individual Passing Leader: 1950, 1952, 1954. NFL Most Valuable Player: 1960. Inducted into the Pro Football Hall of Fame 1971. Career: Passing attempts, 2,895. Passing completions, 1,553. Completion percentage, 53.6. Passing yardage, 23,611. Touchdowns, 173. Interceptions, 178. Rushing attempts, 102. Rushing yardage, 40. Yards per carry, 0.4. Touchdowns (rushing), 11. Punts, 523. Yards per punt, 42.9. Coach: Minnesota Vikings (1961–1966), Atlanta Falcons (1968–1974). Won-lost record: Minnesota Vikings (29–51–4), Atlanta Falcons (37–49–3).

During his NFL tenure, Norm Van Brocklin prevailed as a brilliant but often troubled practitioner of the quarterbacking arts. Though a fitful man by nature, he belied this fact on the field by performing in a consistently superior manner throughout a career beset by controversy and trying conditions.

Norm Van Brocklin

The Dutchman could throw a football as well as anyone ever given the task. He was also a strategist of no mean ability and a gifted punter. Unfortunately, he didn't suffer mistakes very well, his or teammates'. Such is the disposition of a perfectionist. When under center he expected the game plan to be executed flawlessly. And woe unto the receiver who dropped the catchable ball or the lineman guilty of missing a block, thereby allowing a defender to hammer the quarterback of note.

"Look, friend," he would intone, confronting the offending party with a narrowed gaze, "if you don't wanna work today, then get the [bleep] off the field. We got a football game goin' on here."

In 1949, he emerged from the University of Oregon with All-America credentials and a reputation for being outspoken. His opinions were seldom suffered in silence, and this propensity for frank expression did little to win friends and influence people. When the Los Angeles Rams made him their fourth pick of the college draft, they already had a superior signal caller in Bob Waterfield. So why, Van Brocklin wondered aloud, did they select him? The problem, to his way of thinking, was that he didn't want to play behind anyone. Not for a moment. He meant to be the coach on the field, and the prospect of this happening in Los Angeles appeared remote at best. And so it went for him.

As a rookie, he gathered splinters on the bench until the last game of the 1949 campaign. Given a chance to display his wares, he put on quite a show. That afternoon he pitched no less than four touchdown strikes, enabling the Rams to humble the bomb-shocked Washington Redskins 53–27.

When Joe Stydahar assumed control of the Rams' coaching reins in 1950, conditions became somewhat more tolerable for Van Brocklin but still far from his liking. Each game he and Waterfield shared the quarter-backing chores. Waterfield played the first and third quarters, and he ran things in the second and fourth. Despite this half-time arrangement, he managed to cop NFL individual passing honors for that season. He lost out to Waterfield for the passing crown in the final outing of the 1951 schedule but regained his top ranking the following year.

Despite losing his league laurels to Waterfield in 1951, Van Brocklin nevertheless distinguished himself that season for two particularly memorable afternoons. The first came during the regular slate when he threw for a record 554 yards at the expense of the New York Yanks. Later, with the NFL championship on the line, his 73-yard payoff peg to end Tom Fears provided the Rams with a 24–17 victory over the Cleveland Browns and a lock, though temporary, on pro football supremacy.

Even after Waterfield retired, Van Brocklin had to contend with a succession of other quarterbacks for playing time. But through it all, he clung tenaciously to his standards of conduct. On one occasion he had absorbed a particularly vicious sacking at the hands of a San Francisco defensive tackle. With vengeance in mind, he twice sent bruising Rams fullback Deacon Dan Towler rumbling head-on into the burly 49ers lineman. But each time Towler was unceremoniously dumped for no gain. The third time, Towler veered off course just before the moment of impact and picked up six yards. When he returned to the huddle, Van Brocklin was waiting. "You yellow [bleep]!" he screamed. "Why did you run away from him?"

Replied Towler, "You got a problem with the guy, see to it yourself."

And Van Brocklin did. On the next snap, he kept the ball and charged full tilt into his antagonist. He was a far cry from the quarterbacks of today.

In 1958, he went to Philadelphia, and the move proved to be the making of him and the Eagles. Under head coach Buck Shaw, he gained almost complete control over the conduct of the offense. Finally, he was the coach on the field. He directed Philadelphia to a tie for second place in the 1959 Eastern Conference race. The following season, he took the Eagles all the way, defeating the Green Bay Packers for the 1960 NFL title. He became the only quarterback ever to beat a Vince Lombardi team in a championship encounter. As a result of these heroics, he earned All-Pro recognition and was named the league's Most Valuable Player.

Just a month after this triumph, he passed for three TDs in his eighth Pro Bowl appearance and then retired as a player. Thereafter, he coached the expansion Minnesota Vikings from 1961 to 1966, then the Atlanta Falcons during the years 1968 to 1974.

Van Brocklin died on May 2, 1983, at 57.

Bob Waterfield

6'2", 200 pounds. Quarterback: Cleveland Rams (1945), Los Angeles Rams (1946–1952). All-Pro: 1945, 1946, 1950. Pro Bowl: Two appearances. NFL Most Valuable Player: 1945. NFL Passing Leader: 1946, 1951. Inducted into the Pro Football Hall of Fame 1965. Career: Passes attempted, 1,617. Passes completed, 814. Completion percentage, 50.3. Passing yardage, 11,849. Touchdowns, 98. Interceptions, 127. Rushing attempts, 75. Rushing yardage, 21. Yards per carry, 0.3. Touchdowns (rushing), 13. Punts, 315. Yards per punt, 42.4. Interceptions, 20. Return yardage, 228. Yards per return, 11.4. Touchdowns, 0. Scoring: TDs, 13. PATs, 315. FGs, 60. Total points, 573. Coach: Los Angeles Rams (1960–1962). Won-lost record: 9–24–1.

A multipurpose scoring machine with a built-in cooling system to overcome the heat of battle, Bob Waterfield went into every game commanding a variety of ways he could beat the opposition. But of all his many attributes perhaps the most impressive were his ability to produce the big play when it was most needed and to remain calm and collected under pressure.

Early on, he had been considered too small, too frail for big-time football. He overcame this misplaced rap as a collegiate standout at UCLA, but some taint of it still clung to him upon his entry into the National Football League. As a rookie with the Cleveland Rams in 1945, he completed 89 of 171 aerial attempts for 1,609 yards and a league-leading 14 touchdowns, all the while admirably withstanding the battering attendant to his position. In the process, he led his team to the NFL championship game against the Washington Redskins and there pitched TD strikes of 37 and 53 yards, which helped ensure a 15–14 Rams victory. His performance on the year earned him recognition as the league's Most Valuable Player, a first for a freshman mercenary, and All-Pro honors.

In 1946, the Rams moved to Los Angeles, and Waterfield celebrated his return to familiar territory by leading the NFL in passing with 127 completions out of 251 attempts for 1,747 yards and 18 touchdowns. During the ensuing years, he triggered an attack considered the most potent in pro football, one which put points on the scoreboard in gross numbers. He could throw long and short with accuracy and was an effective runner. What's more, his superior punting and placekicking skills gave the Rams a decided edge on their opponents any Sunday afternoon they suited up.

From 1949 on, he shared the quarterbacking duties with another passing sensation, Norm Van Brocklin. But still his stamp remained on the team. And during the latter portion of his playing tenure the Rams made three successive appearances in the NFL championship game. They lost to Philadelphia in 1949 by a muddy 14–0 margin, were edged 30–28 on a last-minute field goal by Cleveland in 1950, and finally triumphed 24–17 over the Browns the following year. In 1952, they fell a game shy of the title tilt, dropping a 31–21 decision to the Detroit Lions in the National Conference playoffs.

Waterfield remained a viable factor in the Los Angeles offense right to the end of his career. He could have continued on past the 1952 season but chose to retire. Friends speculated that he seemed tired of being a part-time quarterback and felt there was really nothing more for him to prove.

In 1960, he returned to the Rams as head coach but experienced little success in stemming a losing trend and resigned midway through the 1962 campaign. He died on March 25, 1983, at the age of 62.

TRENCH
TROOPS

Defensive Linemen

Doug Atkins

6'8", 275 pounds. Defensive End: Cleveland Browns (1953, 1954), Chicago Bears (1955–1966), New Orleans Saints (1967–1969). All-Pro: 1960, 1961, 1963. Pro Bowl: Eight appearances. Inducted into the Pro Football Hall of Fame 1982.

There's a quaint little ditty entitled "Bad, Bad Leroy Brown, Baddest man in the Whole Damn Town." And since Chicago was the town of concern in the song, it could well have been penned with the one and only Doug Atkins in mind. However, the lyrics didn't really do him justice.

Hall of Fame quarterback Sonny Jurgensen tells a story about an encounter with Atkins that puts the giant defensive end in a more appropriate perspective. "It's just before the end of the first half, and we [Washington Redskins] are leading by a few points," Jurgensen recalled. "We're down in Bears territory, and they're expecting us to just kill the clock. So I waste a couple of plays, then right before the gun, I stand up and throw one in their end zone, and we get a touchdown. As I turn and start to run off the field, all of a sudden Atkins is at my side. 'I didn't appreciate that, Jurgensen,' he growled. I don't say anything, just keep trotting. Then, his hand on my arm, he kind of whispers, 'Jurgensen, I could come right into your huddle and maim you, end your career. And all I'd get is fifteen yards. Think about it.' I did. That second half, I spent a lot of time just handing the ball off to somebody else."

Curiously enough, Atkins's athletic ambitions lay with basketball

217

Doug Atkins

when he enrolled at the University of Tennessee. He came to the school as a hardwood recruit and a high-jump champion. But once a member of the Vols football staff saw him rambling around the court, he was promptly commandeered for the gridiron. He grudgingly agreed to the switch in his plans and ended up earning All-America honors at tackle as a senior.

That spring, the Cleveland Browns made him their number-one draft pick, and Coach Paul Brown dispatched his top assistant, Weeb Ewbank, to get the big lineman's name on the dotted line. Ewbank was instructed to go as high as $10,000, if necessary. The negotiations took place at a roadhouse near a small Tennessee town. After any number of beers, the two men settled on a contract price of $6,800. It was a blatant steal for the

Browns. Later, Ewbank stated publicly, "He really was worth much more than even the $10,000. He was the most magnificent specimen I have ever seen."

By the time Atkins reported to the Browns camp in the summer of 1953, he had packed 275 pounds in between his 6'8" extremities. Early on, he proved his ability to play in the pros, but Paul Brown's rather demanding rules of conduct didn't sit all that well with him, so by mutual consent, he went to Chicago prior to the 1955 season, and Bears owner and coach George Halas hailed the trade as "one of the best deals I ever made."

Thus was sealed a 12-year relationship that can truly be described as unusual. Atkins liked to speak his mind. Halas also had a bent for freely expressing his feelings. Needless to say, numerous confrontations resulted. According to Halas, they frequently went something like this: "Doug used to call me in the wee hours of the morning after he'd had a few drinks and offer me some coaching advice. Then he'd start cussing me, and I'd cuss him right back. Eventually, the conversation would terminate with me saying, 'Just don't be late for practice, Atkins.' The format was always the same. From time to time, people asked me why I put up with him, why I didn't get rid of him. My reply was always, 'I can't. He's the best defensive end in the league.' I meant it too."

In the course of plying his trade, Atkins used all manner of ploys to get the quarterback's undivided attention. He not infrequently hurdled would-be blockers who had gotten too low in their stance, surprising everyone with such a display of agility for his great size. On other occasions he would simply resort to brute force, picking up an offensive lineman and hurling him into the backfield. And when the passer dropped back to look for a receiver, he would loom above the protective pocket with arms extended overhead, completely obliterating the view downfield.

Observed Hall of Fame quarterback Fran Tarkenton: "When Doug rushes in with those oak-tree arms way up in the air, he's twelve feet tall. There's no throwing over him."

During his tenure with the Bears, Atkins rated All-Pro honors thrice and made eight Pro Bowl appearances. Finally, he and Halas agreed they should part company, so he was traded to the New Orleans Saints, with whom he put in another three seasons before calling it quits at 39.

At that time, Halas said, "Throughout his career Doug played with the zest of a rookie. He was awesome. Once he made up his mind to do something, there was just no stopping him. His dedication during a game can only be described as sensational. The guy was aggressive, no question about it. For years, the word around the league was, 'Don't make him mad.' I don't know anybody who didn't take the warning to heart."

Junious "Buck" Buchanan

6'7", 287 pounds. Defensive Tackle: Kansas City Chiefs (1963–1969, AFL), Kansas City Chiefs (1970–1975, NFL). AFL All-Star Game: Six appearances. Pro Bowl: Two appearances. Inducted into the Pro Football Hall of Fame 1990.

The likes of Buck Buchanan don't happen along very often. So strong was the conviction of the Kansas City Chiefs in this regard that they were intent upon acquiring him, whatever the price. And they did, passing up a Heisman Trophy winner in the process. But he proved to be worth the sacrifice and much more, developing into one of the pro game's premier defensive tackles.

All this took place in 1963, the year Buchanan graduated from Grambling College, a small black school in Louisiana with a reputation for producing NFL stars. He could have gone with the NFL but opted instead to play in the upstart American Football League (AFL).

"I felt my opportunities would be better in the AFL," he explained. "I was drafted in the first round, and it seemed important for me to be picked at the very beginning. That said a lot for the Gramblings, the Prairie Views, and all the other black colleges."

But Buchanan was no more pleased than Chiefs head coach Hank Stram. "When I think of our excitement over having Buck on the team, I still smile," Stram said of late. "Buck had it all—size, speed, quickness and a great, great attitude. He gave us the big player and the big personality we needed."

At 6'7" and 287 pounds, Buchanan presaged what linemen of the future would be like. Despite his dimensions, he could run the 40-yard dash consistently in 4.9 seconds. However, it took more than bulk to make a standout pro pit warrior, a lesson he learned the hard way. Much of this imposed education took place during a long afternoon doing battle with San Diego all-league offensive tackle Ron Mix.

"I'll tell you, it was a rough day," Buchanan recounted. "That Mix showed me every kind of block I had ever heard of, and most of those I hadn't. He really broke me in to the league right. But I came out of it with something. He made me realize that this was a place where I could really express myself through ability. And I never forgot what Mix showed me that day."

Perhaps the point of greatest moment to be impressed upon Buchanan was that might doesn't necessarily get the desired results. Looking back at his early years in the AFL, he admitted to relying on muscle power almost to the complete exclusion of other tactics. Ultimately, he came to understand that just the right blend of finesse and strength made the difference between being a superior performer and something less grand.

Junious "Buck" Buchanan

"You have to learn new moves," he explained. "You have to think with your opponent. You have to keep moving forward. Invariably you get in trouble when you just hit in there and then don't follow through."

Rushing the passer was yet another of his chores that required considerable adjustment in technique. But with hours of pain and perspiration, he acquired the skills to master the many facets of defensing the aerial game. In 1967, he batted down 16 balls on both sides of the scrimmage line and otherwise terrorized opposition quarterbacks.

He played with distinction at both defensive end and tackle as a rookie but finally assumed the latter role full-time in 1964. That season he rated an invite to the AFL All-Star game, an honor to be proffered annually thereafter. From 1966 through 1969, he was named All-AFL as well.

During this same period, he experienced both the bitterest disappointment and the emotional apex of his career. The hardest blow to his pride occurred when Kansas City absorbed a 35–10 beating at the hands of the Green Bay Packers in Super Bowl I. "It was the only time I felt like physically hurting someone," he related, "because of all that was said about our team and the AFL being a Mickey Mouse league. The criticism the team received after that game was disheartening." But all the embarrassment and heartache of that occasion quickly dissolved from memory when the Chiefs made it back to the Super Bowl three years later and defeated the Minnesota Vikings 23–7 for the world championship. Prior to that historic encounter, Stram devised a "triple stack" defense which called for Buchanan to line up opposite All-Pro Minnesota center Mick Tingelhoff. The result was that Buchanan neutralized Tingelhoff and Kansas City took the initiative early and won going away.

When the Chiefs joined the NFL in 1970, Buchanan continued to make his presence felt, earning All-AFC recognition that campaign and Pro Bowl invites for the 1971 and 1972 contests. In 1974, he suffered a broken hand and missed the only game of his 13-year pro tenure. Injuries cut heavily into his playing time throughout 1975, and he felt compelled to retire at the close of the schedule.

Willie Davis

6'3", 245 pounds. Defensive End: Cleveland Browns (1958, 1959), Green Bay Packers (1960–1969). All-Pro: 1962, 1964–1967. Pro Bowl: Five appearances. Inducted into the Pro Football Hall of Fame 1981.

Success stories are not uncommon in professional football. But all too frequently they are confined to deeds performed on the playing field. More often than should be the case, they do not continue on into life after the tumult and the shouting have died away. A happy exception to this rule is Willie Davis, a star in and out of uniform.

After graduating from little Grambling College in his native Louisiana, he was selected by the Cleveland Browns in the 1956 draft but couldn't suit up for them until completing a two-year stint in the army. Then it seemed as though he didn't belong anywhere in the Browns' scheme of things. He worked at a variety of positions before finally settling in at offensive tackle, only to be traded to the Green Bay Packers. Given this jolt to his ego, he seriously contemplated retirement.

But two things prompted him to reconsider continuing his career, and he can be thankful to this day that they did. First, he met and talked with Vince Lombardi, newly come aboard as head coach of the Packers. Lombardi convinced him that he had a future, a very definite future, with Green Bay as a defensive end. Second, he realized that he really didn't have anything going on in his life but football, nothing he could count on to afford him any encouraging long-term prospects or a reasonable degree of financial security. This sudden coming of age shook him up no little bit.

Upon joining the Packers in 1960, he immediately became associated with a winning situation. Green Bay went to the NFL championship game that year and lost there 17–13 to the Philadelphia Eagles. It would be the last time either the Packers or Davis ever came out on the short end of the score in a title game. They would win six division laurels, five league crowns, and two Super Bowls in a period extending through 1969. During the course of this span, he didn't miss a start in 162 games, earning All-Pro recognition five times and as many invites to the Pro Bowl.

But even then Davis did not forget his real mission, preparing himself for life after football. In the offseasons he went back to school, eventually earning a master's degree in business from the University of Chicago. Shortly thereafter, he embarked upon a training program offered by a major corporation. So when it came time for him to peel off his pads for the last time, it was not with the prospect of living in the past but a new and promising future.

Today, it's nice if someone remembers that he recovered 21 enemy fumbles while active in the NFL. On such occasions he smiles and thanks the person for remembering. But his thoughts are on what must be done now and those things that lie ahead, the normal mental processes of a successful executive, which he has become since his retirement from the pro game.

"Yes, being traded to Green Bay back in 1960 made a big difference in my life," he said not long ago. "It was just what I needed to wake me up to reality."

Art Donovan

6'3", 265 pounds. Defensive Tackle: Baltimore Colts (1950), New York Yanks (1951), Dallas Texans (1952), Baltimore Colts (1953–1961). All-Pro: 1954–1957. Pro Bowl: Five appearances. Inducted into the Pro Football Hall of Fame 1968.

A wag once noted that Art Donovan probably did more for the hops-and-yeast industry than the sudsy nectar ever did for him. No secret about it, he loved his beer. But he loved football even more, and the game reciprocated in kind with the many honors it accorded him in the course of his playing career.

Oddly enough, he grew up in a sporting milieu somewhat apart from that of football. His father, Art Donovan, Sr., was a widely renowned prizefight referee, and the influence of boxing much permeated the atmosphere surrounding the family home in the Bronx. But young Art grew up physically endowed more for the gridiron than the sweet science.

After a stint with the marines in World War II, he sought to play for

Notre Dame, but the Fighting Irish turned him down. So he enrolled at Boston College and there acquired glowing football credentials. In 1950, he hooked on with the Baltimore Colts, but the experience was hardly uplifting for the 26-year-old rookie. The following year the franchise became the New York Yanks and in 1952 the Dallas Texans. Meanwhile, under whatever guise, the team lost games in wholesale lots and yielded points as if they were going out of style.

Finally, the new Baltimore Colts took root in 1953, and Donovan again made a roster spot. But this was to be a club on an upward spiral. Provided the wise and able tutelage of head coach Weeb Ewbank, the Colts were inevitably headed for championship status. Ewbank and his staff liked what they saw in Donovan, a big hard–nosed defensive tackle who could harass the passer, penetrate on running plays, break blocks, and pursue with surprising agility. He early proved his ability to do the job required of him, and from 1954 to 1957, he held forth as a consensus All-Pro selection and a perennial Pro Bowl participant.

If the Colts had any problem with him, it concerned his weight. He ballooned to more than 300 pounds on one occasion, and thereafter his contract specified a structure of fines for each pound above 270. So he had to restrict his intake of beer to meet this limit, but never to the point of total abstinence. And each year the onset of preseason training camp was highlighted by his weighing-in ceremony. It quickly assumed a festival air.

Gruff and outspoken, he was a morale builder for the Colts. He afforded comic relief when it was needed in the course of a tension-packed drive for division and league supremacy, and he could effectively chide those players who might be suspected of giving less than their best.

He retired in the summer of 1962 when it became apparent to him that his skills had faded markedly. Early in the season of that year, the Baltimore fans publicly expressed their love for him during an emotional honors day at Memorial Stadium. On that occasion, his number-70 jersey was retired by the club. The big overgrown kid from the Bronx shed more than a few tears in expressing his appreciation to a crowd of some 55,000 well-wishers.

Donovan still lives in Baltimore and remains a popular sports figure among city residents of all ages.

Len Ford

6'5", 260 pounds. Offensive-Defensive End: Los Angeles Dons (1948, 1949, AAFC). Defensive End: Cleveland Browns (1950–1957, NFL), Green Bay Packers (1958). All-Pro: 1952–1955. Pro Bowl: Four appearances. Inducted into the Pro Football Hall of Fame 1976. Career: Receptions, 67. Receiving yardage, 1,175. Yards per reception, 17.5.

Touchdowns, 8. Fumbles recovered, 20. Return yardage, 79. Yards per return, 3.95. Touchdowns, 0. Interceptions, 3 (NFL). Return yardage, 45. Yards per return, 15.0. Touchdowns, 0.

In both size and tactics, Len Ford was the prototype for modern defensive ends. He was the first of his breed regularly to operate from a four-man front and utilize outside-rushing techniques so commonly practiced today. And no one ever sacked a quarterback or grounded a ball carrier any better.

Given his 6'5", 260-pound dimensions, he satisfied perfectly the stereotype which governs what National Football League scouts currently look for in the way of wingmen to defense the aerial game. He used his height and reach to maximum advantage in constricting the throwing lanes and obstructing the passer's view. And his speed, agility, and bulk enabled him to shed run blockers effectively and close off the sidelines to sweeps and counterplays.

Not a few critics accused him of unnecessary roughness, particularly in the way he fended with his elbows and forearms. They were lethal weapons in the helmet-to-helmet wars of the scrimmage line and for hapless backs with pass-protection responsibilities. But Ford was mentally set to function at just one speed—full-out. After all, he reasoned, anyone who put on pads should know what to expect. The gridiron game wasn't for everybody.

He began his pro career in 1948 as a double-duty end with the Los Angeles Dons of the All-America Football Conference (AAFC). For two years he distinguished himself in the City of Angels as a premier performer on both sides of the ball. Offensively, he logged 67 receptions for 1,175 yards, an average of 17.5 yards a catch, and eight touchdowns. On defense, he routinely wreaked havoc in the enemy backfield.

Dons head coach Jimmy Phelan said, "Len can become the greatest all-around end in history. He has everything—size, speed, strength, and great hands."

As soon as the AAFC went defunct after the 1949 season, the Cleveland Browns wasted no time in signing Ford and permanently limited his job description to defensive end. In this capacity he proved so effective that the Browns' entire defensive structure was realigned to make the most of his considerable abilities. They used just two tackles and a pair of ends along their prevent exterior and supported them with a tier of three linebackers— what would come to be known as the 4-3 formation.

With a shortened gap between him and the opposition center, Ford could make quicker penetration and pursue a sharper, more forceful angle to the quarterback. The result was a sharp increase in his sack production. From 1950 through 1957, he had few peers at his position; he earned All-Pro recognition four times and received as many invitations to the Pro Bowl.

But his reign was not without tribulation. Only five weekends into the 1950 season, he suffered a blow to the face that broke his nose, fractured both cheekbones, and dislodged several teeth. Plastic surgery was required to repair the damage, followed by an extensive rehabilitation program. Everyone thought they had seen the last of him on the field that year. But he made it back with the aid of a specially constructed face mask to play in the NFL championship game pitting the Browns against the Los Angeles Rams. It was as though he had never been away, playing a substantive role in Cleveland's 30–28 come-from-behind triumph.

Ford made a habit of being around the ball in the course of his NFL tenure. He recovered 20 opposition fumbles and returned them for a total of 79 yards. Many of these turnovers were a direct consequence of hits he had laid on unsuspecting quarterbacks and overmatched running backs. And although somewhat ponderous in appearance, he commanded an amazing leaping facility and a soft touch commonly associated with gifted receivers. He used these abilities to best advantage in his defensive work, registering five interceptions as a pro. Two such thefts helped the Browns clobber the Detroit Lions 56–10 in the 1954 NFL title showdown.

After spending the 1958 campaign in the service of the Green Bay Packers, he retired. On March 14, 1972, he died at 46.

"Mean Joe" Greene

6'4", 260 pounds. Defensive Tackle: Pittsburgh Steelers (1969–1981). All-Pro: 1970– 1977. Pro Bowl: Ten appearances. NFL Defensive Rookie of the Year: 1969. NFL Most Valuable Defensive Player: 1972, 1974. Inducted into the Pro Football Hall of Fame 1987.

Perhaps no player more typified the Pittsburgh Steelers in their dynasty years of the 1970s than "Mean Joe" Greene, who bulwarked the famed and feared "Steel Curtain" defense of that era. At 6'4" and 260 pounds, he terrorized quarterbacks from his tackle position as few players have done in the history of the National Football League.

Undoubtedly, there was a star quality about the Steelers when they were winning four Super Bowl titles in as many tries. At almost every position on the team, performers of unusual quality held forth. They were destined to leave their mark in football's sands of time.

"It's a rare group," Greene said of his teammates. "And you have a sense that it can't last forever, that this is a particular moment in time, so you want to take advantage of every possible chance. You want to be a part of the group and stay a part of the group. As an individual, you want to live up to their standards."

More often than not, the shoe was on the other foot. The Steelers in general had trouble keeping pace with Greene. No one on that squad was quite so dominant at his job. And that had to do in large part with his degree of intensity. "Every play, you are the one that has to wear the hat," he said. "You have to make things happen. You have to take the responsibility for yourself, and you have to take responsibility for your team. You can't ever let yourself be satisfied. For a defensive tackle, the ideal would be to consistently beat two or three blockers and make plays from sideline to sideline. It's a game I'll never play. But it's a dream I enjoy chasing."

Greene joined the Steelers in 1969 as their number-one draft pick. He came to them from North Texas State where the team had been known to its more ardent backers as the Mean Green. Thus he fell heir to the "Mean Joe" tag, one that he personally didn't care for all that much. "I just wanted people to remember me as a good player," he said, "not a particularly mean one." But his style of play didn't dissuade members of opposing teams from seeing him in any different manner. In his first pro season, he was NFL Defensive Rookie of the Year. Thereafter, he was twice voted the league's Most Valuable Defensive Player in 1972 and 1974, and rated All-Pro recognition from 1970 through 1977. What's more, he received an invitation to 10 Pro Bowls. Not without coincidence, while his football fortunes were soaring, so did those of the Steelers.

"You need to hold clearly in your mind," he said, "that your success is not totally based on your own athletic prowess or your own intellectuality. It's based on your team's scheme of things. It's based on who you play with. And it's based on God."

When he first slipped on his jersey with the block 75, there wasn't much for the Pittsburgh faithful to cheer about, and hadn't been for some years. But it didn't take him long to get them excited again, and they in turn contributed mightily to his attainment level. "I believed that pro ball was supposed to be less emotional than college," he said. "I thought, 'Hey, I'm a pro now, and it's my duty to go out there and play no matter how the fans are acting.' But they changed my head around. Football players are human too; that's what I found out. There were times in the past when the fans were a little critical, and they had a right to be that way. But when you step out there now, they make you feel like you belong. And anytime they start yelling 'Dee-fense! Dee-fense!' it does affect you. You can feel it jack you up. The fans can create their own intensity, and you pick it up from them."

Even after suffering a debilitating injury in 1975 to his left shoulder and arm, a nerve impairment, Greene continued to be a force on the field, though from another means of focus.

"What I had to do was change my whole style of play," he said. "I had to learn new approaches. I couldn't always make the play myself anymore, so I had to funnel the action toward my teammates. Fortunately, the other teams were still respecting me, still putting the blockers on me. So I figured as long as I could fool them and get the attention, I could help my team get the job done. With new guidelines, I felt I came all the way back in 1978 to my previous effectiveness. I was getting the job done again despite the fact I had to do it in a somewhat different fashion."

After he retired in 1981, the accolades poured in, but none were more rewarding than those proffered by Pittsburgh head coach Chuck Noll. "Joe will always be something special," Noll said. "He's the best I've ever seen."

Currently, Greene tutors the Steelers defensive line.

David "Deacon" Jones

6'5", 260 pounds. Defensive End: Los Angeles Rams (1961–1971), San Diego Chargers (1972, 1973), Washington Redskins (1974). All-Pro: 1965–1970. Pro Bowl: Eight appearances. NFL Defensive Player of the Year: 1967, 1968. Inducted into the Pro Football Hall of Fame 1980.

There have been a few players of such stature they actually dictated the course of games. David "Deacon" Jones was of this number—by his own admission. "I'm the best defensive end around," he once proclaimed unabashedly. "I'd hate to have to play against me."

Flamboyant? He was that. Self-assured to the point of arrogance? Uh-huh. And painfully truthful? Give him that too.

At 6'5" and 260 pounds, he was a dominant performer in his time, especially between the years of 1961 and 1971 when his labors were expended on behalf of the Los Angeles Rams. During this period he constituted a very substantive portion of the Rams' "Fearsome Foursome," one of the great defensive fronts in the annals of the National Football League.

Jones played cheek-and-jowl with Merlin "The Magician" Olsen, a mountainous tackle. They worked so well together that the results might have been depicted as poetic were it not for the violence perpetrated upon the opposition, a hapless array of quarterbacks and ball carriers whose respective missions were more often than not prematurely terminated. With the snap of the ball, Jones and Olsen might subject their offensive counterparts to a bone-bending head-on assault or execute an intricate looping maneuver, a bit of deception where one man crosses behind the other before attacking to confuse their opponents' blocking scheme. In either event, they usually ended up in the enemy backfield before the intended play was able to develop effectively.

But Jones didn't really need any help getting his job done. He rushed the passer with intensity and stifled the run only slightly less dramatically.

David "Deacon" Jones

Grabbing, pushing, shoving, throwing, whatever aided his cause and wasn't likely to elicit a reprimanding penalty, is how he proceeded. He always conducted himself within the confines of the rules, disdaining cheap shots and late hits because they weren't worthy of a place in his repertoire of mayhem. Besides, there were so many things one could do legally that proved to be just as memorable, things that would linger on the periphery of a quarterback's consciousness long after the sting of contact had dissipated. Always leave them something to remember you by, something to prey on their minds. That was his style.

In 1967 and 1968 he was NFL Defensive Player of the Year. Small wonder friend and foe alike referred to him as The Secretary of Defense. He reigned as a perennial All-Pro selection from 1965 through 1970 and participated in eight Pro Bowls. Given his combative nature, it's surprising that he never sustained a serious injury in his 14-season career, missing only three starts during this period. "You play the game right," he said, "and you can protect yourself from physical harm."

Even out of uniform he continued to be an object of reportorial interest with his keen and inventive wit. An amateur lexicographer of sorts, he coined words to suit his personal public-relations goals. One of these was *sack*, which he felt adequately defined what a defensive end does to a quarterback who is caught hanging around his own backfield with the ball still in hand. "Why call it a sack?" He grinned and replied, "Because you need a short term that can fit easily into newspaper headlines." As for the origin of the nickname Deacon, he explained, "Yeah, I made it up. It's just that nobody would ever remember a player with the name of David Jones."

The recognition, the attainments, the laurels—not bad for an anonymous 14th-round draft pick out of an institution of higher learning given the title Mississippi Vocational College. Jones lent his personal touch to everything he did. When asked to expound on the intricacies of playing defense, he replied, "It's all got to do with justice, the implementation of justice. You go in there with a mind to hit people. It's like the devastation of a city. I like to think of putting the entire offensive unit in a bag. And then just beating that bag with a baseball bat."

At the close of the 1971 campaign, he went to the San Diego Chargers for two seasons before ending his colorful NFL tenure with the Washington Redskins in 1974.

Bob Lilly

6'5", 260 pounds. Defensive End, Tackle: Dallas Cowboys (1961–1974). All-Pro: 1964–1969, 1971. Pro Bowl: Eleven invitations, Ten appearances. Inducted into the Pro Football Hall of Fame 1980.

Back when the Dallas Cowboys needed a cornerstone, something to build on in their infancy, Bob Lilly bent his back to the task. He gave them an air of legitimacy when they weren't really entitled to it. And around him they constructed the famed "Doomsday Defense," an aggregation that lifted the franchise from a doormat to the heights as "America's team." And through it all he was the mucilage that held the dream together.

In 1961, he came out of Texas Christian University to be the Cowboys' first draft pick ever. He had good size (6'5", 260 pounds), superior strength, unusual agility for a man of his dimensions, and intelligence—everything to recommend him as a standout performer. Early on, he played defensive end, and as such received his first invitation to the Pro Bowl. But Dallas head coach Tom Landry, a defensive innovator of no small moment, perceived that Lilly would prove to be more effective, have more latitude to exercise his many abilities, simply by moving down the line to the tackle slot. The man in the hat couldn't have been more right.

Within a few seasons Lilly emerged as a perennial All-Pro and Pro Bowl selection. At the fullness of his powers, he was nigh unbeatable. He could rush inside or outside with equal facility, whether shutting down the run or pressing the passer, and pursue the ball from the offside of the field like few of his breed before or since. One time after another he would burst out of the melee and angle down on the play just when it appeared the opposition was going to register a sizeable gain. He could make the stop from sideline to sideline.

Though often outsized by his opponents, he used quickness, balance, and exceptional leverage to fight through blocks and disrupt the offensive stratagems. As a result, he was almost routinely double-teamed, the onside guard making first engagement and the center kicking over to help after the snap. If he happened to be enjoying a particularly good afternoon, a back would be kept in on occasion, thus making it a triple-team block. Now and again the opposition even tried running right at him, but this ploy didn't work all that well either. The most effective deterrent to his forays was holding, pure and simple. And never mind it being an illegal maneuver.

Lilly usually reacted to holding in three stages. Initially, he admonished the offender in no uncertain terms. Should this warning go unheeded, he would seek relief from the game officials. This generally assumed the form of a muttered protest.

Pat Harder, for 17 years an umpire in the National Football League, worked any number of Dallas games and readily recalled the Lilly approach. "Bob got held about as much as any lineman I can remember," Harder said. "If it got to be flagrant, he would kind of sidle over to me between downs and say, 'Hey Pat, this guy is really holding me. Wanna give him a look?' He was no complainer, so I knew there must be something to it. And I would keep an eye out for the obvious stuff. You know, the chicken wing [looping an arm outside the defensive player's elbows, thereby "handcuffing" him] and the takedown. But I'd never call an infraction on the very next down unless the foul was pretty bad because you didn't want any player, even Lilly, to feel he was dictating to you."

If Lilly didn't think the official was responding to his request for

Bob Lilly

assistance, he'd take matters into his own hands. This meant resorting to the headslap, which was legal in those days. A few cuffs to the helmet with a meaty forearm promptly convinced the holder to repent of his ways. "You could really hear it pop in there," Harder related. "Especially when somebody with Lilly's strength delivered the shot. It was a sure means of getting the guy's hands off you and up protecting his head. Personally, I'm glad they outlawed the headslap. It could be dangerous. But it sure made life easier for defensive linemen. Lilly didn't use it all that much. Just when he wanted to make a point."

Despite all the attention received from the attack side of the ball, he missed just one outing in a 14-year career, due to a hamstring injury. Overall, he played in 292 games, inclusive of five NFL-NFC championships and Super Bowls V and VI. His biggest thrill as a pro came in the 24–3 loss the Cowboys hung on the Miami Dolphins in Super Bowl VI. During the course of that encounter, he sacked Miami quarterback Bob Griese for a 29-yard reversal and thereby rated an entry in the league playoff record book.

He also enjoyed the distinction of being one of only a handful of defensive linemen to score a touchdown. In fact, he crossed the enemy goal no less than four times in his NFL tenure. Once he intercepted a pass and threaded his way 17 yards to the end zone. Fumble returns produced the other trio of six-pointers. He recovered a total of 16 opposition bobbles and legged them back for 109 yards.

A chronic neck problem forced his retirement following the 1974 campaign. In 1980, he became the first Dallas Cowboy to be inducted into the Hall of Fame.

Gino Marchetti

6'4", 245 pounds. Defensive End: Dallas Texans (1952), Baltimore Colts (1953–1964, 1966). All-Pro: 1957–1962, 1964. Pro Bowl: Eleven appearances. Defensive End: 50-Year, All-Time, All-NFL team. Inducted into the Pro Football Hall of Fame 1972.

All modern standards for rushing the quarterback had their origin in Gino Marchetti, a defensive end of monumental stature. His techniques and aggressive style have been emulated by nearly three generations of defensemen but largely without the singular success he enjoyed in a 14-year career.

Interestingly, he showed very little aptitude for the gridiron sport as a boy. Not until his senior season at Antioch (Calif.) High School did he start to bud as a football performer. That year he was voted the team's Most Valuable Player. World War II then intervened, and he spent the duration in service, much of his tour concerned with the European theater of operations.

Upon being discharged, he returned home to Antioch and organized a semipro football team. From this endeavor he gravitated to Modesto Junior College and then to the University of San Francisco. During his collegiate tenure, he was generally regarded as the best tackle on the Pacific coast. Once graduated, he became the New York Yanks' second-round pick.

But even before he could slip on a uniform, the Yanks franchise transferred to Dallas and became the Texans. So he spent his rookie season laboring in the Lone Star State for a hapless aggregation that went 1–11–0. Not long after the final gun of the last regularly scheduled game, the club went under. Once more he was on the road, this time to Baltimore where his contract had been assigned to the Colts. Though he felt somewhat tentative about the operation, given the Texans debacle, his fears proved groundless. Ever so gradually, the team began building, and always with stability in mind. That year, 1953, he accepted his first invitation to the Pro Bowl. He would participate in 10 others.

From that juncture, he developed into the most feared defensive end in the NFL. His attainments warranted double-, even triple-team attention from the opposition, but he gladly endured it, knowing that his frontline mates were then making the plays usually reserved for him. With each passing campaign he became more a crowd favorite in a city already rabidly devoted to the Colts. He leapt over would-be blockers, hammered them aside with an oaken forearm, and barged into the enemy backfield to leave the quarterback gazing upward and blearily wondering what hit him. Vicious, yes. Dirty, never.

Attesting to this fact was the late great signal caller Bobby Layne, who said, "My goodness gracious, Gino would just knock your butt off every time. He was the toughest, cleanest ball player I can remember my many years in the league. There's never been another one like him."

Marchetti, who served as Colts captain for most of his time in Baltimore, longed to play on a championship team. This he finally did in 1958 when Baltimore bested the New York Giants in the classic sudden-death NFL title tussle at Yankee Stadium. But he suffered a broken leg during the late going of that epic battle and watched some of its most exciting moments sitting on the sidelines with an icepack consoling his fracture. The Colts repeated in 1959, stopping the Giants in Baltimore.

Not one to overstay his welcome, he determined to retire before his great powers had diminished. With this in mind, he was going to bid farewell to the game after the 1963 campaign but played another year at the request of management. The Colts made it to the 1964 NFL championship game again, only to drop a 27–0 decision to the Cleveland Browns.

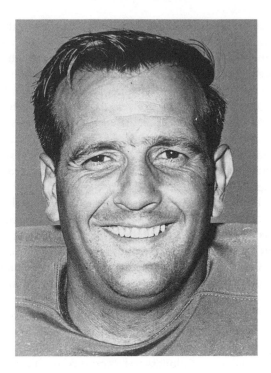

Gino Marchetti

Immediately thereafter, he did retire. But he was out only a single season before club officials asked him to return one more time. He acquiesced but simply wasn't up to his usual snuff. Later he explained, "I'm not making a comeback. I'm just doing the Colts a favor. If they think I can help them, then I have to give it a try. Everything I have I owe to them."

He earned All-Pro recognition 1957–1962 and again in 1964. Perhaps his greatest achievement other than induction into the Hall of Fame was being named as a defensive end to the 50-Year, All-Time, All-NFL squad.

Leo Nomellini

6'3", 284 pounds. Offensive-Defensive Tackle: San Francisco 49ers (1950–1963). All-Pro: 1951–1954, 1957, 1959. Pro Bowl: Ten appearances. Inducted into the Pro Football Hall of Fame 1969. Defensive Tackle: 50-Year, All-Time, All-NFL team.

Leo "The Lion" Nomellini was king of the National Football League jungle for more than a decade, a legend in his own time, dominating the opposition in unparalleled fashion. And even now, years after retirement, his savage habits are still discussed whenever the pro game's big cats are the topic of conversation.

Everything about him could be described as large. He stood 6'3" and weighed 284 pounds. But there was a certain thickness to him, a certain oaken quality to the girth of his body and its appendages that served to dwarf other men of outsize stature. His very presence spoke of power, an innate capacity for brute force the sense of which intimidated opponents even before contact had been initiated. Add to this physical prowess leonine speed and agility along with a fierce competitive spirit, and he loomed an awesome challenge indeed.

Curiously enough, he didn't really become familiar with the game of football until his later teens. He was born in Italy but grew up on the west side of Chicago, the son of working-class parents who didn't have time for boyhood sports. While attending high school, he worked a full shift in a local foundry to help his father support the family. Shortly after the bombing of Pearl Harbor, he joined the marines and was sent to Cherry Point, North Carolina, for basic training. During his tenure there he gained his introduction to the gridiron sport, playing tackle and guard for the post team. Later he saw action in the South Pacific.

Following the war, he accepted an offer to play football at the University of Minnesota. The Golden Gophers coaching staff was more than willing to gamble on his potential, despite a marked lack of experience and playing time. In 1946, freshmen were eligible for varsity competition, so he started at guard and promptly distinguished himself as a rare talent. He later switched to tackle and twice earned All-America recognition at that position.

The San Francisco 49ers, survivors of the defunct All-America Football Conference (AAFC), joined the NFL in 1950 and promptly made Nomellini their number-one pick of that year's draft. It proved to be a most fortuitous selection. Right from the outset, he became a 60-minute performer. On offense he excelled as both a run- and pass-blocker. Defensively, he was particularly adroit at rushing the quarterback and only slightly less effective at blunting enemy ground probes. In 1955, he went both ways in every game, from the opening whistle to the final gun, one of the most notable ironman achievements of the modern era.

Needless to say, his efforts did not go unnoticed. He rated All-Pro honors on six occasions. Twice he was named to the offensive unit and four times to the defensive squad, one of only a few players in NFL annals to be so cited. He also participated in 10 Pro Bowls. Finally, after the 1963 season, he closed out a 14-year career, having done just about everything that could be expected of a tackle offensively and defensively.

In 1969, he was inducted into the Pro Hall of Fame and voted to a defensive-tackle spot on the 50-Year, All-Time, All-NFL team.

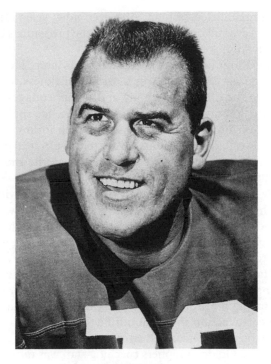

Leo Nomellini

Merlin Olsen

6'5", 270 pounds. Defensive Tackle: Los Angeles Rams (1962–1976). All-Pro: 1966–1970, 1973. Pro-Bowl: Fourteen appearances. Inducted into the Pro Football Hall of Fame 1982.

Although dubbed "Mule" by his teammates, Merlin Olsen was neither stubborn nor weak of mind. Quite the contrary. He was one of the pro game's most cerebral performers, a thinking man who directed his 6'5", 270-pound being in the most calculated manner to prevail for 15 seasons as one of the best defensive tackles ever to ply his skills in the National Football League.

From 1962 to 1976, he bulwarked a defensive front for the Los Angeles Rams that was perennially among the best in the NFL. He took over as the starting left tackle in the third preseason game of his rookie campaign and remained there throughout his career. During this period, he received an invitation to 14 consecutive Pro Bowls and rated All-Pro recognition five times. In the lengthy history of the league, his peers have been few indeed.

Merlin Olsen

With Olsen, football was always mind over matter. Before ever pulling on a uniform, he mentally mapped out his philosophy of play and then religiously adhered to it until success became ensured. "Each game, at the beginning of each new play," he once confided, "I think of it as the most important play of the year. I go into it as if the game depends upon it. I don't think about the preceding play, or the following play, or anything else. I approach every play as if it's an individual, distinct incident—a complete little game of its own. I consider a new play to be only a separate situation but a new challenge. You have to be able to concentrate intently out there. And I am able to concentrate better than most."

From 1962 to 1971, Olsen was an integral cog in a great defensive line colorfully tagged the Fearsome Foursome. Playing alongside him were ends David "Deacon" Jones and Lamar Lundy and Tackle Rosey Grier (later, Roger Brown). Jones, who lined up just outside Olsen, was fast and exceptionally aggressive, so Olsen, in his cognitive manner, determined how he might best abet Jones's style with his own strong points. "One of the reasons why Deacon and I played so well together," Olsen said, "is because he knew what to expect from me and I from him. He was quicker than I, which meant that sometimes he would be leaving some territory uncovered. So I accepted the responsibility of covering that territory. That's how we got the job done."

While Olsen was the Rams' left defensive tackle, they garnered six division titles and were generally regarded as the best in the West. Despite his size and the fact that his position placed him squarely in the most combative area on the field, he managed to avoid giving into his baser instincts. "I believe professionals think too highly of themselves and others in their work to go about hating," he said. "If you are motivated by pride and the desire to win, you will want to dominate your opponent. That is a lot better thing on which to tie your success than hatred. What I'm saying is this—the thing that drives a real pro is simply inner satisfaction. That's all."

Olsen grew up as one of nine children in Logan, Utah. He was a standout tackle at Logan High School and attracted football offers from major universities around the country. But he opted to stay home and play for Utah State. Before spelling finis to his scholastic tenure, he was named a consensus All-American at tackle and winner of the coveted Outland Trophy, emblematic of the best college lineman in the land. He was a Phi Beta Kappa awardee and later earned a master's degree in finance.

Today, he is a much-lauded NBC-TV football commentator, actor, and television advertising personality.

Alan Page

6'4", 225 pounds. Defensive Tackle: Minnesota Vikings (1967–1978), Chicago Bears (1978–1981). All-Pro: 1969–1971, 1973–1975. Pro Bowl: Nine appearances. NFL Most Valuable Player: 1971. NFL Lineman of the Year: 1973. Inducted into the Pro Football Hall of Fame 1988.

Perhaps the appropriate theme for the NFL career of Alan Page would be the popular pop standard "I Did It My Way." The dominating defensive tackle for the Minnesota Vikings and Chicago Bears was a man of singular convictions who both spoke his mind and played his game in a highly individual manner.

Being an iconoclast can be a rough way to go unless one commands the respect of his peers. And Page was an awe-inspiring performer in uniform. He came to the NFL as an All-America defensive end from the University of Notre Dame's 1966 national-championship team. The Vikings made him their number-one pick in the 1967 draft, and he did nothing to disappoint them during his 12 seasons with the club. From 1969 through 1975, he earned All-Pro recognition six times and received nine invitations to the Pro Bowl. In 1971, he became the first defensive player to earn NFL Most Valuable Player of the Year. He also rated the NFL Lineman of the Year in 1973.

Just four games into his rookie season, he took over right tackle and became a fixture there, anchoring a defensive front that became widely known as the Purple People Eaters. In the course of his reign with the Minnesota franchise, the Vikings won nine NFC Central Division titles and participated in the Super Bowl on four occasions. At 6'4" and 225 pounds, he combined strength, speed, and agility in a manner generally unthought of for a lineman. He could power his way to the ball when such an approach was needed, but finesse was his preferred mode of operation. Deftly slipping and shunting would-be blockers, he made the big plays from one sideline to the other. During his 15-year tenure as a pro, he recovered 24 opposition fumbles, blocked 28 kicks, accounted for 164 quarterback sacks, and negotiated 1,431 tackles. He was smart, he was quick, and he could read offensive keys with a jeweler's eye. As a compilation of outstanding talents and abilities, he often controlled play up and down the scrimmage line, frequently forcing opposing coaches to change their game plans.

To be sure, Vikings head coach Bud Grant didn't find him easy to manage within generally unyielding administrative dictates. If Page failed to agree with some of the rules Grant imposed, he made his displeasure known and often deigned not to abide by them. Finally, when he undertook a dedicated running program that dramatically improved his overall conditioning but caused a definitive weight loss, Grant dealt him to Chicago six games into the 1978 campaign. Undaunted, Page reported to the Bears and promptly took over at defensive right tackle. He led the team in sacks that year and again in 1979. At the end of the 1981 campaign, he retired, armed with a law degree and a different agenda for the rest of his life.

Andy Robustelli

6'0", 230 pounds. Defensive End: Los Angeles Rams (1951–1955), New York Giants (1956–1964). All-Pro: 1953, 1955, 1956–1960. Pro Bowl: Seven appearances. Maxwell Club Player of the Year: 1962. Inducted into the Pro Football Hall of Fame 1971.

The pro football prepping of "Handy Andy" Robustelli was so obscure as to be negligible. He played for little Arnold College, a Connecticut preparatory institution for teachers which disappeared from the scene not long after granting him a degree. Largely due to this inauspicious background, he didn't get selected in the 1951 National Football League draft until the 19th round when the Los Angeles Rams finally beckoned to him. Unknown to them at the time, they had found a virtual diamond in the rough.

Right from the outset, he had doubts about his ability to make the grade in the pro game. So it took no little soul-searching before he decided to pass up a high school coaching opportunity for a trip to California and a shot at the NFL brass ring. Upon his arrival at the Rams' preseason camp, head coach Joe Stydahar informed him that his best chance, perhaps his only chance, was at defensive end.

This wasn't what Robustelli wanted to hear. He had always considered himself better adapted to offense than defense, and hence his doubts were further magnified, so much so that he refused even to unpack his clothes, half expecting to get cut at any time. But all such dour forebodings, his and those of the coaching staff, were dispelled for good on the occasion of the Rams' initial full-scale scrimmage. That afternoon he blocked kicks, slapped down passes, and strewed members of the offensive unit around the greensward like so much dirty laundry. Afterward, he unpacked his bags and stayed awhile—14 years to be exact.

To be a rookie and nail down a job with a team that had just finished atop the National Conference standings the season before amounted to quite a feat for Robustelli. He made his presence felt almost immediately as the Rams won the NFL crown in 1951. The next year he became a regular and went on to earn All-Pro recognition and a Pro Bowl invitation in 1953. He continued to play spectacularly and in 1955 keyed a strong defensive effort that paced the Rams to still another appearance in the league-championship contest. Again he rated All-Pro and Pro Bowl selection.

In 1956, he moved to the New York Giants, just in time to help them win NFL honors. Things couldn't have been better. He had returned home and was playing for a club with one of the most illustrious pedigrees in the annals of pro football, his favorite team since boyhood. During the next eight seasons, he would head up one of the finest defensive aggregations in the history of the league. The Giants would hold sway over their conference and division five times but be frustrated in as many NFL championship games. Meanwhile, Robustelli reigned as a perennial All-Pro choice from 1956 to 1960 and a Pro Bowl participant as many times between 1956 and 1961. The Maxwell Club chose him as its Player of the Year in 1962.

Strong, intelligent, quick of hand and foot, and of fiery determination, he prevailed as a premier pass-rusher throughout his lengthy tenure, a model of consistency in all phases of defensive play. "It's knowing when to rush," he said by way of explaining his success. "And knowing when is just a matter of experience, nothing else. Otherwise, you've got to play hard and tough as you can all the time."

Following his retirement in 1964, Robustelli remained briefly with the Giants as an assistant coach, tutoring the defensive ends. Currently, he is a successful businessman in Stamford, Connecticut.

Arnold College would have been proud.

Ernie Stautner

6'2", 235 pounds. Defensive Tackle, End: Pittsburgh Steelers (1950–1963). All-Pro: 1956, 1958. Pro Bowl: Nine appearances. Inducted into the Pro Football Hall of Fame 1969.

If ever there was a pro football prototype, it had to be Ernie Stautner. He looked the part and played the part, a rough-and-tumble pit fighter who always showed up for work despite fractures, fissures, and other physical failings.

For 14 years, 1950 to 1963, he held forth as a defensive tackle for the Pittsburgh Steelers, during which time the team enjoyed only four winning seasons. But no matter how disappointing the circumstances, he played as though it were that championship season. Ever eager to be in the thick of the fray, he frequently doubled as a defensive end or even a guard on offense to ensure that the quality of play was the best the club could provide. The game was what counted most to him. All the rest of it fell under "peripheral."

Pain and infirmity were just part of the job description for a pro football player in Stautner's estimation. He missed starting assignments only six times in his lengthy tenure with the Steel City franchise. He viewed the games as miniature wars, the degree of play reduced to the most primal level for the best results. The members of the loyal opposition did not often share this vision of their means of livelihood.

Perhaps Hall of Fame running back Bobby Mitchell put this basic difference of opinion in best perspective. "You'd come out on the field all pumped up and ready to play," he recalled, "and then Ernie Stautner would hit you in the mouth. Right away you forgot everything else and just concentrated on survival."

Curiously enough, there were some members of the NFL establishment who felt that as a rookie prospect, Stautner was too undersized for a pro lineman and sought to discourage him from embarking upon a play-for-pay career. When he inquired of the New York Giants as to their possible interest in his services, then head coach Steve Owen drawled paternally, "Why, son, my smallest tackle is 248 pounds, and you're nowhere near that big. I'm afraid you're just too small for this league."

The Steelers took a chance and drafted him in the third round as their number-two pick. He repaid their vote of confidence with a caliber of play that earned him nine invitations to the Pro Bowl and All-Pro recognition twice. And he always made it a point to give one of his best performances when lined up against the Giants.

But being rejected was nothing new to Stautner. Following a laudatory football experience in high school and a World War II stint in the Marine Corps, he applied for a scholarship at the University of Notre Dame. The Fighting Irish turned him down. So their loss became Boston College's gain. He was a varsity standout on both sides of the ball from day one at the Beantown institution.

Squat and powerful at 6'2" and 235 pounds, he used his brawny arms and shoulders to forge a path through enemy linemen usually much larger than himself. His strength became legend around the NFL; anyone who ever caught an oaken forearm alongside his helmet didn't soon forget it.

"Weight training wasn't a part of the conditioning regimen back then," Mitchell said, "but Stautner didn't need it. He was strong enough to pull up trees anyway."

In 1988, Stautner ended a 23-year association with the Dallas Cowboys as their defensive coordinator and line coach. He developed the famed "Doomsday Defense" that played an integral role in the Cowboys' march to the Super Bowl in 1970, 1971, and 1975. Then, in 1977, his "Doomsday II" aggregation mightily assisted Dallas to its second Super Bowl triumph as well as a record fifth appearance in the 1978 big game. In all, he contributed significantly to "America's team" when it was compiling 20 consecutive winning seasons.

Ernie Stautner

Shortly before departing the Cowboys, he considered the changes of note that had been wrought in defensive play since his heyday with the Steelers. "The rules have taken so much away from defensive linemen," he lamented. "There's just no comparison between my time and today. When I played, the headslap could be used to discourage the other guy from holding you. If you were being tied up on the inside, a couple of slaps to the helmet got the guy to thinking about protecting his head instead of grabbing you. But that's been outlawed. You can still use the shoulder slap, but it just isn't as effective. Now that offensive linemen are allowed to use their hands, they can do anything short of tackling you. So a defensive linemen has to be a super athlete. He's got to have good speed and make a lot of moves before contacting the opposition in order to penetrate the defense. And still he doesn't have much of a chance to do his job. Naw, I'm glad I played when I did. I don't have any regrets."

The same can't be said for the people that played against Ernie Stautner.

Arnie Weinmeister

6'4", 235 pounds. Defensive Tackle, End: New York Yankees (1948, AAFC), Brooklyn–New York Yankees (1949, AAFC), New York Giants (1950–1953, NFL). All-AAFC: 1949. All-Pro: 1950–1953. Pro Bowl: Four appearances. Inducted into the Pro Football Hall of Fame 1984.

The word *dominant*, used indiscriminately all too often, applied in its most legitimate sense to Arnie Weinmeister, that good big man much sought after but so rarely found. Blessed with both size and speed, he held forth as the finest lineman of his era, perhaps any era.

Although a native of Canada, he attended the University of Washington and from there matriculated into the U.S. brand of the play-for-pay game. The National Football League Boston Yanks bid for his services, but he joined the New York Yankees of the fledgling All-America Football Conference (AAFC) in 1948 when they offered him a contract for $8,000, a munificent sum in those days, particularly for a rookie.

He stood 6'4", weighed 235 pounds, and could play tackle offensively and defensively with consummate skill. This ability was abetted by a truly eye-opening fleetness of foot. While a member of the Yankees, he regularly outran all of his teammates, save only Buddy Young, a diminutive halfback possessed of Olympic sprinter's speed. A regular feature of the Yankees preseason training camp was a 100-yard dash pitting the outsize Canadian import against the fastest rookie recruits. He never failed to finish ahead of the competition in these matchups.

New York head coach Ray Flaherty once observed, "Arnie is the best fullback prospect in the country." But Weinmeister remained at tackle where his explosive charges kept the opposition in a constant state of anxiety. In 1949, he earned All-AAFC honors. The following year, the conference folded, and he jumped to the New York Giants of the NFL, along with a pretty good back by the name of Tom Landry, who would later become a Hall of Fame member as coach of the Dallas Cowboys.

"Arnie was bigger than most who played at that time," Landry recalled. "He could operate all over the field because he was probably the fastest lineman in the league."

During the 1950s, the Cleveland Browns boasted the most versatile and potent offense in the pro game. But the Giants' prevent corps, spearheaded by Weinmeister, consistently frustrated the likes of such Hall-of-Famers as quarterback Otto Graham and fullback Marion Motley. He now concentrated all of his energies on playing defense, frequently doubling as end in pass-rushing situations. Given his height, speed, and reach, he was a formidable force indeed, rating All-Pro recognition on four occasions. He participated in as many Pro Bowls.

In the wake of the 1953 campaign, he received a $15,000 offer from the British Columbia Lions of the Canadian Football League (CFL). When the Giants failed to meet this asking price, he left the NFL to close out his gridiron career north of the border.

He played just six seasons in the American version of pro football. Still, the board of selectors for the Hall of Fame found this no impediment to his induction, stating, "Arnie Weinmeister definitely does belong. He was to the defensive tackle spot what Gale Sayers was to halfbacks—in a class by himself."

SPECIAL
FORCES

Linebackers

Chuck Bednarik

6'3", 230 pounds. Center, Linebacker: Philadelphia Eagles (1949–1962). All-Pro: 1951–1955, 1957–1960. Pro Bowl: Eight appearances. Inducted into the Pro Football Hall of Fame 1967. Center: 50-Year, All-Time, All-NFL team. Career: Interceptions, 20. Return yardage, 268. Yards per return, 13.4. Touchdowns, 1. Punts, 12. Yards per punt, 40.3. Punt returns, 2. Return yardage, 26. Yards per return, 13.0. Touchdowns, 0. Kickoff returns, 4. Return yardage, 57. Yards per return, 14.3. Touchdowns, 0. Last of the NFL's two-way performers (ironmen).

The horse and buggy, the steam engine, the electric car, and Chuck Bednarik all had one thing in common. Each represented a distinctive period in the development of the American way of life. And with their respective passing a colorful era became history, just so many facts consigned to the impermanence of yellowing pages and fading memories.

Football aficionados perhaps best remember Bednarik as the last of the pro game's ironmen, the storied two-way players who performed on both offense and defense during the course of an afternoon. In his heyday he held forth offensively at center and defensively as a linebacker, though only 6'3" and 230 pounds. When not so employed, he often punted and did the placekicking chores.

On December 26, 1960, the age of the ironman officially came to an end with the playing of the NFL championship game between the Philadelphia Eagles and the Green Bay Packers. Up in the press box of Philadelphia's

Franklin Field, famed New York sportswriter Jimmy Cannon leaned back in his chair, a finger pensively plying his chin. "A league title would be a fitting present for the old guy," he thought aloud.

"You're referring to a going-away present?" a fellow writer inquired.

Cannon nodded. "I believe we're witnessing the death of an era."

Beyond the press box it was dank, dreary, and spitting snow as dusk settled over the 67,235 spectators who peered through the gloom at the hostilities unfolding before them. Less than three minutes remained in the struggle, the Eagles leading the Packers by a slim 17–13 margin. Yet the outcome was still very much in doubt, with Green Bay in possession of the ball at the Philadelphia 16-yard line.

Members of the Packers offensive line hunkered down in their three-point stance as the Eagles defenders quickly aligned themselves, cleats anxiously pawing the lacerated turf. All the while, Green Bay quarterback Bart Starr barked signals in a martial cadence, his gaze sweeping to and fro. Taking the snap, he pivoted crisply and laid the ball in the belly of hard-charging fullback Jim Taylor.

Legs churning like well-oiled pistons, Taylor burst from a pile of writhing bodies and turned upfield toward the Philadelphia end zone. But at just that moment his progress was rudely halted by an Eagles linebacker, the large numeral 60 barely visible on the back of his muddied jersey. With a muted crunching sound, Taylor crumpled to the ground and lay there under the weight of his attacker. The crisis had passed, and the City of Brotherly Love could now celebrate winning another NFL title.

"I was thirty-five years old at the time," Bednarik recalled of late. "When Taylor broke through, I made the stop on him at the nine-yard line with about sixteen seconds left in the game. From where I was sitting on him, I could see the clock running down. Taylor asked me to get off him in strong language. I didn't do it, though, not until time had expired. Then I said, "All right, get up. The blankety-blank game is over." We had won the league championship seventeen to thirteen. Whenever people ask me what game I remember most of all the ones I've played in, my answer is always the same. 'The championship game of 1960.' It was the high point of my fourteen-year career."

On that wintry afternoon, as Cannon had predicted, the world of pro football saw in Bednarik the last of the 60-minute performers. Although he remained active for another two seasons, it was never again as a two-way player. "That day [1960 championship game]," he said, "I played fifty-eight and a half minutes at center and left-side linebacker. I did everything in that game but go down on kickoffs. Yeah, I was the last guy to play sixty minutes. Besides going both ways, I snapped the ball on punts, extra points, and field goals. . . . A few years ago, old Baltimore Colts tackle Art Donovan said about me, 'Bednarik? He's crazy.' And I guess that's right."

Chuck Bednarik

Now 64, Bednarik still looks with mixed feelings on an incident that occurred nearly 30 years ago in which Frank Gifford, currently a celebrated network sportscaster, nearly lost his life. "We [Eagles] played our first game in 1960 against the New York Giants in Yankee Stadium," Bednarik said. "In that one I knocked out Frank Gifford to preserve a 17–10 win for us. Gifford [running back, receiver] ran a little down-and-in pattern, and I was coming from the left side, and we met head-on. I think of that situation being like a one-way street with a Mack truck hitting a Volkswagen. As a result of that injury, he was out of football for more than a year."

The day after, sports pages all across the land displayed a photo of Bednarik exulting over the fallen Gifford. But Bednarik was celebrating that Gifford had fumbled and an Eagles teammate made the recovery. Not until the Giants trainers carried Gifford off the field on a stretcher did Bednarik realize the magnitude of the injury. Only days later did he learn that Gifford had suffered a fractured skull and intracranial bleeding.

"Despite what happened," Bednarik said, "Frank and I are good friends, close friends. I see him all the time. On occasion we'll discuss that day, and he'll say, 'That was a heck of a tackle, Chuck.' Some people say it was a cheap shot, that I blindsided him. But that's simply not true. I hit him a clean, legitimate shot. The films will show that."

Even today, people still come up to Bednarik and want to talk about the hit he put on Gifford.

"If it had been somebody else and another game against a team other than the Giants in Yankee Stadium," Bednarik said, "the play would have gone unnoticed. But it was the Giants in Yankee Stadium and Gifford, who later became a national celebrity. So I'm still getting a lot of publicity from it. I'm still living it today. The fractured skull I gave Gifford and my iron-man play are the two things by which people still relate to me."

Currently, Bednarik lives in Coopersburg, Pennsylvania, a small community located not far north of Philadelphia. He still maintains an interest in pro football and from 1976 to 1982 was a part-time assistant coach with the Eagles under then field boss Dick Vermeil.

All things considered, Bednarik is satisfied with the way his football career turned out. "I never suffered a serious injury," he said, "and I got my share of notoriety. I only hope I performed as well as my record and statistics suggest I did. Like most athletes, I was reluctant to quit doing what I did best, what I loved doing. But that's the way it goes. Still, I reached the pinnacle of pro football. I was inducted into the Pro Football Hall of Fame in 1967. After that I made the 50-Year, All-Time, All-NFL team at center. Only three of us on that team—Don Hutson [Green Bay Packers], Jim Thorpe [Canton Bulldogs], and myself—played both ways. Those are the kinds of things that stay with you forever."

Bobby Bell

6'4", 225 pounds. Defensive End, Linebacker: Kansas City Chiefs (1963–1969, AFL), Kansas City Chiefs (1970–1974, NFL). All-AFL: 1966–1969. AFL All-Star Game: Six appearances. Pro Bowl: Two appearances. Linebacker: All-Time, All-AFL team. Inducted into the Pro Football Hall of Fame 1983. Career: Interceptions, 26. Return yardage, 479. Yards per return, 18.4. Touchdowns, 6.

Call Bobby Bell a man for all seasons, and the chances are good the naysayers would number few. He commanded the size and the speed to be effective if not outstanding at a variety of positions. And this is what he did throughout a football career that had its culmination with the Kansas City Chiefs.

He commenced his gridiron sojourn as an all-state selection at quarterback in high school. Then he did a complete turnabout at the University of Minnesota, starring there as an All-America tackle in a prevent-minded program. Following graduation, he went to Kansas City of the American

Football League (AFL) and began his pro career as a defensive end. When not occupied with rushing the opposition passer or shutting down the run, he would tend to the Chiefs' snapping chores in punting and field-goal situations.

But after he had spent a couple of years on the wing, Kansas City head coach Hank Stram changed his job description once more to outside linebacker. How could this be done so easily? Well, if you're 225 pounds, have 4.5 speed in the 40-yard dash, and possess the upper-body build and strength of a super heavyweight, making such impromptu switches is very possible indeed.

Necessity was always the reasoning behind the many roles he played. As a performer of several abilities, assuming new guises on a moment's notice is all part of the business. However, few of this breed ever proved as successful at each assignment as Bell. But he really shone on the outside of the second line of defense. From this vista he could better discern the intent of the offense, not having to contend with a blocker at the moment of the snap. Given this few seconds, he was able to react more quickly when the opposition's purpose had become more completely defined. His duties were also greatly expanded, and he enjoyed this phase of his new assignment.

"I loved the game of football no matter where I played," he once said. "But if forced to pick a position, my favorite would have to be outside linebacker. It's the most challenging spot because there are so many things that need doing out there. You have to be able to deal with the run and the pass. When it's a run, that means turning the ball carrier inside or stuffing the draw up the middle. And if it's a pass, you may find yourself covering a receiver man-for-man or faced with breaking up a screen. There are a lot of responsibilities that come with the job."

During the Chiefs' existence in the early years of the AFL, real football talent was sometimes in short supply at key places. Bell was always ready and more than able to do the task imposed upon him. He wanted to be out on the field, even if it meant functioning while hurt. Then, as the league matured, he gained stature with it, the fans in the stands and members of the media becoming aware of what his contributions really meant to the club.

He was named to All-AFL status four times and the league All-Star game on six occasions. When the Kansas City franchise became part of the National Football League in 1970, he participated in two Pro Bowl games.

He retired after the 1974 campaign and in 1983 became the first Chiefs player to gain induction into the Hall of Fame.

Dick Butkus

6'3", 245 pounds. Middle Linebacker: Chicago Bears (1965–1973). All-Pro: 1966–1973. Pro Bowl: Eight appearances. Inducted into the Pro Football Hall of Fame 1979. Linebacker: 50-Year, All-Time, All-NFL team. Career: Interceptions, 22. Return yardage, 166. Average yards per return, 7.5. Touchdowns, 0. Fumbles recovered, 25. Return yardage, 22. Yards per return, 0.88. Touchdowns, 0. Kickoff returns, 12. Return yardage, 120. Yards per return, 10.0. Touchdowns (kickoff returns), 1.

In the 1960s the Green Bay Packers prided themselves on beating opposing teams at their strength. Such was the philosophy of head coach Vince Lombardi.

But there is an exception to every rule. And in the case of the Packers' harsh offensive dictum, it was Dick Butkus. "Yeah, it's true," said Fuzzy Thurston, one of the Packers' great pulling guards during their championship era. "Whenever we played the Bears, the game plan was to run away from Butkus. That was the only case in which Lombardi would make that kind of adjustment."

Listed as a middle linebacker on the Chicago depth chart, Butkus was viewed by teammates and opponents alike as the very embodiment of mob violence, for it seemed at times that he was more than one person. The malevolent glint that inhabited his eyes, once likened to cold steel reflecting a winter sun, was for real. Fellow Bears linebacker Joe Fortunato testified candidly, "Butkus mean? Naw, Richie's all right, after he gets his cup of blood for the day."

When asked by an intrepid reporter about his conduct on the field, Butkus said, "Naw, I don't try to hurt anyone, except maybe on special occasions." Sucking up his courage, the reporter inquired more pointedly about such special occasions. Given some thought, Butkus replied offhandedly, "Oh, league games, usually."

By comparative measure, Butkus's tenure in the National Football League was relatively short, from 1965 to 1973, nine short but glorious years. "My knees were so bad the last two seasons of my career," he said, "that I almost never practiced. It took me from one game to the next just to recover to the point where I could play effectively. My one regret is that I didn't get to play longer."

When Butkus came to the Bears from the University of Illinois, it was with the highest recommendations by the Chicago scouting corps. He had been a standout performer for the Fighting Illini at center offensively and linebacker defensively. Besides that, he possessed the requisite size—6'3", 245 pounds—for the pro game as well as noteworthy speed for these dimensions. It was attitude, however, that set him apart from the other members of his graduating class who harbored NFL ambitions. "You have to have the body to play football," he has said. "That's not something you can do anything about. You're either born with it or you're not. And you also have to have the skill to play the game. You can work to improve this aspect of your makeup, but the basics still have to be there. From my schoolboy days I wanted to play professional football. I wanted to be the best that ever played my position."

This drive to be the best translated into everything Butkus did on the field, and much of what he did off it. "I loved practice, the games, the hitting," he said. "I loved all there was about football. When you put on that uniform, you ought to know what it means, what you're getting into out there. I did, and I loved it."

Back in the 1960s and early 1970s, NFL teams didn't employ strength coaches, and weight training was largely unknown in pro football. That didn't deter Butkus from devising his own training regimen. In the off-season he would load up an old junker of a car with the heaviest objects at his disposal. Then he proceeded to push the entire assemblage up and down the hills of his suburban Chicago neighborhood. He did this rain or shine and no matter the temperature level. "Yeah, if I had been able to train with weights the way they do now, my career might've been extended a few years," he said. "I think I might have been able to strengthen my knees a little more, cut down on the effects of the injuries a little more. But that's all water under the bridge."

Unlike many of his teammates, Butkus went all out in practice, just as he did on game days. This unbridled enthusiasm posed no small problem for those less fortunate individuals consigned to scrimmage with him. Star running back Gale Sayers was one such hapless sort. "Dick didn't just tackle you," Sayers said. "He ran right over you, up your legs, knees, back. After a couple of days of this, I went to Coach [George] Halas and complained, 'If we keep this up, there isn't going to be anybody left to play on Sunday.' I was serious."

Psychology had as much a part in Butkus's on-field strategy as brute force. And he sought to use it to ultimate advantage. "When I hit a guy, I wanted to make an impression on him," he said. "I wanted to punish him. I wanted him to know who hit him without his ever having to look around and check a number. And I wanted him to know I'd be back. I wanted him to think about me instead of what he was supposed to be doing."

Despite this dispassionate approach to his duties, he had a soft spot in his heart for an opponent with a chronic injury. "I never cheap-shot a guy with a bad leg or knee, nothing like that," he said. "When I tackled him, it would be up around the shoulders, up high. Oh, I'd rough him up a little, throw him down. But I wouldn't give his knee a twist or that kind of thing. He was playing the game because he loved it, just like me. I respected that and wanted to be treated the same."

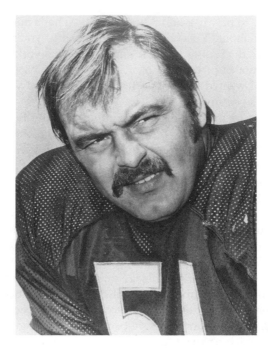

Dick Butkus

Conversely, Butkus displayed scant mercy on any member of the opposition who took a shot at his tender knees. "If a guy rolled up the back of my legs," he said, "and I thought he was trying to hurt me, that was it. I went after him, to get him out of the game before he got me."

Today, Butkus is a successful actor, frequently appears in nationally televised commercials, and serves as a football commentator with CBS Sports. When he retired from the Bears, it was assumed his thoughts would turn to coaching. Halas even invited him to join the Chicago staff. But he politely declined. "The attitude of many of the players entering the league when I was finishing up bothered me," he explained. "I just felt I would have a very difficult time coaching these type of players because of their attitude and practice habits. I would have expected them to be like me. I really loved the game, and I knew that wasn't true with everybody. A lot of them always had this question, 'Why? Why do I have to do this? Why do I have to do that?' That question wasn't asked much in my era. If you were told to go down there and break up the wedge [on a kickoff], then that's what you did. You went down there, and when you saw those four guys [forming the wedge], you barreled into them and tried to knock them all down. I just didn't feel many of the players had the attitude and desire that I did, and I would've had a problem coaching under those circumstances."

Bill George

Bill George

6'2", 230 pounds. Middle Guard/Linebacker: Chicago Bears (1952–1965), Los Angeles Rams (1966). All-Pro: 1952, 1953, 1957, 1958, 1960–1963. Pro Bowl: Eight appearances. Inducted into the Pro Football Hall of Fame 1974. Career: Interceptions, 18. Return yardage, 144. Yards per return, 8.0. Touchdowns, 0. Scoring: TDs, 0. PATs, 14. FGs, 4. Total points, 26.

No one ever accused Bill George of being an inventor, but for all intents and purposes, that was his proper designation. He evolved into one of the first middle linebackers if not the original of this genre, and played the position as though it had been especially designed for him.

During the 1954 NFL season, he held forth as the middle guard in the Chicago Bears' standard five-man defensive front. He had experienced no small success at the spot, earning All-Pro honors in 1952 and 1953. Still, the Philadelphia Eagles were having a field day at his expense, completing little passes over his head with monotonous regularity. In keeping with his defined duties, he first checked the opposing center at the snap of the ball and then, if he read pass, quickly dropped back to cover the short zone immediately behind him. But he was getting beat consistently.

Frustrated, he wisely called a time-out and went over to discuss his plight with George Connor, the Bears defensive captain. Between the two of them they determined that the best resolution of the problem involved coming off the scrimmage line as soon as possible in passing situations, and never mind the Eagles center. This would enable George that extra step or two he needed to get the jump on the encroaching receiver.

Good theory. Now would it wash in practice? On the very next play, George diagnosed a pass once again. This time, he backpedaled furiously, and moments later he had an interception; 17 more were to follow in his playing career.

And so the middle linebacker position was born. It remained largely embryonic for the remainder of that campaign. Still, things would never be the same again defensively for the Bears or any of the other teams in the league. With the advent of the 1956 schedule, George became the defensive signal caller, having abandoned the three-point stance many months previous. He would retain this role until leaving the Bears at the close of the 1965 season.

Under defensive coordinator Clark Shaughnessy, the Bears had more than 100 prevent formations and variations at their command. It was up to George to know them all and to use the proper one at a moment's notice. He mastered the entire repertoire and introduced a few innovations of his own as circumstances dictated. A classic example of this brainstorming ability occurred in the early 1960s.

Back then, the San Francisco 49ers used an early version of the shotgun set to pass their opponents into submission. Taking the long snap from center gave the quarterback the extra time he needed for his receivers to get open downfield. This aerial bombardment paid big dividends on the scoreboard. But George, a gifted blitzer, readily perceived how this threat could be effectively neutralized. When the 49ers went into the shotgun, he merely moved up to the scrimmage line and at the snap of the ball, blew past the center and into the backfield. He was on the quarterback before the play could get underway. Other teams adopted this tactic, and San Francisco's reign of terror was over.

Blitzing and George went together like peanut butter and jelly. He firmly believed no defense could allow a quarterback time to adjust his sights and still survive. He once observed, "You've got to put pressure on a good quarterback. Give a guy like Johnny Unitas that extra second to throw, and he'll beat you every time. The idea is to force him to put the ball up before he's ready or make him eat it."

George earned All-Pro recognition six times as a middle linebacker, eight times overall, and participated in eight successive Pro Bowls. After leaving the Bears, he played with the Los Angeles Rams in 1966 and then retired. He died on September 30, 1982, at 51.

Jack Ham

6'1", 225 pounds. Linebacker: Pittsburgh Steelers (1971–1982). All-Pro: 1973–1979. Pro Bowl: Eight appearances. NFL Defensive Player of the Year: 1975. Inducted into the Pro Football Hall of Fame 1988. Career: Interceptions, 32. Return yardage, 218. Yards per return, 6.8. Touchdowns (interception returns), 1.

When the red dog was on, Jack Ham was a harrier among hounds, a whippet who could hunt alone or as a member of the pack with equal efficiency. He was the prototype outside linebacker—swift enough to cover the clutch catchers coming underneath in must-yardage situations and physical enough to strip blockers and stuff the run. Just what the Pittsburgh Steelers needed in their glory years of the 1970s.

Even as a collegian at Pennsylvania State University, he had a reputation for being a big-play performer. It was a quality that attracted Steelers head coach Chuck Noll to him in the second round of the 1971 National Football League draft. At 6'1" and 225 pounds, he didn't seem to be cut out for linebacking in the pros. But his quickness and intelligence more than compensated for what he lacked in size. And he could diagnose plays with the best of his breed, enabling him to get the jump on the opposition before the play ever reached the point of fruition.

Another ability that served Ham well in his 12-year NFL tenure was his effectiveness as an open-field tackler. Time and again he prevented long gainers or potential touchdown rambles by bringing a receiver or ball carrier to an abrupt halt in a man-on-man situation. Still another facet of his defensive repertoire was a unique penchant for blocking punts. Using the Steelers' big linemen as something of a blind, he cheated up into position at the moment of the snap and then, upon spotting a chink in the blocking front, burst through it just soon enough to get a hand on the ball before it could begin its spiraling flight downfield.

Despite his agility and preceptive play, he took a goodly number of hits but proved remarkably durable for his relatively slight physique. Only five times during his first 10 years in the league did he fail to suit up for a game. Not one to complain, he simply endured the usual array of bumps and bruises that go with being a linebacker and continued to be aggressive. His quiet, unassuming nature endeared him to teammates and fans alike. Once the final gun had sounded, he would head for the dressing room, quickly shower, and be en route to the parking lot before the media hordes could converge for a lengthy postmortem session. People making a fuss over him were merely a source of embarrassment he preferred to avoid.

From 1973 through 1979, he was a perennial All-Pro selection and participated in eight Pro Bowls. In 1975, he earned recognition as NFL Defensive Player of the Year. And this honor was due him for the heroics as he displayed in the 1974 AFC Championship contest. Twice in the course of that encounter he came up with key interceptions that ensured Pittsburgh's initial trip to the Super Bowl. Again, in 1976, he produced another of his patented blocked punts to give the Steelers a much-needed win over the Cleveland Browns. Overall, he intercepted 32 passes and picked up 19 enemy fumbles.

He retired following the 1982 campaign.

Ted Hendricks

6'7", 220 pounds. Linebacker: Baltimore Colts (1969–1973), Green Bay Packers (1974), Oakland–Los Angeles Raiders (1975–1983). All-Pro: 1971, 1974, 1980, 1982. Pro Bowl: Eight appearances. Inducted into the Pro Football Hall of Fame 1990. Career: Interceptions, 26. Return yardage, 332. Yards per return, 12.8. Touchdowns, 1.

Ted Hendricks was different. That's why his contemporaries referred to him as The Mad Stork. He stood 6'7" and weighed only 220 pounds. As for his on-field deportment, it was freewheeling in nature and characterized by a derring-do which more conventional strategists might well consider to be mad. By any measure, he qualified as different.

The Baltimore Colts made him their number-two draft pick out of the University of Miami in 1969. As a lean, lank, and boyish-looking rookie, he seemed out of place in the National Football League and hardly destined for a playing career that would span 15 seasons. There was just too much distance between his head and feet that lacked a layer of meat and and gristle sufficient to withstand the calculated violence sure to be directed against it. The first good hit bode to snap him in half, or so went the thinking of certain uninformed types who critized his preferred status.

But before long, they learned he was composed of jerky and whalebone bound in close proximity by yards of piano wire. He could be bent but not broken. He proved to be one of the most resilient and durable performers ever at the outside linebacker position. As a matter of course, he played with all manner of injuries and could be numbered among the league's fiercest competitors. Weight training didn't meet with his approval, and he

Ted Hendricks

avoided it to the extent that team conditioning regulations allowed. He held finesse and perception of more value than raw power, and who can say he wasn't correct in this assumption. After all, results are the ultimate measure of success.

Despite his ungainly appearance, he was agile and relatively quick, consistently able to frustrate would-be receivers running shallow-out patterns or crossing over the middle. Given his height and reach, he presented a formidable barrier to such aerial intrusions. He was even used effectively on occasion to cover deep drop zones.

On the next snap he could just as readily be draped around the quarterback's neck, having skirted end or slipped through a gap in the protective pocket like an undernourished wraith. He commanded exceptional lateral mobility, which enabled him to help back up the center of the line and blunt sweeps wide to his side of the field. Reading offensive keys and reacting to them were two of his strongest attributes. He always seemed to be in the right place at the right time. This was particularly true when it came to blocking kicks, both the punt and placement varieties. In addition, he scored three touchdowns and logged a record-equaling four safeties.

During his lengthy tenure in the NFL, he earned All-Pro recognition in 1971, 1974, 1980, and 1982, and received eight Pro Bowl invitations. He also had the distinction of playing with the winning team in four Super Bowls, one with the Colts (V) and three as a member of the Oakland–Los Angeles Raiders (XI, XV, and XVIII).

Following the 1983 season, he decided not to subject his body to the rigors of another campaign and retired. There would not be another Mad Stork.

Recently he noted, "They didn't think I could play linebacker at my weight. Well, that is really quite silly. If you're good, you're good."

Sam Huff

6'1", 230 pounds. Middle Linebacker: New York Giants (1956–1963), Washington Redskins (1964–1967, 1969). All-Pro: 1958, 1959. Pro Bowl: Four appearances. Inducted into the Pro Football Hall of Fame 1982. Career: Interceptions, 30 (second-best total among Hall of Fame linebackers). Return yardage, 381. Yards per return, 12.7. Touchdowns (interception returns), 2.

Just mention the name Sam Huff and observe the reaction.

Whisper it in the ear of one-time Green Bay fullback Jim Taylor, and a frown will doubtless darken his broad brow. And his hands might even knot themselves into hard fists. He and Sam had that kind of relationship.

In the 1962 National Football League Championship game played between the Packers and the New York Giants on a frozen field at wind-whipped Yankee Stadium, Taylor and Huff were at their most savage. As the trigger of a standout Giants defensive unit, Huff moved from his middle-linebacker spot again and again to thwart Taylor's pile-driving forays. Each time, before they unlocked bodies on the ice-cold turf, Huff would apply an extra twist to a knee or an arm. In retaliation, Taylor butted and battered and, yes, even bit. The afternoon wore on without either man giving quarter until Taylor finally burst into the New York end zone to give Green Bay a 16–7 victory and the league title. Taylor sprang to his feet and thrust the game ball into Huff's face mask. They exchanged words again, and the afternoon was history.

"Sam was always trying to give you that little extra something in there," Taylor said later. "The elbow, the forearm, the late hit. He kept trying to intimidate you all the time."

Huff, recalling his 13-year playing career, admitted, "Yeah, I made some late hits, all right. But it was nothing illegal. I always got there before the whistle."

Insert his name into a conversation with famed Cleveland Browns running back Jim Brown and watch a knowing smile form on his handsome features. Then, very likely, it will expand into a satisfied grin. He and Huff faced each other over a line of scrimmge at least twice a season for nearly a decade. But there is one incident that remains firmly planted in Brown's memory. "The Browns and the Giants were playing at Municipal Stadium in Cleveland," he recalled. "I don't remember the year, but we were both in the title hunt. Twice in a row I carried the ball, and each time I got stopped for short yardage. After the last time, we were unpiling, and Sam sticks his face right in mine and says, 'You stink.' A couple of plays later, I break a big one for a touchdown. In the end zone I turn around and there's Sam coming up. So I smile and yell, 'How do I smell from here, Sam?' I'll never forget that day, and I don't think he will either."

Huff played every game full-out—mentally, physically, and vocally. If there was a way to rattle an opposing quarterback or ball carrier, he would exploit it to fullest advantage.

From 1956 to 1963, he personified a Giants defense that was perennially the best in the NFL. With the likes of Andy Robustelli, Jim Katcavage, Dick Modzelewiski, Roosevelt Grier, and Jim Patton around him, he was free to exercise his special penchant for mayhem. He became the darling of the New York fans, who, when the Giants needed the ball, would give rousing chorus to the chant of "Huff! Huff! Huff!" At the peak of his prowess, he was featured on the cover of *Time* magazine and as the subject of a network television special entitled "The Violent World of Sam Huff."

In 1964 he went to the Washington Redskins and continued to perform in headline fashion until 1967. Then he retired to pursue business interests, but only for a year. When Vince Lombardi took over as head coach and general manager of the Redskins in 1969, he coaxed Huff back into uniform for one final fling.

During his last season in the league, he split his time between playing and coaching. But like so many of his breed, he was loath to concede that time had passed him by. Thus the task of reminding him fell to Lombardi. "Lombardi and I were sitting in the projection room watching game film from the previous week," Huff said. "All of a sudden he sits up in his chair and points to the screen at a player wearing number seventy. 'That guy is terrible,' he said. 'It's time for him to retire.' Without thinking, I replied, 'Yeah, he's terrible, all right.' Then I realized the guy he indicated was me. I got the message."

Today, he is vice president of special marketing for Marriott Hotels and Resorts. He also works as a color commentator for Washington radio station WMAL, which broadcasts all the Redskins games. When not so occupied, he raises horses on his Middleburg, Virginia, spread and often races them in nearby West Virginia.

From his lofty position in the broadcast booth during the NFL

Sam Huff

campaign, Huff is a somewhat outspoken critic of the modern pro game. "Personally, I feel there have been too many rules changes within the past ten years," he said. "The problem is the rules are being made largely by people who have never played the game. Maybe they like to see a lot of scoring and thought more points would hold the fans' interest. But I don't think this has proven to be the case. I played in the highest-scoring game in NFL history when the Redskins beat the Giants 72–41. It wasn't exciting. It was a joke. It was like NBA basketball—run and dunk. You can't make me believe the fans enjoyed that at all."

With a wink, he added, "The worst changes have to be those that protect the quarterback. Now, with the in-the-grasp rule and the two-step rule and whatever, the defensive guys can't really do their job. There's nothing quite like the feeling when you see an opening in the pass protection and the quarterback just standing there looking downfield. You break through there and lay it on him before he even knows you're there. Nothing quite like it."

Seated next to Huff in the booth is Sonny Jurgensen, fellow commentator and Hall of Fame quarterback. He savors a cigar for several moments before noting, "Spoken like a true linebacker, Sam."

Jack Lambert

6'4", 225 pounds. Middle Linebacker: Pittsburgh Steelers (1974–1984). All-Pro: 1975, 1976, 1979–1983. Pro Bowl: Nine appearances. NFL Defensive Rookie of the Year: 1974. NFL Defensive Player of the Year: 1976, 1979. Inducted into the Pro Football Hall of Fame 1990. Career: Interceptions, 28. Return yardage, 243. Yards per return, 8.7. Touchdowns (interception returns), 0.

The public image of Jack Lambert was best exemplified by a widely circulated photograph of him glaring malevolently from behind his face mask, lips parted in a gap-toothed snarl beneath a Fu Manchu mustache. He played middle linebacker for the Pittsburgh Steelers in their Super Bowl years with the unbridled ferocity his appearance portended.

Psyched to the max, he held forth as a man in motion before each snap, his arms and legs gyrating violently, all the while barking signals and encouragement to other members of the prevent unit. He prevailed as the pivotal player in Pittsburgh's famed "Steel Curtain" defense of the 1970s, earning All-Pro recognition six times and NFL Defensive Player of the Year in both 1976 and 1979. He also participated in nine consecutive Pro Bowls.

"I play the way that suits me best," he said at the height of his career. "I weigh about 218 pounds, while most of your middle linebackers are 20

Jack Lambert

to 30 pounds heavier. Because of my size, I have to be active and aggressive, but that's as far as it goes. I tackle somebody as hard as I can and then get up and go back to the huddle. I'll play clean if they play clean."

But he wasn't above becoming involved in mind games with an opponent or otherwise attempting to intimidate him. Strong evidence of this is indicated in a graphic NFL Films clip which shows Lambert breaking free from a jumble of humanity and applying a withering tackle on a Houston running back, throwing him for a jolting loss. Rising off his fallen foe, he was distinctly heard to comment, "That oughta cool off your [bleep], hotshot."

If the Steelers had any doubts about drafting Lambert, it was not his ability but where to play him. At 6'4" and only 215 pounds, his dimensions as a senior linebacker out of Kent State University, he posed a problem for the Pittsburgh braintrust.

"We thought Jack was a lot like Ted Hendricks [also a 1990 inductee into the Hall of Fame], an outside linebacker," said Dick Haley, Steelers director of player personnel. "We knew Jack was undersized, be we didn't have any reservations about his being a football player. We felt he was good enough to overcome any weight problems he might have. He had the intensity and instincts to play somewhere."

After being selected by Pittsburgh in the second round of the 1974 National Football League draft, Lambert drove from his Ohio home to Steelers headquarters every weekend before the start of the summer camp to view films and prepare himself for the transition to pro football. "I didn't feel I was big enough for the middle," he said, "and from watching films, I knew I couldn't beat out Jack Ham or Andy Russell on the outside. But after watching the middle linebacker [Harry Davis] on film, I felt I could play as well as he did. I mentioned it to [linebackers] Coach [Woody] Widenhofer, and he assured me I would get a trial at both the middle and the outside."

When Davis went down with an injury in the third preseason game, Lambert stepped into the middle linebacker spot and became a starter from that moment on. In the early going, the opposition tested him severely, pounding his position with big running backs and still larger blockers. His fortunes waxed and waned for a few weeks until he proved instrumental in sustaining the Steelers in a five-game winning streak. By the end of the campaign, they ranked first in the NFL for total defense, scoring prevention, sacks, and takeaways. They went on to capture the AFC title and win Super Bowl IX. And he was named 1974 NFL Defensive Rookie of the Year, averaging 11 tackles for the last five contests of the regular schedule. From that juncture on, there was no more talk about the "undersize kid at middle linebacker."

During the next five years, Pittsburgh won three more Super Bowl championships, and Lambert played an integral role in each of these victory quests. In addition to being a native hitter and a tremendous team leader, he proved to be an exceptional defender against the passing game. His height and speed forced quarterbacks to throw higher and sooner than anticipated, so their aerials often didn't have all the power and trajectory desired. This gave the Steelers defensive backs a much better opportunity to get a play on the ball and intercept it.

His lanky build notwithstanding, he missed only six starts in 10 years with Pittsburgh due to injuries, shaking off the beatings absorbed every weekend with a surprising display of resilience. But in the Steelers' season opening game of the 1984 campaign he suffered a severely dislocated toe. He tried to tough it out for eight games, but his effectiveness was cut in half. Finally, before the onset of the 1985 slate, he reluctantly retired.

Willie Lanier

6'1", 245 pounds. Middle Linebacker: Kansas City Chiefs (1967–1969, AFL), Kansas City Chiefs (1970–1977, NFL). All-AFL: 1968. Pro Bowl: Six appearances. Inducted into the Pro Football Hall of Fame 1986. Career: Interceptions, 27. Return yardage, 440. Yards per return, 16.3. Touchdowns (interception returns), 2.

Willie Lanier played middle linebacker like a fist clenched in malice. He was such a fierce tackler that teammates nicknamed him Contact. To him, impact was the very meaning of football.

"I've always enjoyed contact a great deal," he once said. "A good hit is beautiful. But you have to attack people under control. You can't play recklessly in this league. I get several good hits in every game—only I select the hits. I make sure everything is the way I want it. Essentially, I enjoy the concept of competing, of matching my body against that of another man. I've always played the game that way."

Control wasn't a key word in Lanier's football lexicon initially. As a rookie with the Kansas City Chiefs, he was consumed with standing out, attracting attention. The best method to this end, he figured, had to be hitting people with a distinctive lethalness, much as Dick Butkus did. It nearly proved to be a fatal point of view.

"I attacked somebody head-first," he recalled, "and I took the punishment. I was out cold on the field. I spent a week at the Mayo Clinic being tested and a lot longer worrying if I'd ever be right again. Thereafter I determined I wasn't going to simply throw myself into the action in just any shape or form. I decided I'd never again take any unnecessary chances on a fractured neck. There's just no way I was ever going to hit anybody head-on again."

Following his accident, he wore a specially padded helmet designed to protect that portion of his head which had suffered the most trauma. "It's really a standard helmet," he said at the time, "but it has extra rubber padding on the outside. I don't really know if it has any technical merit, if it really disseminates the shock. It's basically a psychological thing, to remind me not to use my head for tackling at all."

At 6'1" and 245 pounds, he posed a serious impediment to the offensive plans of any opponent the Chiefs faced. But size, speed, and mind-set weren't the only aspects of his play that made him so difficult to block. He was very intelligent and methodical in his approach to playing middle linebacker. "There are angles and lines of approach to be considered," he said. "It all has to do with the most effective means of pursuit. When you've made the proper estimate, the proper mathematical evaluation, then a big hit usually results. You've got everything in your favor."

The highlight of Lanier's lengthy career came in Super Bowl IV, the last time the champions of the American Football League (AFL) challenged the best team in the National Football League for world supremacy. The date was January 11, 1970, and the Minnesota Vikings were the NFL representative. Some 80,000 spectators jammed Tulane Stadium in New Orleans for the showdown, and millions of other fans watched on national television. Kansas City won convincingly, 23–7, and principal to the Chiefs' victory was a powerful defensive effort that held the Vikings' vaunted ground attack to a paltry 67 yards. Lanier spearheaded this yeoman effort and accounted for one of three timely pass interceptions to make it the most memorable day of his career. The next year, the NFL absorbed the AFL and was split into NFC and AFC conferences.

"One of the most important lessons I learned in football," he said, "is that you have to stress involvement in the game rather than the final result. Get back to the sandlot attitude, where you're trying to score points because it's fun. If you let pressure of winning get to you, it can tie you up. You become too afraid of making mistakes. You aren't free to play your best. You get away from the basics of human nature; you are human, and it is human to err."

In the course of 11 years plying his considerable football skills, Lanier earned All-American Football Conference honors five times and played in two AFL All-Star games and six Pro Bowls.

Ray Nitschke

6'3", 235 pounds. Middle Linebacker: Green Bay Packers (1958–1972). All-Pro: 1964–1966. Pro Bowl: One appearance. Most Valuable Player: 1962 NFL Championship game. Inducted into the Pro Football Hall of Fame 1978. Linebacker: 50-Year, All-Time, All-NFL team. Career: Interceptions, 25. Return yardage, 385. Yards per return, 15.4. Touchdowns (interception returns), 2. Kickoff returns, 4. Return yardage, 40. Yards per return, 10.0. Touchdowns, 0.

The Bears offensive linemen trotted up to the ball and hunkered down in their three-point stances. Green Bay middle linebacker Ray Nitschke peered into the Chicago backfield, eyes fixed on the elusive Gale Sayers. At the snap, Nitschke began sidestepping to his left in reaction to the flow of activity along the blocking front. He watched Sayers take a handoff and belly out wide. "Got to get over in front of him," Nitschke's football sense screamed in his mental ear. "Can't give him room to maneuver."

Now the Packers outside defenders surged against the thrust of interference, effectively blunting its impact. Like a skittish rabbit, Sayers quickly turned back to the inside, and Nitschke smiled to himself. From the corner of his eye, Sayers discerned a sliver of daylight in the seething mass of bodies and darted for it. Just then, Nitschke and tackle Henry Jordan pinched in from opposite sides, each man appropriating one of Sayers's legs. As they unceremoniously upended the fleet-footed running back with a powerful splitting action, Nitschke inquired of Jordan, "Wanna make a wish?"

If hard times make for hard guys, Nitschke was a prime product of this process. By age 13, he had experienced the loss of both his parents, a thoroughly depressing situation which technically qualified him as an orphan. And while an older brother raised him, he still resented the awful intrusion death had made into his life and displayed this anger in his interpersonal relationships. He was, in a word, a bully.

Looking back on his youth, he said, "Yeah, I was always knocking other kids around. My brother made a good home for me, but I still felt that I had somehow been shorted, that I didn't have anything. I wasn't very well disciplined."

Later, sports provided Nitschke with an acceptable outlet for his frustrations. In addition, they afforded him a vehicle for recognition that he had previously lacked. When his natural aggressiveness became conformed to the format of combative athletics, he developed into an all-star quarterback in high school. He also played baseball well enough to contemplate a professional career. But when a football scholarship was forthcoming from the University of Illinois, he decided to continue his education. With the Fighting Illini he performed with distinction as a fullback and a linebacker.

When invited to join the Green Bay Packers in 1958 as a rookie, Nitschke had doubts about his ability to make the grade, even though the franchise perennially posted a losing record. "Back then, not many rookies made it in the NFL," he said. "There just weren't that many opportunities. When I looked around me, I saw a lot of veterans who had been playing for a while."

Despite the usual rookie mistakes, Nitschke impressed the coaching staff with his determined, hard-nosed play, and in 1959 he proved to be just what the Packers needed defensively when Vince Lombardi came to Green Bay and began changing the team into the scourge of the NFL. Whether in practice or a game, Nitschke always seemed to have a liberal sprinkling of blood on his hand wraps and uniform, a condition Lombardi invariably viewed with his famous gap-toothed grin.

This feeling of admiration was reciprocated by Nitschke. "Lombardi had an enthusiasm about him that was infectious," he said. "He would be the first person on the field at practice every day. When we got beat, he expected us to take it like men. You just went back to work, corrected your mistakes, and you got it right the next time."

During the Packers' dynasty years (1960–1967), Nitschke served as the pivot around which the awesome Green Bay defense functioned. Often his true effectiveness was overlooked due to the caliber of players who performed alongside him. But he cared less about honors than commanding the respect of the opposition. "You wanted them to be aware that you were out there," he said. "You wanted them to remember who you were and what you could do."

When finally it came time to retire, Nitschke confessed to having

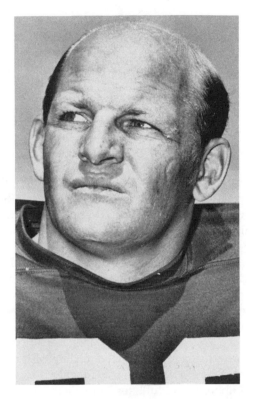

Ray Nitschke

withdrawal symptoms for several years. "On Sundays during the season," he said, "I would get up and head for the garage like I was going to the stadium. My wife would say, 'Hey, you're not playing anymore.' I still felt like I could play, but in my mind I knew I couldn't."

Now a successful businessman, Nitschke remains an avid Packers fan, but he is not entirely pleased with the way the pro game had evolved of late. "I think anybody who loves football, who knows football, wants to see the game get back to being a little more physical," he said. "It's a contact sport, and there are guys out there avoiding contact. There are not too many really good hits now, not the basic good blocking and tackling. I think the rules changes have allowed the players to get a little sloppy fundamentally. As a player, I always felt I had to be improving fundamentally all the time. I had to be able to properly play off a blocker, read my keys, pursue at the right angles, and be available to help out in passing situations. Today, I don't see a lot of guys who can play the whole game."

Maybe the problem is they just don't make them like Ray Nitschke anymore.

Joe Schmidt

6'0", 220 pounds. Middle Linebacker: Detroit Lions (1953–1965). All-Pro: 1955–1962. Pro Bowl: Ten appearances. Inducted into the Pro Football Hall of Fame 1973. Career: Interceptions, 24. Return yardage, 294. Yards per return, 12.3. Touchdowns, 2. Coach: Detroit Lions (1967–1972). Won-Lost Record: 43–35–7.

"Too small and too slow" is what the scouts wrote in their reports. But Joe Schmidt had been subjected to that kind of cursory judgment before and proved it ill advised.

No agility test, no stopwatch, no physical examination, could adequately measure heart size, resolve, or the will to prevail. So he just smiled that little smile of his and waited, waited until it was time to put on the pads, until the hitting commenced. That's when everybody came down to his size, and the toughest guys made their mark.

During 13 seasons in the National Football League, Schmidt made the most of his 6'0", 220-pound dimensions to the extent that he earned an invitation to 10 Pro Bowls and was voted All-Pro status eight times. He became the Detroit Lions' starting middle linebacker as a rookie and played an integral role in bringing two NFL titles to the Motor City. When he first slipped on a Detroit uniform, Bobby Layne was still the Lions' signal caller. Before retiring in 1965, he teamed up with the likes of cornerback Dick "Night Train" Lane, defensive tackle Alex Karras, ends Gail Cogdill and Jim Gibbons, and fullback Nick Pietrosante to usher in a new era for the pro game.

"I dearly loved to play football," he said. "And because a coach once told me that my calves were too small to play football didn't change my mind about the game. Football was my life. I simply couldn't think of anything better to do. Tiger Stadium on Sundays with snow piled up on the sidelines; cold, frozen ground; hits that numbed your bones—it was beautiful. I just loved it. To me, it was a privilege and an honor to play in the National Football League."

As the defensive quarterback, Schmidt had to be intimately familiar with the offensive formations of the opposing team each weekend and know almost instantly how to counter them effectively. To do this, he made ample use of a tactic called red-dogging, shooting linebackers through gaps in the blocking front to trap a ball carrier or quarterback behind the scrimmage line or simply force the play out of its pattern. In any event, he was a master at being in front of the ball and frustrating its advance. "We did a lot of dogging, a lot of blitzing," he said. "This made it difficult for the blockers to get their angles down and generally confused the offense."

No sooner did Schmidt doff his helmet for the last time than he took up a clipboard, accepting a coaching position with the Lions. He tutored

Joe Schmidt

the linebackers until taking over as head coach in 1967. In this capacity he compiled a 43–35–7 record during a six-year tenure, leading Detroit to four consecutive second-place finishes in the NFC's Central Division. Today, he is a successful sales executive and continues to follow pro football with a keen eye.

"In drafting players, you want people with good football intuition," he said. "The best athlete may not be the best football player. Believe me, there's a difference. You want people who are tough, intelligent and have good character. If a guy runs a four-point-two or four-point-three for forty yards, that's fine. Speed is good if he has the other qualities I mentioned. You've got to have the tenacity to play the game. For the most part, the players today are bigger, faster, stronger, and better trained than we were in our day. But a lot of them don't play with the same intensity we did. The thing is, you've got to want to hit somebody. Reduced to basics, that's what football is all about."

Schmidt is of the opinion that escalating salaries in the modern pro game have served to dilute some of the players' desire. "Back when I played, you only made $5,000 to maybe $10,000 a year," he said. "But you had such a camaraderie with your teammates that you never wanted to be embarrassed, to have anybody talk behind your back and say, 'He could have played but he didn't.' I never want that said about me. But a lot of guys today look at if differently. Inwardly, they say, 'I want to play twelve or thirteen years, only I don't want to hurt myself; I don't want to jeopardize my career. I want to make my half a million for as long as I can.' So they don't play hurt like we used to do. It's a difference in mentality. And economics has a lot to do with it."

Despite the bigger, faster, and stronger players currently holding forth in the NFL, Schmidt still feels he could perform as effectively today as in his time. "Yeah, I could make it now," he said without hesitation. "They'd have to find a place for me. Football is a game the eleven toughest guys are supposed to win. And that's the kind of game I always played."

REARGUARD BRIGADE

Defensive Backs

Herb Adderley

6'1", 200 pounds. Cornerback: Green Bay Packers (1961–1969), Dallas Cowboys (1970–1972). All-Pro: 1962, 1963, 1965, 1966, 1969. Pro Bowl: Five appearances. NFL Interception Return Leader: 1965, 1969. Inducted into the Pro Football Hall of Fame 1980. Career: Interceptions, 48. Return yardage, 1,046. Yards per return, 21.8. Touchdowns (interception returns), 7. Kickoff returns, 120. Return yardage, 3,080. Yards per return, 25.7. Touchdowns (kickoff returns), 2.

The time was right for Herb Adderley. Man-to-man coverage prevailed as the order of the day, and the gloves were off out back, with possession being nine-tenths of the law. Quickness and toughness counted heavily as winning attributes, and so he prospered, his native speed and a faro player's sense of knowing when to go for the bank giving him the house edge. Indeed, he was a man for his era.

Not all that long ago in the National Football League, the name of the game was reach out and touch someone—hard. Only members of the defense could use their hands, the fingers often being closed to protect one's manicure, and contact went on anywhere from sideline to sideline with relative impunity, save for that brief interlude it took a pass to proceed downfield, those fleeting moments a receiver and defender were supposed to cease hostilities and just concentrate on the ball. Under conditions such as these, Adderley established himself as one of the finest cornerbacks ever.

Curious it is, then, that he became a secondary practitioner by the most

273

indirect of means. He had been a running back of note at Michigan State University, and that's what Green Bay head coach Vince Lombardi had in mind when the club selected him in the first round of the 1961 college draft. And when he arrived at the Packers' preseason training camp, his name graced the depth chart as a ball carrier. Nothing unexpected there surely.

But once he had embarked upon his rookie campaign, Henry Greminger, the regular left cornerback, went down with an injury, and his status changed with mind-boggling suddenness. He commenced the 1961 season on special teams, returning three San Francisco kickoffs for big yardage in only his second outing as a pro. With a ball under his arm, he posed a significant problem for the opposition. But with Greminger out, circumstances dictated that he perform in a capacity other than his specialty. Hence it was he who harbored a few misgivings and grumbled no little bit under his breath. Still, he who didn't do Lombardi's bidding didn't have a football future in Green Bay.

In his very first start as a cornerback, Adderley logged an interception and from that juncture on conducted himself as if born to the spot. His attainments were such that Lombardi felt compelled to acknowledge publicly that he very nearly made a grievous error. "It scares me to think how I almost mishandled him," the great man testified. "It was just a case of me being stubborn, of already having my mind made up."

On the other hand, Adderley happily voiced his confession. "Hey, I'll be the first to admit I didn't look foward to playing defense all that much," he said. "But when I got out there and was challenging the best receivers in the league head-to-head, there's no way I ever wanted to go back on offense."

Almost from the beginning he set his sights on becoming the classic cornerman, one of the best, if not the best ever, at the position. Endowed with a "nose for the ball," he early demonstrated a willingness to take chances to steal an enemy aerial. Needless to say, he also understood the odds were good that this aggressive approach could just as easily result in a quick touchdown for his opponent. But he was a gambler on the field and coveted a philosophy that supported this role. "Sure, you're going to get beat, give up the score now and then," he said. "Only you can't dwell on it. The idea is not to let the same guy beat you again."

Blessed with speed and agility to complement his 6'1", 200-pound frame, he could be physical and still not lose out in a footrace. No one better appreciated what a rare combination of talents he possessed than diminutive pass-catching ace Tommy McDonald of the Philadelphia Eagles, Dallas Cowboys, and Los Angeles Rams. "Herb Adderley simply wouldn't let me get to the outside," McDonald once lamented. "He'd just beat me up, force me to run the underneath routes all the time. That made it very

Herb Adderley

difficult for me to do my job. Other guys tried the same tactic, but he was the only one tough enough and fast enough to get it done."

In Super Bowl II Adderley closed out the scoring for Green Bay by picking off an Oakland Raiders pass and returning it 60 yards for a touchdown to give the Packers a 33–14 victory. Overall, he played in four Super Bowls, two each with Green Bay and Dallas, and five NFL title games. He also earned All-Pro recognition five times and participated in as many Pro Bowls.

He retired after the 1972 schedule.

Mel Blount

6'3", 203 pounds. Cornerback: Pittsburgh Steelers (1970–1983). All-Pro: 1975, 1977, 1981. Pro Bowl: Five appearances. NFL Most Valuable Defensive Player: 1975. Pro Bowl Most Valuable Player: 1977. Inducted into the Pro Football Hall of Fame 1989. Career: Interceptions, 57. Return yardage, 736. Yards per return, 12.9. Touchdowns (interception returns), 2. Fumbles recovered, 13. Touchdowns (fumble returns), 2. Kickoff returns, 36. Return yardage, 911. Yards per return, 25.3. Touchdowns, 0.

Nothing under the sun is perfect, but when cornerbacks are the subject, Mel Blount can be said to have pushed the limits of divine quality control to the max. Size, speed, and toughness—he had it all. And he used it
all to the best advantage.

Pushing the bounds of perfection was his intent from day one in the
National Football League. As he put it, "I didn't want to be second to
anyone. I wanted to set the standards for my position."

Few members of his defensive breed were ever so bountifully endowed
with the physical skills to excel. He had 4.5 speed couched in a body that
stretched 6'3" and tipped the beam at 205 pounds. The name of his game
was intimidation, and he dominated it by any standard.

When Blount joined the Pittsburgh Steelers in 1970, members of the
secondary could all but commit mayhem on receivers downfield until the
ball was thrown. Given his fleetness of foot, he could pick up his man at
the scrimmage line and then "bump and run" him all the way to the reception area.

Without exception, the top catch guys in the league got a little weak
in the knees when they lined up on the side of Steel City's destroyer. In
the opinion of Pittsburgh assistant coach Jon Kolb, "Mel could just walk
out there, look down on the guy, and then control him. That's intimidation."

During the late 1970s, NFL rulemakers became alarmed at the way the
passing game was being shut down, so they instituted a hands-off policy for
secondary defenders aimed at putting more points on the scoreboard. But
Blount changed his tactics with chameleonlike ease. Given his height and
native quickness, he would lay off the receiver until the ball drew near and
then come swooping in to make the theft. He could ably dispatch his responsibilities by whatever dictum.

Interestingly, he experienced no few problems in adjusting to the pro
game at the outset of his career. The physical abilities were all there, but
he lacked savvy, the acute sense of knowing when and how to react under
a variety of circumstances. His first two seasons were precarious at best,
giving rise to doubts that he could successfully make the transition from
college to play-for-pay football. Quarterbacks picked on him, as did about
every receiver in the American Football Conference (AFC). One afternoon
the Miami Dolphins' Paul Warfield beat him three times for touchdown
romps of 12, 86, and 60 yards. His future in the NFL seemed limited indeed. "Yeah, I thought about quitting," he recalled. "I thought a whole lot
about it."

What made things worse, the Steelers fans were on him the moment
he made an appearance on the field. They stood ready to excoriate him at
the slightest hint of human frailty. Finally, prior to the onset of the 1972
season, he came to a necessary accommodation with himself. "I realized

that the football I played in college hadn't given me the preparation for the pros that I needed," he said, looking back on that trying time. "In college the game was more physical but less complex. So I came to rely too much on natural ability to get me by."

He decided that every mistake would be a lesson learned rather than a cause for morbid deliberation. "Instead of thinking about how many times I had been beaten," he said, "I decided to think of how many lessons I had learned."

Fortified with this new mind-set, he went to work with a vengeance, and shortly thereafter his fortunes took a markedly upward turn. He was named the NFL's Most Valuable Defensive Player in 1975. That year he earned All-Pro recognition, an honor that would be accorded him in 1977 and 1981. He also rated five invitations to the Pro Bowl and was the most valuable player of that postseason classic in 1977.

He was one of the most durable players in Steelers history, failing to suit up only once in 201 regular-season contests. In the playoffs, he missed just a single start in 14 years. He appeared in six AFC championship encounters and four triumphant Super Bowl outings (IX, X, XIII, and XIV).

Following his retirement after the 1983 campaign, he said, "If the scales were balanced, there was nobody I couldn't cover. That's what motivated me, drove me to be as good as I was. I was in front of fifty thousand people in the stands and millions more on television. I didn't want to be embarrassed." And, with few exceptions, he wasn't.

Blount later served as director of NFL player relations.

Willie Brown

6'1", 215 pounds. Cornerback: Denver Broncos (1963–1966, AFL), Oakland Raiders (1967–1969, AFL), Oakland Raiders (1970–1978, NFL). All-AFL: 1964, 1968, 1969. AFL All-Star Game: Five appearances. All-Time, All-AFL team: 1969. All-Pro: 1970–1973. Pro Bowl: Four appearances. Inducted into the Pro Football Hall of Fame 1984. Career: Interceptions, 54. Return yardage, 472. Yards per return, 8.7. Touchdowns (interception returns), 2. Punt returns, 3. Return yardage, 29. Yards per return, 9.7. Touchdowns, 0. Kickoff returns, 3. Return yardage, 70. Yards per return, 23.3. Touchdowns, 0.

Life on the corner is lonely, highly combative, and seldom subject to relief. It's a hardship post in the fullest sense. When the action commences, it's intense, concentrated, and all-consuming. Should defeat result, it must be endured with a certain naked humiliation, every eye privy to the disgrace imposed. But Willie Brown made a name for himself out there in a most individual fashion.

Other than quarterback, the most difficult position to fill adequately on any football team is cornerback. Paramount among the attributes required for success in this regard are speed, intelligence, size, determination, mobility, and an innately hard-nosed demeanor. Now and again, such players can be recruited. Even less frequently, they may adapt successfully to the duties required by switching from another mode of the game. But almost never do they just walk up and present themselves, needing only a little fine-tuning and experience to be adjudged among the greatest. However, such was the case with Brown when he joined the Denver Broncos of the American Football League (AFL) in 1963 as a rookie fresh from little Grambling College.

Usually it takes a few seasons for even a superior talent to become completely operational at cornerback. Brown required only six weeks into his freshman campaign to acquire starter status. And he needed until just the remainder of the schedule that year to establish himself as an exceptional performer. He earned All-AFL recognition as a sophomore sensation and went on to become Most Valuable Player in the 1965 league All-Star game.

In 1967, he went to the Oakland Raiders in a trade and so began an association that would ultimately lead to the Hall of Fame. His style of play was physical and audacious, a modus operandi tailor-made for the silver-and-black mentality. At the snap of the ball, he would challenge the receiver right at the scrimmage line, hand-fighting him for an advantage. Then he ran stride for stride with his man, bumping and jostling him out of his pattern. Just as the ball began its descent, he made his move, strong hands and arms stretching overhead to pull down the interception and blunt another offensive threat.

During one afternoon he thieved no less than four of Joe Namath's aerial offerings, prompting the New York Jets Hall of Fame signal caller to observe, "Willie gives you nothing. Unless you throw a perfect pass, you can't complete it. He's the vest best."

All of this was by design, to be sure. "I wanted to be the best," he confessed. "I never tried to intimidate receivers, but I always wanted to let them know it wouldn't be easy."

For 10 of his 12 seasons with the Raiders he held forth as their defensive captain. It is not coincidental that in the course of this tenure Oakland compiled a most impressive 125–35–7 won-lost record and had the finest secondary in all of pro football. He set the tone for his running mates in all they did, particularly concerning mental toughness. In 1971 he played with an arm encased in a cast, a broken thumb, and a painful groin pull, permitting only 10 receptions in his area of responsibility. This he did in the face of 359 passes put up by the opposition during that period.

Brown had only one real goal as a professional, and that was the pursuit of perfection.

"I worked at it," he said. "Desire. Concentration. I guess you could say it's total dedication. Off-season, I did a lot of drills, defensive drills. Twisting. Cutting. I'd go to the practice field, draw a line, set up five yards away, then imagine a guy running a post pattern on me. Things like that."

He intercepted at least one pass in each of 16 seasons, for a pro mark. In 1964, he had nine thefts and seven in 1967. While in the AFL he received an invitation to five All-Star games, being voted MVP of the 1965 contest, and was designated all-league three times. He rated a berth on the All-Time, All-AFL team in 1969. Following the NFL merger a year later, he participated in four Pro Bowls and earned All-Pro status as many times.

Among his greatest thrills were two Super Bowl appearances (II and XI). In Super Bowl XI against the Minnesota Vikings, he intercepted a pass and returned it 75 yards for a touchdown and record in the postseason classic. The Raiders won 32–14 for their first victory in the big game.

Brown retired before the 1979 season and joined the Raiders coaching staff as an assistant in charge of the defensive backfield. He remained in this capacity through the 1988 campaign.

Jack Christiansen

6'1", 185 pounds. Defensive Back: Detroit Lions (1951–1958). All-Pro: 1952–1957. Pro Bowl: Five appearances. NFL Interception Leader: 1953, 1957. NFL Punt Return Leader: 1951, 1952, 1954, 1956. Inducted into the Pro Football Hall of Fame 1970. Career: Interceptions, 46. Return yardage, 717. Yards per return, 15.6. Touchdowns (interception returns), 3. Punt returns, 85. Return yardage, 1,084. Yards per return, 12.8. Touchdowns (punt returns), 8. Kickoff returns, 59. Return yardage, 1,329. Yards per return, 22.5. Touchdowns, 0. Rushing attempts, 20. Rushing yardage, 143. Yards per carry, 7.2. Touchdowns (rushing), 2.

Early on, it appeared that Jack Christiansen was playing against a stacked deck. His boyhood years were spent in an orphanage without benefit of a family, and then as a teenager he suffered a crippling injury to his arm. Nonetheless, he prevailed over these negative influences to become one of the finest defensive backs ever to play in the National Football League.

He grew up calling home the Odd Fellows Orphanage in Canon City, Colorado. Sports-oriented from his youth, he developed into a fine football player in high school and harbored aspirations of acquiring an athletic scholarship to a major university. However, in his senior year, he was accidentally shot in the left arm, and doctors pronounced the damage so severe as to preclude any further participation in contact sports.

When Christiansen enrolled at Colorado State University, he confined

Jack Christiansen

his freshman athletic endeavors to running sprints with the track team. But as a sophomore he succumbed to his love for football and went out for the varsity, choosing to disregard all medical advice to the contrary. He won a spot on the roster as a reserve defensive back. When the regular safety went down in the season opener. He suddenly found himself elevated to a starter. He would maintain that status for the rest of his college tenure, earning all-conference recognition in the process. What's more, he was a highly regarded kick-return specialist.

After graduation, he gave little thought to the prospect of making it in the NFL. There just wasn't much call for pro safeties who tipped the beam at barely 162 pounds. Still, Detroit Hall of Fame quarterback Dutch Clark thought he could do the job, as did erstwhile teammate Thurman McGraw, then a rookie with the Lions. Together they persuaded the club hierarchy to select the Colorado State standout in the sixth round of the 1951 college draft. So commenced a most memorable career.

From day one, Christiansen left no doubt that he belonged in the money game. His first year with Detroit he doubled as a punt returner and tallied four touchdowns, tops in the NFL for this category. Against the Los Angeles Rams that season he registered scoring runbacks of 69 and 47 yards, swiveling through the opposition with electrifying ease. In 1952, his punt-return average of 21.5 yards led the league. By that time, opposing teams had developed a special spread formation for punting situations with the hope of containing him. Unfortunately for them, it didn't prove all that effective.

Despite his kick-return success, he's still best remembered as a secondary defender. He was the key element in Detroit's deep prevent corps, so much so that the Motor City sportswriting fraternity referred to this quartet as Chris's Crew. In 1953 and 1957, he paced the NFL with 12 and 10 aerial thefts, respectively, and pulled down 46 interceptions overall during his eight years on the backline. Once again, the opposition found it necessary to employ special tactics to cope with his defensive prowess.

In his heyday, the word to the wise around the league was "Don't pass in Chris's area and don't punt to him." He rated All-Pro honors six consecutive years (1952 to 1957) and participated in five Pro Bowls. During this period, the Lions won four division titles and three NFL championships.

Following the 1958 campaign, Christiansen retired as a player and later was an assistant coach with several league teams. He died on June 29, 1986, at 57.

Ken Houston

6'3", 198 pounds. Strong Safety: Houston Oilers (1967–1969, AFL), Houston Oilers (1970–1972, NFL), Washington Redskins (1973–1980). All-Pro: 1971–1973, 1975–1977. AFL All-Star Game: Two appearances. Pro Bowl: Ten appearances. Inducted into the Pro Football Hall of Fame 1986. Career: Interceptions, 49. Return yardage, 898. Yards per return, 18.3. Touchdowns (interception returns), 9 (NFL record). Punt returns, 51. Return yardage, 333. Yards per return, 6.5. Touchdowns (punt returns), 1. Kickoff returns, 3. Return yardage, 53. Yards per return, 17.7. Touchdowns, 0.

October 8, 1973: The master scoreboard at RFK Stadium told the story: Washington 14, Dallas 7. Time remaining: 16 seconds. With a punctuality born of the 30-second clock, the Cowboys broke out of their huddle and trotted to the scrimmage line. Just a few steps beyond a waiting wall of burgundy-and-gold jerseys lay the end zone and a much-desired "kiss-your-sister" ending to a long night's work—a tie game. And ABC-TV would record the face-saving heroics for millions to see.

Dallas fullback Walt Garrison took his three-point stance and strained to hear the quarterback's cadence above the deafening din of the highly partisan crowd. At the snap-count, he ventured an influence step toward the line of scrimmage, which was now obscured by a violent melding of writhing bodies. Then he turned toward the sideline and looked back to his inside. With a graceful looping flight, the little swing pass came in soft and easy to handle. But just as he gathered the ball to him and prepared to take the few required steps toward the goal line, a mind-numbing hit abruptly terminated his forward movement. For a brief, blurred interlude he lost all sense of orientation before crumpling to the scarred turf under the weight of his oppressor.

Overhead the scoreboard glared accusingly 14–7 Washington, and no time was left on the clock. Garrison rolled reluctantly to a sitting position and watched Redskins strong safety Ken Houston head toward the home-team dugout, his mode of departure almost matter-of-fact. Garrison shook his head. He had fooled everybody in the house except the one man who counted most—Houston.

During an illustrious career in pro football that spanned 14 seasons, Houston made many a saving tackle, but none more dramatic than the one against Dallas on that electric October night with a national television audience looking on. With that single savage act, he introduced himself to fans and members of the media the land over, apprising them of what his opponents in the National Football League had known for years. He was voted the finest strong safety in the NFL for the decade of the 1970s. In that time he held forth as a premier defender against both the pass and the run. Lean and lanky of build but bound together by baling wire and gifted with sprinter speed, he could match steps or shots with anybody who came his way. Throughout the course of his playing tenure, he earned All-Pro recognition six times and participated in 10 Pro Bowls. Today, his nine touchdown returns of stolen aerials remains a league record.

Prior to joining the pro ranks, he performed as a linebacker for a nondescript institution of higher learning in Texas billed as Prairie View A & M College. He went in the ninth round of the 1967 American Football League (AFL) draft to the Houston Oilers, who envisioned him as a strong safety. Once in their preseason camp, he quickly convinced them of his ability to make the transition without a hitch. Just three games into his rookie campaign, he took over as a starter on the backline. Then, two weeks later, he notched a pair of touchdowns at the expense of the New York Jets. His first score resulted when he blocked a field goal attempt, then scooped up the loose ball and ported it 45 yards to the end zone. Not long thereafter, he picked off an enemy pass and returned it 43 yards for another six points.

He spent an eventful six years with the Oilers, appearing in two AFL

All-Star contests between 1967 and 1969. Immediately following the merger of 1970, he was twice an all-league selection in 1971 and 1972. In 1973 he was traded to the Washington Redskins for five players, three of whom became regulars from day one in uniform. Once suited up for the Redskins, he rated All-Pro honors again in 1973, 1975, 1976, and 1977.

In the wake of the 1980 season, he retired with 49 interceptions, good for 898 return yards and 9 TDs.

Dick "Night Train" Lane

6'2", 210 pounds. Cornerback: Los Angeles Rams (1952, 1953), Chicago Cardinals (1954–1959), Detroit Lions (1960–1965). All-Pro: 1956, 1960–1963. Pro Bowl: Six appearances. NFL Interception Leader: 1952, 1954. Cornerback: 50-Year, All-Time, All-NFL team. Inducted into the Pro Football Hall of Fame 1974. Career: Interceptions, 68. Return yardage, 1,207. Yards per return, 17.8. Touchdowns (interception returns), 5. Receptions, 8. Receiving yardage, 253. Yards per reception, 31.6. Touchdowns (receiving), 1. Punt returns, 4. Return yardage, 14. Yards per return, 3.5. Touchdowns, 0. Scoring: TDs, 7. Safeties, 1. Total points, 44.

Taking a chance is what got Dick "Night Train" Lane an opportunity to play in the National Football League, and this same willingness to gamble set him apart from his contemporaries as a standout performer.

His football pedigree wasn't all that extensive. It amounted to playing in high school, at Scottsbluff (Nebr.) Junior College and a little in the army. But then again, his alternatives outside of the game were bleak indeed. So, with a collection of old newsclips under arm, he walked off the street into the administrative office of the Los Angeles Rams in search of a future in the NFL. Essentially, he had nothing more going for him than the dog-eared scrapbook and his ability as a self-salesman. By any measure, his gambit qualified as a long shot.

Perhaps something in the clips caught the eye of Rams head coach Joe Stydahar, or maybe it was simply a gut feeling that this young man with the burglar's cool just might be a find. In any event, he agreed to give Lane a look, and thus commenced one of the most unusual and illustrious of pro football careers.

At the outset, he was given a try as an end because of his size and speed, but the prospects of getting much playing time in this category seemed slight. Preceding him on the depth chart were the likes of Elroy "Crazylegs" Hirsch and Tom Fears, both proven big-catch guys commanding Pro Bowl potential. So his stay with the offensive unit proved brief. But before undergoing a transplant to the other side of the ball, he and Fears formed a student-mentor relationship, which led to the acquisition of his famous nickname. While they conferred, Fears's phonograph would be continuously

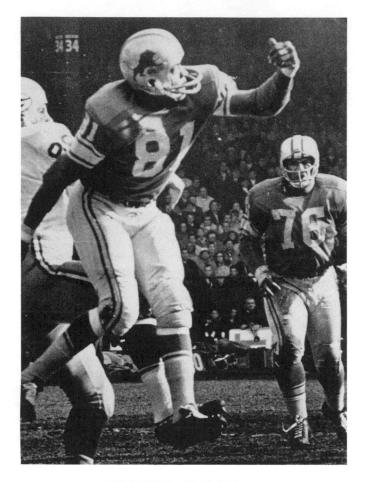

Dick "Night Train" Lane

spinning the then popular recording of "Night Train." One day a member
of the team came into the room where they were conversing and remarked,
"Hey, there's Night Train Lane." From that moment on, the colorful
designation became a permanent part of his mystique.

Finally he found a home in the Rams' deep prevent corps as a cornerback. In this spot he could utilize his penchant for derring-do and fleetness
of foot to best advantage. He quickly developed into an excellent cover man
and early on distinguished himself as a sure and savage tackler in the open
field. During his rookie year of 1952, he logged 14 interceptions in a
12-game slate, a single-season record that remains on the books to this day.
And against the run he showed himself equally effective, regularly forcing
turnovers with his native hitting capability.

Prior to the 1954 campaign, he went to the Chicago Cardinals in a trade and remained with the Windy City franchise for six seasons. In 1956, he earned All-Pro recognition for the first time. Come 1960, he moved on to Detroit and a place with the Lions on their defensive backline. His six years in the Motor City would be glorious ones. The first four were marked by his perennial selection to the all-league team and successive invitations to the Pro Bowl. And his swashbuckling play, matching the game's top receivers step for step and routinely stealing the ball from their grasp, captured the imagination and the hearts of Motown fans.

"Sure, Dick gets burned once in a while," noted Lions Hall of Fame linebacker Joe Schmidt. "But he makes the big play a lot of times, too. I'd say, percentage-wise, he's way ahead of the game."

During an era in which man-for-man coverage prevailed, Lane reigned supreme. "The idea is to let the guy [receiver] think you've been conned," he said. "So when he makes his big move, you do the same, and suddenly there's no room for him to catch the ball. I like seeing the expression on their faces. That's a reward just in itself."

He retired following the close of the 1965 schedule. Not long thereafter, he was picked as a cornerback on the 50-Year, All-Time, All-NFL team.

Yale Lary

5'11", 189 pounds. Safety, Punter: Detroit Lions (1952, 1953, 1956–1964). All-Pro: 1952, 1953, 1956, 1957. Pro Bowl: Nine appearances. NFL Punting Leader: 1959, 1961, 1963. Inducted into the Pro Football Hall of Fame 1979. Career: Interceptions, 50. Return yardage, 787. Yards per return, 15.7. Touchdowns (interception returns), 2. Punt returns, 126. Return yardage, 758. Yards per return, 6.0. Touchdowns (punt returns), 3. Kickoff returns, 22. Return yardage, 495. Yards per return, 22.5. Touchdowns, 0. Rushing attempts, 10. Rushing yardage, 153. Yards per carry, 15.3. Touchdowns, 0. Punts, 503. Yards per punt, 44.3.

Hall of Fame admission was accorded Yale Lary on the basis of his play as a defensive back and only secondarily because he happened to be one of the best punters ever in the annals of pro football. Through the years, the reverse of this situation has often been thought true.

For the duration of his 11 years in the National Football League he held forth as a starter on the backline of the Detroit Lions secondary. He played what is now known as the free-safety spot, the last bastion of defense against the aerial bomb and the rampaging ball carrier. Seldom did he fail in the execution of his duties.

At 5'11" and 189 pounds, he had enough bulk to hold his own against the bigger ends and running backs while possessing the speed to match the deep receivers step for step. His presence as a preventive force out back contributed substantively to the success the Lions enjoyed during the 1950s when they won three NFL titles out of four appearances in the league-championship game.

In the course of his career, he logged 50 interceptions, but speculation that this number could have been appreciably greater is based upon the knowledge that many a quarterback opted not to throw into his area of coverage for fear of having the pass stolen. Further credence is given this assertion by no less an authority than Hall of Fame signal caller Bobby Layne, not only a longtime admirer of Lary but a former teammate. "If I had to pick one defensive back who had everything, it would have to be Yale," said Layne. "He was smart, but the big thing was his quickness and his ability to recover and intercept a pass after lulling the quarterback into thinking he had an open receiver."

Lary plied his trade in an era when the bump-and-run tactic downfield not only didn't elicit a whistle but was accepted practice. He worked receivers in a more overt manner than he did quarterbacks, jostling the former off stride just as they made their break, conning the latter with equal subtlety into putting up the ball under seemingly opportune circumstances. In either endeavor he excelled, his timing and staging uniformly impeccable.

He maintained a top level of performance at his post probably as long as anyone in league history. From his rookie year to the day of retirement, he held forth among the best of his breed.

Unlike many a football luminary, great and near-great, he didn't gradually slide down to the end but without apparent loss of facility simply chose to step off the glitzy merry-go-round of big-time sport, having a sense that enough was enough.

When back to punt, he presented a problem of much different dimension to the opposition, for two reasons. First, he could lay the ball in the coffin corner with unerring accuracy or simply boom it, his lifetime average a healthy 44.3 yards. He won NFL punting honors three times and missed making it four by little more than three inches. Second, he commanded the speed to fake a kick and then go the distance. He ran only 10 times under these conditions for a per-attempt average of 15.3 yards, but the threat was always there. As a result, opponents had to rush guardedly lest he loop outside them and take off along the sideline for their end zone.

He put his fleetness of foot to further good use returning punts and kickoffs. Each time the ball settled into his grasp, he became a potential six points.

Truly, he could do it all. He retired following the 1964 campaign.

Emlen Tunnell

6'1", 200 pounds. Safety: New York Giants (1948–1958), Green Bay Packers (1959–1961). All-Pro: 1951, 1952, 1955, 1956. Pro Bowl: Eight appearances. Inducted into the Pro Football Hall of Fame 1967. Career: Interceptions, 79. Return yardage, 1,282. Yards per return, 16.2. Touchdowns (interception returns), 4. Punt returns, 258. Return yardage, 2,209. Yards per return, 8.6. Touchdowns (punt returns), 5. Kickoff returns, 46. Return yardage, 1,215. Yards per return, 26.4. Touchdowns (kickoff returns), 1. Rushing attempts, 17. Rushing yardage, 43. Yards per carry, 2.5. Touchdowns, 0.

Whoever coined the phrase "The best defense is a good offense" quite possibly had Emlen Tunnel in mind. No one before or since has been able to match his knack for routinely turning an intercepted pass into a game-breaking defensive-offensive play. The Em was truly one of a kind.

His football career nearly came to an unceremonious end before it had really gotten under way. While a freshman gridiron aspirant at the University of Toledo, he broke his neck, and all future contact seemed out of the question. Further confirmation of this dour prospect came when both the army and the navy refused to enlist him because of his condition, despite the fact the armed services needed manpower in the worst way with World War II threatening global stability. He finally did manage to get accepted by the coast guard.

When hostilities were over, he enrolled at the University of Iowa and promptly went out for the football team. With no thoughts of dire consequences, he waded through a surfeit of returned veterans to nail down a spot on the Hawkeyes roster as a largely defense-oriented performer. Though always giving his best on the prevent side of the ball, he still harbored a desire to play on the offensive unit. When the opportunity for so doing seemed next to nil, he dropped out of school after the 1947 season and sought to market his skills in the pro game.

Because he had a year of eligibility remaining at Iowa, the great majority of the NFL teams didn't think to include him in that year's college draft; they were unaware of his availability. Undaunted, he set out to call on the league clubs with hopes of cutting his own deal. His knock resulted in an open door at the office of New York Giants owner Tim Mara. Right from the outset, the two men hit it off, and Mara offered to sign Tunnell for $5,000 with bonuses totaling $1,000 thrown in as an incentive. It would turn out to be one of the best deals Mara ever made.

Tunnell became the first black man to wear a Giants uniform. Once again he fell into the defensive mold, his solid dimensions (6'1", 200 pounds), strong hitting ability, and standout speed eminently qualifying him for a safety spot. He also proved to be a gifted kick returner, endowed with a particular elusiveness and the ability to work even the most minimal advantage into good field position. Before long, sportswriters referred to him as the team's "offense on defense."

In 1952, he outgained powerful running back Deacon Dan Towler of the Los Angeles Rams, the leading rusher in the NFL that season. And he did it without ever being in on an offensive down. Towler plowed for 894 yards and a sparkling per-carry average of 5.7 yards. But Tunnell, handling the ball just 52 times, scampered for 923 yards and averaged an even more spectacular 17.8 yards. He picked up 411 yards shagging punts, ran back kickoffs for another 364 yards, and logged 149 yards returning seven intercepted aerials. By virtue of these startling stats, reporters wondered in print why Tunnell wouldn't be better used on offense.

New York head coach Steve Owen's standard reply was "Em is more valuable to us on defense. With him back there, we have the potential to get the ball on any play the entire game."

His special-teams magic notwithstanding, Tunnell made his greatest contribution as the key man in the Giants' innovative 4-1-6 "umbrella defense." In passing situations the New York ends would drop off the scrimmage line and assume the role of linebackers with shallow-coverage responsibilities. Joining the regular middle linebacker and the two cornerbacks, they formed the configuration of an open umbrella. The shaft of the umbrella extended backward with Tunnell, in the deep safety spot, serving as the handle of the alignment. From this vantage point, he could see the receivers run their patterns and get a quick jump on the ball when it showed.

During his tenure in New York, he earned All-Pro honors four times. After the 1958 schedule, he went to the Green Bay Packers, providing them the needed vintage in a young and developing secondary. Ironically, he helped the Packers beat the Giants for the NFL championship in 1961. Thereafter he retired, claiming the then-NFL interception record (79) and the career high for return yardage (1,282). He was also tops in the all-time categories of punt returns (258) and runback yardage (2,209). In 1967, he became the first black inducted into the Hall of Fame.

Tunnell died on July 22, 1975, at the age of 50.

Larry Wilson

6'0", 190 pounds. Free Safety: St. Louis Cardinals (1960–1972). All-Pro: 1963, 1966–1970. Pro Bowl: Eight appearances. NFL Interception Leader: 1966. Inducted into the Pro Football Hall of Fame 1978. Safety: 50-Year, All-Time, All-NFL team. Career: Interceptions, 52. Return yardage, 800. Yards per return, 15.4. Touchdowns (interception returns), 5. Rushing attempts, 5. Rushing yardage, 36. Yards per carry, 7.2. Touchdowns (rushing), 1. Punt returns, 3. Return yardage, 26. Average yards per return, 8.7. Touchdowns, 0. Kickoff returns, 11. Return yardage, 198. Yards per return, 18.0. Touchdowns, 0.

For 13 seasons, from 1960 to 1972, Larry Wilson was widely regarded as the "toughest player in the National Football League." At times it seemed as though the term *playing hurt* had been specially coined for him. Not fractures, not lacerations, not busted teeth, not stitches, not bumps, bruises, or contusions of varying magnitudes could deter him from lining up at his free-safety position for the St. Louis Cardinals. During a portion of one season he played with a pair of broken hands until team physicians finally convinced him that further trauma could irreparably damage the affected tissue and prevent proper healing. Only then did he repair to the bench, grousing and protesting all the while.

"My first year in the league," he recalled, "I got kind of banged up in practice, so I went to see the trainer. He just gave me a Band-Aid and said, 'Shake it off, rookie. You're in the NFL now.' I got the idea. Besides, playing was too much fun. You didn't want to miss anything sitting on the sidelines. And you might just lose your job, too."

At the University of Utah, he had played on both sides of the ball. But once in the pros, it became abundantly clear to him that his future lay with the defensive unit. And even then it was touch-and-go for a spell. Initially he tried to make it as a cornerback, but he quickly proved to himself and the coaching staff that his speed was not sufficient unto covering fleet-footed wide receivers and backs. So he gravitated to free safety where his hitting ability, nose for the ball, and general savvy could be utilized to best advantage.

Under the tutelage of St. Louis defensive coordinator Chuck Drulis, Wilson perfected a daring maneuver that came to be known as the safety blitz. It required an aggressive, hard-nosed individual who was a superior tackler and not afraid to take his licks. He fit the qualifications as though they were tailor-made for him. On downs in which a pass was indicated, particularly in third-and-long situations, he would "cheat up" from his normal position in the defensive alignment with an eye to picking an appropriate opening in the blocking front. With the snap of the ball, he would burst through the elected breach and confront the startled quarterback. The result was more often than not a sack, and sometimes a forced turnover. "I remember the first time I did it," he said, chuckling. "You should have seen the quarterback's face. His eyes were practically bugging out of his head."

But the triumphs were bought dearly, with pain and infirmity. When the newness of the safety blitz wore off, opposing quarterbacks began to read it like any other bit of defensive trickery. For blitzing circumstances blocking schemes were devised whereby a big back, a tight end, or even an

Larry Wilson

offside guard would trap down behind the offensive line and meet the safety man coming through the opening. The difference in size plus the blindside approach invariably worked severe damage on the blitzer. Today, Wilson has very few original teeth in his head, the majority having been lost to forearms and elbows thrown with malice.

Still, he gave as good as he got. He was a ferocious tackler, intimidating even the largest and hardest-running backs. Dan Dierdorf, who played tackle and center for the Cardinals, has a favorite Wilson story he likes to tell. "There was this hotshot rookie-receiver who came into our game with a pretty good catching average and talking a lot," Dierdorf related. "Early in the first quarter, he goes up for the ball, and Larry hits him in midair, knocking him cold. I said, 'Hey, welcome to the NFL.' That was the kind of hits Larry put on people."

When Wilson retired, the Cardinals did the same for his jersey with the familiar block number 8. He stayed with the organization in a front-office capacity and is now the team's general manager. Like most former defensive performers, he isn't happy with the rules lately devised to keep quarterbacks out of harm's way. "If they want to protect them," he has often said, "then they ought to put skirts on them."

As is the case with many an old pro, Wilson tends to be critical of NFL players today who display an unwillingness to line up when hurt. "They're packing guys off the field now with injuries we used to just shake off," he said. "You see guys rolling around on the ground like they're really in pain, then, a couple of downs later, they're back out there going like nothing had happened. It kind of makes you wonder."

He also wonders about the techniques employed by some of the defensive backs today. "It used to be a hitter was a guy who could really tackle," he said. "Now there's a difference between hitters and tacklers. You see guys who try to block people down. I've seen them try this stunt and succeed in only knocking the offensive player into the end zone. They give them shoulder pads to put right on the ball carrier. And then you have to wrap your arms around them and drive them to the ground. But you don't see a whole lot of that anymore."

When Bud Wilkinson was fired as head coach of the Cardinals with three games left on the 1979 schedule, Wilson finished out the season as the field boss. Under his direction, St. Louis defeated San Francisco and New York in convincing fashion but took a bad beating at the hands of the Chicago Bears. "No, I didn't like that at all," he said. "I felt pretty good about the first two games, but the Bears convinced me that I didn't want to be a coach. In the front office I can stay close to pro football, and I appreciate that. But there's nothing like being out on the field, actually playing the game. I miss being out there."

And the Cardinals miss Larry Wilson being out there too.

Willie Wood

5'10", 190 pounds. Safety: Green Bay Packers (1960–1971). All-Pro: 1963–1968. Pro Bowl: Eight appearances. NFL Punt Return Leader: 1961. NFL Interception Leader: 1962. Inducted into the Pro Football Hall of Fame 1989. Career: Interceptions, 48. Return yardage, 699. Yards per return, 14.6. Touchdowns (interception returns), 2. Punt returns, 187. Return yardage, 1,391. Yards per return, 7.5. Touchdowns (punt returns), 2.

It seemed to Willie Wood that he spent most of his life waiting for the recognition he deserved. First it was getting to play college football. Then it was gaining entrance into the National Football League. And finally it was being accepted into the Hall of Fame. But he believed that all things would come in good time, and they did, in abundance.

After graduating from high school, he tried to interest a major California university in his football potential but found no takers. So he enrolled at Coalings (Calif.) Junior College to hone both his classroom and gridiron skills. Then he was able to transfer to the University of Southern California. While there, he performed at both quarterback and defensive back.

Once finished at USC, he turned to the NFL, but again there was no interest in his talents. Black quarterbacks were not a priority item back then, and he was small, just 5'10" and 160 pounds. What's more, he had played with a debilitating collarbone injury his last two years in college and never did show to best advantage. For these reasons, he wasn't drafted. Undaunted, he enlisted the aid of a friend to contact the various pro clubs, seeking an opportunity for a tryout. At length the Green Bay Packers agreed to take a look, but only if he would compete for a job as a defensive back.

"There were twenty-four defensive backs in camp that first year [1960]," he recalled, "and I knew the Packers would only keep six of them. I had a lot of sleepless nights, a lot of anxiety. I didn't know much about playing safety, but my experience as a quarterback helped me because I could understand what the quarterback was thinking."

Despite his lack of savvy, he made the regular season roster, due primarily to a couple of outstanding attributes. He had tremendous jumping capability, being able to "dunk" a football over the crossbar of the goalposts with ease. And he demonstrated a willingness to tackle anybody, regardless of reputation and size, and did so with verve. The coaching staff also took note of the fact that he possessed a knack for being in the right place at the right time.

"My first chance in the NFL came in a preseason game against Bobby Layne and the Pittsburgh Steelers," he said. "I was able to intercept one of Layne's passes, and that gave me a little confidence that I might have a chance to stick around."

Wood commenced his rookie campaign in 1960 as a punt returner with a desire to excel at whatever was asked of him. "I understood," he said, "that when you join a pro club, the more things you can do for your team, the better your chances are for fitting in."

But the future came upon him very quickly. That November, veteran Jess Whittenton went down with an injury, and he suddenly found himself out on the field with a mission to stop the best receivers in all of football. "My first starting assignment was against the Baltimore Colts," he said. "Johnny Unitas [Colts Hall of Fame quarterback] picked on me right away, and Ray Berry [Hall of Fame end] caught two early touchdown passes. I was scared just guarding Berry. After that, I thought my pro career had come to an end. I figured my mistakes cost us the game." To his relief, such wasn't the case. Defensive backfield coach Norb Hecker merely said, "Those things happen. Forget it."

When preseason training camp opened the following summer, Wood got the chance he had been anticipating so ardently. He became a regular when Emlen Tunnell (Hall of Fame safety), a 14-year veteran, was moved to a backup spot. Now he would play full-time but his duties were somewhat awesome. As the right safety in the Packers secondary, he played as a "roving centerfielder," the onus on him to make the big play, to come

Willie Wood

up with the saving interception or tackle. He proved aptly suited for the
role.

In 1961, his initial season as a regular, Wood stole five passes, one of
them coming at the expense of Unitas. How sweet it was. A year later, he
denied the New York Giants a key touchdown with a fine open-field tackle
in the NFL championship contest. But his most memorable defensive gem
occurred in Super Bowl I when he snatched a third-quarter Kansas City
aerial and legged it back half the field to the Chiefs' five-yard line, thereby
giving Green Bay the momentum to break away to a 35–10 win.

During his 12-year tenure with the Packers, he earned All-Pro honors
six times and made eight appearances in the Pro Bowl. In 1961, he led the
league in interceptions, and a year later did likewise as a punt returner. He
retired following the 1971 season, and then the waiting began all over again.
As one after another of Green Bay's former greats went into the Hall of
Fame and he was passed over, it made him wonder, once again, if his hour
had passed, his contribution forgotten. At last, in 1989, he got the long-
awaited call.

"No, I didn't lose faith," he said. "There were so many fine players
with the Packers in those days, it's difficult really to define who did more

than someone else. I have no regrets. Interceptions and punt returns both gave me a thrill. Those are the big plays that pep up a team. And I always enjoyed tackling, too. You've got to accept the punishment. That's the name of the game."

Currently he is a successful businessman in his hometown of Washington, D.C.

HEADQUARTERS COMPANY

Coaches

Paul Brown

Coach: Cleveland Browns (1946–1962), Cincinnati Bengals (1968–1975). General Manager: Cleveland Browns (1946–1962), Cincinnati Bengals (1968–1991). Inducted into the Pro Football Hall of Fame 1967. Career: Won-lost record: Cleveland Browns (167–53–8), Cincinnati Bengals (55–59–1). Championships: AAFC, 1946, 1947, 1948, 1949. Eastern Division (NFL), 1950, 1951, 1952, 1953, 1954, 1955, 1957. AFC Central Division, 1970, 1973. NFL, 1950, 1954, 1955.

A wag once remarked, "With all the sparklers Paul Brown owns, he should've been a jeweler." The reference was to championship rings because "The Master" had his teams in pro-title tilts for a solid decade, winning seven of them. But his influence on the play-for-pay game extends far beyond won-lost records and statistical references.

Prior to gravitating into professional football, he enjoyed noteworthy success coaching on both the high school and collegiate levels, and in the armed services. It was during his tenure directing the outstanding Great Lakes naval teams in the course of World War II that he attracted the attention of Mickey McBride, a Cleveland entrepreneur. When Brown left the navy in 1945, McBride made him an offer he couldn't refuse. All he had to do was coach McBride's entry in a new pro league called the All-America Football Conference (AAFC) for a salary of $20,000 a year and a 15 percent cut of the profits. Needless to say, he "took the bait."

Brown immediately began recruiting players, a good number of them having performed for him at Great Lakes. Always a perfectionist, he organized the Cleveland organization from top to bottom with a meticulous eye for detail. When he was done, his Browns annexed four consecutive AAFC crowns while amassing a slightly spectacular overall regular-season mark of 47–4–3. But because his teams were so much better than the opposition, fans in other league cities lost hope that their clubs could ever compete effectively. This attitude had much to do with dwindling attendance at the games which preceded the AAFC's collapse following the 1949 campaign.

The success of the Cleveland franchise was watched closely by team owners and administrators in the National Football League. And some of them even made derogatory remarks about the Browns for the benefit of the newspapers. Of course, none of this was lost on Brown. "I remember the attitude of some people in the NFL toward us quite well," he said some years later. "They figured we had done pretty well with the teams in AAFC, but they also figured the worst team in their league could beat us."

Early in 1950, the Browns and a few other AAFC survivors were absorbed into the NFL, and suddenly it was put-up-or-shut-up time for pro football's old guard. The schedule maker must have felt there was no use in putting off the inevitable because the Browns and the defending NFL champion Philadelphia Eagles were pitted against each other in the season opener for both clubs. As might be expected, the impending confrontation drew a lot of media attention.

The game took place in Philadelphia's huge Municipal Stadium before more than 70,000 members of the paying public on the night of September 16, 1950. Just before the kickoff, Brown told reporters, "The Eagles may chase us off the gridiron, but we're going out there with no alibis. Truthfully, I don't know what to expect tonight."

Looking back on that time, he observed, "I was just trying to keep us from crystallizing emotionally before we got on the field. We had a couple of years to think about playing in the NFL, about getting an opportunity to play against the clubs that had ridiculed us, and that made us a very aroused group. So we, the coaches, tried kiddingly to get the players not to take the game too seriously. But there just wasn't any way they weren't taking the game seriously."

Both teams were like fighters feeling each other out in the early going. The Eagles took a 3–0 lead in the first quarter, only to have the Browns forge ahead 7–3. From that point, Cleveland kept building on its advantage to win going away by a 35–10 margin. It could have been even worse for Philadelphia as a pair of Browns' touchdowns were nullified by penalties. "The two disallowed scores were because of clipping infractions," Brown recalled. "Afterwards, the game films clearly showed they were missed calls."

Paul Brown

Said Philadelphia tackle Bucko Kilroy, "Cleveland completely dominated the game. It was no contest. The score could have been much greater. It could have been 61–10."

From that juncture, the Browns went on to finish the season with a 10–2 record, deadlocking the New York Giants for Eastern Division honors. In the playoff, Cleveland bested New York 8–3, then proceeded to claim the NFL championship with a 30–28 triumph over the Los Angeles Rams. The Browns proved in no uncertain terms that they belonged — in any league.

Cleveland annexed five more division titles and two additional league crowns from 1951 through 1955. In 1956, Brown experienced his only losing campaign during a 17-year tenure with the Browns. Following the 1962 slate, he was dismissed by new club owner Art Modell and remained on the sidelines for five years.

He was inducted into the Pro Football Hall of Fame in 1967. The next year he joined the American Football League (AFL) as head coach and general manager of the Cincinnati Bengals. In 1970, Cincinnati entered the NFL. Under his tutelage, the Bengals won 55 games against 59 losses and a lone tie from 1968 to 1975. At the time of his death on August 5, 1991, at 82, he served as general manager of the Cincinnati franchise.

Standings and numbers aside, Brown had as much influence on pro football as any individual in the history of the money game. He was the first coach to retain a staff of assistants the year around, to use intelligence tests to measure players' learning capabilities, to use classroom techniques extensively, and to introduce the use of statistics for the purpose of rating player performance and film evaluation.

On the field, he instituted the practice of sending in plays from the bench by a system of rotating guards. He did as much as any innovator to develop the spread formation and the intricate passing patterns that made it function. Then he worked out defensive alignments that could stymie his offensive inventions. And in the area of personnel he inaugurated the practice of converting running backs with the desired "hitting instincts" to defensive secondary positions, so their native speed and agility could be exploited to maximum advantage.

Perhaps Cleveland Hall of Fame quarterback Otto Graham said it best: "I think Paul Brown was as good a coach as there's ever been in the pro game."

Jimmy Conzelman

6'0", 180 pounds. Quarterback, Coach, Owner: Decatur Staleys (1920), Rock Island Independents (1921, 1922), Milwaukee Badgers (1923, 1924), Detroit Panthers (1925, 1926), Providence Steam Roller (1927–1930), Chicago Cardinals (1940–1942, 1946–1948). Career: Coach: Rock Island Independents (1922), Milwaukee Badgers (1923, 1924), Detroit Panthers (1925, 1926), Providence Steam Roller (1927–1930), Chicago Cardinals (1940–1942, 1946–1948). Won-lost record: Rock Island Independents (4–2–1), Milwaukee Badgers (12–10–3), Detroit Panthers (12–8–4), Providence Steam Roller (26–16–6), Chicago Cardinals (34–31–0). Championships: Western Division, 1947, 1948. NFL: 1928, 1947. Inducted into the Pro Football Hall of Fame 1964.

Perhaps Jimmy Conzelman can best be depicted as a man for all season, a Renaissance type in tweed who could do many things well, football being just one such area of notable attainment.

By nature he was born to lead rather than follow, to innovate rather than imitate. Following his student-athlete days at Washington University of St. Louis, he entered the navy as America was involved in World War I and played with the Great Lakes team that won the 1919 Rose Bowl. Upon receiving his discharge, he was recruited by George Halas, a teammate at the training center, to play quarterback for the Decatur (Ill.) Staleys of the newly formed American Professional Football Association (APFA). This loose confederation of teams would ultimately evolve into the National Football League with Halas, player-coach of the Staleys, as its guiding light.

Conzelman left the Staleys after the 1920 season and joined the Rock Island (Ill.) Independents. While so employed, he suddenly fell heir to the club's head-coach position. It all happened rather abruptly one day early in the second half of a game. He was huddling with his teammates when a substitute ran in from the sidelines bearing a message from the team owner: "You're the new coach. So get busy."

After serving as player-coach through 1922, he made yet another career move. This time he signed on with the Milwaukee Badgers for a two-year stint from 1923 to 1924. Shortly thereafter, he became not only the player-coach of the Detroit Panthers but their owner. He doffed his owner's hat at the end of the 1926 campaign and journeyed on to Providence (R.I.) and the Steam Roller organization, which now belonged to the newly realigned National Football League. Given Conzelman's impetus as a player-coach, the Providence franchise improved markedly to an 8–5–1 record in 1927 and won the 1928 NFL title. But during that championship campaign, he incurred a knee injury which permanently relegated him to the bench. He coached the team through the 1930 schedule, then departed the league to try his hand at other endeavors.

A decade elapsed while he busied himself as a songwriter, singer, pianist, and actor. When not indulging his artistic bent, he held forth as a newspaper editor and publisher, a successful business executive, and a silver-tongued orator. In 1940, he returned to pro football as head coach of the Chicago Cardinals. It was not a fulfilling experience. With a paucity of talent to work with, he struggled through the 1942 season, amassing an unenviable 8–22–3 mark, and resigned once more. From 1943 to 1945, he served in the front office of the St. Louis Browns baseball club.

He gravitated back to the NFL and the Cardinals in 1946, lured by club owner Charlie Bidwell and the challenge of turning around another franchise with potential. That first year, the team improved dramatically, finishing just a half game out of second place in the Western Division with a 6–5 showing. In the spring of 1947, he acquired a phenomenal rookie ball carrier named Charley Trippi who joined the likes of quarterback Paul Christman, fullback Pat Harder, and halfback Elmer Angsman to compose what would be eulogized as the Dream Backfield.

Loaded for bear, the Cardinals sprinted to the top of the 1947 Western Division standings with a 9–3 record and faced the Philadelphia Eagles for the NFL championship. With the game to be contested on the frozen turf of Chicago's Comiskey Park, Conzelman gave his charges a big advantage by outfitting them in basketball shoes. Provided better traction, they were able to outmaneuver the Eagles consistently and came away with a 28–21 victory and the league crown. They repeated as division winners in 1948 and met the Eagles again, this time in Philadelphia, for pro football supremacy. A driving snowstorm all but obliterated the yard markers, and the Eagles prevailed 7–0 on a much-disputed short-yardage touchdown plunge.

But the Cardinals' success was bittersweet to Conzelman. In 1947, Bidwell died unexpectedly, as did halfback Jeff Burkett. Then tackle Stan Mauldin dropped dead in the Chicago dressing room following the season-opening contest of 1948. These deaths preyed heavily upon Conzelman, deeply saddening him at a time when he should have been reveling in the fruits of his labors. He quit football for good in the wake of the 1948 season.

On July 31, 1970, he passed away at 72.

Weeb Ewbank

Coach: Baltimore Colts (1954–1962), New York Jets (1963–1969, AFL), New York Jets (1970–1973, NFL). Inducted into the Pro Football Hall of Fame 1978. Career: Won-lost record: Baltimore Colts (61–52–1), New York Jets (73–78–6). Championships: Western Conference (NFL), 1958, 1959. Eastern Division (AFL), 1968, 1969. NFL, 1958, 1959. AFL, 1968. Super Bowl III.

Unlike most of his more-publicized coaching contemporaries, Weeb Ewbank didn't display any clearly definable character traits—no jutting jaw, no glowering gaze, no readily quotable phrases. In fact, he looked and acted more like the man on the street than a lot of people thought was good for his image. He didn't care. The only two things which set him apart from his peers were the way he could discern talent and the way he could win championships. And that's what his business was all about.

During a career which spanned 20 years, he tutored teams which won two National Football League titles, an American Football League (AFL) crown (the only field boss in the history of the pro game to accomplish this double), and a Super Bowl which served to ensure the vitality of this postseason extravaganza and prompted the eventual merger of the NFL and AFL. And along the way, he developed two of the finest quarterbacks ever in Johnny Unitas and Joe Namath.

When Ewbank came to the Baltimore Colts in 1954, the club was without tradition or direction, having undergone two changes of identity and a somewhat vagabond existence since 1950. Right from the outset, the club's majority owner, Carroll Rosenbloom, put him on the spot, demanding to know how long it would take to build a champion. The studied response put the target date at five years. It would be a difficult task, acquiring the needed players and acclimating them to a system that best fit their several abilities, and no one knew this better than the little round man with the butch haircut.

Weeb Ewbank

First, Ewbank put together a good teaching staff of assistants. Then he began to fit the personnel pieces together via the draft and trades, ever careful in the latter endeavor not to get further crippled in the exchange. One such piece, a most integral addition to the club puzzle, fell into place with no more than a phone call to Pittsburgh. That's where Unitas was playing semipro sandlot football with a team titled the Bloomfield Rams in hopes of getting another shot at the big time. Ever so gradually, the Colts began to meld into a well-schooled, savvy gridiron machine. But the process wasn't going fast enough for Rosenbloom. He had it in mind to fire his head coach even as the club was headed for league laurels in 1958 and the onset of a new era.

That year, Baltimore met the New York Giants in storied Yankee Stadium on a cold December day to contend for the NFL title. Early on, the Colts jumped out to a substantive lead, only to have their mistakes and the Giants come back to haunt them. A last-minute field goal by Baltimore kicker Steve Myhra sent the epic battle into a sudden-death overtime, the first of its kind in the annals of the championship contest. During the extra session, Unitas led a dramatic touchdown drive that settled the issue 23–17.

Even today, that classic matchup is generally referred to as "the greatest game ever played." It was the first nationally televised pro game and supplied the excitement necessary to turn on the American people to what would become the "Sunday afternoon madness."

In 1959, the Colts under Ewbank claimed a second NFL crown, whipping the Giants 31–16 in Baltimore to give the little coach back-to-back titles. And in so doing, he had kept his word to the team management. It took exactly five years to win a championship and six years to win two of them. So what was the secret to his success? The number of theories equaled the quantity of sportswriters to espouse them. But perhaps Lenny Moore, the Colts' standout running back and receiver, best put his finger on the pulse of the matter. "You can take fifty guys and run them a couple of laps around a ping-pong table," he said, "and Coach Ewbank will pick out the football players. He knows talent like nobody I've ever seen."

All his contributions to the Baltimore franchise notwithstanding, he was let go following the 1962 campaign. He promptly moved over to the rival AFL as head coach of the New York Jets. The situation was very similar to that when he joined the Colts. In 1963, the Jets had just come under new management, thereby being rescued from receivership, with the club in general disarray. So the careful rebuilding program began anew. Once more, he needed a quarterback of note to take charge of the offense and got him. Joe Namath signed on with the club in 1965, and three seasons hence the New York franchise owned an AFL championship.

This set the stage for a bit of pro football history. Given their league title, the Jets were to meet the NFL Colts in Super Bowl III. No one really expected the representative of the AFL to do any better than their predecessors in the first two Super Bowls. But Ewbank knew how the game was played in the older league, and he wanted to show Baltimore owner Rosenbloom that a serious mistake had been made in firing him. With Namath boldly predicting, even guaranteeing victory, the Jets made good on his boasting with a 16–7 victory, and Ewbank enjoyed a measure of revenge at the expense of the Colts' braintrust.

An innately loyal man, he never revealed his feelings about what the momentous win meant to him. But it clearly demonstrated to the NFL hierarchy the necessity for seeking peace rather than further confrontation with the AFL. A merger followed in 1970, and pro football moved on to new heights of popularity.

When asked to compare his quarterbacks Unitas and Namath, Ewbank did so guardedly. "Both of them had great arms and could throw long effectively," he said. "John [Unitas] was probably the best quarterback I've ever seen at throwing those little crossing patterns over the middle, and Joe [Namath] had the quickest release of any quarterback I've known. John could move out of the pocket better, but Joe, of course, had two bad knees.

Who was best? I really don't know. Both of them could do everything you could want a quarterback to do. They were in a class by themselves."

As times changed, so did Ewbank. He ran the Colts much in keeping with the conservative tenor of the 1950s but held the coaching reins of the Jets at the height of a cultural revolution. "I remember the time John Riggins [Jets fullback] came in to sign his contract just before preseason camp got underway," Ewbank recalled. "His head was shaved, and he wore a derby with an Indian feather stuck in the band. He had on a vest but no shirt. And his motorcycle was parked outside. You could talk to John when he wasn't out hunting or fishing somewhere."

Whatever the motif in which he found himself, Ewbank could cope. At the close of the 1973 season, he retired, two decades on the sidelines having been enough for him. But even then, he continued to boost the cause of pro football at every opportunity.

Ray Flaherty

6'1", 190 pounds. End, Coach: Los Angeles Wildcats (1926, AFL), New York Yankees (1927, 1928, NFL), New York Giants (1928, 1929, 1931–1935). All-Pro: 1928, 1932. Career: Coach: Boston Redskins (1936), Washington Redskins (1937–1942), New York Yankees (1946–1948, AAFC), Chicago Hornets (1949). Won-lost record: Boston Redskins (7–5–0), Washington Redskins (49–18–3), New York Yankees (22–10–2), Chicago Hornets (4–8–0). Championships: Eastern Division (NFL), 1936, 1937, 1940, 1942. Eastern Division (AAFC), 1946, 1947. NFL, 1937, 1942. Inducted into the Pro Football Hall of Fame 1976.

Few coaches would have offered to resign and put it in writing before their first season ever got under way, but Ray Flaherty did. His teams also won two National Football League titles and six division crowns in 11 years on the job. Needless to say, it takes all kinds to make a Hall of Fame.

Prior to becoming a coach, Flaherty spent nine seasons plying his considerable skills as an end for the Los Angeles Wildcats of the first American Football League (AFL) and then the New York Yankees and New York Giants of the NFL. So when he took over as the tutor of the Boston Redskins in 1936, it was with no little knowledge of how important a top wingman can be to a club. Thus the acquisition in that year's draft of Wayne Millner, an All-America end from Notre Dame, prompted him to dash off a letter to Redskins owner George Preston Marshall saying, "Please accept my resignation if we do not win the championship."

Impetuous, yes. Braggadocio, no. In any event, the Redskins topped the Eastern Division standings in 1936 but lost league honors to the Green Bay Packers 21–6. However, Flaherty did not resign, and Marshall didn't ask him to make good on his offer. And a fortunate thing it was for both men as the team embarked upon one of the most successful eras of its long existence.

Come 1937, the Redskins adopted Washington, D.C., as their new base of operations and signed a rookie quarterback by the name of Sammy Baugh who would lead them to unprecedented football heights. That campaign, the team boasted an 8–3 record and again headed the Eastern Conference. Now it was on to the NFL championship game once more and a confrontation with the powerful Chicago Bears.

Just for the occasion, Flaherty demonstrated his innovative penchant by devising a behind-the-line screen pass for his freshman quarterback. He knew the Bears would be intent upon pressuring the youthful signal caller in hopes of forcing costly turnovers. To counter this tactic, he inserted a little looping pitch into the flat which would then enable the receiver to proceed unchallenged through the area left vacant by the opposition's all-out pass rush. It worked perfectly as Baugh threw for three touchdowns and Washington prevailed 28–21.

The Redskins and the Bears renewed their intense rivalry in the 1942 battle for league honors, and Flaherty prepared yet another offensive wrinkle to give his charges the edge. When the Chicago defenders lined up, they found themselves having to contend with a two-platoon system of sorts. One Washington attack unit featured Baugh and his receivers, and a second group contained the club's best ball carriers and run-blockers. During the afternoon, the Redskins' ground troops controlled the clock and wore down the enemy resistance, allowing Baugh and company to negotiate a pair of scoring strikes, all the hometown favorites needed for a 14–6 victory.

Sandwiched in between these high points, Flaherty's squad absorbed the worst beating in the annals of pro football. In the 1940 NFL title tilt, the Bears sprang some surprises of their own, the T-Formation complete with a man-in-motion and a devastating counter series, and waxed the Redskins by an unbelievable margin of 73–0. But in a six-season span the Washington gridders under Flaherty bested the Bears, then the scourge of the pro game, two games to one with the league championship on the line.

Following the 1942 schedule, he entered the navy and remained in service for the duration of World War II. After discharge from active duty, he coached the New York Yankees of the All-America Football Conference (AAFC) from 1946 to 1948, winning division laurels in his first two years. He closed out his career with the AAFC Chicago Hornets in 1949.

Sid Gillman

Coach: Los Angeles Rams (1955–1959, NFL), Los Angeles Chargers (1960, AFL), San Diego Chargers (1961–1969, AFL), San Diego Chargers (1971, NFL), Houston Oilers (1973, 1974). First coach to win divisional titles in the NFL and AFL. Inducted into the Pro Football Hall of Fame 1983. Career: Won-lost record: Los Angeles Rams (28–32–1), Los Angeles Chargers (10–5–0), San Diego Chargers (77–52–6), Houston Oilers (8–15–0). Championships: Western Division (NFL), 1955. Western Division (AFL), 1960, 1961, 1963, 1964, 1965. AFL, 1963.

It can be postulated mathematically that there are only so many ways to get the football downfield. But Sid Gillman never believed the limit couldn't be extended indefinitely, and he did his best to prove it during a coaching career that straddled two leagues.

He was espousing his theories on the collegiate scene more than 50 years ago. But his ideas were many years ahead of the times. No one better appreciated the value of the running game: Control the ball and the game clock, get the first down and short yardage as necessary, and keep the opposition's defense on the field, thereby markedly enhancing the potential for errors due to the fatigue factor. But he knew rushing could never be more than just half of the offensive arsenal.

"The big play comes from the pass," he preached. "It's for sure running is essential to winning. But when you want to put points on the scoreboard, you have to pass."

Long before the multiple offense was even so named, he devised ways to send four and five receivers into the enemy secondary on almost every down. "We want people to fear our long game," he said. "Once we have success throwing deep, then we can be assured our short-passing attack will work, too. Every time our receivers go out, they know any one of them has the potential to score. And the opposition knows that as well."

In the late 1950s and the 1960s, man-to-man coverage prevailed as the textbook method for defending against the pass. Needless to say, Gillman's genius in designing varied routes for a flock of receivers at any one time played havoc with man-to-man defensive tactics. He first became a pro head coach with the Los Angeles Rams in 1955. That year he led the club to the NFL Western Division title.

After the 1959 campaign, he moved across town to become head coach and general manager of the American Football League (AFL) Chargers. They played one season in Los Angeles and then relocated to San Diego. Under Gillman's direction, they won five divisional crowns during their first six years of existence and the 1963 AFL championship. Footballs filled the air every weekend, and fans filled the stadium seats to cheer the Chargers' highly imaginative and prolific offense.

Gillman took a leave of absence from his coaching duties in 1970 for health reasons. The AFL and NFL had already merged when he returned to the team for the next season. Not long thereafter, friction developed between him and the front office and intensified to the point where he elected to leave the Chargers for good late in the 1971 schedule. After a year away from the game, he signed on to coach the Houston Oilers. He was named 1974 American Football Conference (AFC) Coach of the Year, his last hurrah as a field boss in pro football.

Much of what he had implemented while guiding the Chargers became the subject of imitation throughout the NFL. His penchant for devising aerial schemes of intricate but effective design served as a prototype for what the professional game has become today. Perhaps no one put it better than Al Davis, president of the Los Angeles Raiders, when he said, "Sid Gillman brought class to the AFL. Just being a part of Sid's organization [1960–1962 as an assistant coach] was, for me, like going to a laboratory for the highly developed science of organized football."

In truth, all of pro football went to school with Sid Gillman.

George Halas

6'2", 195 pounds. End, Coach: Hammond Pros (1919), Decatur Staleys (1920), Chicago Staleys (1921), Chicago Bears (1922–1929). Career: Coach: Decatur Staleys (1920), Chicago Staleys (1921), Chicago Bears (1922–1929, 1933–1942, 1946–1955, 1958–1967). Won-lost record: Decatur Staleys (10–1–2), Chicago Staleys (9–1–1), Chicago Bears (306–149–28). Championships: Western Division-Conference, 1933, 1934, 1937, 1940, 1941, 1942, 1943, 1946, 1956, 1963. NFL, 1932, 1933, 1940, 1941, 1943, 1946, 1963. Inducted into the Pro Football Hall of Fame 1963.

George Halas was there In The Beginning. When pro football subsisted as little more than a brawl with a pigskin, he played it. Later, he coached it, improved it, and promoted it. Still later, he administered it and nurtured it. Then, at the time of his death, he bequeathed it to the masses for their continued enjoyment, a living legacy of one man's monumental devotion to a beloved brainchild. In essence, the National Football League was his baby.

While working to get the league organized and on a sound financial footing, he labored tirelessly to do the same for the present and future fortunes of his Chicago Bears. They were an extension of his personality, his alter ego. So it was that they held forth as the "Monsters of the Midway," perennially rough and tough, and imbued with a certain sense of destiny.

He first came by them in 1920 when they answered to the name of the

George Halas

Decatur Staleys. Back then, they belonged to a loose confederation of clubs joined under the American Professional Football Association (APFA) banner. In those days, he was a player-coach. Upon moving the franchise to Chicago in 1921 he acquired another title, that of owner. The following year he helped found the NFL, and the designation Bears became firmly affixed to his team.

Right from the outset, he proved to be a shrewd appraiser of football flesh. He openly recruited the best talent available, but his earliest coup, and certainly one of his most significant, involved the acquisition of the incomparable Red Grange. The famed "Galloping Ghost" joined the Bears shortly after playing his last game for the University of Illinois. Given his already considerable reputation, he was just what the league and the Bears needed in the way of a premier gate attraction, that catalyst which afforded them both instant respectability and financial stability. Just leave it to George.

At the close of the 1929 campaign, he retired as a player after 11 seasons at end. He also fired himself as coach, hired Ralph Jones to be his replacement, and retreated to the front office. In 1932, the Bears won their first official NFL championship, besting the Portsmouth Spartans 9–0 in a game played on an indoor 80-yard field and attended by more than 11,000 fans. Particularly frigid December weather in the Windy City forced the contest to be conducted under the roof of Chicago Stadium, an arena normally used for professional hockey.

Halas returned to the sidelines full-time in 1933 and remained there through 1942 when World War II intervened and he was called to active duty with the navy. Following his discharge from the service, he picked up his clipboard again in time for the onset of the 1946 season. He stepped down as head coach once more in the wake of the 1955 schedule to give old friend John "Paddy" Driscoll an opportunity to guide the Bears. In 1958, he became the field boss again and this time stayed until 1967 when he left the bench for good at 73.

During his 42 years as head coach, the Staleys-Bears compiled a 325–151–31 record. They also won 7 NFL championships—1932, 1933, 1940, 1941, 1943, 1946, 1963—and 10 division-conference crowns. In the course of his lengthy tenure, he was the first to institute daily practice sessions, to study the game films of opposing clubs, to have radio broadcasts of his team's games, and to arrange a coast-to-coast barnstorming tour.

But his most significant contribution to the pro game had to be the introduction of the T-Formation. Given the substantial input of Ralph Jones and consultant Clark Shaughnessy, he developed an offensive format which launched the NFL into a new and exciting era, and forever ensured that the league would be a lucrative attraction at the gate.

The T-Formation, as applied by the Bears, enjoyed only moderate success before quarterback Sid Luckman joined the organization in 1938. From that juncture on, with Halas ever looking over his shoulder, he directed the team to four league championships in 13 seasons with a quick-strike attack that left the opposition fairly reeling. But man and system never came together better than in the 1940 NFL title tilt against the Washington Redskins. That afternoon, the Bears showcased the T with the man-in-motion variation that devastated the Redskins by 73–0, the worst beating ever administered in league annals. Halas considered this victory his biggest thrill in 64 years as an owner, coach and player.

Stories depicting him as a gruff, heavy-handed manipulator of staff and players frequently appeared in the media during his stewardship of the Bears. He was often pictured as reluctant to reward on-field performance at contract-negotiating time. But this reputation didn't hold with the men who had been subject to his tutelage. "The public Halas was nothing like the private man," Grange said. "I can't tell you how many of his former players he helped to get a start in business. And he gave generously to all manner of charities. He was always ready with a helping hand."

Added Hall of Fame running back Gale Sayers: "He fought you for every thousand dollars. I signed a four-year contract with the Bears in my rookie year. But after each one of those years, he gave me a substantial bonus. He didn't have to do that, but he did it. I'm quite sure he did the same thing with [Hall of Fame linebacker] Dick Butkus. That was just the way he showed his appreciation for our contribution to the team. I always found him to be a very, very fair person."

Luckman said, "I could never, never repay him for all he did for me."

In 1963, the Bears won their last league championship under Halas's leadership. That year he was inducted into the Hall of Fame as a charter member. He died on October 31, 1983, at 88.

Earl "Curly" Lambeau

Coach: Green Bay Packers (1919–1949), Chicago Cardinals (1950, 1951), Washington Redskins (1952, 1953). Inducted into the Pro Football Hall of Fame 1963 (charter member). Career: Won-lost record: Green Bay Packers (212–106–21), Chicago Cardinals (7–15–0), Washington Redskins (10–13–1). Championships: Western Division, 1936, 1938, 1939, 1944. NFL, 1929–1931, 1936, 1939, 1944.

What at first appeared to be a broken dream for Earl "Curly" Lambeau developed into a blessing in disguise, the upshot a notable coaching career and a favored place in National Football League history.

From earliest boyhood he had a love affair with the game of football. As an elementary student, he suffered his only real injury in the sport, a broken ankle. On the secondary level, he was a bona fide standout at East High School in Green Bay. His ability and reputation earned him an invitation to ply his skills at Notre Dame. While playing fullback on the freshman squad, he contracted a tonsil infection which forced him to drop out of the university. His dream was summarily shattered, or so it seemed at the time.

He returned to Green Bay and began working for a local packing firm, given the munificent sum of $250 a month. A year later, he was afforded the opportunity to organize a company football team. He threw himself into the task with a will, becoming both the playing coach and captain of the loose-knit group. In 1921, the Green Bay Packers joined the American Professional Football Association (to become the National Football League), and he sought to field the best personnel. His fervor to do so prompted him to indulge in a common practice of that time—using college players who performed under assumed names. But league officials learned of his duplicity and canceled the Packers' franchise.

Repentant, Lambeau appealed for reinstatement, and it was granted provided he agreed to abide by league rules. He promised, and then, using $50 of his own money, bought the Packers outright. When he went broke

Earl "Curly" Lambeau

trying to sustain the club, some local merchants arranged for him to get a $2,500 loan. Thereafter, a public nonprofit corporation was established to operate the team, and he was retained as head coach and general manager.

The Packers were back on the field in 1922 as a full-fledged member of the NFL (so named in June of that year). In addition to his coaching and front-office duties, Lambeau played halfback and held forth as an exceptionally fine passer in the innovative Green Bay aerial attack. He pioneered the overhead game in pro football, stocking his team with the best receivers available. It can be said he was much ahead of his time in using complex passing patterns and advocating a quick-strike mentality. The entire roster consisted of the finest talent to be had at every position.

By the time he had retired to the bench following the 1927 campaign, the Packers were on the rise to football supremacy. They dominated the league from 1929 through 1931, winning the NFL championship three successive seasons. Later, when the teams were separated into two divisions, he led Green Bay to another trio of titles in 1936, 1939, and 1944. Overall, his teams won six league crowns, topped the Western Division four times, and were second in the standings on six occasions. No less than eight Hall of Fame inductees—Johnny "Blood" McNally, Don Hutson, Robert "Cal" Hubbard, Clarke Hinkle, Mike Michalske, Arnier Herber, Walt Kiesling, and Tony Canadeo—flourished under his tutelage.

After the 1949 season, Lambeau became frustrated with a downswing in the Packers' gridiron fortunes and the club's board of directors and tendered his resignation. Thus he ended a 31-year affiliation with the Green Bay franchise during which it grew from a company-owned team to one of the most illustrious entries in the NFL. He would coach the Chicago Cardinals (1950, 1951) and the Washington Redskins (1952, 1953) with disappointing results before leaving the game entirely.

He died on June 1, 1965, at 67. Currently, his 229 career victories put him fifth on the list of pro football's winningest coaches.

Tom Landry

Coach: Dallas Cowboys (1960–1988). Inducted into the Pro Football Hall of Fame 1990. Career: Won-lost record: Dallas Cowboys (270–178–6). Championships: Capitol Division, 1967, 1968, 1969. Eastern Division, 1970, 1971, 1973, 1976, 1977, 1978, 1979, 1981, 1985. Eastern Conference, 1966, 1967. NFC, 1970, 1971, 1977. Super Bowl VI, XII.

To countless devotees of the pro game, former Dallas Cowboys coach Tom Landry was the National Football League's version of the Sphinx.

Like the ancient monolith of the Egyptian desert, he presided over the sidelines with a stony veneer. And though pandemonium swirled around him as do sandy winds about his famous look-alike, he maintained a pose of practiced dispassion. Because of this demeanor, he was often accused of being cold and aloof, unable to empathize effectively with the emotional tenor of his players. Nothing could have been further from the truth.

So why the facade?

"Because what the players see in me, hopefully, is that I'm always in control of the situation," Landry once explained, "and that I'm confident it will work out the way it should. That's leadership in a strong way. Players look at the coach first. If he doesn't appear confident, or looks defeated, then all of a sudden they are defeated. That's the one thing I hope they see in me—that I am in command of the situation, that I am confident things will work out."

And that's precisely what they saw. "He projects confidence, poise and composure," said Cowboys linebacker Lee Roy Jordan of his boss. "If we thought he was throwing tantrums and screaming, we might lose control out there."

Deliberate and contemplative, Landry had no time for thoughts of rancor, only those pertaining to the next move that needed to be made on the field. He did nothing that wasn't precipitated by the most meticulous study. This penchant for thoroughness was evidenced throughout his association with football.

As a collegian, he performed offensively as a fullback and defensively in the secondary for University of Texas teams that won the 1948 Sugar Bowl and the 1949 Orange Bowl. Following graduation, he joined the New York Yankees of the All-America Football Conference (AAFC). When that league folded, he crossed over to the NFL and the New York Giants. During seven seasons as cornerback, he stole 32 enemy aerials and returned them a total of 404 yards. This he accomplished with only average speed and a comprehensive knowledge of the opposition's offensive tendencies gained via hours of scrutinizing game films. He was selected All-Pro in 1954 and received an invite to the 1955 Pro Bowl.

In addition, he averaged 40.9 yards for 389 punts and helped with the coaching chores. Prior to the onset of the 1956 season, he joined the club staff as a full-time defensive assistant. In this capacity he began to make contributions that helped to shape the pro game the way it is played today. "Tom was very instrumental in helping to develop the revolutionary umbrella defense," said Jim Lee Howell, then offensive coordinator for the Giants and later the head coach. "He always anticipated what the opposition was going to do and then devised an effective means to stop it. Sometimes he would put in plays, new plays, right from the sidelines."

While still an assistant coach, Landry found himself matching wits with Cleveland Browns mentor Paul Brown, already hailed as an offensive genius. No one recalls those early days of Landry's career any better than Al DeRogatis, an All-Pro defensive tackle with the Giants of that era. "Tom institutionalized defense as we know it now," DeRogatis said. "When Paul Brown devised the spread formation to allow Cleveland quarterback Otto Graham more time to make optimal use of his receivers, Tom devised the proper antidote. We lined up against the Browns in a standard 6-1 set, but once Graham went into his cadence, both of our ends dropped off the scrimmage line to become linebackers while we [tackles] played as ends. We shut them down cold. Tom was always a master tactician."

Shortly afterward, Landry converted a guard-tackle named Sam Huff into a middle linebacker and made both him and the Giants' defense the envy of the NFL. "Landry built the 4-3 [defense] around me," Huff said. "It revolutionized defense and opened the door for all the variations of zones and man-to-man coverages which are used in conjunction with it today. Back in 1956, we'd get our defensive plays during a game by hand signals from Landry over on the sidelines. It's a big thing now. He also designated offensive formations by colors. This way, the defensive players had an easy reference as to what the opposition was running. We just called out the designated color."

Dick Nolan played in the New York defensive secondary with Landry and then came under his tutelage. Years later, he joined his staff in Dallas. "Tom committed to memory a tremendous number of offensive patterns," Nolan said, "and could pull them right out of his head. We did a great deal of film work under him. Because of his study habits, he was in a class by himself when it came to reading receivers. He took the system of keys farther than anyone else. By simplifying them, he enabled players who were quick enough and smart enough to utilize them to great advantage. He also started the inside-outside secondary alignment. The cornerback on the short side of the field had the job of covering the underneath routes while leaving the deep responsibility to the safey paired with him. On the opposite side, the other cornerback took everything deep, leaving the shallow coverage to the fourth back."

Jim Katcavage and Andy Robustelli were perennial All-Pro defensive ends under Landry's auspices. "Tom gave us keys to all the offensive formations in the book," said Katcavage. "We had defenses for third-down-long and third-down-short situations. If on a sweep the near guard pulled, we'd automatically look for the fullback coming through, look for him to block down. But if the guard came straight ahead, you closed in, looking for a trap block. Tom had it down to perfection."

Added Robustelli: "Back then, Tom was just beginning to fool with the flex defense. The tackle up and the tackle off the line of scrimmage as later became standard with his Dallas teams. He experimented playing one tackle off the line so you could set the defensive front to point toward the offense's weakness. No matter what the opposition did, Tom always seemed to be just one step ahead of them."

Come 1960, Landry was hired as head coach of the newly formed Dallas franchise. As expected, he struggled to formulate a team that could complete in the NFL. It wasn't until 1965 that the Cowboys managed to break even with a 7–7 record. Then they put together a succession of 20 winning seasons. During the course of this phenomenal streak, they annexed 12 division titles, five conference championships, and Super Bowls VI and XII. And through it all, he continued to be an innovator.

"Tom was the first coach in the league to use the multiple offense exclusively," Nolan said. "And when the defense went multiple, he was right there in the forefront of the action. He devised more combinations of zones and man-to-man coverages than any other coach in modern times."

Said Huff: "Nothing changed with him through the years. He was always playing cat and mouse with himself. He would devise a new form of offense and then turn right around and counter it with just the right defensive adjustment. That's the way it always was with him."

Tom Landry

From 1986 through 1988, the Dallas franchise fell on hard times, and the Cowboys departed from their all-conquering ways. In the wake of the 1988 season, the club came under new ownership, and Landry was let go, the only coach in the team's 29-year history. He quietly gathered the physical remnants of his lengthy tenure, gave a tearful farewell to his players, and departed. Some weeks after his dismissal, the people of Dallas turned out by the tens of thousands to make public their feelings for him.

Since then, he has been kept busy making personal appearances and conducting a variety of business ventures. "I'm doing a lot of different things," he said, "and they are interesting. There's always life after football. We had some great years, and they can't take that away from us."

Another thing that can't be taken away is his 270–178–6 coaching record, third best such mark, all-time.

Vince Lombardi

Coach: Green Bay Packers (1959–1967), Washington Redskins (1969). NFL Man of the Decade (1960s). Inducted into the Pro Football Hall of Fame 1971. Career: Won-lost record: Green Bay Packers (98–30–4), Washington Redskins (7–5–2). Championships: Western Conference, 1960, 1961, 1962, 1965, 1966 (central division), 1967. NFL, 1961, 1962, 1965, 1966, 1967. Super Bowl I, II.

After the Green Bay Packers had been defeated 17–13 in the 1960 National Football League title contest, Vince Lombardi told his players, "We will never lose another championship game as long as I am coach of this team." And he was true to his word.

From 1961 to 1967, the Packers won five league crowns and Super Bowls I and II. Given this accomplishment, Lombardi was named NFL Man of the Decade (1960s). Within two years of his arrival in Green Bay, he took a franchise that had been losing for 11 seasons to the top of the NFL heap. This transformation was all but miraculous.

Unlike most of the other coaches in the Hall of Fame, he didn't get his big chance in the pros until the rather advanced age of 45. Before going to Green Bay, he served five years with the New York Giants offense. Prior to that, he was an assistant to Earl "Red" Blake, the famed field boss of the U.S. Military Academy football team at West Point during the 1940s and 1950s.

While working under Blake, Lombardi gained a measure of control over his temper, although he was still subject to angry outbursts of volcanic magnitude on occasion. Blake once characterized Lombardi as "very intelligent, very determined and very violent."

In the employ of the Giants, Lombardi early displayed the fixation for fundamental perfection that later would mark his tenure with the Packers. He wanted to get every detail letter perfect and had precious little tolerance for players who were not similarly dedicated.

Another member of the New York coaching staff at that time was Tom Landry, who had charge of the defense. He became both a close friend and observer of Lombardi. "Vince wanted to win in the worst way even then," Landry recalled. "If the Giants defense had played better, or was more of a factor in a victory than the offensive unit, then he wouldn't speak to me for days. I knew he wanted to run all aspects of the football operation. There aren't too many opportunities in the NFL to do that, so Green Bay was the perfect situation for him. And he made the most of it. Everything done there during the time he was head coach and general manager had his stamp on it. That's the way he wanted it."

A lifelong resident of the New York City area, Lombardi had attended Fordham University and was a standout lineman with its football team, one

Vince Lombardi

of the legendary "Seven Blocks of Granite." Following graduation, he coached and taught at a parochial school in Englewood, New Jersey. Then came his stints at Army and the Giants. So when it was time to call Green Bay home, he found moving away from his Big Apple roots a heartrending experience. But he undertook the task with his usual show of enthusiasm.

Vince Lombardi, Jr., will always remember that fateful day he drove across the George Washington Bridge with his parents en route to the Midwest, his mother particularly morose about leaving New York for the unknown.

"Dad extolled the virtues of Green Bay all the way there," Vince, Jr., said. "He could have been working for the chamber of commerce. He was intent upon putting the best face on the situation. That's the way he approached everything."

Once among the Packers, Lombardi announced that he had never been associated with a losing team and didn't intend to start now. And he meant it. His first season as head coach, they posted a highly creditable 7–5–0 record. In 1960 they were 8–4, Western Conference winners, and met the Philadelphia Eagles for the NFL championship. The dynasty years had begun.

Gruff, demanding, vocal, and demonstrative—Lombardi exemplified all of these characteristics. The element of fear as well as respect played a key role in his relationship with the Packers. But his methods were not so entrenched that they couldn't be altered for the sake of winning. One time he chewed out Bart Starr during a practice session, then later, in a private meeting with the quarterback, apologized for his outburst and promised to take a different tack in the future. "I told him that if he was going to belittle me in front of my teammates," Starr said, "they would soon lose respect for me on the field. I asked him to correct me in his office after that, and he always did."

But when Lombardi spoke, everybody jumped. Everybody. Willie Davis, a Hall of Fame defensive end, said, "If the coach told you to take a seat, you took a seat. And never mind a chair."

With the acquisition of his second successive Super Bowl triumph, Lombardi gave up the Green Bay coaching reins but soon found that the duties of a general manager were not sufficient unto salving his restless spirit. In 1969 he joined the Washington Redskins as head coach and general manager. The franchise, much like Green Bay 10 years earlier, had fallen upon losing ways. Again he effected an immediate turnaround, leading the team to a 7–5–2 mark in his first season on the sidelines. But it was to be his last hurrah.

On September 3, 1970, cancer claimed his life at the age of 57. Many of his players, past and present, sat by his bedside and prayed for him. One of them was Frank Gifford, a Hall of Fame running back and flanker with the Giants, now a network sportscaster. He had been tutored in New York by Lombardi, and a special chemistry developed between them. Whenever questioned about his former mentor, Gifford said, "I gave up trying to explain to people about him a long time ago. They have their image of the man, and that's it. But they don't have a clue about what he was really like. They only saw his public side."

Earle "Greasy" Neale

Coach: Philadelphia Eagles (1941–1950). Inducted into the Pro Football Hall of Fame 1969. Career: Won-lost record: Philadelphia Eagles (66–44–5). Championships: Eastern Division, 1947, 1948, 1949. NFL, 1948, 1949.

The Philadelphia Eagles owe much of their glossy heritage to Earle "Greasy" Neale. Without him, the big green-and-white would not have enjoyed one of the most illustrious decades in the history of the National Football League.

From 1941 to 1950, the Eagles won two NFL championships and three

Eastern Division titles while fashioning a fine 66–44–5 record. But during the years 1944 through 1949, they flourished at a sizzling 48–16–3 pace, the hottest team in the league, and never finished lower than second in their division. And for this success they can largely thank Neale, a peripatetic offensive genius whose philosophy of defense was only slightly less sensational.

He began his football as captain of the Parkersburg (West Virginia) High School team, which would later benefit from his coaching ministrations. As a collegian, he starred at end for little West Virginia Wesleyan, plying his skills with equal distinction on offense and defense. Thereafter, he labored under an assumed name for the Canton Bulldogs when both the club and the pro game were still in their infancy. Ever so briefly he switched to baseball, hitting .357 for the Cincinnati Reds as an outfielder in the infamous "Black Sox" World Series.

But football was his real love, and he coached early on at six colleges. All the while he maintained something of a hit-and-run romance with the play-for-pay version of the sport. In 1930, he directed the semipro Ironton (Ohio) Tanks to four victories in five outings against NFL clubs in the area. Then 39, he put in a full 60 minutes at end as a player-coach when the Tanks upset the heavily favored Portsmouth Spartans by a 16–15 margin. Needless to say, his teaching and organizational abilities did not go unnoticed by members of the "big league" hierarchy. But they wouldn't get him to join them until 1941.

That year, the Eagles' new owner, Alexis Thompson, finally got Neale's name on the dotted line. As head coach, he wasted little time in familiarizing himself with all the nuances of the T-Formation, seeing in it the wave of the future. He acquired films of the Chicago Bears' monumental 73–0 beating of the Washington Redskins in the NFL championship game of the previous season and studied them for hours. On that occasion, the Bears had utilized the T to perfection, complete with a motion man and a counter series. There was much to know.

By 1944, he had the Eagles in the runner-up spot of the Eastern Division, a position they would maintain for three successive seasons. In 1947, he led Philadelphia to the division crown for the first time ever, beating the Pittsburgh Steelers 21–0 after the two clubs had finished in a deadlock atop the standings. The Eagles lost the league championship game to the Chicago Cardinals, but a new era had dawned in the City of Brotherly Love.

In a rematch for the league title the following year, Philadelphia bested the Cardinals 7–0 in a snowstorm that all but obliterated the field and its markings. Anxious to prove their triumph was no fluke, the Eagles captured Eastern Division honors once more in 1949 and then took on the Los Angeles Rams for NFL superiority. This time the confrontation took place

Earle "Greasy" Neale

in a sea of mud, the Eagles prevailing 14–0 for back-to-back wins in the big one, the first team in league annals to register a double shutout.

With the advent of the 1950 schedule, Philadelphia was squarely in the limelight again, but for a different reason. The Cleveland Browns, perennial champions of the then defunct All-America Football Conference (AAFC), had come over to the NFL with a glint in their eye. Having been badmouthed through the years by certain owners and officials of the senior league, they were looking for a measure of revenge, and what better way to exact it than by whipping their detractors' titleholder, the Eagles? The showdown took place in the season opener for both clubs in Philadelphia's mammoth Municipal Stadium before more than 71,000 spectators. After a relatively close first quarter, the Browns pulled away for a convincing 35–10 victory. The loss went down hard with the old guard.

Even before the Browns tiff, the Eagles suffered from two maladies — injuries to key players and age. These same factors weighed heavily on Neale throughout the campaign, and his best efforts could do no more than effect a 6–6 break-even mark. Given the traditional "what-have-you-done-for-us-lately" mind-set of management, he was fired at season's end. Yet no one, before or since, has done so much for the Philadelphia franchise.

During his tenure with the Eagles, Neale coached a number of outstanding performers, including Hall of Fame inductees Pete Pihos, Steve Van Buren, and Chuck Bednarik.

On November 2, 1973, he died at 81.

Steve Owen

6'2", 235 pounds. Tackle, Coach: Kansas City Cowboys (1924, 1925), New York Giants (1926–1932). Career: Coach: New York Giants (1931–1953). Won-lost record: New York Giants (153–108–17). Championships: Eastern Division, 1934, 1935, 1936, 1938, 1939, 1941, 1944, 1946. NFL, 1935, 1938. Inducted into the Pro Football Hall of Fame 1966.

The school of hard knocks never graduated a more astute pupil than Steve Owen. Lessons learned as a grit-and-grapple lineman in the National Football League's brawny youth served him well years later when as head coach of the New York Giants he proved to be one of the most successful and innovative of his breed.

He was there in the infancy of the NFL, a pit warrior first for the Kansas City Cowboys and later his beloved Giants. A hard, ham-handed tackle from the Cherokee Strip of Oklahoma, he came to grips with most of pro football's early greats and more than held his own. He butted heads with George Halas (Chicago Bears end, coach, and owner), ran interference for Jim Thorpe (Hall of Fame running back), and tutored the likes of Mel Hein (Hall of Fame center). If the money game had a foundation, he was one of the most substantive stones in its base.

"Football is a game played down in the dirt," he once observed, "and it always will be that way. So there's no use getting fancy about it."

This simple but realistic view sufficed as the matrix of his coaching philosophy for 23 years. In 1931 and 1932, he performed the dual function of player and coach for the Giants. Thereafter, he concentrated solely on his role as field boss of the New York franchise through the 1953 season. During this lengthy tenure, he emphasized fundamentals, hard work, and

Steve Owen

sacrifice, running and defense being the staples of his operation. The result was two NFL championships, eight divisional titles, and 153 victories. His teams were perennially among the most feared in the league, and with good reason.

Despite his success, Owen was not without critics. In the main they complained that his Giants were too conservative, even boring. They simply lent greater credence to the old adage "An empty barrel makes the loudest noise" because if they had known anything about the game of football, it would have been apparent to them that he was an innovator of no small stature. His most noteworthy and enduring contributions were the A-formation offense, the umbrella defense, and the two-platoon system.

The A-formation offense featured overpowering but intricate line play (trapping, pulling, and blocking down) as well as imaginative ball handling and running variations out of a backfield set which fathered such later ploys as the quarterback option and countergap series. Owen believed in possession being nine-tenths of the law and the value of controlling the clock. A full decade later, Vince Lombardi made use of the same thesis to sustain his Green Bay Packers dynasty.

Conversely, the umbrella defense revolved around a revolutionary idea of masking intent, or what today is referred to as giving a "different look." So unusual was the concept that *Life* magazine devoted a centerfold spread, complete with diagrams, to inform the committed fan about this latest gridiron artifice. Just before the snap, the Giants would line up in a 6-1-4 alignment. When the ball was centered and the opposition maneuvered to pass, the defensive ends would drop off the scrimmage line to perform as linebackers with shallow-coverage responsibilities. Meanwhile, the tackles became ends and pressured the quarterback, effecting a strong outside rush. In the secondary the backs formed an open umbrella, an elementary zone arrangement designed to keep the receivers inside and in front of them.

How well did it work? Al DeRogatis, an All-Pro tackle with the Giants from 1949 to 1952, remembers precisely. "When the ends dropped off the line to cover the outside receivers," he recalled, "and Arnie Weinmeister [Hall of Fame tackle] and I became ends, the defensive linemen didn't know who to block, or quite what to do. We thoroughly confused their assignments and got good pressure on the passer. And the defensive back right behind me was Tom Landry [later Hall of Fame coach of the Dallas Cowboys]. He would take this idea even further and make it into the standard 4-3 defense most of the teams in the NFL use today."

In 1950, New York's unique defense restricted the prolific Cleveland Browns to a total of 21 points in three games. And in their first encounter of that year, the Giants held the Browns scoreless, something that wouldn't happen again in regular play for more than a decade.

The two-platoon system provided New York with a pair of completely cohesive self-sustaining units that could operate with equal effectiveness in an offensive or defensive capacity. Prime advantages of this stratagem were that it kept fresh troops on the field at all times and greatly reduced the incidence of injuries.

Following the 1953 campaign, Owen turned in his clipboard, and so ended a glorious era in New York Giants history. On that occasion, old foe Halas said, "Steve was the first to stress the importance of defense and settling for field goals instead of touchdowns in certain circumstances. Every team strives today to do what Owen was doing twenty years ago."

He died on May 17, 1964, at 66.

GENERAL
STAFF

Team Owners, League Officials

Bert Bell

NFL Commissioner (1946–1959). Team Owner: Philadelphia Eagles (1933–1940), Pittsburgh Steelers (1941, 1942), Phil-Pitt (1943), Pittsburgh Steelers (1944–1946). Inducted into the Pro Football Hall of Fame 1963 (charter member).

When the National Football League needed good administrative acumen, devotion to duty, a strong sense of justice, and dogged perseverance in the face of adversity, Bert Bell was there to provide them. In every respect he qualified as the right man at the right time.

He was chosen commissioner of the NFL in 1946, a time marked by the onset of a bitter battle for talent between the league and the newly organized All-America Football Conference (AAFC). Within four years, it became apparent that the AAFC would rather switch than fight, especially since a number of its members were experiencing serious financial difficulties. Amid talk of merger, he held out for the inclusion of just those AAFC clubs which were solvent and could successfully compete in the NFL. Only three teams fit this profile—the Cleveland Browns, New York Yanks (ultimately the Baltimore Colts), and the San Francisco 49ers. Each would contribute significantly to the growth and prosperity of the NFL. In the end, his judgment proved sage.

Even as the AAFC war was heating up, Bell had another controversial matter to contend with, the deleterious effect of gambling on professional sport. He could foresee that the NFL, still very much in the developmental

Bert Bell

stage, could not hope to withstand a setback of the magnitude that the "Black Sox" scandle imposed on baseball. As soon as it had been verified that two New York Giants stars, Frank Filchock and Merle Hapes, were approached by gamblers with an offer to fix the point spread on the upcoming 1946 league title game, he knew decisive action was mandated. True, Filchock and Hapes hadn't accepted the bribe, but they failed to notify the proper authorities of the incident, so both players drew suspensions that prevented them from participating in the championship contest, which the Chicago Bears won, 24–14. Harsh treatment, surely, but Bell understood that the NFL couldn't afford even a taint of wrongdoing if pro football was to retain the public trust.

Next came the lure of television, with promises of money to be made the easy way. The club owners, many of whom were struggling to meet expenses, became upset with Bell when he urged caution. His response was "You can't expect people to buy tickets at the ballpark if they can watch the same game at home for free." On the other hand, he grasped what TV could eventually mean to the success of the NFL—national exposure. But for the time being he recommended that only the fans of teams playing away on a particular Sunday should be allowed to watch the proceedings on the tube while the area immediately surrounding the game site ought to be blacked out. This arrangement persisted for years until home games were routinely fully attended, the balance of the seats going to season-ticket holders. By then, pro football had become the opiate of the people. Once again, the little round man with a voice like gravel in a tin can proved to be right.

Nobody cowed Bell, even the proprietors of the teams who had hired him. A classic example of this independent attitude involved his decision to recognize the NFL Players Association as the legitimate bargaining agent for its constituency. Ignoring the angry protests of his employers, he merely cited the clause in the NFL Constitution which permitted the commissioner to "act in the best interest of the league" as his source of authority. He survived that crisis as well.

As a matter of fact, crisis was nothing new to him. In 1933, he bought the Philadelphia Eagles franchise and struggled to make it a going concern until 1940. That year, with World War II on the horizon and hard times on the land, the Eagles moved to Pittsburgh in an unusual franchise shift with the Steelers. In 1943, the clubs were joined; then, the following year, they returned to independent operation. He was part owner of the Steelers until 1946 when the league tapped him as commissioner.

On October 11, 1959, Bell died of a heart attack while watching the Eagles and Steelers play at Franklin Field in Philadelphia. He was 64.

Charles W. Bidwell, Sr.

Team Owner: Chicago Cardinals (1933–1947). Inducted into the Pro Football Hall of Fame 1967.

It can truly be said that Charles Bidwell, Sr., never realized a tangible return on his investment. But because of him the National Football League has been able not only to survive but prosper, with no limit to its potential growth in sight.

A native of Chicago, Bidwell was an ardent Bears fan almost from the club's inception. He even intervened on behalf of owner-coach George Halas following the 1932 season when it appeared the Bears might slip from his grasp. On that occasion, he saw to it that Halas got the needed up-front cash and an extended loan to maintain control of the franchise. He was that kind of a man.

In 1933, Bidwell purchased the Chicago Cardinals for $50,000 and promptly became a competitor of the Bears. Despite this natural crosstown rivalry, he maintained a lifelong affection for his old team. And this wasn't an easy thing to do as the Bears perennially lorded it over the Cardinals, besting them on the field and at the box office. This status remained quo all the way through World War II.

Shortly after the hostilities ended, the All-America Football Conference (AAFC) commenced operations, and the upstart league put a team, the Rockets, in Chicago. It immediately became a financial threat to the lowly Cardinals. But Bidwell had never been one to shy away from competition, be it the Bears or whoever. With a bidding war raging between the NFL and the AAFC, he pulled off no small coup by signing University of Georgia All-America running back Charley Trippi right out from under the nose of the opposition New York Yankees. The price tag was $100,000, large money in those days.

Trippi joined quarterback Paul Christman, fullback Pat Harder, and halfback Marshall Goldberg to form what would become the "Dream Backfield." That year, 1947, the Cardinals edged the Bears for the Western Division title and went on to defeat the Philadelphia Eagles 28–21 for the NFL championship. In 1948, they repeated as division winners before losing their world crown to the Eagles 7–0 in a blizzard-plagued rematch.

Unfortunately, Bidwell didn't live to see any of these good things. Early in 1947, on April 19, he succumbed to the ravages of pneumonia at the age of 51. Up to that time, his Cardinals had not experienced so much as even one financially rewarding season. But success is gauged in ways other than money. His sons put it best when they said of their father, "Without people like him, there would be no NFL today."

And amen.

Joe Carr

President: American Professional Football Association (1921), National Football League (1922–1939). Inducted into the Pro Football Hall of Fame 1963 (charter member).

Bluntly put, Joe Carr adhered to the rules, and he expected everybody else to do the same. As president of the National Football League in its brawling youth, this was his mission, one he pursued with zeal.

No one better understood how important law and order were to pro football in the 1920s than he. Prior to heading up the NFL, he had been a newspaperman and manager of the Columbus (Ohio) Panhandle football team since 1904. During those early days, the pro game amounted to little more than structured mayhem which barely escaped prosecution under local statutes governing aggravated assault and battery. Back then, the rules could be numbered on one hand, and the game officials served more as bouncers than arbitrators.

In 1920, he was a prime mover in the formation of the American

Professional Football Association (APFA), the immediate forerunner of the NFL. That year, the league presidency went to Jim Thorpe, the most publicized player of the era. However, it soon became apparent that more than a figurehead would be needed if pro football was to enjoy anything resembling longevity, let alone prosperity, so the game's hierarchy turned to Carr, and he responded with dauntless efficiency and attention to detail.

He became president of the APFA in 1921. The following year it became the National Football League. Right from the outset of his 18-year administrative tenure, he concerned himself with pro football's public image—how the people in the stands perceived the sport. He felt the ticket buyer had a right to be assured that everything was done honestly and aboveboard. With this as a foremost objective, he didn't hesitate to come down hard on team owners who were inclined to cut corners to get the edge on their competition. Before he took office, the signing of college players to perform under assumed names was a fairly common practice. One of his first official acts involved dealing with this bit of subterfuge. When the Green Bay Packers were found to have "ringers" in their lineup, after fair warning he summarily cancelled the franchise. And it wasn't restored until team founder Earl "Curly" Lambeau made an appeal, personally promising to abide by the rules, and then turned over club ownership to a board of Green Bay businessmen.

Carr also initiated the use of a standard player contract modeled after the form of agreement adopted by baseball. He insisted that players and owners treat one another in a professional manner and worked tirelessly to close off those legal loopholes that had allowed team management to deal dishonestly with its employees.

In 1925, Red Grange appeared in his first game with the Chicago Bears just 10 days after completing his collegiate playing career at the University of Illinois. Carr moved quickly to curtail this practice, fearing that the recruiting of players from campuses before they had graduated would ultimately antagonize the college community. He ruled that henceforth no NFL club could contact a player until his undergraduate eligibility had fully expired. The pro teams that failed to comply in this regard were subject to a stiff fine and expulsion from the league.

Fan support was absolutely vital to the economic survival of the NFL, he knew, and this meant taking the pro game to major metropolitan areas where it could be properly showcased. Through his efforts, the New York Giants were formed in 1925. Later that year, the Grange-led Bears took on the Giants at the Polo Grounds in New York before an SRO crowd of 70,000. As a result, more franchises began operating in major markets, and money football soon became as avidly watched as any sporting attraction.

When the NFL most needed strong leadership, Carr supplied it in abundance. He died in office on May 20, 1939, at 58.

Lamar Hunt

League Founder–Team Owner: Dallas Texans (1960–1962, AFL), Kansas City Chiefs (1963–1969, AFL), Kansas City Chiefs (1970 to the present, NFL). Inducted into the Pro Football Hall of Fame 1972.

Not often does success grow out of repeated frustration and disappointment, but Lamar Hunt proved the exception to this rule. And given his unflagging determination, the National Football League benefited not only by growing in dimension but in stature.

As a young man, he had harbored a burning desire to acquire an NFL club, to be a pro football owner, but circumstances just never so dictated. Finally, while contemplating the futility of his ambition, it suddenly occurred to him that there was a viable alternative to attaining his goal. He would start a league of his own. Consumed with this idea, he approached fellow Texan and Houston businessman K. S. "Bud" Adams, Jr., also a frustrated would-be pro-team proprietor, and suggested a new league was the answer to their collective lament. They quickly gathered other entrepreneurs of like disposition, and thus the American Football League (AFL) was born in mid–August of 1959.

It wasn't until a year later that the AFL actually became an on-field entity comprising clubs located in Boston, Buffalo, Dallas, Denver, Houston, Los Angeles, New York, and Oakland. Hunt's team was titled the Texans and played in his hometown, Dallas. He knew, as did his fellow partners, that signing players meant an all-out economic war with the NFL. This competition got under way immediately, and the AFL more than held its own, stocking its team rosters with many a big-name performer and any number of solid less-talented football practitioners.

Hunt ran head-to-head with the NFL Cowboys in Dallas for three years (1960–1962) before deciding that it made good fiscal sense to strike out in search of his own gridiron domain. He found it in Kansas City. Once settled there, he dubbed his team the Chiefs and set about establishing the most successful of the original clubs in the AFL. His Chiefs accumulated an 87–48–5 record for the 10-year life of the league and appeared in two of the four Super Bowls contested with the NFL. In 1966, fittingly enough, Hunt saw his team meet the NFL champion Green Bay Packers in Super Bowl I. When the smoke of the hostilities had cleared, Kansas City had been vanquished by a 35–10 score, hardly indicative of the evenness of the contest.

Looking back on that encounter, Chiefs quarterback Len Dawson said, "Super Bowl I was a war of the worlds. It was the AFL's chance to prove we belonged, but we were embarrassed. I knew we would have to live with that beating until the time we had another opportunity to play in the Super Bowl."

That time came in Super Bowl IV, conducted at New Orleans' Tulane Stadium, between Kansas City and the Minnesota Vikings of the NFL. It was an occasion of sweet revenge for Hunt as his Chiefs mauled the Vikings 23–7. He had the last laugh, as that constituted the final meeting between clubs from the two leagues. Later that year, 1969, he became the AFL representative in merger talks with the NFL, a wedding which formally took place in the fall of 1970. Back then, the new, expanded NFL consisted of American and National Conference groupings of teams into Eastern, Central and Western divisions. So the war ended, but the memories lingered on.

"Whenever a team from the American Conference takes on a team from the National Conference, one of the old AFL clubs against an old NFL club," he said, "the pride and spirit is still there. We still want to beat them, and they know it."

Hunt remains the owner of the Kansas City Chiefs and serves as president of the American Football Conference (AFC).

Tim Mara

Franchise Founder, Administrator: New York Giants (1925–1959). Inducted into the Pro Football Hall of Fame 1963 (charter member).

Gambling on the National Football League was not a short-odds venture for Tim Mara, but he bet with his heart and the knowledge that staying power often made the difference between winning and losing. Pro football generally, and the New York Giants specifically, owe much to the big Irishman and his penchant for risk taking.

In 1925, NFL president Joe Carr sought to market his product in major metropolitan areas so the game would have the needed opportunity to grow and prosper. When he approached Billy Gibson about buying a football franchise, the New York City fight promoter declined but suggested that his friend Tim Mara, a noted bookmaker, commanded both the interest and the money for such a project.

Mara paid $2,500 for the right to represent the NFL in New York City. Once the deal had been made, he turned his new acquisition, the Giants, over to experienced football executive Dr. Harry March, who promptly set about hiring a coach, former Navy field boss Robert Folwell, and signing as many All-America collegians as possible.

The Giants won more games than they lost that first season, but the New York sporting public paid them scant attention, preferring big-time college football to the pro version. As a result, Mara found himself $40,000 in the hole and looking to lose even more. Desperate for a crowd attraction,

Tim Mara

he attempted to sign up former Illini superstar Red Grange, only to learn that his playing rights had already been acquired by the Chicago Bears.

Undaunted, the quick-witted Mara determined there was more than one way to achieve the desired result. If he couldn't get Grange into a Giants uniform, the next best thing was to get Grange in a Bears uniform to play against his team at New York's Polo Grounds. This he did. On December 6, 1925, more than 70,000 fans swarmed into the confines of the big horseshoe-shaped stadium in the upper Bronx, sending the turnstiles clicking in record fashion for an NFL contest. With people literally hanging from the rafters and looking on from the roofs of nearby buildings, the Bears prevailed over the Giants by a 19–7 margin, but Mara couldn't have been happier. From the game proceeds he netted $143,000 and at least temporarily saved his franchise from an early death.

In 1926, there came a new challenge which took the form of a rival league started by Grange and his agent C. C. "Cash and Carry" Pyle. The American Football League (AFL) put two teams in New York City, one at Yankee Stadium and the other at Brooklyn's Ebbets Field. Poor weather conditions and a bidding war for players with the AFL cost Mara heavily, but he hung on with a gambler's innate belief in miracles. By the end of the year, he had lost a bundle, but the other league fared even worse and went out of business. Once again, the Giants managed to survive, but just barely.

During the next two seasons, Mara practiced all manner of economies. The Giants, like the rest of the clubs in the NFL, made do with worn uniforms, coach train travel, cheap hotels, and smaller team rosters so as not to cut into their meager gate receipts any more than absolutely necessary. Meanwhile, they won their first league title in 1927 with an enviable 11–1–1 record.

Finally, in 1929, Mara acquired triple-threat quarterback Benny Friedman, a genuine star talent and former University of Michigan standout. But as usual, it wasn't an easy process. Since Friedman was under contract to the Detroit Wolverines, Mara had to buy the entire franchise to get the pivotal player he needed for the Giants. The sacrifice proved well worth the expense incurred. With Friedman in New York and Grange back in Chicago, the NFL began to solidify its ranks. Schedules were formalized, and player agreements became standardized on an annual basis. Then rivalries between the Giants, Bears, and Green Bay Packers were established and served as a focal point for fan interest. Before long, newspapers began to carry game reports on their sports pages routinely, along with league standings and statistical information.

Mara never passed up a chance to gain a little publicity for his Giants and the NFL in general. When New York mayor Jimmy Walker approached him in 1930 with the suggestion for an exhibition game to benefit the city's unemployment fund, he put together an extravaganza with all the public-relations trappings that earned $115,153 for the cause. His club went on to win two more league crowns in 1934 and 1938.

The 1940s brought World War II and more lean times for the duration of the conflict. Immediately thereafter, the All-America Football Conference (AAFC) arose to challenge the NFL, and the burden of bidding for players took its toll once again. But as before, Mara led the Giants through this trying period and back into a state of solvency. In 1956, the team moved to Yankee Stadium for its home games and celebrated this transition by crushing the Bears 47–7 for yet another NFL championship.

At the time of Mara's death on February 17, 1959, at 71, the Giants had annexed four league titles and logged 13 division-conference firsts. The franchise continues to thrive under the stewardship of his son. But none of this would have been possible had not the big Irishman made book on his own ability to come up a winner when the chips were down.

George Preston Marshall

Founder-Team Owner: Boston Braves (1932), Boston Redskins (1933–1936), Washington Redskins (1937–1969). Inducted into the Pro Football Hall of Fame 1963 (charter member).

Some critics thought George Preston Marshall belonged in the circus business rather than the National Football League, but his irrepressible spirit was the moving force behind a number of changes that made the pro game more marketable as a major spectator attraction.

On July 9, 1932, he headed a four-man syndicate that bought a new NFL franchise for the city of Boston. This was a marked departure from the norm for the proprietor of a Washington, D.C., laundry, but he had always been a free thinker. He and his co-owners named their team the Braves, as all home games were to be played at the field of the National Baseball League Boston Braves. This liaison lasted one season, and then the NFL club moved down the street to Fenway Park, its official designation becoming the Redskins.

At this juncture of the proceedings, Marshall bought out his three partners to become solely responsible for the $46,000 debt incurred during the first year of operation. Undaunted, he became a prime agitator to have the league teams split into two divisions, East and West, with the leaders of each to meet in a playoff contest to determine a universally recognized champion. He felt this would incite more specator interest and provide the NFL with a higher profile in the media. This ultimately proved to be the outcome.

From 1933 on, the Redskins played an ever-improving brand of football and culminated their climb by winning the Eastern Division title in 1936. But when the reaction to this accomplishment by the Boston populace proved to be less than overwhelming, Marshall lobbied to have the league title game played at New York's Polo Grounds. It was, and the Redskins lost to the Green Bay Packers 21–6. Shortly thereafter, he moved all his gridiron bags and baggage to the nation's capital. On February 13, 1937, the team underwent still another identification change to the Washington Redskins.

In that year's college draft, the Redskins made Texas Christian University passing sensation Sammy Baugh their number-one pick. Marshall, utilizing professional public-relations techniques, promptly set about familiarizing anyone who could see and read with his latest acquisition. Even before Baugh had thrown a ball in an official capacity that year, he held forth as the most widely recognized NFL player the land over. Needless to say, given this publicity blitz, another first for the league, the rest of the team owners quickly instituted similar outreach programs.

George Preston Marshall

Come the night of September 16, the Redskins opened their inaugural campaign in Griffith Stadium under banks of floodlights. Nearly 20,000 fans turned out for the event, and in addition to the on-field action they were entertained by the Redskins band, an aggregation of musicians in Indian attire who had been assembled strictly for this purpose. They would also play the team fight song, especially composed at Marshall's request, yet another unprecedented attainment. Out of this beginning were added regular halftime shows which would prove to be a most colorful addendum to the game, particularly with the advent of television in the 1950s.

Under Marshall's guidance during those early years, the Redskins became one of the league's most successful clubs on and off the field. They won five division crowns, and NFL championships in 1937 and 1942. Given shrewd promotional gimmicks, their attendance figures were heartening and provided the club with a sound financial foundation upon which to function. And even during the lean 1950s and 1960s when losses often outnumbered wins, fan loyalty remained high as a result of careful and consistent seeding begun more than a decade earlier.

Above all, Marshall realized that excelling in the marketplace meant more than just making a good product available to the consumer. Sales were also heavily dependent upon proper packaging and other embellishments that attracted the buyer and served the sense of pleasure as well as that of necessity. He added the element of showmanship to pro football just when the game most required it. For this contribution alone, the NFL owes him undying gratitude.

On August 9, 1969, he died at 71.

Hugh "Shorty" Ray

Technical Advisor on Rules, Supervisor of Officials: NFL (1938–1952). Inducted into the Pro Football Hall of Fame 1966.

There was a time in the late 1930s when the National Football League finally began to come of age, a crucial time when the pro game had commenced to establish itself in the sporting marketplace as a legitimate attraction. But it badly needed direction and refinement, a strong sense of control, the institution of a civilizing and maturing process that would guarantee long-term acceptance, even interest, by the paying public. And that's where Hugh "Shorty" Ray entered, stage left, and none too soon.

Although only 5'6" and 138 pounds, he joined the NFL in 1938 as the "cop on the block." He was no newcomer to the realm of football. Despite his diminutive stature, he had been a four-sport standout at the University of Illinois nearly 20 years earlier. Back then, the gridiron sport was little more than sanctioned mayhem, barely satisfying local ordinances governing assault and battery. He was painfully aware of this regrettable condition and could foresee serious trouble in the offing if corrective remedies weren't taken.

Following his collegiate career, he turned to coaching on the high school level, a commitment which absorbed him for some two decades. While so occupied, he also became concerned with better defining football as an institution. He attempted to achieve this end by founding the American Officials Association, which sought to clarify conduct-of-play and rules-interpretation problems by means of clinics and conferences. Not long thereafter, he was approached by the State High School Athletic Association to write a football code which would have universal application. He did, and it served as the foundation for the conduct of the game at all strata of achievement.

Fortified with this background, he accepted a position with the NFL as the supervisor of officials. His job was to police the pro game and recommend changes that would enhance its salability to the fans. Right from the outset, he established demanding qualifications for would-be officials. They had to score better than 95 percent on the written tests he devised and then submit to intense instruction concerning on-field procedures. Each of them was then graded on his performance during the course of a season. If he failed to measure up, more tutoring ensued; in some cases, dismissal resulted.

Ray annually made recommendations to the league hierarchy regarding changes in the rules, suggesting that some be eliminated and others implemented. He also considered it an important part of his routine to visit every club once a year to educate the coaches and players about the regulations governing their means of livelihood. It was everybody's responsibility, he felt, to put the best possible face on the game for public consumption.

No one better appreciated the necessity of presenting the fans with a fast-paced competitive contest than he. To realize this objective, he took an estimated 300,000 stopwatch readings during his 15-year tenure in the NFL. By insisting that officials merely toss the ball back onto the field after an out-of-bounds call as opposed to personally returning it, he managed to add 12 additional downs to every league game.

He once observed, "The faster you play, the more plays you create. The more plays you create, the more situations you develop in which the clock can be stopped"—something akin to the old paradox "The faster I go, the behinder I get."

When Ray retired because of poor health in 1952, he left the NFL with an exciting product that would become the most successful sporting venture of all time.

On September 16, 1956, he died at 71.

Dan Reeves

Team Owner: Cleveland Rams (1941–1945), Los Angeles Rams (1946–1971). Inducted into the Pro Football Hall of Fame 1967.

Foresight and conviction played as much a part in establishing the current success of the National Football League as time, talent, and money. Dan Reeves was an especially perceptive administrator who heeded Horace Greeley's advice, "Go West, young man, go West" and thus ushered the play-for-pay gridiron game into an era of unprecedented popularity and financial stability.

It all began on January 14, 1946, just a few weeks after the Cleveland Rams had won the NFL championship. At that time Reeves announced his intention to relocate the franchise in Los Angeles, some 2,000 miles from the nearest league city. Was it a rash decision? One made without proper reflection? Hardly. That just wasn't his style. If anything, he tended to be a mite conservative, a singularly thorough individual.

What, then?

He and a partner bought the Rams in 1941 with visions of making them the class of the league. But as one year melded into another and the team steadily improved, attendance did not. Finally, in 1945, the Rams reached the NFL title game and there defeated the Washington Redskins 15–14 to become world champions. On that occasion, only 32,178 paying customers made their way into Cleveland Municipal Stadium, a cavernous structure that could have accommodated more than twice this number. What's more, the city fathers charged Reeves three times the usual rental rate for use of the ballpark to host the contest.

Enough is enough, he concluded, and determined to split for the West Coast. Immediately, he found himself at odds with the other nine club owners. They fumed about the added expense involved to transport their players, coaches, and other personnel all the way to Los Angeles for a single Sunday outing and then just turn around and come back. And because air travel wasn't all that developed in those days, it meant taking the better part of a week going to and fro by train. No way, they vowed.

But Reeves stood his ground. He didn't have to be ripped off by a town that wouldn't even support a winner. Angrily, he told the other owners that if they didn't sanction his plan, the Rams were prepared to withdraw from the league. Realizing that he wasn't making an idle threat, they reluctantly approved the move. After finally clearing this hurdle, he found more of the same awaiting him in Los Angeles.

Initially he learned that the Rams weren't the only pro team in town. They would be sharing center stage with the Los Angeles Dons of the rival All-America Football Conference (AAFC) and unlike the Dons, who were largely local in origin, they were as interlopers, so to speak, composed of unfamiliar names and reputations from a far country. It meant open war-fare for fans and a costly competition to acquire and keep quality players. While in Cleveland operating capital was drained off slowly but steadily, Reeves now lost money in alarming gushes. But the point of no return had long been passed.

Late in 1949, the AAFC and the Dons went under as the Rams were coming into their own with an exciting offense that featured the likes of standout receivers Elroy "Crazylegs" Hirsch and Tom Fears, as well as the explosive quarterbacking duo of Bob Waterfield and Norm Van Brocklin. In the course of the next seven seasons, they would register four Western Division firsts and annex the 1951 NFL crown in the process. During this period, the people of Los Angeles turned out in droves to watch their team perform. The Rams drew crowds of 80,000 or better 22 times during their first two decades in the City of the Angeles. And in 1957 more than 102,000 spectators jammed the Coliseum to see them confront the San Francisco 49ers.

But even as the club was flourishing, Reeves concerned himself with building for the future. He instituted the Free Football for Kids program, which enabled youngsters to attend games and form an affinity for the Rams that promised to remain intact into adulthood, the fans who would keep the turnstiles clicking in the years ahead. Also, his experimenting with television in the early days of the medium did much to help the NFL form sound TV policies that would later successfully introduce the game to an entire nation.

Of all Reeves's innovative contributions, the most significant had to be his move to the West Coast at a time when conventional wisdom cried out against it. It proved to be a most fortuitous act of courage which opened a brave new world to the then struggling young giant of professional football. There was indeed "gold in them thar hills."

He died on April 15, 1971, at 58.

Arthur Joseph Rooney

Founder-Team Owner: Pittsburgh Pirates (1933–1939), Pittsburgh Steelers (1940–1988). Inducted into the Pro Football Hall of Fame 1964.

An open hand, an open heart, and an open mind were the attributes brought to every human relationship by Arthur Joseph Rooney until his death as a patriarch of the National Football League and the owner and patron saint of the Pittsburgh Steelers. There may have been a more admired and beloved figure in the annals of professional sport, but that person has yet to be revealed.

On July 8, 1933, "The Chief" brought his team into being for the price of $2,500, funds appropriated from a good day at the track, or so the story goes. He christened them the Pittsburgh Pirates, a designation they bore for seven seasons while accumulating just 22 victories and totally frustrating the efforts of five head coaches. Back then, they resided in the Eastern Division of the NFL's restructured 10-member league.

Forbes Field served as the Pirates' home turf, but they didn't draw well there, given the presence of major league baseball and the popularity of the local University of Pittsburgh football team, so Rooney often took his charges to the area hinterlands—places like Latrobe, Johnstown, and Youngston (Ohio)—and occasionally to such far flung sites of adventure as New Orleans and Louisville. He had a twofold purpose: to build a market for the pro gridiron product and to make a few extra bucks on his investment. Neither one of these purposes realized anything like fulfillment.

Come 1940, he renamed the team the Pittsburgh Steelers in honor of the industry that largely subsidized western Pennsylvania. But this rebirth of sorts didn't generate any marked change in the club's mode of operations, on or off the field. The only tangible rewards for his long-suffering support took the form of a winning season in 1942, a first, and a share of the 1947 Eastern Division lead. Other than that, his lot was disappointment and no little embarrassment. Lesser men would have thrown in the towel, but not Rooney. He had his reason and enunciated it some years later. "I'll tell you something from the bottom of my heart," he told a reporter. "I'd pay to lose money just to keep in this game. I love it that much."

There was another underlying factor. He had grown up in a sporting environment and possessed the heart of an athlete, that something down deep that won't let a real competitor quit. In 1920, he earned a berth on the U.S. Olympic boxing team and also won AAU championships in the welterweight and middleweight classes. From 1921 to 1925, he played minor-league baseball until an arm injury cut short a promising career. Thereafter, he continued to submit health and welfare to the rigors of semipro football. Later, he sponsored such western Pennsylvania semipro teams as the J. P. Rooneys, the North Side Majestics, and Hope Harveys. And always he dreamed his dreams.

It wasn't until the hand of age lay heavy upon him that he finally realized his fondest ambitions. With the arrival of Chuck Noll as the Steelers' 14th head coach in 1969, the franchise underwent a not so gradual upswing in fortune. During the decade of the 1970s, Rooney would see his club win four Super Bowl championships, an accomplishment that was equaled only in January 1990 by the San Francisco 49ers. Through it all, the vindication of 40 years' faithful service to his team and the NFL, he remained a humble, quiet-spoken man with thoughts more of others than himself.

When the NFL rode the uncertain tide of infancy, he was a beacon that kept the rest of his fellow owners on course until a safe harbor finally hove into view. He spent top dollar for the best talent available and to promote the game when folding legal tender was in very short supply, always believing that the hoped-for point of turnaround lay just ahead. Through it all, he prevailed as a galvanizing force, uniting friends in an ever-closer bond and bringing adversaries together in mutual forgiveness.

Arthur Joseph Rooney

He passed from the scene on August 25, 1988, and even in death the healing effect of his personality was felt. During his funeral proceedings, NFL commissioner Pete Rozelle and Los Angeles Raiders owner Al Davis, bitter foes for some years, shook hands and buried the hatchet in honor of their departed friend. Art Rooney was a very special man indeed.

Pete Rozelle

Commissioner of the NFL (1960–1989). Inducted into the Pro Football Hall of Fame 1985.

In the words of Winston Churchill, "Power can be acquired in three ways. One can fall heir to it, seize it or have it thrust upon him." The latter instance perfectly describes Pete Rozelle's ascent to power as commissioner of the National Football League.

He was a 33-year-old general manager of the Los Angeles Rams in January 1960 when the NFL team owners gathered for their annual meeting. The principal order of business concerned the election of a new league executive. Former commissioner Bert Bell, a popular and respected leader, had died in office three months earlier, and now a successor had to be found. There were no clear favorites for the position, so the deliberations bode to be lengthy and even acrimonious.

No less than 23 rounds of balloting took place, and still no candidate could gain the needed majority for confirmation. At that juncture, Rozelle was asked to leave the gathering so further caucusing could take place. When he exited the meeting, none of the media representatives gathered in the corridor outside so much as glanced in his direction. He wasn't exactly a news item in his own right.

Unsure of what to do with himself, Rozelle wandered into a nearby men's lounge and waited, periodically making a show of washing his hands if anyone entered the room so as not to seem loitering. After a couple of hours, he was bid to rejoin the owners. Upon returning to the conference table, he received the startling news of his election as the new commissioner of the NFL.

To say his elevation to the most influential and powerful post in the league was most fortuitous for money football is to state the obvious. His backers assured the team owners at large that he would grow into the job. He did nothing to disappoint them, acclimatizing himself to the dictates of the assignment more quickly and completely than anyone could have foreseen. Within a relatively few years, he became recognized as the most effective commissioner in all professional sport.

Not only did he possess the leadership qualities necessary for success as the league's top executive, but he also commanded a singular appeal that engendered the trust, respect, and in most cases, the friendship of the owners on an individual basis. The weight of his personality, as much as any other factor, enabled him to negotiate and conciliate so successfully during his lengthy tenure in office. Many a crisis was averted simply by his ability to placate and mollify the 28 diverse egos which composed the governing body of the NFL.

Under his direction, the NFL became the most financially profitable sporting endeavor of all time. His skill at deriving lucrative television contracts from the major networks ensured the stability of every club in the league. And given both regional and national TV game coverage for 26 or more weekends out of the year, pro football became the most watched of all

Pete Rozelle

athletic events. Millions of fans, young and old the land over, identified with the teams of their choice via shirts, caps, jackets, and other paraphernalia bearing the league seal and trademark. NFL films and highlights became much in demand not only as general TV viewing fare but as sources of entertainment for business and professional gatherings. All of this added up to fiscal security for the game and the fealty of the masses.

Rozelle served in an era of unequaled prosperity for the league and one of unparalleled change. He began the job of commissioner even as the NFL and the American Football League (AFL) were embarking upon a costly and destructive rivalry. Ultimately, he would work to bring this confrontation to an amicable merger, the result being an immense profit for both factions, and still managed to retain his place at the head of the table. Out of this mating the Super Bowl emerged as a sports extravaganza that dwarfed all others. Then came the United States Football League (USFL) and another costly bidding war. Out of this ruckus grew divisive litigation, not to mention suits and countersuits within the league over the unofficial movement of franchises from city to city. There were intermittent player strikes, threatened strikes, and still more court action. It was the best of times; it was the worst of times.

Through it all, Rozelle presided over an unprecedented period of growth for the NFL in dollars and cents, number and quality of teams, fan commitment, and player participation. He was a man who very definitely grew to the magnitude required of him by the dictates of his position.

In December 1989 he retired as commissioner of professional football.

Tex Schramm

General Manager–President: Dallas Cowboys (1960–1988), Chairman: NFL Competition Committee (1966–1988). President–Chief Executive Officer: World League of American Football (1989–1990). Inducted into the Pro Football Hall of Fame 1991.

With the exception of the patriarchs—George Halas, Art Rooney, et al.—few men have contributed more to the growth and prosperity of the National Football League than Tex Schramm.

He commenced his affiliation with the NFL in 1947 when the Los Angeles Rams took him on as the team's publicity director. In the course of a decade, he steadily climbed the administrative ladder until reaching first assistant to the president and then general manager. While heading up the club staff, he hired a young man named Pete Rozelle who was destined to become commissioner of the league.

In 1957, Schramm left the Rams and joined the Columbia Broadcasting System as an assistant director of sports. With CBS he quickly distinguished himself as an innovator and ultimately arranged for comprehensive coverage of the 1960 Winter Olympics, a notable coup as the famous games had never before been the subject of a live network telecast.

Later that year when Dallas was awarded an NFL franchise, he returned to pro football, becoming president and general manager of the newly formed organization. He remained in this dual role for the next 28 years, a period during which the Cowboys became perennial challengers for the league crown and gained wide acclaim as "America's team."

Given his impetus, Tom Landry was selected as head coach, and the club's front office soon became the envy of the NFL. Early on, the Cowboys began utilizing computers and the latest technology to enhance their scouting and statistical inference capabilities, advancing the then hit-or-miss process to a rather exact science. As a result, the team made five Super Bowl appearances, emerging victorious on two of these occasions; claimed five National Football Conference championships; and reached the playoffs 18 times during a span of 20 consecutive winning seasons.

When the destructive bidding war for players between the NFL and the rival American Football League reached its peak in 1966, Schramm undertook a series of secret negotiations with AFL Kansas City Chiefs owner Lamar Hunt, the objective a peaceful settlement of their differences. The result was a merging of the two leagues into a 26-team NFL which officially began operation in 1970.

As chairman of the influential competition committee, Schramm introduced the concept of a six-division format, three in the National Football Conference and a like number for the American Football Conference, and a wild-card postseason scheme. These changes established a series of natural regional rivalries while maintaining the strong competitive feelings that existed between the old NFL and AFL clubs. It proved to be a stroke of genius as game attendance and television revenues soared.

He also advocated a referee's microphone for better communicating on-field decisions to the fans in the stands and watching on TV, a 30-second clock for assuring consistency of the intervals between plays, extra-wide sideline borders, wind-direction strips on the goalpost uprights, and multicolored lines demarcating the 20- and 50-yard lines.

When the Cowboys came under new ownership in 1989, Schramm left the organization to accept an appointment as president and chief executive officer of the World League of American Football, a developmental system sponsored by the NFL and composed of teams based in the United States and a few major European cities. After setting up the groundwork for the WLAF, he relinquished his duties in 1990.

An Epilogue

Dave Butz was a weekend warrior for 16 years, a trench soldier (defensive tackle) in the service of the St. Louis Cardinals (1973, 1974) and the Washington Redskins (1975–1988). He stood 6'7" and weighed 315 pounds. Football had been a part of his life since childhood.

"My high school coach took me aside one day when I was just a junior," Butz recalled, "and he said, 'Dave, you were made to play football.' At the time I was 6'5" and 267 pounds. From then on, I began preparing myself to play in the pros."

The 1988 season was Butz's last as an NFL gladiator. He left the battle, the grit and the gore of it, most reluctantly, feeling that his time had not really passed, that his skills had not really diminished appreciably. Those of his breed who had gone before him could smile knowingly, for precious few of them stripped off their armor on their last day of active duty with anything resembling a sense of willingness.

But Butz fared better than many of his predecessors. He played on two Super Bowl championship teams, three conference winners, and several division titlists. Ornate rings commemorating these attainments adorn his massive hands. Still, there is an honor he yet seeks. "If you don't want to be in the Hall of Fame," he said, "then you shouldn't be in pro football. That's the ultimate goal. Everybody who plays in the NFL should desire that above all else."

As his first year of eligibility for induction approaches, the importance of belonging will play more heavily on his thoughts and emotions. He'll try to block out of his mind reports of the selection process, telling himself that

345

it doesn't really matter. Down deep, however, he knows it does—terribly. To be enshrined with one's peers, other noted men of valor who fought the weekend wars in so distinguished a fashion, is the quest of every warrior. Even now, would-be football immortals set out along the road to Canton, confident in their youth and blithely oblivious to the carnage, the broken dreams and ambitions, that litter the way. For in truth, "Many are called, but few are chosen." And so must it be.

Index

347